Dear Scott, Dearest Zelda

Dear Scott, Dearest Zelda

THE LOVE LETTERS
of F. SCOTT *and* ZELDA FITZGERALD

With an introduction by their
granddaughter ELEANOR LANAHAN

Edited by JACKSON R. BRYER
and CATHY W. BARKS

BLOOMSBURY
LONDON · NEW DELHI · NEW YORK · SYDNEY

First published in Great Britain 2002
This paperback edition published 2003

The moral right of the author has been asserted

Bloomsbury Publishing Plc, 50 Bedford Square, London WC1B 3DP

A CIP catalogue record for this book is available from the British Library

ISBN 978 07475 6601 4

10 9 8 7 6 5 4

Printed and bound by CPI Group (UK) Ltd, Croydon CR0 4YY

To Mary and David —

"Happily, happily foreverafterwards
— the best we could."

ACKNOWLEDGMENTS

In preparing this book, we received assistance from a number of people. Ronald Goldfarb and Kristen Auclair found us a publisher. At St. Martin's Press, Diane Higgins, our editor, was a consistent voice of support and encouragement, along with her assistant, Nichole Argyres. Carol Edwards not only copyedited our manuscript expertly; she improved it significantly. Mary C. Hartig, Marc Singer, Sarah Barks, and David Bryan Barks helped prepare the text. Eleanor Lanahan, Wendy Schmalz, AnnaLee Pauls, Don C. Skemer, Ruth Prigozy, Judith Baughman, Tom Adams, David Bryan Barks, Rosemary Mizener Colt, Mary Anne Neeley, and Lisa Hartjens assisted us in securing photographs.

CONTENTS

LIST OF ILLUSTRATIONS

Insert

PREFACE

The most important relationship that either F. Scott or Zelda Sayre Fitzgerald had was that with each other; it was the catalyst for and foremost theme of much of their fiction. The letters they exchanged tell the story of this central relationship in their own words; those that have been previously published in editions of Scott's correspondence and in Zelda's *Collected Writings* have never before appeared together in one volume. In addition, there are many unpublished letters in the Princeton University library, and these deserve to be part of the record, as well. The Fitzgeralds' courtship and marriage has become a compelling and enduring part of our literary history. The new letters, placed chronologically with those collected previously, allow us to view their relationship in a more evenhanded manner than heretofore has been possible.

The most detailed and accurate account of the Fitzgeralds' relationship is still Nancy Milford's best-selling *Zelda: A Biography* (1970). Milford was the first not only to explore the many letters Zelda wrote to Scott but also to attempt putting them in some kind of order. In the prologue to *Zelda*, Milford recalls how she and her husband read the letters aloud to each other "as if they had just arrived, not knowing from what terrain of their lives they had been written or what the next one would say. They were hopelessly mixed up and undated, without, in most cases, envelopes to give them dates. . . . I had somewhat innocently . . . entered into something I neither could nor would put down for six years . . ." (xiii). Much of Milford's account is based on these letters, from which she quotes extensively; yet only a sampling of them could appear in her biography, and even then only in a highly truncated form. Now, for the first time, we can read those intriguing letters from Zelda to Scott for ourselves.

Over thirty years have passed since the Milford biography, and, as a society, we have learned much (though still not enough) about the nature of mental illness (from which Zelda suffered) and alcoholism (from which Scott suffered). Yet this knowledge has not been reflected in what has been written about the Fitzgeralds. The tendency has been to sensationalize their lives and illnesses.

Scott and Zelda's lives were indisputably dramatic and tragic, and therefore all too easy to distort. Perhaps the most sensational myth of all is the persistent claim that Scott, jealous of his wife's creativity, suppressed her talents and drove her mad. Koula Svokos Hartnett's view of the Fitzgeralds' marriage, in *Zelda Fitzgerald and the Failure of the American Dream for Women* (1991), regrettably is all too representative: "As his appendage, [Zelda] was to become the victim of [Scott's] self-destructive urge. In denying her the right to be her own person . . . , by refusing to permit her the use of her *own* material . . . , by rebuking her for attempting to create a life of her own—he gradually causes her to emotionally wither and die" (187). Such an assertion defies common sense as well as even the most fundamental understanding of mental illness; yet it has gained some general acceptance. For further evidence that this view persists, one has only to look at the most recent biography of the Fitzgeralds, published in 2001 and claiming to be definitive, in which Kendall Taylor asserts:

> She [Zelda] had used up her life providing material for a writer who to this day is considered one of America's greatest, yet as a man and husband was cunningly controlling. When she finally tried to make a life for herself, apart from the marriage, it was too late. She had scant resources left. The only way out was through the insanity to which her family was prone. In writing the epigram "sometimes madness is wisdom"* she was revealing the paradigm of her life. (*Sometimes Madness Is Wisdom* 372–373)

The suggestion of mental illness as an escape ("[t]he only way out") echoes this passage from *Zelda* in which Milford makes the same suggestion when discussing Zelda's first breakdown in 1930:

> Ahead of them [Scott and Zelda] would be the slow agony of putting the pieces of their lives together again. . . . She was diagnosed . . . as a schizophrenic, and not simply as a neurotic or hysterical woman. It was as if once Zelda had collapsed there

---

* When, in January of 1934, Zelda's paintings were shown in New York, she used the French aphorism *Parfois la Folie Est la Sagesse* (Sometimes Madness Is Wisdom) as the title for her exhibition (see color insert).

was no escape other than her spiraling descent into madness. . . .
To record her breakdown is to give witness to her helplessness
and terror, as well as to explore again the bonds that inextrica-
bly linked the Fitzgeralds. (161)

Despite this somewhat vague insinuation, Milford's biography
remains well researched and the most trustworthy exploration of
Zelda's side of the Fitzgeralds' relationship to date, far more careful
and accurate than Taylor's, which contains factual errors as well as
insupportable assertions.

The new Taylor biography probably is not all that important in
itself, but it does represent for the first time a full-length study guided
by a viewpoint that has ridden the wave of contemporary criticism
for the past thirty years. The Fitzgeralds' marriage was a chaotic one,
but it is no more reasonable to say that Scott drove his wife mad than
it is to say that Zelda drove her husband to drink. Although Zelda
and Scott married young, their inherited predispositions to mental illness and alcoholism, respectively, were already present. These traits
were apparent in the impulsive behavior that characterized their
courtship and actually fed their attraction for each other from the
beginning. Although stories of the descent into madness and alcoholic binges may create exciting reading, they do little to further our
understanding and appreciation of these two gifted and troubled
human beings who have captured and held our attention as readers
all these years.

Even more disturbing is Taylor's statement that her argument is
substantiated by Zelda's letters, indicating that her biography presents Zelda's point of view regarding the marriage:

Nowhere is the reality of the Fitzgeralds' marital situation
more evident than in Zelda's superbly crafted letters to Scott.
These number in the thousands, and Fitzgerald saved all of them.
Much of my book has been drawn from them, because they provide the greatest understanding of Zelda's character. (xiv)

This assertion is disturbing because it is inaccurate. The total number
of Zelda's letters to Scott that survive at Princeton is closer to five
hundred than to thousands; and although we agree that the letters are
superb, they are not "crafted": Zelda wrote spontaneously, impres-
sionistically, and quickly. *Dear Scott, Dearest Zelda,* which features
virtually all of Zelda's previously published letters, along with a

substantial selection of those previously unpublished, allows readers to see for themselves just how Zelda viewed her marriage to Scott at each stage of the relationship.

At times, the Fitzgeralds did blame each other for the things that went wrong in their lives, including problems in their marriage. During the years 1932 through 1934, they often had bitter arguments over who had the right to fictionalize material based on their lives. Their letters certainly represent these periods of anger, but the greater portion express concern over the hardships endured by the other and an appreciation of each other's accomplishments despite formidable obstacles. Although conflict is an important aspect of their relationship, and not to be minimized, when we look at the entire relationship, we can see that it is not competition that emerges as the defining characteristic of their marriage, but love and mutual support, hampered as that support might have been by the serious illnesses the Fitzgeralds struggled with, which, unfortunately, *did* dominate their lives.

Although Zelda's painful struggle with mental illness has been viewed sympathetically, such has not been the case with Fitzgerald's alcoholism (and the deterioration of his physical health it caused), which has often been viewed as disgraceful behavior on his part, not as the devastating disease we understand it to be today. Scott himself, of course, did not understand the disease, either, only the humiliation it caused. In addition to being insensitive to Scott's alcoholism, the view that he cruelly stifled Zelda's creativity neglects the dire position he was in, struggling to pay bills (including those for Zelda's doctors and hospitalizations) by practicing the only profession he knew—writing. Despite the decline of his reputation and health, he somehow continued to write, just as Zelda, despite the crippling disintegration of her personality, continued to write and paint, and to dream of getting a job and being able to support herself. Ironically, the central value this sensationalized couple held in common was the work ethic; as their letters attest, it was the guiding principle they ultimately valued above all others. Perhaps the most enduring impression of the Fitzgeralds that emerges from their letters is the courage, beauty, and insight born of their deep but tormented love.

EDITORS' NOTE

In an effort to retain the distinctive flavor of Scott's and Zelda's epistolary styles, we have attempted to transcribe their letters as literally as possible, consistent with a reader's ability to understand them. Thus, we have not corrected spelling errors—of which they both made many—and have inserted corrected spelling (of full words or of letters within words) in brackets only in cases where we felt it necessary to make meaning clear. Similarly, their punctuation is frequently erratic and inconsistent; we have inserted bracketed punctuation only to clarify meaning. All ellipses in the texts of letters are in the originals, unless otherwise indicated. Zelda also used dashes of varying lengths throughout her letters; her use of them is more pervasive in her early correspondence, however, then diminishes in the letters she wrote during the 1930s. Our practice has been to retain many of these (standardized to a one-em dash in length) but to convert some to periods when they occur at the ends of sentences.

Conjectural readings and omitted, obliterated, or illegible words are also indicated in brackets in the text. All words underlined by the Fitzgeralds, either with one line or several, are rendered in italics. In the headings for each letter, we have indicated the date and return address; these are almost always indicated in brackets and are based on internal evidence, because most often such information was not supplied in the original. The following abbreviations have been used in the headings to denote the true form of any given letter: AL—autograph letter unsigned; AL (draft)—unsigned autograph letter found only in draft form; AL (fragment)—autograph letter found only in a fragment; ALS—autograph letter signed; AN—autograph note unsigned; TL—typewritten letter unsigned; TL (CC)—typewritten letter found only in a carbon copy; TLS—typed letter signed; and Wire—telegram. The number of pages cited at the head of each letter refers to the number of sides of paper on which the letter was written. The original copies of all but a very few items of the correspondence in this edition are in the Princeton University library, either in the F. Scott or Zelda Fitzgerald Papers; items found in the Fitzgeralds' scrapbooks, which are also at Princeton, are so indicated. The location of the very few original items not at Princeton is footnoted.

In providing footnotes, we have attempted to strike a balance between giving needed information and overburdening the reader with excessive scholarly apparatus. We have not identified persons we deemed familiar to most readers; nor have we attempted to do so when a general identification is obvious from context—for example, the many Montgomery friends Zelda mentions in her early letters. Generally, those persons, places, and events we have footnoted are identified only once; if persons, places, and events have been identified in our introductions and narrative passages, we do not reidentify them in footnotes. Nationalities of persons footnoted are given only when such persons are not American.

In order to make our narratives more concise, sources for quoted material are indicated in parentheses in abbreviated form. The full references (and the abbreviation) for such citations are as follows:

Bruccoli, Matthew J. *Some Sort of Epic Grandeur: The Life of F. Scott Fitzgerald*. New York: Harcourt Brace Jovanovich, 1981: *Some Sort of Epic Grandeur.*

———, ed. *F. Scott Fitzgerald: A Life in Letters*. New York: Scribners, 1994: *Life in Letters.*

———, ed., with the assistance of Jennifer McCabe Atkinson. *As Ever, Scott Fitz—: Letters Between F. Scott Fitzgerald and His Literary Agent Harold Ober 1919–1940*. Philadelphia: J. B. Lippincott, 1972: *As Ever, Scott Fitz—.*

———, and Margaret M. Duggan, eds., with the assistance of Susan Walker. *Correspondence of F. Scott Fitzgerald*. New York: Random House, 1980: *Correspondence.*

———, Scottie Fitzgerald Smith, and Joan P. Kerr, eds. *The Romantic Egoists: A Pictorial Autobiography from the Scrapbooks and Albums of Scott and Zelda Fitzgerald*. New York: Scribners, 1974: *Romantic Egoists.*

Fitzgerald, F. Scott. *Afternoon of an Author: A Selection of Uncollected Stories and Essays*. New York: Scribners, 1958: *Afternoon of an Author.*

———. *F. Scott Fitzgerald's Ledger: A Facsimile*. Washington, DC: NCR/Microcard, 1973: *Ledger.*

———. *The Great Gatsby*. New York: Scribners, 1995; originally published in 1925.

————. *The Notebooks of F. Scott Fitzgerald.* Edited by Matthew J. Bruccoli. New York: Harcourt Brace Jovanovich/Bruccoli Clark, 1978: *Notebooks.*

————. *The Stories of F. Scott Fitzgerald.* New York: Scribners, 1951: *Stories.*

Fitzgerald, Zelda. *The Collected Writings.* Edited by Matthew J. Bruccoli. New York: Scribners, 1991: *Collected Writings.*

Hartnett, Koula Svokos. *Zelda Fitzgerald and the Failure of the American Dream for Women.* New York: Peter Lang, 1991.

Hemingway, Ernest. *A Moveable Feast.* New York: Scribners, 1964.

Kuehl, John, and Jackson R. Bryer, eds. *Dear Scott/Dear Max: The Fitzgerald-Perkins Correspondence.* New York: Scribners, 1971: *Dear Scott/Dear Max.*

Lanahan, Eleanor. *Zelda: An Illustrated Life.* New York: Abrams, 1996.

Milford, Nancy. *Zelda: A Biography.* New York: Harper & Row, 1970: *Zelda.*

Mizener, Arthur. *The Far Side of Paradise: A Biography of F. Scott Fitzgerald.* Revised ed. Boston: Houghton Mifflin, 1965.

Taylor, Kendall. *Sometimes Madness Is Wisdom — Zelda and Scott Fitzgerald: A Marriage.* New York: Ballantine, 2001.

Turnbull, Andrew, ed. *The Letters of F. Scott Fitzgerald.* New York: Scribners, 1963: *Letters.*

Wilson, Edmund, ed. *The Crack-Up.* New York: New Directions, 1964; originally published in 1945: *Crack-Up.*

The state of the previously published Scott and Zelda letters is as follows:

Andrew Turnbull's *The Letters of F. Scott Fitzgerald* (1963) contains thirty-five letters from Scott to Zelda, many of which are not printed in their entirety; Matthew J. Bruccoli's *Correspondence of F. Scott Fitzgerald* (1980) has twenty-three letters from Scott to Zelda and sixty-two letters from Zelda to Scott; Bruccoli's *The Collected Writings* of Zelda Fitzgerald (1991) reprints the same Zelda letters as *Correspondence,* plus an additional one; and Bruccoli's *F. Scott Fitzgerald: A Life in Letters* (1994) contains twenty-four letters from Scott to Zelda, bringing the total number of published letters from Scott to Zelda to fifty-eight and those from Zelda to Scott to sixty-three.

At the Princeton University library, there are twenty-two previously unpublished letters from Scott to Zelda, eleven previously unpublished telegrams from Scott to Zelda, and approximately 430 previously unpublished letters from Zelda to Scott. These deserve to be part of their story. All of Scott's letters and telegrams to

Zelda appear in this book, and 189 new letters from Zelda are included.

As indicated by these statistics, many of Scott's letters to Zelda have undoubtedly been lost. This is not surprising when one considers that Zelda, never highly organized, was in and out of hospitals during the 1930s and 1940s and that fires oddly punctuated her life — the fire at the Fitzgeralds' Baltimore home in 1933; the fire at Highland Hospital that killed Zelda in 1948; and the fire in which her sister Marjorie burned many of Zelda's possessions (including several of her paintings) at their mother's home in Montgomery after Zelda's death. Scott, however, was meticulous in keeping all correspondence that related in any way to his life, and his letters from Zelda were certainly central to that life. Despite the missing letters to Zelda, we know Scott's side of the story from existing letters to friends and editors and to Scottie, all of which have been published. It is Zelda's view of their lives that has been seriously underrepresented, and one of the purposes behind this book is to display her talents as a letter writer.

The organization and breakdown of the letters is as follows:

PART I Courtship and Marriage: 1918–1920 (letters 1–49). Eight telegrams from Scott to Zelda and six letters from Zelda to Scott from this period have been previously published. Scott's letters to Zelda from these years are lost, but we have included twelve additional telegrams from him, which Zelda pasted in her scrapbook. We have also included twenty-three previously unpublished letters from Zelda to Scott during this period.

PART II The Years Together: 1920–1929 (letters 50–51). The Fitzgeralds lived together throughout the twenties and therefore did not exchange letters. However, in 1930, the Fitzgeralds each wrote a long letter looking back on the twenties, in an attempt to discover why they faced the new decade in such terrible straits. Because these two letters are retrospective, lengthy, and contain references to many of the important events and people in the Fitzgeralds' lives during the preceding decade, we have placed them in this section.

PART III Breaking Down: 1930–1939 (letters 52–209). We have included two previously unpublished letters that Scott wrote to Zelda during the first eight years of the thirties, and we have selected 106 out of the 260 previously unpublished letters from Zelda to Scott to include in this section. These letters give a much fuller picture of Zelda's life as she lived intermittently in a series of institutions and in her hometown of Montgomery, Alabama.

PART IV The Final Years: 1939–1940 (letters 210–333) From 1939, there are seven letters from Scott to Zelda and four letters from Zelda to Scott that have been previously published. We have included eleven additional letters from Scott to Zelda and sixty-nine previously unpublished letters from Zelda to Scott. From 1940, there are thirty-seven previously published letters from Scott to Zelda, and we have found an additional nine. Astonishingly, none of Zelda's letters to Scott from 1940 has ever been published—only an unsigned Valentine's Day card—thereby giving the impression that she no longer wrote to him. This impression is far from accurate; we have found fifty-seven letters and telegrams that Zelda wrote to Scott during the last year of his life, and we have selected thirty-three of them.

We have followed two principles in selecting which letters to include in this book. First, we have included those letters that sustain the narrative—that tell what actually happened. Second, we wanted to include those letters that convey the varied and complex emotional nature of the Fitzgeralds' relationship. Their letters to each other often communicate these difficult-to-describe emotional nuances in passages of startling beauty and clarity as they wrote about the present and reevaluated the past.

INTRODUCTION

Eleanor Lanahan

To mention F. Scott and Zelda Fitzgerald is to invoke the twenties, the Jazz Age, romance, and outrageous early success, with all its attendant perils. The names Scott and Zelda can summon taxis at dusk, conjure gleaming hotel lobbies and smoky speakeasies, flappers, yellow phaetons, white suits, large tips, expatriates, and nostalgia for the Lost Generation. And even though they are my grandparents, I can't fail to mention that Scott's alcoholism and Zelda's madness are a powerful part of the myth.

My grandparents' lives are as fascinating to me as their artistic achievements. I've always been amazed by their ability to express their love for each other in original and poignant ways. Despite their short and nomadic lives—Scott was born in 1896 and died in 1940, at the age of forty-four, eight years before Zelda—they left an abundance of correspondence, a window into an extraordinary romance. Their letters reveal two people possessed of an incredible life force and an urge to communicate to the fullest of their powers. Scott's are astoundingly intimate; they are testimony to his frankness, his caring, his extraordinary ear, and his virtuosity with the English language. Zelda's are poetic, full of metaphor and descriptions. How they must have loved to open each other's envelopes! Sometimes.

Several collections of Scott's letters have already been published, as have single volumes of letters to his agent Harold Ober, his editor Maxwell Perkins, and to my mother, Scottie. Scott and Zelda did not need to write to one another during the ten most famous years of their lives, and the idea of assembling both of their letters in one volume has always presented a problem. The editors of this book, Jackson R. Bryer and Cathy W. Barks, have done a painstaking and graceful job of bridging this gap with letters, insights, and information from many sources.

This compilation is timely. Now that Zelda's role as wife, as artist, and as a person who struggled with mental illness can be viewed in a more modern and compassionate light, her talents are becoming more widely respected—although Scott apparently appreciated them all along. With this volume, he may regain some stature with his critics. The record confirms that he offered Zelda support and encouragement for her writing. He also shared his editorial skills, his high standards, and his hope when it was needed most. Scott is revealed as a man of profound loyalty and responsibility—far from his usual image.

What emerges from this collection are the Fitzgeralds' natural gifts, their charms, and their vast reservoirs of love, tenderness, and devotion. This is an emotional biography—a record of their successes and tragedies, as well as a firsthand glimpse at the first half of the twentieth century through the eyes of two people at the center of its artistic life.

I was two months old when my grandmother died in a fire at Highland Hospital in Asheville, North Carolina. Zelda's last letter to my mother in 1948 said that she longed to meet the baby. For me, that letter has been an important thread to the past, an almost accidental link between the generations; it's a comfort that my grandmother knew of my existence.

Zelda's letters abound with metaphor. The sky over a lake closes "like a gray oyster shell." The mountains cover "their necks in pink tulle like coquettish old ladies." Her prose is lush and multisensory, as when she reminds Scott of the smells of July by the sea. Occasionally, her persona gets scrambled with that of Daisy Buchanan, who appears in *The Great Gatsby* as a languid and careless member of the idle rich. But in the novel, please note, Scott saved his scorn for the Buchanans, whose vast resources allowed them to have other people clean up their messes. Scott, too, is often confused with his own creation, the ludicrously rich Jay Gatsby. But the novel is a cautionary tale, in which Gatsby tries to use his ill-gotten wealth to recreate the past. Although Scott frequently wrote about high society, to the end of his days he retained a firm midwestern belief in honesty and hard work, as well as a desperately low bank balance.

These letters reveal how little money kept them afloat. And it's miraculous how much they accomplished on such a tiny budget. When they had it, they spent it. The need for money motivated Scott to write much of his short fiction. Not until the depths of the Depression, when he was forced to take employment in the Hollywood screenwriting factories, did Scott waver from his true vocation. By the time he died, he had completed four novels, 160 short stories (including many self-described formulaic potboilers, which provided the major part of his sustenance), numerous essays and reviews, and a full-length play, *The Vegetable* — not to mention the hundreds of letters that consumed much of his creative energy, as well as his unfinished novel, *The Last Tycoon*.

At critical junctures, when Scott had no money at all, he borrowed from his agent, his editor, and his friends, which forced him into a cycle of writing to eradicate debt and then borrowing to write. In 1923, he reported that he had worked twelve-hour days for five weeks to "rise from abject poverty back into the middle class."

My mother, their only child, knew this cycle well. She described Scott's relationship to money: "He worshipped, despised, was awed by, was 'crippled by his inability to handle' (as he put it), threw away, slaved for, and had a lifelong love-hate relationship with, money . . . money and alcohol were the two great adversaries with which he battled all his life."

Because Scott's books were on a proscribed list at the time of his death, authorities of the Catholic St. Mary's Church in Rockville, Maryland, denied him burial in ancestral plots. Instead, he was laid to rest in the nearby Rockville Union Cemetery. Eight years later, when Zelda died, the family decided they should be buried together in a double vault. My mother wrote to her grandmother Sayre just after Zelda's funeral:

> I was so glad you decided she should stay with Daddy, as seeing them buried there together gave the tragedy of their lives a sort of classic unity and it was very touching and reassuring to think of their two high-flying and generous spirits being at peace together at last — Mama was such an extraordinary person that had things continued as perfect and romantic as they began the story of her life would have been more like a fairy-tale than a reality.

The fairy tale began when Scott and Zelda met in 1918, at a country club dance in Montgomery, Alabama. Lt. F. Scott Fitzgerald was among the many soldiers stationed at nearby Fort Sheridan, awaiting orders to fight overseas. Zelda, gifted with beauty, grace, high spirits, and expert skills of flirtation, was one of the most popular belles in the region. Her earliest letters to Scott are distinctly girlish. She sounds awash, agoggle in love. Young women of the South, barely free of their Victorian chaperones, still cultivated an utter femininity, a "pink helplessness," as Zelda calls it. She also refers merrily to her desire for merged identities, for Scott to define her existence. In taking a man's name, a woman assumed his whole identity, including his career and his social standing—an abject dependency that today would make both sexes wary. Zelda's declarations of loneliness, of her "nothingness without him" might be alarming to the modern reader, but they are reflections of the time. The Nineteenth Amendment, guaranteeing women the right to vote, was not even ratified until August 1920.

In Montgomery the ratio of soldiers to young women was tipped heavily in favor of the women, and competition was fierce among suitors. Scott's insecurity about losing the woman who had captured his heart is reflected in her mail. Because his side of the correspondence is underrepresented, I'm taking the liberty of including the poem that opens *The Great Gatsby*, one that few people know he wrote, because he attributed it to a fictitious poet, Thomas Parke D'Invilliers:

> Then wear the gold hat, if that will move her;
>   If you can bounce high, bounce for her too,
> Till she cry "Lover, gold-hatted, high-bouncing lover,
>   I must have you!"

To win her hand, Scott certainly wore the gold hat and bounced.

The Fitzgeralds arrived in New York for the kickoff of the Roaring Twenties. In the boom years, it seemed, the entire city was having one big party. The ticker tape had barely settled along the Fifth Avenue parade route from welcoming the troops home from World War I when Scott's first novel, *This Side of Paradise*, astonished his publishers and sold out of its entire first printing. A week after publication, on April 3, 1920, he and Zelda were married.

Twenty-three-year-old Scott, an overnight celebrity, told the press that his greatest ambitions were to write the best novel that ever was and to stay in love with his wife forever. With instinctive media savvy, the newlyweds set about giving America a fresh image of itself as youthful, fun-loving, free-spending, hardworking, and innovative. And they weren't too sophisticated to plunge in the Plaza fountain or to spin to their hearts' content in the hotel doors. Scott described the excitement of those early days in the East: "New York had all the iridescence of the beginning of the world." And he recalled (an important and too often overlooked ingredient to this fairy tale) "writing all night and all night again."

My mother was born on October 26, 1921, and was immediately

assigned to the care of a nanny. "Children shouldn't be a bother," Zelda explained. On the subject of the domestic arts, when Harper & Brothers asked Zelda to contribute to *Favorite Recipes of Famous Women*, she wrote:

> See if there is any bacon, and if there is ask the cook which pan to fry it in. Then ask if there are any eggs, and if so try and persuade the cook to poach two of them. It is better not to attempt toast, as it burns very easily. Also, in the case of bacon do not turn the fire too high, or you will have to get out of the house for a week. Serve preferably on china plates, though gold or wood will do if handy.

Scott's second novel, *The Beautiful and Damned*, was published a few months after my mother's birth. The Fitzgeralds were still enraptured. Scott inscribed his first edition to Zelda:

> For my darling wife, my dearest sweetest
> baboo, without whose love and aid
> neither this book nor any other
> would ever have been possible.
> From me, who loves her more
> every day, with a heartful of
> worship for her lovely self.
>
> Scott
>
> St. Paul, Minn.
> Feb 6th 1922

A lock of Zelda's hair, bound with a blue ribbon, was pressed inside the cover, where it remains to this day. During the early years of their marriage, Zelda seemed content to toss her talents aside and become a reckless and decorative wife, although a jovial strain of competition ran through a review she wrote of *The Beautiful and Damned* for the *New York Tribune*:

> To begin with, every one must buy this book for the following aesthetic reasons: First, because I know where there is the cutest cloth of gold dress for only $300 in a store on Forty-second Street, and also if enough people buy it where there is a

platinum ring with a complete circlet, and also if loads of people buy it my husband needs a new winter overcoat, although the one he has has done well enough for the last three years. . . .

It seems to me that on one page I recognized a portion of an old diary of mine which mysteriously disappeared shortly after my marriage, and also scraps of letters which, though considerably edited, sound to me vaguely familiar. In fact, Mr. Fitzgerald—I believe that is how he spells his name—seems to believe that plagiarism begins at home.

Scott's use of Zelda's letters is sometimes cited as evidence of his gross misappropriation of Zelda's talent. At the time, however, it was generally considered a husband's job to be a provider, and a wife's job to tend to amenities. Maybe Zelda wanted to give herself a bit of credit for authorship, but at this point there was no serious rivalry between them. A reporter interviewed Zelda a year and a half after the review appeared. For fun, Scott posed several of the questions:

"What do you want your daughter to do, Mrs. Fitzgerald, when she grows up?" Scott Fitzgerald inquired in his best reportorial manner, "not that you'll try to make her, of course, but—"

"Not great and serious and melancholy and inhospitable, but rich and happy and artistic. I don't mean that money means happiness, necessarily. But having things, just things, objects makes a woman happy. The right kind of perfume, the smart pair of shoes. They are great comforts to the feminine soul."

Later, in France, where my grandparents were immersed in an entirely artistic crowd, Zelda's ambitions sparked. For three agonizing years, she threw all of her creative energy into ballet. That a married woman would try to establish her own artistic identity was unusual, and the strain of such physical discipline, begun at the late age of twenty-seven, is thought to have contributed to Zelda's exhausted mental state.

When she suffered her first breakdown, ten years after the wedding, in 1930, the fairy tale ended. Her first letters from the Prangins Clinic in Switzerland, and Scott's first letters from Paris, are bitter, blameful reinterpretations of their whole relationship. Very little was understood about the nature of Zelda's suffering. Treatment for schizophrenia, identified as an illness only nineteen years earlier, was in its infancy.

No helpful drugs existed, only grim and largely ineffective therapies.

By this time, my grandfather's alcoholism was also full-blown. It's no secret that F. Scott Fitzgerald was one of the most famous alcoholics who ever lived. But he was a "high-functioning" alcoholic, which made it even more difficult for him to acknowledge or treat his problem. In 1931, little insight had been gained about the negative effects of alcohol. Alcoholism was not regarded as a disease so much as a shameful weakness of character. The AA program, as millions now know it, wasn't founded until 1935, and it did not become widespread until several years after Scott's death.

Although no one knew the cause or cure for either of their maladies, there was much reproach. Mrs. Sayre blamed Scott for drinking too much and for not providing stability for her daughter. Scott blamed Zelda's mother for spoiling her. He also blamed Zelda for being too preoccupied with ballet, while she blamed him for his drunken carousing. Their confusion is poignant, especially when Zelda begged forgiveness for whatever mysterious part of it was her own fault.

The myth persists that Scott drove Zelda crazy. My mother, who was eight years old when Zelda was first hospitalized, and who visited her mother in various clinics over the next seventeen years, wrote to a biographer: "I think I think (short of documentary evidence to the contrary) that if people are not crazy, they get themselves out of crazy situations, so I have never been able to buy the notion that it was my father's drinking which led her to the sanitarium. Nor do I think she led him to the drinking. I simply don't know the answer, and of course, that is the conundrum that keeps the legend going. . . ."

In 1932, Zelda, yearning to earn her own way in the world, wrote a novel, *Save Me the Waltz*. Before showing it to Scott, she rushed it to his agent. Scott was understandably irate. It had taken her only a few months of furious activity to write the book. He had been working on *Tender Is the Night* for several years, had torn up draft after draft, and had read her various passages from it. Clearly, Zelda anticipated that Scott would not want her to use exactly the same material that he was using in *Tender Is the Night*—the years they had spent in France and her own mental breakdown.

Her project inspired their most fierce territorial struggle. At issue was their individual right to use their shared autobiographical material. Scott was also furious that Zelda had named a character Amory

Blaine, after the protagonist in *This Side of Paradise*. He was certain, as the bill-payer of the family, that her wholesale borrowing would lead to ridicule from his readers and financial ruin. In the end, Zelda removed the parts of her manuscript that overlapped (or, to Scott's mind, were directly imitative of) *Tender Is the Night*.

One admirable thing about my grandparents was their ability to forgive infinitely. In the end, Scott helped Zelda with revisions of her novel. He also arranged publication of various articles she wrote and helped produce her play, *Scandalabra*, written when she was an out-patient in Baltimore. When Zelda began painting seriously, he arranged an exhibition of her work at a New York gallery.

I don't purport to understand my grandparents better than they did themselves. Nor do I believe in latter-day diagnoses, based only on letters and art. Nonetheless, I've been exposed to many amateur diagnoses of my grandmother: bipolar disorder, schizophrenia, or simple depression. A therapist at a panel I recently attended took the microphone and proceeded to give definitive diagnostic code numbers for my grandparents' disorders, apparently comfortable diagnosing both of them on the basis of letters and biographies. Perfect strangers have volunteered with straight faces that Zelda had all the talent and Scott simply stole her ideas—an injustice that, of course, drove her crazy!

Zelda had many periods of lucidity and she was never declared legally insane. Her illness had many phases. When she was well, she wrote lyrical, haunting, loving, and nostalgic prose. When she was ill, she sent terribly convoluted warnings to friends about the Second Coming. The strain on Scott was enormous. He tried to be both father and mother to his daughter, to provide the best possible treatment for his wife, and to keep the family financially afloat. But, as he admitted publicly in *The Crack-Up*, he now faced his own emotional bankruptcy. The wellspring of his story ideas had dried up. Until he was hired as a scriptwriter by MGM, he faced despair.

A trait of Scott's, made crystal-clear in these letters, was his tendency to overmanage, and, occasionally, to be downright domineering. My mother felt he would have made a fine headmaster of a school. The summer before she entered Vassar College, he warned her:

> You have reached the age when one is of interest to an adult only insofar as one seems to have a future. The mind of a little child is fascinating, for it looks on old things with new eyes—

but at about twelve this changes. The adolescent offers nothing, can do nothing, say nothing that the adult cannot do better. . . .

To sum up: What you have done to please me or make me proud is practically negligible since the time you made yourself a good diver at camp (and now you are softer than you have ever been). In your career as a "wild society girl," vintage of 1925, I'm not interested. I don't want any of it—it would bore me, like dining with the Ritz Brothers. When I do not feel you are "going somewhere," your company tends to depress me for the silly waste and triviality involved. On the other hand, when occasionally I see signs of life and intention in you, there is no company in the world I would prefer.

Scott wrote weekly to my mother at college. Rather than send her $50 allowance once a month, he insisted on sending her a check for $13.85 every week, probably as a vehicle for his missives. He told her which courses to take, what extracurricular activities were worthwhile, whom to date, her duties toward Zelda, what to read, and how to wear her hair. He critiqued her behavior, her academic performance, and her choice of roommates. Clearly, he loved Scottie very much and his self-confessed desire to preach now had an outlet.

From California, Scott also wrote to Zelda, loyally, warmly, and sometimes perfunctorily. During the last three years of his life, while working as a scriptwriter in Hollywood and, later, on his fifth novel, he began an affair with the gossip columnist Sheilah Graham. Sheilah gave a healthy structure and domesticity to Scott's last years, but he never completely relinquished his love for Zelda. "You are the finest, loveliest, tenderest, and most beautiful person I have ever known," Scott wrote to her after their last trip together in 1939, "but even that is an understatement."

I believe, as did my mother, that Scott and Zelda stayed in love until the day they died. Perhaps it became an impossible and impractical love—part nostalgia and part hope. Perhaps it was a longing for a reunion of all the best qualities in each other that they had once celebrated, and the happy times they had shared, but it was a bond that united them forever. This collection, at last, allows Scott and Zelda, two magnificent songbirds, to sing their own duet.

Lt. F. Scott Fitzgerald and Zelda Sayre, as they looked when they met at a country club dance in Montgomery, Alabama, in July 1918. Photograph of Zelda Sayre courtesy of Princeton University Library

PART I

Courtship and Marriage: 1918–1920

The good things and the first years . . . will stay with me forever. . . .
—SCOTT TO ZELDA, APRIL 26, 1934

Scott and Zelda first met in Montgomery, Alabama, Zelda's hometown, in July 1918, probably at a country club dance. Zelda, who had just graduated from high school and was still the town's most popular girl, turned eighteen that month; Scott, who had attended Princeton and was now a lieutenant in the infantry, would be twenty-two that fall. In her autobiographical novel, *Save Me the Waltz* (1932), Zelda recalled that Scott, so handsome in his tailor-made Brooks Brothers uniform, had "smelled like new goods" as she nestled her "face in the space between his ear and his stiff army collar" while they danced (*Collected Writings* 39). Just two months later, Scott recorded in his Ledger the event that would shape the rest of his life and much of his work: "Sept.: Fell in love on the 7*th*" (*Ledger* 173). That same month, Scott summed up his twenty-first year: On his birthday, he wrote, "A year of enormous importance. Work, and Zelda. Last year as a Catholic" (*Ledger* 172). The major decisions that a young man coming of age makes—matters of vocation, love, and faith—had been decided.

Scott, although still untried and immature in many ways, had adamantly committed himself to becoming "one of the greatest writers who ever lived" (as he told his college friend Edmund "Bunny" Wilson) and to having the "top girl" at his side to share the storybook life he envisioned. During his years at Princeton University, his academic life had taken a backseat to his social ambitions; realizing that he probably would never graduate, Scott had enlisted in the army in October 1917. His military training eventually brought him to Camp Sheridan, near Montgomery, and to Zelda—the most beautiful, confident, and sought-after girl in town. Scott then devoted himself to becoming the "top man" among her many suitors, intending to vanquish the other young college boys and soldiers by marrying this most desirable girl.

Zelda, being younger, was less clear about particulars, but she certainly shared Scott's romantic sense of a special destiny. Other than teaching, careers for women were still discouraged. Courtship and marriage were the areas in which young women such as Zelda, the daughter of a prominent judge, were expected to achieve distinction. Her three older sisters, Marjorie, Rosalind, and Clothilde, were already married; Zelda intended to make the absolute most of her own days as a southern belle, relishing her role in the spotlight. Montgomery may have been a small, provincial city, but it was surrounded by college towns, as well as being crowded with young soldiers from nearby training camps. The war imbued the local courtship rituals with an even greater sense of urgency and romanticism than usual. The crowds of young people necessitated numerous forms of entertainment—parties, dances, sports, plays, and Friday-night vaudeville shows—to keep them occupied. The Sayres' front porch, replete with every sort of southern flower and a porch swing for Zelda and her beaux, was locally famous. Zelda had already filled a glove box with the small colorful badges of masculine honor the young soldiers took from their uniforms and gave to her as tokens of their affection. Scott soon added his own insignia to this collection. Young aviators from Taylor Field executed dangerous stunts as they flew their airplanes over Zelda's house to impress her. Scott competed with such exploits by bragging about the famous writer he was going to become. Although Scott did not "get over" to fight the war, that summer and fall, as he vied for Zelda's heart, the two no doubt believed that he would be sent overseas and perhaps face death. He continued to write, hoping that in the event of his death, he would become the American counterpart of Rupert Brooke, the handsome young English poet, who in death had become the romantic hero—forever young, beautiful, and full of promise.

The war, however, ended just as Scott was preparing to embark for France. When he was discharged in February 1919, he went to New York City to find a job and to become a famous *living* writer, instead of a dead one. He hoped to find work with a newspaper but had to settle for a low-paying job with an advertising firm. He missed Zelda terribly, told his family about her, and asked his mother to write to Zelda, which she did. Then, on March 24, Scott sent Zelda the engagement ring that had been his mother's. Zelda couldn't have been more thrilled. But although her letters are full of enthusiastic assurances of her love, her life in Montgomery continued pretty much the same as before—a whirlwind of social engagements, which included continuing to go out with other boys—and she wrote Scott all about it. Zelda especially loved the rounds of college parties, dances, and commencement activities beginning in May and the exciting football weekends in the fall. Scott's daily life, on the other hand, was at total odds with his idealized conception of himself. He hated his job, hated having so little money, and especially hated how his clothes were becoming threadbare. And, worse yet, his stories weren't selling. Later, in "My Lost City" (1936), he would look back and write, ". . . I was haunted always by my other life . . . my fixation upon the day's letter from Alabama—would it come and what would it say?—my shabby suits, my poverty, and love. . . . I was a failure— mediocre at advertising work and unable to get started as a writer" (*Crack-Up* 25–26).

Despite his sense of failure, Scott was actually quite productive. Although he sold only one story in the spring of 1919—"Babes in the Woods," for which *The Smart Set* paid him thirty dollars—he continued his apprenticeship and produced over nineteen stories that winter and spring. All were rejected by the magazines to which he submitted them; many, however, were later revised and published. Although Scott was being unrealistic in his expectations of immediate fame—who, after all, is a blazing success at the age of twenty-two?—his sense of failure, anxiety, and loss was keen and would remain with him the rest of his life. When Scott visited Zelda in Montgomery in mid-April, he was depressed and losing confidence in himself. Zelda tried to reassure him in her letters, but she also continued to report on all the fun she was having.

By June 1919, Scott and Zelda's engagement was in serious jeopardy. When Scott received a note that Zelda had written to another suitor and then accidentally put into the wrong envelope, one addressed to Scott, he was enraged and ordered her never to write to him again. But as soon as he received Zelda's brief explanation, he went to Montgomery and begged her to marry him right away. Zelda cried in his arms, but she turned him down and broke the engagement. Scott returned to New York feeling utterly defeated as a writer and a lover. He wrote to a friend: "I've done my best and I've failed—it's a great tragedy to me and I feel I have very little left to live for. . . . Unless someday she will marry me I will never marry" (*Letters* 455–456). He quit his job, went on a three-week bender, returned to his parents' home in St. Paul, and went to work revising "The Romantic Egotist," the novel that had been rejected by Charles Scribner's Sons in 1918. During this period of a little over two months, Scott and Zelda exchanged no letters. But when Scribners accepted his novel, now entitled *This Side of Paradise,* on September 16, 1919, Scott immediately wrote to Zelda again and planned a visit to Montgomery; the couple soon resumed their engagement. More letters and visits to Montgomery followed, and Zelda and Scott were married the following April, only one year after Scott had first sent Zelda the engagement ring.

In his imagination, Scott attached the acquisition of Zelda to the acquisition of material success, thereby identifying what were already the twin themes of his writing—love and money—as the twin themes of his life, as well. Later, he looked back on the summer of his broken engagement in "Pasting It Together" (1936) and wrote, "It was one of those tragic loves doomed for lack of money" and that although when he became "the man with the jingle of money in his pocket," he "married the girl" after all, he would never trust either money or love—the same elements of life to which he was most drawn (*Crack-Up* 77). Zelda's imagination, however, was committed solely to the enchantment of love. Her letters from this period offer evidence that dispels two enduring but misleading myths about her marriage to Scott: first, that Zelda would not marry him until he had money; second, that one of the reasons Scott interested her was because she was eager to leave her small town for the larger social stage of New York City. It is true that Zelda's parents certainly had reservations about their daughter marrying a young man with no secure prospects for the future, but Zelda repeatedly reassures Scott in these letters that *love*, not money, is what she wants most out of life. Although they resumed their engagement after Scribners accepted Scott's novel, it hadn't been published yet and there was no assurance that it would be a moneymaker. Once the engagement was settled, Zelda eagerly anticipated joining Scott in New York, but her enthusiasm again was for being with Scott and not the larger possibilities the so-called glittering city offered. Zelda loved Montgomery, especially its beautiful flowers, and she knew she would miss the way of life she had always known.

While these letters challenge the myths, they also offer a vivid portrait of Zelda at eighteen—a flirtatious, audacious young woman, whose life was full of friends, practical jokes, and parties. Her letters indicate that although she believed that provoking jealousy was an important ritual in courtship, she did not feel that she was being unfaithful to Scott by dating other men; they also reveal that she felt no hesitation in reporting it all to him. In addition to telling Scott about an endless stream of social engagements, she also articulated her ideas about life and love—that women were intended be "a disturbing element among" men and that even though she loved to appear all "pink and helpless," the men who thought her "purely decorative" were "fools for not knowing better" (letters 16 and 28). Scott, who had a wonderful ear for words, freely borrowed passages from these letters for his fiction.

Certain themes emerge from the events and letters of this period that foreshadow characteristics and conflicts that will persist throughout the Fitzgeralds' lives together. Jealousy was certainly a factor. According to Fitzgerald biographer Arthur Mizener, when Scott and Zelda first started seeing each other, she pulled another date into a lighted phone booth and initiated a spirited kissing session, which ended when she said, "Scott was coming and I wanted to make him jealous" (83). As Scott Donaldson and others have suggested, one of the reasons Scott was attracted to Zelda (as well as to earlier girlfriends, such as the Chicago socialite Ginevra King) was *because* of their many suitors. In order to be the "top girl" he wanted, she had to be popular with other men. Yet when Scott tried to play the same game and wrote to her from New York that he found a young woman very attractive, Zelda called his bluff, giving him the go-head to kiss the girl, a response guaranteed to turn the tables and make Scott worry even more about what Zelda herself might be doing in Montgomery. When Scott looked back on this period in "Early Success" (1937), he recalled that some of his friends had "arrangements with 'sensible' girls," but he noted, "Not I—I was in love with a whirlwind and I must spin a net big enough to catch it . . ." (*Crack-Up* 86). The great paradox of their love affair is that the same traits that attracted them to each other would also create chaos and conflict in their lives. Just as the jealousies so playful during courtship would take on a more destructive role in their marriage, alcohol, considered a harmless rite of passage for the young, would become an increasingly destructive factor, one that would continue to haunt them.

In addition to jealousy and alcohol as troubling factors in their relationship, each had a distinct personality sharply divided and pulled in opposing directions. The split in Scott's personality has been thoroughly analyzed and much written about. His contemporary Malcolm Cowley perceptively argued that Scott possessed a "double vision," by which he meant that he had the ability to throw himself wholeheartedly into dissipation, despite his deeply embedded puritanism. Scott gave Nick Carraway, the narrator of *The Great Gatsby*, this trait, as well: "I was within and without," states Nick, "simultaneously enchanted and repelled by the inexhaustible variety of life" (40). Such double vision would help make Scott a great writer, but it would also allow him to become an emblem of the material excesses and moral corruption of the 1920s, at the same time that his writing provided a prophetic judgment against the period. The divided aspect of Zelda's personality, however, has not been adequately recognized or analyzed.

Zelda most aptly described her own divided personality in *Save Me the Waltz,* saying that it was "very difficult to be two simple people at once, one who wants to have a law to itself and the other who wants to . . . be loved and safe and protected" (*Collected Writings* 56). Although Zelda, age thirty at the time she wrote the novel, was looking backward at the young girl she had once been, this conflicting pull between dependency and independence also emerges vividly in the letters she wrote at eighteen, in passionate declarations of love expressed by a willful, spirited young woman, but one who, in the ardor of youth, desired to merge with the beloved as closely and completely as possible. These expressions, along with her equally passionate expressions of independence, also represent a more deeply embedded aspect of Zelda's personality, one that will reemerge in her letters in the 1930s, in which she vacillated between valiant struggles to establish herself as a writer (and therefore create economic independence) and her deeply felt gratitude for and need of Scott's continued provisions for her care.

Sadly, Scott's letters to Zelda from this period do not survive. We have only urgent telegrams he sent to Zelda (which she pasted in her scrapbook), announcing the numerous visits he hurriedly planned to make to Montgomery, afraid that if he was not around, another suitor would win her. Scott did express his view of her in a letter to a friend; writing in February 1920, just before his marriage, he admitted, "My friends are unanimous in frankly advising me not to marry a wild, pleasure loving girl like Zelda so I'm quite used to it." Notwithstanding such warnings, Scott, in this same letter, clearly expressed his understanding of Zelda's temperament and his commitment to her:

> No personality as strong as Zelda's could go without getting critisisms and as you say she is not above approach. I've always known that. . . . But . . . I fell in love with her courage, her sincerity and her flaming self respect and its these things I'd believe in even if the whole world indulged in wild suspicions that she wasn't all that she should be.
>
> But of course the real reason . . . is that I love her and that's the beginning and end of everything. (*Correspondence* 53)

While the loss of Scott's courtship letters to Zelda is a great one, perhaps there are some advantages to be gained from Zelda's letters standing nearly on their own here. We know so much about Scott from his published correspondence, from his insightful essays of self-analysis collected in *The Crack-Up,* and from the numerous biographies and scholarship his life and work have justifiably generated. Zelda, on the other hand, has too often remained a cultural icon, cast in a series of feminine roles: first as a tempestuous and beautiful southern belle, then as a trendsetting flapper of the twenties, and ultimately as a woman who has gone mad (another myth, as her later letters will attest). In these letters, however, Zelda emerges as a wonderfully vivacious and articulate young woman, someone with interesting and original things to say.

1. TO ZELDA
[August 1918]

ALS, 1 p. Scrapbook
Hq. 67th
[Camp] Sheridan[, Montgomery,
Alabama]

Zelda:

Here is the mentioned chapter . . . . . a document in youthful melancholy . . . . .[1]

However . . . . . the heroine does resemble you in more ways than four . . . . .

Needlessly I may add that the chapter and the sending of it are events for your knowledge alone . . . . —Show it not to man woman or child.

I am frightfully bored today—

Desirously

F. Scott Fit—

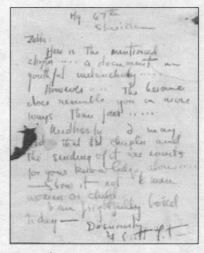

Courtesy of Princeton University Library

---

1. Scott sent Zelda a chapter from his novel, "The Romantic Egotist," the summer that they first met. Although Scribners returned Scott's manuscript the same month (August 1918), Maxwell Perkins, who would become his editor, wrote Scott an encouraging letter, suggesting that he revise and resubmit the novel.

2. TO ZELDA Wire. Scrapbook

CHARLOTTE NC   122 AM   FEB 21ST 1919
MISS TELDA FAYRE[2]
    CARE FRANCES STUBBS[3]
        AUBURN ALA
YOU KNOW I DO NOT [DOUBT?] YOU DARLING
    SCOTT
    1103AM

Auburn football star Francis Stubbs;
Zelda pasted this picture in her scrap-
book. Courtesy of Princeton University
Library

---

2. All wires in the book are reproduced as transmitted by the telegraph service. Mis-
spellings, such as those in Zelda's name here, have not been corrected.
3. Francis Stubbs, with whom Zelda had a date, was one of Auburn University's star foot-
ball players. Scott, discharged from the military, was on his way to New York when he
wired Zelda, who was at Auburn with Stubbs, perhaps hoping to ensure her fidelity by
expressing trust in her.

3. TO ZELDA   Wire. Scrapbook
[After February 22, 1919]   [New York City]

MISS SELDA SAYRE
       6 PLEASANT AVE   MONTGOMERY   ALA
DARLING HEART AMBITION ENTHUSIASM AND CONFI-
DENCE I DECLARE EVERYTHING GLORIOUS THIS WORLD
IS A GAME AND WHITE [WHILE] I FEEL SURE OF YOU LOVE
EVERYTHING IS POSSIBLE I AM IN THE LAND OF AMIBI-
TION AND SUCCESS AND MY ONLY HOPE AND FAITH IS
THAT MY DARLING HEART WILL BE WITH ME SOON.

4. TO SCOTT   ALS, 3 pp.
[February 1919]   [Montgomery, Alabama]

Lover—

I drifted into school this morning, and delivered a most enlight-
ening talk on Browning. Of cource I was well qualified, having read,
approximately, two poems. However, the class declared themselves
delighted and I departed with honors—I almost wish there were nothing to think of but to-morrow's lessons and to-day's lunch—I'd feel so
to-no-purpose if it werent for you—and I know you wouldnt keep
going just as well without me—that damn school is so depressing—

I s'pose you knew your Mother's anxiously anticipated epistle at
last arrived—I really am so glad she wrote—Just a nice little note—
untranslatable, but she called me "Zelda"—

Sweetheart, please dont worry about me—I want to always be a
help—You know I am all yours and love you with all my heart. Physically—I am prone to exaggerate my sylphiness—I'd so love to be 5 ft
4" × 2"—Maybe I'll accomplish it swimming. To-morrow, I'm breaking the ice—I can already feel the icicles. But the creek is delightfully
clean, and me and the sun are getting hot—

Last night a small crowd of practical jokers reversed calls to University, Sewanee and Auburn[4]—telegraphed collect all over the U.S.,

---

4. Prank calls to boys they knew who were attending southern colleges—the University of
Alabama in Tuscaloosa, the University of the South in Sewanee, Tennessee, and Auburn
University in Alabama—and were a part of the social circuit of football games and parties.

and were barely restrained by me from getting New York on the wire—O, you're quite welcome—It would've been a good joke, but I couldn't see the point—

Darling—lover—You know—
　　Zelda

5. TO SCOTT　　　　　　　　　ALS, 7 pp.
[March 1919]　　　　　　　　　　[Montgomery, Alabama]

Darling, I've nearly sat it off in the Strand to-day and all because W. E. Lawrence of the Movies is your physical counter-part.[5] So I was informed by half a dozen girls before I could slam on a hat and see for myself—He made me so homesick—I thought at first waiting must grow easier later—but every day I want you more—

All these soft, warm nights going to waste when I ought to be lying in your arms under the moon—the dearest arms in all the world—darling arms that I love so to feel around me—How much longer—before they'll be there to stay? When I do get home again, you'll certainly have a most awful time ever moving me one inch from you—

I'm glad you liked those films[6]—I wanted them to serve as maps of your property—The best is being finished for you—Monday—but if you're going to be so flattering, my head'll be swelled so big then, it won't look like me—Anyway, I am acquiring myriad wrinkles pondering over a reply to your Mother's note—I'm so dreadfully afraid of appearing fresh or presuming or casual—Most of my correspondents have always been boys, so I am at a loss—now in my hour of need—I really believe this is my first letter to a lady—It's really heart-rending—my frenzied efforts—Mid-night oil is burning by the well-full—O God!

An old flame from the Stone Ages is calling to-night—He'll probably leave in disgust because I just must talk about you—I love you so, and I'm *so* lonesome—

---

5. Actor who starred in sixty-seven movies from 1912 to 1947; his 1919 films included *The Girl-Woman, Caleb Piper's Girl,* and *Common Clay.*

6. Zelda had sent Scott pictures of herself.

Tilde[7] leaves to-morrow at 6. A.M.—It seems as though I should be going too—I'm sure she isnt half as anxious to leave as I am—O Lover, lover you are mine—and before long—I'll be coming to you because you are my darlin husband, and I am

Your Wife—

6. TO SCOTT   AL, 8 pp.
[March 1919]   [Montgomery, Alabama]

They're the most adorably moon-shiny things on earth[8]—I feel like a Vogue cover in 'em—I do wish yours were touching—But I feel sure I'll never be able to keep off the street in 'em—Does one take a lunch to bed with one in one's pockets? One has always used her pockets for biscuit—with butter! It was waiting for me when I came home from Selma to-day—What is it? It feels like a cloud and looks like a dream—Thanks, darling—

There are two or three nice men in New York, and he is expecting me near the 11th—so I am going—travelling—I shall probably arrive with a numerous coterie collected en route, but when my husband meets me, it will dissolve, and I shall dissolve, too, in his arms—and we shall live happily ever after—I don't care where.

"My Soldier Girl" was playing in Selma—so my male escort and I attended a rehearsal. I taught the chorus how to sling [swing?] a little, and so visited upon myself the profuse thanks of the manager—But the pool I went *particularly* to swim in, *was closed*—

> Aint no use in livin'—
> Just die
> Aint no use in eatin'—
> 'Taint pie
> Aint no use in kissin'—
> He'll tell
> Aint no use in nothin'—
> Aw Hell!

---

7. Clothilde, the third of Zelda's three older sisters, married to John Palmer; she was to join him in New York.
8. Scott sent Zelda a gift of a glamorous pair of pajamas.

You really mustn't say short hair thrills you—Just after I've lived in Vaseline, thereby turning mine dark, to make it long like you wanted it—But anyway, it didn't grow, so I really am glad you're becoming reconciled to the ways of convenience—I still think how nice the back of my neck *would* feel—Then, I think of Porphuria's Lover—and between the two, I am remaining *somewhat* sane—

Darling, I guess—I know—Mamma knows that we are going to be married some day—But she keeps leaving stories of young authors, turned out on a dark and stormy night, on my pillow—I wonder if you hadn't better write to my Daddy—just before I leave—I wish I were detached—sorter without relatives. I'm not exactly *scared* of 'em, but they *could* be so unpleasant about what I'm going to do—

But you know we will, my Sweetheart—when you're ready—your funny little pants sorter are coming home—for you to wrinkle with the dearest arms I know—I hope you squeeze me so hard, I'll be just as full of wrinkles as it—I hope so—

I dont see how you can carry around as much love as I've given you—

7. TO SCOTT   ALS, 11 pp.
[March 1919]   [Montgomery, Alabama]

Sweetheart,

Please, please don't be so depressed—We'll be married soon, and then these lonesome nights will be over forever—and until we are, I am loving, loving every tiny minute of the day and night—Maybe you won't understand this, but sometimes when I miss you most, it's hardest to write—and you always know when I make myself—Just the ache of it all—and I *can't* tell you. If we were together, you'd feel how strong it is—you're so sweet when you're melancholy. I love your sad tenderness—when I've hurt you—That's one of the reasons I could never be sorry for our quarrels—and they bothered you so—Those dear, dear little fusses, when I always tried so hard to make you kiss and forget—

Scott—there's nothing in all the world I want but you—and your precious love. All the material things are nothing. I'd just hate to live a sordid, colorless existence—because you'd soon love me less—and less—and I'd do anything—anything—to keep your heart for my own—I don't want to live—I want to love first, and live incidentally—Why don't you feel that I'm waiting—I'll come to you, Lover, when you're ready—Don't—don't ever think of the things you can't give me. You've trusted me with the dearest heart of all—and it's so damn much more than anybody else in all the world has ever had—

How can you think deliberately of life without me—If you should die—O Darling—darling Scot—It'd be like going blind. I know I would, too,—I'd have no purpose in life—just a pretty—decoration. Don't you think I was made for you? I feel like you had me ordered—and I was delivered to you—to be worn. I want you to wear me, like a watch-charm or a button hole boquet—to the world. And then, when we're alone, I want to help—to know that you can't do *anything* without me.

I'm glad you wrote Mamma. It was such a nice sincere letter—and mine to St Paul was very evasive and rambling. I've never, in all my life, been able to say anything to people older than me. Somehow I just instinctively avoid personal things with them—even my family. Kids are so much nicer. Livye[9] and a model from New York and I have been modelling in the Fashion Show—I had a misconceived idea that it was easy work—Two hours a day exhausts the most pig-iron of females—after twenty minutes, you feel like ten cents worth of fifty-dollar a yard lace—Some old fool had the sheer audacity to buy my favorite dress, so now what'll I do to-morrow? I've discovered something very, very comforting by this attempt at work—that I'm really smaller than average, and I am *delighted*!

I mailed your picture to-day—It's not a very characteristic pose, but maybe, if you look hard enough, there will be a little resemblance between me and the madonna—

This is Thursday, and the ring hasn't come—I want to wear it so people can see—

All my heart—
I love you
Zelda

---

9. Livye Hart, a popular friend of Zelda's, whose family, along with the Sayres, belonged to Montgomery's society club, *Les Mysterieuses*, an organization that planned entertainments and balls featuring the town's eligible young women.

8. TO ZELDA   Wire. Scrapbook
[March 1919]   [New York City]

Miss Lelda Sayre[10]
    Six Pleasant Ave   Montgy-Ala.
Sweetheart I have been frightfully busy but you know I have thought
of you every minute will write at length tomorrow got your letter and
loved it everything looks fine you seem with me always hope and
pray to be together soon good night darling.

9. TO ZELDA   Wire. Scrapbook

NEWYORK NY   MAR 22 1919
MISS LILDA SAYRE
        6 PLEASANT AVE   MONTGOMERY   ALA
DARLING I SENT YOU A LITTLE PRESENT FRIDAY THE
RING ARRIVED TONIGHT AND I AM SENDING IT
MONDAY[11] I LOVE YOU AND I THOUGHT I WOULD TELL
YOU HOW MUCH ON THIS SATURDAY NIGHT WHEN WE
OUGHT TO BE TOGETHER DONT LET YOUR FAMILY BE
SHOCKED AT MY PRESENT
SCOTT

---

10. Unlike most of the other telegrams from Scott that Zelda pasted in her scrapbook, this
one was not fully in capital letters. See also no. 27.
11. Scott sent Zelda an engagement ring that had been his mother's.

10. TO ZELDA   AN,[12] 1 p. Scrapbook
[March 24, 1919]   [New York City]

Darling: I am sending this just the way it came—I hope it fits and I wish I were there to put it on. I love you so much, much, much that it just hurts every minute I'm without you—Do write every day because I love your letters so—Goodbye, my own wife.

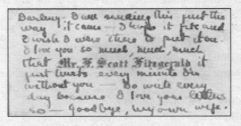

Courtesy of Princeton University Library

11. TO SCOTT   ALS, 8 pp.
[March 1919]   [Montgomery, Alabama]

Tootsie[13] opened it, of cource, and I wanted to so much. She says she wants Cappy Tan[14] to give her one like it. Scott, Darling, it really is beautiful. Every time I see it on my finger I am rather startled—I've never worn a ring before, they've always seemed so inappropriate—but I love to see this shining there so nice and white like our love—And it sorter says "soon" to me all the time— Just sings it all day long.

Thank goodness, the Fashion Show is over—wearing $500 dresses is the most strenuous task I've ever performed—There's always so much hanging on to be switched around—Aren't you glad I look like Hell in trains and slick jet dotties? Seems to me it'd be a constant source of pleasure to you that I am pink and blue.

Auburn has turned loose her R.O.T.C. with 60 loves in Mont-

---

12. Scott wrote this note to Zelda on his calling card and enclosed it with the engagement ring.
13. Rosalind, the second of Zelda's three older sisters.
14. Newman Smith, Rosalind's husband, who served in France during the war.

gomery—May's is completely devastated as the result. People may be thrown out of New York restaurants for squirmy dancing, but absolutely, those boys must have studied "Popular Mechanics" for months to be able to accomplish some of their favorite feats—Can't even be called "Chimey"—And every night I get very loud and coarse, and then I always wish for you so—so I wouldn't be such a kid—

Darlin, I don't know whether I *exactly* like the fact of having aged so perceptibly in one year. But, if you do, cource I'm glad—I'm glad "Peevie"[15] is back, too, because I've always thought I'd like him best of all the people you know—

Your feet—that you liked so much—are ruined. I've been toe-dancing again, and nearly broke my right foot—The doctor is trying, [of] cource, but they'll always look ugly, I guess—and I'd give half my life to have even little things like toes please you—I love you so—Sweetheart—so—

Hank Young arrived yesterday—to see me parade around in fine feathers. He was just telling me how proud of me you'd be—then May[16] dragged him away.

    Zelda

12. TO SCOTT   AL, 9 pp.
[March 1919]   [Montgomery, Alabama]

Dearest Scott—

I like your letter to A. D.[17] and I'm slowly mustering courage to deliver it—He's so blind, it'll probably be a terrible shock to him but it seems the only straight-forward thing to do—I dont see how you can write such nice family letters—and really, your mother was just sparing your feelings, or else she isn't a literary critic—I hope she'll like me—I'll be as nice as possible and try to make her—but I am afraid I'm losing all pretense of femininity, and I imagine she

---

15. Stephan Parrott, a friend of Scott's, whom he met at the Newman School, a Catholic prep school in New Jersey.
16. Either May Inglis, a popular girl who graduated from Sidney Lanier High School with Zelda in 1918, or May Steiner, a Montgomery girl whom Scott was dating when he met Zelda.
17. Zelda's father, Judge Anthony Dickinson Sayre, was sometimes called "A.D."

will demand it. Eleanor Browder[18] and I have formed a syndicate—
and we're "best friends" to more college boys than Solomon had
wives—Just sorter buddying with 'em and I really am enjoying it—
as much as I could anything without you—I have always been
inclined toward masculinity. It's such a cheery atmosphere boys
radiate—And we do such unique things—Yesterday, when the University boys took their belated departure, John Sellers wheeled me
thru a vast throng of people at the station, crying intermittently
"The lady hasn't walked in five years"—"God bless those who help
the poor," the lady would echo, much to the amazement and amusement of the station at large—We had collected fo'bits when our
innocent past-time was rudely interrupted by a somewhat brawny
arm-of-the-law being thrust between me and the rolling-chair—I
was rather vehemently denounced by the police force—In fact, we
are tinting the town a crimson line—and having a delightful time
acquiring a bad name—and Ed Hale has left us his cut-down
Flivver while he pursue[s] educational muses at Auburn. Of
cource, our lives are in continual danger, and our mothers are frantic, but Eleanor and I are enjoying the sensations we create
immensely—

I guess you can tell it's turned colder'n Blackegions by my
Spencerian method—That scrawly, wiggly fist seems so inappropriate for winter. I labored for quite a while accomplishing a sun-
burned, open-air looking script, and almost forgot my cold-weather
hand mean-time—

The fire burning again, and the old bench looking so lonesome
without us, make things mighty hard—If I weren't so *sure*—If I didn't
know we just *had* to have each other—I think I'd cry an awful lot—I
can just feel those darling, darling hands—and see your shiny hair—
not slick, but *wrinkled*, like I did it—

Good night, Sweetheart—

---

18. A friend of Zelda's from high school. In the "Composite Picture of an Ideal Senior Girl,"
Zelda was voted the best mouth and Eleanor the wittiest.

13. TO SCOTT   AL, 3 pp.
[March 1919]   [Montgomery, Alabama]

I am about to sink into a sleep of utter exhaustion — Eleanor B. and I have been *actually* running the Street-Car all day — We were quite a success in our business career until we ran it off the track. Then we got fired — but we were tired, anyway! Mothers of our associates just stood by and gasped — much to our glee, of cource — Things like the preceeding incident are our only amusement —

Darling heart, I love you — truly. You are my sweetheart — and I do — I do

I must leave or my date (awful boob) will come before I can escape —

Good Night, Lover

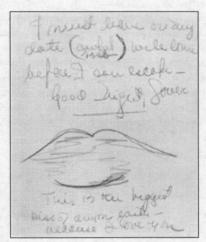

Courtesy of Princeton University Library

This is the biggest kiss of any on earth — because I love you

14. TO SCOTT
[March 1919]

AL, 4 pp.
[Montgomery, Alabama]
Sunday—

Darling, darling I love you so—To-day seems like Easter, and I wish we were together walking slow thru the sunshine and the crowds from Church—Everything smells so good and warm, and your ring shines so white in the sun—like one of the church lillies with a little yellow dust on it—We ought to be together [in] the Spring—It seems made for us to love in—

You can't imagine what havoc the ring wrought—a whole dance was completely upset last night—Everybody thinks its lovely—and I am so proud to be your girl—to have everybody know we are in love. It's so good to know youre always loving me—and that before long we'll be together for all our lives—

The Ohio troops have started a wild and heated correspondence with Montgomery damsels—From all I can gather, the whole 37th Div will be down in May—Then I guess the butterflies will flitter a trifle more— It seems dreadfully peculiar not to be worried over the prospects of the return of at least three or four fiancées. My brain is stagnating owing to the lack of scrapes—I havent had to exercise it in so long—

Sweetheart, I love you most of all the earth—and I want to be married soon—soon—Lover—Don't say I'm not enthusiastic—You ought to know—

15. TO ZELDA
[April 1919]

Wire. Scrapbook
[New York City]

MISS TELDA SAYRE
    SIX PLEASANT AVE   MONTGOMERY   ALA
TELDA FOUND KNOCKOUT LITTLE APARTMENT REA-
SONABLE RATES I HAVE TAKEN IT FROM TWENTY SIXTH
SHE MOVES INTO SAME BUILDING[19] EARLY IN MAY BET-

---

19. Scott visited Zelda's sister Clothilde in New York while looking for an apartment for himself and Zelda.

TER GIVE LETTER TO YOUR FATHER IM SORRY YOURE
NERVOUS DONT WRITE UNLESS YOU WANT TO I LOVE
YOU DEAR EVERTHING WILL BE MIGHTY FINE ALL
MY LOVE

16. TO SCOTT   ALS, 7 pp.
[April 1919]   6 Pleasant Ave.,
                                      Montgomery, Ala.

Dearest—

Your letters make things seem so close—and you always said I'd
wire I was "scared, Scott"—I'm really not one bit afraid—I love you
so—and April has already started!

I'm glad you went to see *Tilde*—I guess you are too, now that it's
over—she already writes Mamma of moving—says she never sees a
single tree from her windows, and it makes her homesick—This
end of the family just sits around straining their ears for Miss Boot-
sie's[20] little grunts and squeals—the Judge has relapsed into his
usual grouch since she left—I guess they'll be pretty lonesome
without me to disturb them—Toots[21] is taking an uproarious departure in about a week—She certainly makes life obnoxious sometimes. I hate people who *can't* do *anything* calmly. When I meet
persons who act as if everything, anything, were exactly what they
expected and wanted, I always gasp with admiration—They always
make me feel so irresponsible—and rather objects to be pitied—
they love to fancy themselves suffering—they're nearly all moral
and mental hypo-crondiacs. If they'd just awake to the fact that
their excuse and explanation is the necessity for a disturbing element among men—they'd be much happier, and the men much
more miserable—which is exactly what they need for the improvement of things in general.

I've just found, in Major Smith's[22] old books a Masonic Chart, in
hieroglyphics, of cource, which is puzzling me sorely—It's a very
queer—religion?—and with the help of pencilled notes, I am about to

---

20. The Sayres' cat, which apparently moved to New York with Clothilde.
21. Same as Tootsie, Zelda's sister Rosalind.
22. Newman Smith, Rosalind's husband.

fathom unfathomable secrets — If I could just stop reading "Scott" in every line I'd make more progress —

Kiss me, Lover — one darling kiss — I need you so —
Zelda

17. TO ZELDA　　　　　　　Wire. Scrapbook

S1 NEWYORK NY　250PM　APRIL 14 1919
MISS TELDA SAYRE
　　6 PLEASANT AVE　MONTGOMERY ALA
AM TAKING APARTMENT IMMEDIATELY RIGHT UNDER
TILDES NEW APARTMENT LOVE
　　SCOTT

18. TO SCOTT　　　　　　　ALS, 8 pp.
[April 1919]　　　　　　　　　[Montgomery, Alabama]

I feel like a full-fledged traveller — by the 18th I'll be well qualified for my trip — In desperation, yesterday Bill LeGrand and I drove his car to Auburn and came back with *ten* boys to liven things up — Of cource, the day was vastly exciting — and the night more so — Thanks to a jazz band that's been performing at Mays between Keith shows. The boys thought I'd be a charming addition to their act, and I nearly entered upon a theatrical career —

Scott, you're really awfully silly — In the first place, I haven't kissed anybody good-bye, and in the second place, nobody's left in the first place — You know, darling, that I love you too much to want to. If I did have an honest — or dishonest — desire to kiss just one or two people, I *might* — but I couldn't ever want to — my mouth is yours. But s'pose I did — Don't you know it'd just be absolutely *nothing* — Why can't you understand that nothing means anything except your darling self and your love — I wish we'd hurry and I'd be yours so you'd *know* — Sometimes I almost despair of making you feel sure — so sure that nothing could ever make you doubt like I do —

Charlie Johnson has arisen from the depths of oblivion — I thought he was dead — and he'll be home Easter. Seems almost like old times again—I wish you could get a glimpse of Montgomery like it really is—without the camp disturbing things so—and you'd know why I love it so—

We are donning men's clothing to-night—to take in some picture on Commerce St. It promises disaster, but it's by far the most madcap of my escapades, so I'm looking forward to the dusk with great excitement. We are dragging Willie Persons along for *protection*—he's effeminate—and won't show us up so much. I could knock him out in one round—but my fertile brain is certainly being cooked over-time thinking up sure-deaths to reputations—

Darling—darling I love you so—and I'm going to—all my life—
Zelda

19. TO ZELDA   Wire. Scrapbook

> NEWYORK NY   APRIL 15 1919   3AM
> MISS TILDA SAYRE
>   SIX PLEASANT AVE MONTGOMERY ALA
> ARRIVE MONTGOMERY WEDNESDAY EVENING

20. TO SCOTT   AL, 8 pp.
[After April 15, 1919]   [Montgomery, Alabama]

Scott, my darling lover—everything seems so smooth and restful, like this yellow dusk. Knowing that I'll always be yours—that you really own me—that nothing can keep us apart—is such a relief after the strain and nervous excitement of the last month. I'm so glad you came—like Summer, just when I needed you most—and took me back with you. Waiting doesn't seem so hard now. The vague despondency has gone—I love you Sweetheart.

Why did you buy the "best at the Exchange"?[23]—I'd rather have had 10¢ a quart variety—I wanted it just to know you loved the

---

23. The Hotel Exchange in Montgomery, where Scott bought a bottle of gin when he visited Zelda.

sweetness—To breathe and know you loved the smell—I think I like breathing twilit gardens and moths more than beautiful pictures or good books—It seems the most sensual of all the sences. Something in me vibrates to a dusky, dreamy smell—a smell of dying moons and shadows—

I've spent to-day in the grave-yard. It really isn't a cemetery, you know,—trying to unlock a rusty iron vault built in the side of the hill. It's all washed and covered with weepy, watery blue flowers that might have grown from dead eyes—sticky to touch with a sickening odor— The boys wanted to get in to test my nerve—to-night—I wanted to *feel* "William Wreford, 1864." Why should graves make people feel in vain? I've heard that so much, and Grey is so convincing, but somehow I can't find anything hopeless in having lived—All the broken columnes and clasped hands and doves and angels mean romances— and in an hundred years I think I shall like having young people spec- ulate on whether my eyes were brown or blue—of cource, they are neither—I hope my grave has an air of many, many years ago about it—Isn't it funny how, out of a row of Confederate soldiers, two or three will make you think of dead lovers and dead loves—when they're exactly like the others, even to the yellowish moss?[24] Old death is so beautiful—so very beautiful—We will die together—I know—

Sweetheart—

21. TO SCOTT   AL, 5 pp.
[April 1919]   [Montgomery, Alabama]

Those feathers—those wonderful, wonderful feathers are the most beautiful things on earth—so soft like little chickens, and rosy like fire-light. I feel so rich and pompous waving them around in the air and covering up myself with 'em. Darling, it is the prettiest thing in the world, and you were so sweet to send it—That color is rather becoming.[25]

---

24. Scott took this romantic description of a graveyard and used it nearly verbatim as the thoughts of the protagonist Amory Blaine, a thinly disguised fictional version of himself, in the final two pages of *This Side of Paradise*.

25. Nancy Milford says that Scott, "[t]ouched by the beauty of" Zelda's previous letter (let- ter 20), "sent her a marvelous flamingo-colored feather fan. It was the perfect gift for Zelda, frivolous and entirely beautiful; she was delighted by it" (*Zelda* 46).

Aunt Annabel[26] is certainly a procrastinator—I was wondering if pop-calls were hereditary, but I guess you just acquired the fancy. I don't s'pose now, tho, her visit's very momentous—except, of cource, that you'll be glad to see her. I know, Sweetheart, that we aren't going to need her—Don't ask me to have more faith—I love you most of everything on earth, and somehow you[r] visit made things so much saner, and I *do* believe in you—Just the wild rush and knowing what you did was distasteful to you made me afraid—I'd die rather than see you miserable, and you know you hated looking incessantly at banannas and ice-cream before lunch.

I want to go to Italy—with you, Darling—It seems so yellow—dull, mellow yellow—and that's your color—and I'd feel so like there was nobody else is [in] existence but just you'n me—

Les Mysterieurs[27] is holding a rehearsal on me—I think I'm going [to] look cute in my ballet-dress—

I love you, Scott, with all my heart—

22. TO SCOTT   ALS, 8 pp.
[April 1919]   [Montgomery, Alabama]

Sweetheart, Sweetheart, I love you so—and I get so lonesome when I *never* get a letter—you were very sweet and thoughtful to send the music—but I wish you had just scribbled on the cover what I live to hear you say. I can 't tell you in "ten words"—or ten volumes, or ten years. I can't even tell you a new way—But, please, Darling, try not to get tired of the old one—

We're having the Vaudeville[28] to-night—and I'm leading "Down on the Farm"—in overalls—And, thank Goodness I've lost my sandals, so I guess I'll have to dance bare-foot—and probably suffer more injuries thereby. I think I could do so much better if you were in the audience—Everytime I look nice—or do anything I mentally applaud, I always wish for you—just to hear you say you like it—

---

26. Scott's maiden aunt, who had helped finance his education.
27. *Les Mysterieuses*: Zelda's mother and sister Rosalind wrote a skit for the April "Folly Ball," in which Zelda performed.
28. The local Junior League put on a variety show, the proceeds of which were to be sent to "the Alabama boys in France."

"Marcus Aurelius"[29] is my literature in the absence of your let-ters—Tootsie thinks he's most remarkable. I guess he was, for his day, but now it's all just platitudes. All philosophy is, more or less—It seems as if there's no *new* wisdom—and surely people haven't stopped thinking. I guess morality has relinquished it's claim on the intel-lect—and the thinkers think dollars and wars and politics—I don't know whether it's evolution or degeneration—

Look at this communication from Mamma—all on account of a wine-stained dress—Darling heart—I won't drink *any* if you object—Sometimes I get so bored—and sick for you—It helps then—and afterwards, I'm just more bored and sicker for you—and ashamed—

When are you going to marry me—I don't want to repeat those two months—but I've just got to have you—when you can—because I love you, my husband—

     Zelda

Zelda[30]

If you have added whiskey to your tobacco you can substract your Mother. I am no Mrs. Guinvan however much you are like Susie. If you prefer the habits of a prostitute don't try to mix them with gentil-ity. Oil and water do not mix.

23. TO SCOTT   ALS, 8 pp.
[May 1919]   [Montgomery, Alabama]

Dearest Scott—

T. G. that's over! The vaudeville, I mean, and I am a complete wreck—but everybody says the dance was a success. It nearly broke my heart to take off those lovely Oriental pants—Some actor with this week's Keiths tried to take me and Livye on the road with him—but I can't ignore physical characteristics enough to elope with a pos-itive *ape.* And now I've got just two weeks to train a Folly Ballet for Les Mysterieurs—

29. The philosopher and emperor of ancient Rome, who wrote *Meditations,* a classic work of stoicism.
30. This two-page handwritten note from Zelda's mother to her daughter was enclosed.

"Plasher's Mead"[31] has been carefully perused—Thanks awfully for it. I haven't read in so long—but I don't really like it—People seldom interest me except in their relations to things, and I like men to be just incidents in books so I can imagine their characters. Nothing annoys me more than having the most trivial action analyzed and explained. Besides, Pauline is positively atrociously uninteresting—I'll save the book and re-read it in rainy weather in the Fall—I think I'll appreciate it more—

Scott, you've been so sweet about writing—but I'm so damned tired of being told that you "used to wonder why they kept princesses in towers"[32]—you've written that verbatim, in your last *six* letters! It's dreadfully hard to write so very much—and so many of your letters sound forced—I know you love me, Darling, and I love you more than anything in the world, but if its going to be so much longer, we just *can't* keep up this frantic writing. It's like the last week we were to-gether—and I'd like to feel that you know I am thinking of you and loving you always. I hate writing when I haven't time, and I just have to scribble a few lines. I'm saying all this so you'll understand—Hectic affairs of any kind are rather trying, so *please* let's write calmly and whenever we feel like it.

I'd probably aggravate you to death to day. There's no skin on my lips, and I have relapsed into a nervous stupor. It feels like going crazy knowing everything you do and being utterly powerless not to do it—and thinking you'll surely scream next minute. You used to blame it all on poor Bill—and all the time, it was just my nastiness—

Mamma gave me this[33] to-day—I s'pose it's another of her subtle suggestions—

All my love
　　　Zelda

---

31. A novel by the popular English writer Compton Mackenzie.

32. When Scott returned to New York after his April 15 visit to Zelda, he wrote in his Ledger: "Failure. I used to wonder why they locked princesses in towers" (*Ledger* 173). He apparently liked the sentence so much that he used it in letters to Zelda as well.

33. Whatever Zelda's mother had given her has been lost. Mrs. Sayre, however, was in the habit of giving her daughter clippings of news articles about failed writers, and perhaps this was one.

24. TO SCOTT   AL, 8 pp.
[May 1919]   [Montgomery, Alabama]

The Fourth Alabama[34] arrives Tuesday, and town looks like Mardi Gras — Perry St. is just one long booth with flags and confetti everywhere — The houses for three blocks around the Governor's are open — or will be — and everybody's dragging out old costumes and masks — and Good Lord, it's hot! Commerce St. is just a long arch — Rosemont Garden's has turned over it's greenhouse for a flower-barage. I wish you could see it — but, of cource, everybody's asleep all up and down the streets. Everything is so delightfully slow, even now. Major Smith's company that he took over is going to march with the ranks unfilled — Twenty-three men — It almost makes me cry[35] — I would if I weren't expending all my energy on gum — I've started a continuous chew again. Your disapproval used to put me on the wagon, but now I've got the habit again —

To-morrow, a man's going to make some Kodak snaps of me in my Folly dress,[36] and cource I'll send them to you — Mamma gets rather annoying about her rose-bushes at times, so I s'pose I'll be perched on the topmost thorn on one of 'em. She bids me tell you how beautiful they are — Even if you didn't go into ecstacies over Mrs. McKurneys when they weren't bloomed —

My poor limbs have suffered another accident. Jumping off a sandbank tall as the moon — nearly — and landing in a pile of rocks almost makes me wish them amputated. Little boys are almost too strenuous for my old age. Darling Sweetheart, I'll be *so* glad to see you again —

Are you coming on the 20th, or had you rather wait till early June when I'll be going to Georgia Tech commencement and can go as far as Atlanta with you on your way back? The family threatens to depart for Asheville, N.C.[37] in July — Wouldn't it be nice if you needed a rest about then and spent a week or two in the mountains with me? However, I cordially loathe consumptives and

---

34. A regiment that had been serving in France.
35. Twenty-three of the men in her brother-in-law's regiment died in France.
36. Zelda had her picture taken in her costume for the April "Folly Ball" in her backyard, sitting among Mrs. Sayre's rose bushes, and sent it to Scott.
37. Ironically, Highland Hospital — where Zelda was a patient in the 1930s and 1940s and where she died tragically in a fire in 1948 — was in Asheville, North Carolina.

Zelda in her costume for the "Folly Ball"—photo she sent to Scott. Courtesy of Princeton University Library

babies with heat, which constitu[t]e one's circle of acquaintances there—

I've tried so many times to think of a new way to say it—and its still I love you—love you—love you—my Sweetheart—

25. TO SCOTT　　　　　　AL, 9 pp.
[May 1919]　　　　　　　　[Montgomery, Alabama]

A beautiful golden kitty would be nice—but I wouldn't swap my cat for two of 'em, and he would probably kill the new one—Besides, I lost my brush and mirror at Cobb's Ford, and I'd love to have one with pink flowers around the edge. Just so you come, Darling—

Mrs. Francesca—who never heard of you—got a message from Ouija[38] for me. Nobody's hands were on it but her's—and it told us to

---

38. Mrs. Francesca, a local spiritualist, who claimed to receive messages from the "other world" on a Ouija board.

be married—that we were soul mates. Theosophists think that two souls are incarnated to-gether—not necessarily at the same time, but are mated—since the time when people were bi-sexual, so you see "soul-mate" isn't exactly Snappy-Storyish,[39] after all. I can't get messages, but it really moved for me last night—only it couldn't say anything but "dead, dead"—so, of cource, I got scared and quit. It's really most remarkable, even if you do scoff. I wish you wouldn't, it's so easy, and believing is much more intelligent.

We are going to Asheville in July—definitely—but we'll have some trouble over the "thirty *moonlights*"—I'm afraid some of the nights may be lacking the moon—But, Sweetheart, we'll be to-gether a whole month,—and moons dont really matter, anyway. I *think* I'm going to bob my hair, and that may evoke a furor. I wish you'd tell me if you'll like it—Everybody's so discouraging—but think how good it'd feel in the water! I'll probably look like Hell.

"Red" said last night that I was the pinkest-whitest person he ever saw, so I went to sleep in his lap. Of cource, you dont mind because it was really very fraternal, and we were chaperoned by three girls—

Darling Scott—please come—I love you with all of me—and I'll be so very, very glad to see you—We're going to repeat the Vaudeville on the 20th—maybe you'd like to see it—but we're in the midst of terrible upheaval—The cast is being revised—and I dont think they're going to let me sing—It's funny, but I really do think I sing well—

Look at this fist—It's grown rusty and dreadfully spasmodic—Just translate it into what I'm always thinking—Sweetheart—

26. TO SCOTT ALS, 8 pp.
[Late May 1919] [Montgomery, Alabama]

One more afternoon as strenuous as this, and I'll be [a] fit inmate for the morgue—Having seen the Vaudeville last night, Livye and I went again to-day to see the dance in the last act so we could put it on for the League show—We were discussing the costumes—very calmly and not one bit drunk or disorderly, when a howling hussy over the foot-lights

---

39. *Snappy Stories*, a popular bimonthly pulp magazine, published formulaic short stories, articles, cartoons, and reviews of movies and plays.

stopped the orchestra, and demanded in her loudest voice whether "*she* was going to talk, or *we* were" — Of cource, the audience went into an uproar instantly, and pandemonium broke loose — After glaring at us for five minutes, she continued the song — to the best of her ability above the noise. The first three rows are already bought for to-morrow's matinée — the boys are indignant, and I am expecting no less than a ten-round bout — Here's the point to the joke: We *really* weren't annoying a soul. May was back of us, and even she says she couldn't hear us talking.

She asked me to say she'd be in New York the end of this week, and that she'd call you up. All her beautiful hair came out when she had Flu, and she's coming up to have it treated. It makes me sorter sick at heart to see her head. It used to be so pretty and curly.

Joel Massie, too, is sending his utmost. He makes a desperate effort at ragging me — as if I could be teased — you'd probably like this now — lots of boys like Jo are back, and things seem more dignified.

Toots is packing her truck — nearly — Cincinnati the first week in May — then New York — Please hurry — I want so much to come — and if that man feels that he must bust loose, for Lawd's sake shield our timidity from his generosity — He evidently isn't acquainted with my habits, or he'd realize that meals by lamp-light aren't exactly *breakfasts* —

I love you, Darling — and I'm waiting —
    Zelda

Please — *please* — aren't you *ever* going to learn that boys never appreciate things other men tell them on their girls? At least five men have suffered a bout behind the Baptist Church for no other offense than you are about to committ, only I was the lady concerned — in the dim past — Anyway, if she is good-looking, and you want to one bit — I know you could and love me just the same —

27. TO ZELDA   Wire. Scrapbook

Newyork May 14–19
    Miss Lelda Sayre
        6 Pleasant Ave MONTGY ALA
    Arrive Montgomery eight thirty thursday night love
        Scott

28. TO SCOTT   AL, 8 pp.
[May 1919]   [Montgomery, Alabama]

Darling Scott, you don't know how I miss your letters—This morning, I thought you'd written me such a nice fat one, and it was your story—I haven't heard but once since you left—But I like the little tale[40]—"Clayton" has just been here with Keith's and even the stage-setting was identical. He suffered a broken head and a hasty departure from here by shrieking, in answer to Mrs. Byar's question "Is my daughter all right" that her daughter was three months *all wrong.* The town has been in a dreadful uproar. I think he's fine, tho, cause he said I'd be in New York before October—It seems so far away, and I love you so—

The sweater is perfectly delicious—and I'm going to save it till you come in June so you can tell me how nice I look. It's funny, but I like being "pink and helpless"—When I know I seem that way, I feel terribly competent—and superior. I keep thinking, "Now those men think I'm purely decorative, and they're just fools for not knowing better"—and I love being rather unfathomable. You are the only person on earth, Lover, who has ever known and loved all of me—Men love me cause I'm pretty—and they're always afraid of mental wickedness—and men love me cause I'm clever, and they're always afraid of my prettiness—One or two have even loved me cause I'm lovable, and then, of cource, I was acting. But you just *do*, darling—and I *do*—so very, very much—

I think I'm beginning to realize the seriousness of us—Little things, like[41] and small familiarities—I used to do them thoughtlessly—and now I can't, because I love you, so I've quit Chummying. I'll never learn the combination.[42] Maybe I'm getting tired—I can't think of anything but nights with you—I want them warm and silvery—when we can be to-gether all our lives—Which will probably be long, as I've recovered from the cough, much to my disgust. I don't want you to see me growing old and ugly—I know you'll be a beautiful old man—romantic and dreamy—and I'll probably be most

---

40. Perhaps Scott had sent her his short story "Babes in the Woods"; he had just sold the story to *The Smart Set* for thirty dollars, out of which he bought a sweater for Zelda and white flannel trousers for himself.

41. At this point in the letter, Zelda drew a picture of two stick figures dancing.

42. Zelda inserted "I'll never learn the combination" above "Chummying" and drew an arrow circling these words and pointing to the two stick figures that she had drawn.

prosaic and wrinkled. We will just *have* to die when we're thirty. I wish your name were Paul—or Jacquelyn. I'm going to name all our children that—and Peter—yours and mine—because we love each other—

---

29. TO SCOTT   AL, 4 pp.
[June 1919]   [Montgomery, Alabama]

No wonder I never hear from you—The New York post-office has been communicating wildly regarding two letters with no postage. Circumstantial evidence against you—looks like wild nights and headachy mornings—I was scared you had forgotten me—It's been so long since I had a letter. I've been seeking consolation in a perfectly *delightful* golf-tournament—Perry Adair and all the Atlanta celebrities were over, so of cource, I wouldn't miss Tech commencement for a million. I'll be in Atlanta till Wednesday, and I hope—I want you to so much—you'll come down soon as I get back. Darling heart, I love you—It's been so long since you left me—much more than the three weeks you promised—and sometimes I feel like I'll die without you—But you're coming—and please take me with you.

Your pictures are ready—but I haven't got any money, as usual, so I wish you'd send for 'em.

I do—hope I get a letter to-morrow—and

I do—love you with all my heart.

---

30. TO SCOTT   ALS, 6 pp.
[June 1919]   [Montgomery, Alabama]

Dearest Ole Dear—

I'm back home again—and, as usual, had the most fun I *ever* had. God, Scott, if you waited till I got *tired* we'd certainly both be bachelors—Every time, it improves, and I'll never feel grown. I absolutely despair of it. But if I wait much more I'd have to go in a wheel-chair and return in a hearse. This time the casualty list was unusually long—both eyes and a leg, a couple of tonsils and a suit-case full of clothes: all lost in action. And still I'm so mighty happy—It's just sort of a "thankful" feeling—that I'm alive and that people are glad I am.

There's nothing to say—you know everything about me, and that's mostly what I think about. I seem always curiously interested in myself, and it's so much fun to stand off and look at me—

But this:

I know you've worried—and enjoyed doing it thoroughly—and I didn't want you to *because* something always makes things the way they ought to be—Even this time—*and its all right*—Somehow, I rather hate to tell you that—I know its depriving you of an idea that horrifies and fascinates—you're so morbidly exaggerative—Your mind dwells on things that don't make people happy—I can't explain, but its rather kin to the way kids 13 feel when everybody goes off and leaves them at home—if they aren't scary, of cource. Sort of deliberately experimental and wiggly—

In Tuscaloosa I saw Katherine Ellesberry's baby. It's darling and it's gotten round. I'm so *glad*—I hate long children. I felt like I'd sorter like to have it.

Scott, dear boy, I love you—and, thank Heavens, events can take a natural cource—

Write me, please—

Zelda

31. TO SCOTT   ALS, 5 pp.
[June 1919]   [Montgomery, Alabama]

Dearest Scott—

I certainly appreciated your last letter. It must have been a desperate struggle to write it, but your efforts were not wasted on an unreceptive audience. Just the same, the only thing that carried me thru a muddy, rainy, boring Auburn commencement was the knowledge that I'd have a note, at least, from you when I got home—but I didn't. I was so sure—because I left Wed. and you hadn't written in a week—Not that letters make so much difference, and if you don't want to write we'll stop, but I love you so—and I hate being disappointed day after day.

I'm glad you're coming. Make it any time except the week of June 13. I'm going to Georgia Tech to try my hand in new fields—You might come on the 20th and stay till we go to North Carolina—or come before I go to Atlanta, only I'll be mighty tired, and they always dance till breakfast.

The picture in the hat is an awful bother—Tresslar won't make less than three, and won't send a fifteen-dollar bill to New York, so please remit, and I'll send my beaming likeness when I get it—next week.

Zelda—

32. TO SCOTT   ALS, 2 pp.
[June 1919]   [Montgomery, Alabama]

You asked me not to write—but I do want to explain—That note belonged with Perry Adair's fraternity pin which I was returning. Hence, the sentimental tone. He has very thoughtfully contributed a letter to you to the general mix-up. It went to him, with his pin.[43]

I'm so sorry, Scott, and if you want the pictures, I'll mail them to you.

Zelda

33. TO SCOTT   ALS, 8 pp.
[October 1919]   [Montgomery, Alabama]

Dearest Scott—
Nov. 1—Columbus—sponsor Auburn-Ga. game THANKSGIV-ING—ATLANTA ditto AUBURN-TECH—
So, you see, you'll be down just about the right time. It's awfully hard to do everything by a foot-ball schedule, but I've been making a frantic effort at it for the last month. Between the games and my *piano-lessons* I'll probably be a mere shadow of the girl I once was

---

43. When Zelda returned home from Georgia Tech, she was pinned to the golfer Perry Adair but she soon regretted it and returned Adair's fraternity pin by mail. She inadvertently mixed up a "sentimental" note she had written to him with a letter she was writing to Scott. Unfortunately, Scott got the note intended for Adair and was so hurt and angry that Zelda had been disloyal to him that he demanded that she never write to him again. Zelda could not comply, and she sent this brief explanation and apology. After receiving this letter, Scott made a frantic trip to Montgomery to try to patch up the relationship. He begged Zelda to marry him immediately, but she refused and broke their engagement. There were no more letters until they resumed their relationship in the fall.

by the time you come, but I guess you'll recognize me. Anyway, in case of emergency, you can notify my parents at the same old Six Pleasant.

I'm mighty glad you're coming—I've been wanting to see you (which you probably knew) but I *couldn't* ask you—and besides Mrs. McKinney has run me positively crazy planning weddings in her atrocious magnolia hall until I was almost wishing you'd never come anymore. It's fine, and I'm tickled to death.

And another thing:

I'm just recovering from a wholesome amour with Auburn's "starting quarter-back" so my disposition is excellent as well as my health. Mentally, you'll find me dreadfully detiorated—but you never seemed to know when I was stupid and when I wasn't, anyway—

Please bring me a quart of gin—I haven't had a drink all summer, and you're already *ruined* along alcoholic lines with Mrs. Sayre. After you left, every corner the nigger started cleaning was occupied by a bottle (or bottles). Tootsie, of cource, is largely responsible—but it was just one of those incidents that cant be explained. She thought you drank at least 12 qts. in two days.

'S funny, Scott, I don't feel a bit shaky and "do-don't" ish like I used to when you came. I really want to see you—that's all—

Zelda

Beautiful color scheme—n'est-ce pas? [I'm a madamoiselle][44]

34. TO SCOTT　　　　　　AL, 8 pp.
[Fall 1919]　　　　　　　　[Montgomery, Alabama]

I am very proud of you—I hate to say this, but I, don't *think* I had much confidence in you at first—I was just coming anyway—It's so nice to know that you really *can* do things—*anything*—and I love to feel that maybe I can help just a little—I want to so much—Don't ask Mr. Hooker about me—I might try and be *dreadful* and then you'd be so ashamed of me—Why don't you write the things? Lyrics sound easy—but you know best, of cource. I'm so damn glad I love you—I

---

44. These brackets were supplied by Zelda.

wouldn't love any other man on earth—I b'lieve if I had deliberately decided on a sweetheart, he'd have been you—I thought that at first when we couldn't find each other—Years ago, when you wouldn't pretend, and I called you Don Juan—and you thought I was Eleanor—and discovered that I really wasn't a thing on earth but your own true sweetheart—

Don't—please—accumulate a lot of furniture. Really, Scott, I'd just as soon live *anywhere*—and can't we find a bed ready-made? Someday, you know we'll want rugs and wicker furniture and a home—I'm terribly afraid it'll just be in the way now. I wish New York were a little tiny town—so I could imagine how it'd be. I haven't the remotest idea of what it's like, so I am afraid to make any suggestions—What became of the apartment the men decorated? I liked that—I was picturing walls covered with huge orange and black fruit—and yellow ceilings—

Mrs Hayden is bringing her daughter, Edwine, down Easter—Tilde and Tootsie have both visited them, and, of cource, we're obligated—Toots is threatening to go with Mrs. DeFuniac to Michigan—She leaves Friday—If she does, I'll *have* to stay and entertain Edwine—Then, when they leave, I could come North with them—That's why I wanted you to write Mamma. You see, I can't tell them *why* Tootsie just *can't* go to Michigan—What must I do?

Craighead telegraphed he was coming from Gordon for the weekend. I'll be glad to see him—There're absolutely no males in this vicinity and, besides, I can tell him about you. I love talking of you—Darling—you're all—everything in the world—I love you so—

In case of, emergency—

Here's Tilde—

520 W 124th St Apt. 51

Lover—lover—I want you—always—

35. TO SCOTT   ALS, 9 pp.

[Fall 1919]   [Montgomery, Alabama]

I'm writing on this beautiful paper which everybody thinks is so awful and which I hate to use for fear it'll use up to thank you—so you know how much I like the "two little junks"—But I'm so distressed over not finding a place to put the picture in the case that I'm going to glue it somewhere even if it's on the outside. Please don't look so horrified. It's a company case, anyway—The chain is just like a hat on a lady, shrieking "take me somewhere—take me somewhere," and I do love to take it—You know how I like things that nobody around's ever had, and the tassel on the other thing has elevated me to a most superior position.

Yesterday I almost wrote a book or story, I hadn't decided which, but after two pages on my heroine I discovered that I hadn't even started her, and, since I couldn't just write forever about a charmingly impossible creature, I began to despair. "Vamping Romeo" was the name, and I guess a man would have had to appear somewhere before the end. But there wasn't any plot, so I thought I'd ask you how to decide what they're going to do. Mamma answered my S.O.S. with one of O. Henry's, verbatum, which I discarded because he never *created* people—just things to happen to the same old kind of folks and unexpected ends, and I like stories with all the ladies like Constance Talmadge and the men just sorter strong, silent characters or college boys—but I know I'm going to be rather fond of Margery See[45] and maybe she'll fire me with enough ambition to carry Romeo thru two more pages—And so you see, Scott, I'll never be able to do anything because I'm much too lazy to care whether it's done or not—and I don't want to be famous and fêted—all I want is to be very young always and very irresponsible and to feel that my life is my own—to live and be happy and die in my own way—to please myself.

And, Scott, Darlin' *don't* try so hard to convince yourself that we're very old people who've lost their most precious possession. We really havent found it yet—and only weaklings like the St. Paul girl you told me about who lack courage and the power to feel they're right when the whole world says they're wrong, ever lose—All the fire and sweetness—the emotional strength that we're capable of is growing—growing and just because sanity and wisdom are growing too and we're building our love-castle on a firm foundation, nothing is lost—That first abandon *couldn't* last, but the things that went to make it are tremendously alive—just like blowing bubbles—they burst, but more bubbles just as beautiful can be blown—and burst—till the soap and water is gone—and that's the way we'll be, I guess—so don't mourn for a poor little forlorn, wonderful memory when we've got each other—Because I know I love you—and you'll come

---

45. Most likely the heroine of her story.

in January to tell me that you do—and we won't worry any more about anything—Zelda

36. TO ZELDA   Wire. Scrapbook
[Before January 9, 1920]   [New York City]

I FIND THAT I CANNOT GET A BERTH SOUTH UNTIL FRI-
DAY OR POSSIBLY SATURDAY NIGHT WHICH MEANS I
WON'T ARRIVE UNTIL THE ELEVENTH OR TWELFTH
PERIOD AS SOON AS I KNOW I WILL WIRE YOU THE SAT-
URDAY EVENING POST HAS JUST TAKEN TWO MORE STO-
RIES PERIOD ALL MY LOVE.

37. TO ZELDA   Wire. Scrapbook
[January 1920]   STPAUL MINN 254P 10

MISS LELDA SAYRE
    6 PLEASANT AVE. MONTGOMERY ALA.
ARRIVE MONDAY
    SCOTT FITZGERALD

38. TO ZELDA   Wire. Scrapbook

NEWORLEANS LA[46] 1213P   JAN 19 1920
MISS ZELDA SAYRE
    SIX PLEASANT AVE MONTGOMERY ALA
SEND MANUSCRIPT[47] SPECIAL DELIVERY LOVE
    SCOTT

---

46. Concerned about tuberculosis, Scott went to New Orleans in January to write and to avoid the St. Paul winter. While there, he visited Zelda in Montgomery twice, during which Scott and Zelda made love, probably for the first time. Scott moved back to New York in February; then, toward the end of February, he moved to the Cottage Club at Princeton to await the publication of *This Side of Paradise*.
47. Perhaps Scott was asking Zelda to send him the story that she was working on (mentioned in letter 35).

39. TO ZELDA   Wire. Scrapbook

> NEWORLEANS LA   530P   JAN 29 1920
> MISS ZELDA SAYRE
>   6 PLEASANT AVE MONTGOMERY ALA
> COMING UP SATURDAY AND SUNDAY WIRE ME ONLY IF
> IN-CONVENIENT
>   SCOTT

40. TO ZELDA   Wire. Scrapbook

> NEWYORK NY   FEB 24 1920
> MISS LIDA SAYRE
>   SIX PLEASANT AVE MONTGOMERY ALA
> I HAVE SOLD THE MOVIE RIGHTS OF HEAD AND SHOUL-
> DERS TO THE METRO COMPANY FOR TWENTY FIVE HUN-
> DRED DOLLARS I LOVE YOU DEAREST GIRL
>   SCOTT

41. TO SCOTT   AL, 6 pp.
[February 1920][48]   [Montgomery, Alabama]

Darling Heart, our fairy tale is almost ended, and we're going to marry and live happily ever afterward just like the princess in her tower who worried you so much—and made me so very cross by her constant recurrence—I'm so sorry for all the times I've been mean and hateful—for all the miserable minutes I've caused you when we could have been so happy. You deserve so much—so very much—

I think our life together will be like these last four days—and I

---

48. Nancy Milford dates this letter March 1920 and believes that it was the last letter Zelda wrote to Scott before their marriage. Scott's biographer Matthew J. Bruccoli, however, believes that the letter was written earlier in February. The editors agree with the February date because Zelda's writing "and next time I'm going back with you" indicates that Scott was still making trips to Montgomery.

do want to marry you—even if you do think I "dread" it—I wish you hadn't said that—I'm not afraid of anything. To be afraid a person has either to be a coward or very great and big. I am neither. Besides, I know you can take much better care of me than I can, and I'll always be very, very happy with you—except sometimes when we engage in our weekly debates—and even then I rather enjoy myself. I like being very calm and masterful, while you become emotional and sulky. I don't care whether you think so or not—I do.

There are 3 more pictures I unearthed from a heap of débris under my bed. Our honored mother had disposed of 'em for reasons of her own, but personally I like the attitude of my emaciated limbs, so I solict your approval. Only I waxed artistic, and ruined one.

Sweetheart—I miss you so—I love you so—and next time I'm going back with you—I'm absolutely nothing without you—Just the doll that I should have been born. You're a necessity and a luxury and a darling, precious lover—and you're going to be a husband to your wife—

42. TO SCOTT   AL, 8 pp.
[February 1920]   [Montgomery, Alabama]

O, Scott, its so be-au-ti-ful[49]—and the back's just as pretty as the front. I think maybe I like it a little better, and I've turned it over four hundred times to see "from Scott to Zelda." I try to feel so rich and fine but I'm so tickled I can't feel any way but happy—happy enough to bubble completely over and flow away into a sweet-smelling nothing. And I've decided, like I do every night before I go to sleep, that you're the dearest, dearest man on earth and that I love you even more than this delicious little thing ticking on my wrist.

Mamma came in with the package, and I thought maybe it might interest her to know, so she sat on the edge of the bed while I told her we were going to marry each other pretty soon. She wants me to

---

49. When Scott sold "Head and Shoulders" to the movies for $2,500, he sent Zelda a $600 platinum and diamond watch.

come to New York, because she says you'd like to do it in St. Patrick's. Now that she knows, everything seems mighty definite and nice; and I'm not a bit scared or shaky—What I dreaded most was telling her—somehow I just didn't think I could—Both of us are very splashy vivid pictures, those kind with the details left out, but I know our colors will blend, and I think we'll look very well hanging beside each other in the gallery of life [This is *not* just another one of my "subterranean river" thoughts][50]

And I love you so terribly that I'm going to read "McTeague"[51]— but you may have to marry a corpse when I finish. It certainly makes a miserable start—I don't see how any girl could be pretty with her front teeth lost in action, and besides, it outrages my sense of delicacy to have him violently proposing when she's got one of those nasty rubber things on her face. All authors who want to make things true to life make them *smell bad*—like McTeague's room—and that's my most sensitive sense. I do hope you'll never be a realist—one of those kind that thinks being ugly is being forceful—

When my wedding's going to be, write to me again—and if you'd rather have me come up there I will—I told Mamma I might just come and surprise you, but she said you mightn't like to be surprised about "your own wedding"—I rather think it's *my* wedding—

"Till Death do us part"

43. **TO SCOTT**   ALS, 4 pp.
[March 1920]   [Montgomery, Alabama]

Dearest—

I wanted to for your sake, because I know what a mess I'm making and how inconvenient it's all going to be—but I simply *can't* and *won't* take those awful pills[52]—so I've thrown them away. I'd rather

---

50. These brackets were supplied by Zelda.
51. In *McTeague* (1899), a novel by Frank Norris, who belonged to the literary school of naturalism, the protagonist is a dentist smitten by a young woman named Trina, whose gaping smile he corrects with bridges and crowns, after which he marries Trina, then murders her. Zelda apparently found Norris's naturalism so repulsive as to be amusing.
52. Zelda mistakenly believed that she might be pregnant.

take carbolic acid. You see, as long as I feel that I had the right, I don't much mind what happens—and besides, I'd rather have a *whole family* than sacrifice my self-respect. They just seem to place everything on the wrong basis—and I'd feel like a damned whore if I took even one, so you'll try to understand, please Scott—and do what you think best—but don't do *anything* till we *know* because God—or something—has always made things right, and maybe this will be.

I love you, Darling Scott, and you love me, and we can be thankful for that anyway—

Thanks for the book—I don't like it—

    Zelda Sayre

44. TO ZELDA   Wire. Scrapbook

  [PRI]NCETON NJ   1117AM   MAR 23 1920
  MISS ZELDA SAYRE
     6 PLEASANT AVE MONTGOMERY ALA
  GOOD MORNING ZELDA DEAR YOU KNOW I DO
     SCOTT

45. TO ZELDA   Wire. Scrapbook
[March 1920]   [Princeton, New Jersey]

  MISS ZELDA SAYRE
     SIX PLEASANT AVE MONTGOMERY ALA
  DEAR YOUR LETTER JUST CAME I HAD COUNTED ON
  YOUR LEAVING MONTGOMERY ON THE THIRTIETH OF
  THIS MONTH BUT IF YOU ARE READY TO COME EARLIER
  SAY ON THE TWENTIETH WIRE ME TODAY YOU KNOW I
  WANT YOU ALL THE TIME DEAREST GIRL YOUR PICTURE
  HAS NOT COME AM WRITING

46. TO ZELDA   Wire. Scrapbook
[March 1920]

 PRINCETON NJ 1042A 17
 MISS TILDA SAYRE
    SIX PLEASANT AVE MONTGOMERY ALA
 THE PICTURE IS LOVELY AND SO ARE YOU DARLING

47. TO ZELDA   Wire. Scrapbook

 PRINCETON NJ   MARCH 28 1920
 MISS ZELDA SAYRE
    6 PLEASANT AVE MONTGOMERY ALABAMA
 YOUR TELEGRAM CAME TONIGHT I HAVE TAKEN
 ROOMS AT THE BALTIMORE [BILTMORE?] AND WILL
 EXPECT YOU FRIDAY OR SATURDAY WIRE ME EXACTLY
 WHEN WILL CALL TOOTSIE TOMORROW MORNING
 BOOK SELLING[53] ALL MY LOVE
    SCOTT

48. TO ZELDA   Wire. Scrapbook

 [Princeton] NJ
 NEWYORK NY MAR 30 1920
 MISS TILLA SAYRE
    6 PLEASANT AVE MONTGOMERY ALA
 TALKED WITH JOHN PALMER AND ROSALIND[54] AND WE
 THINK BEST TO GET MARRIED SATURDAY NOON WE
 WILL BE AWFULLY NERVOUS UNTIL IT IS OVER AND

---

53. *This Side of Paradise* was published on March 26, 1920.
54. John Palmer (Clothilde's husband) and Rosalind (Zelda's sister) apparently helped Scott with the last-minute wedding arrangements. Zelda's other sister, Marjorie, accompanied her to New York for the wedding. Neither Scott's nor Zelda's parents attended. The small wedding party consisted of Zelda's three sisters; her brothers-in-law, Newman Smith and John Palmer; and Scott's best man, Ludlow Fowler, his friend from Princeton. Scott was so nervous he began the ceremony before John and Clothilde arrived.

WOULD GET NO REST BY WAITING UNTIL MONDAY FIRST
EDITION OF THE BOOK IS SOLD OUT ADDRESS COTTAGE
UNTIL THURSDAY AND SCRIBNERS AFTER THAT
LOVE
SCOTT

Scott and Zelda in Montgomery, March 1921. ©Bettmann/Corbis

PART II

The Years Together: 1920–1929

❦

The things that we have done together and the awful splits that have broken us. . . .
—Scott to Zelda, April 26, 1934

Following their marriage and the triumphant publication of *This Side of Paradise* (the first printing of three thousand copies sold out in three days; by the end of 1921, it had gone through twelve printings, totaling more than 49,000 copies), the newlyweds found themselves celebrities at the beginning of the Roaring Twenties in the city that was at the center of the party. As Scott later wrote in "My Lost City" (1932), "To my bewilderment, I was adopted, not as a Middle Westerner, not even as a detached observer, but as the arch type of what New York wanted" (*Crack-Up* 26). What New York wanted was an attractive couple who drank and partied endlessly and whose escapades—diving into fountains, riding on top of taxicabs, disrobing during a performance of *George White's Sandals*, and brawling with policemen—became staples of the gossip columns. "We felt," Scott recalled in "My Lost City," "like small children in a great bright unexplored barn." But he also remembered in the same essay "riding in a taxi one afternoon between very tall buildings under a mauve and rosy sky; I began to bawl because I had everything I wanted and knew I would never be so happy again" (*Crack-Up* 28–29).

After living in a succession of New York hotels, from at least one of which they were expelled for disturbing other guests, the Fitzgeralds, in the spring of 1920, rented a house in Westport, Connecticut, where Scott worked on stories and began a second novel. During that summer, they drove to Montgomery in their secondhand Marmon sports coupe to visit Zelda's family, a trip that Scott later immortalized in his comic essay "The Cruise of the Rolling Junk" (1924). In September, Scribners published his first collection of short stories, *Flappers and Philosophers*. Although the reviews were mixed, it sold remarkably well, probably because of the popularity of *This Side of Paradise*. But the Fitzgeralds were already quarreling, often after drinking heavily. The following is a fragment of a letter Zelda gave to Scott after one such episode:

Embarking on "The Cruise of the Rolling Junk." Courtesy of Princeton University Library

49. TO SCOTT   ALS, 2 pp.
[September 1920]   [Westport, Connecticut]

I look down the tracks and see you coming—and out of every haze
+ mist your darling rumpled trousers are hurrying to me—Without
you, dearest dearest I couldn't see or hear or feel or think—or live—I
love you so and I'm never in all our lives going to let us be apart
another night. It's like begging for mercy of a storm or killing Beauty
or growing old, without you. I want to kiss you so—and in the back
where your dear hair starts and your chest—I love you—and I cant
tell you how much—To think that I'll *die* without your knowing—
Goofo, you've *got* to try [to] feel how much I do—how inanimate I am
when you're gone—I can't even hate these damnable people—
nobodys got any right to live but us—and they're dirtying up our
world and I can't hate them because I want you so—Come Quick—
Come Quick to me—I could never do without you if you hated me and
were covered with sores like a leper—if you ran away with another
woman and starved me and beat me—I still would want you *I know*—
    Lover, Lover, Darling—
    Your Wife

Frances Scott Fitzgerald

The dramatic quarrels may have encouraged rather than discouraged the Fitzgeralds about the success of their marriage. When Scott summed up the year in his *Ledger*, he wrote: "Revelry and Marriage. The rewards of the year before. The happiest year since I was 18." (*Ledger* 174); and he continued to work on his second novel after they moved back into New York.

In February of 1921, when Zelda discovered she was pregnant, they decided to take their first trip abroad, sailing first-class on the *Acquitania* on May 3 for England. Just before their departure, Scott delivered a draft of his new novel, *The Beautiful and Damned*, to his agent, Harold Ober, for serial publication.

In London, the Fitzgeralds dined with English novelist John Galsworthy, playwright and critic St. John Ervine, and Irish playwright Lennox Robinson, and had lunch with Lady Randolph Churchill and her son Winston. They went on to Paris, Venice, and Rome, and then went back to London before returning to America in July. This first trip to Europe had not impressed them, as Scott later emphasized in a letter to his college friend Edmund Wilson:

God damn the continent of Europe. It is of merely antiquarian interest. Rome is only a few years behind Tyre + Babylon. . . . France made me sick. It's silly pose as the thing the world has to save. I think its a shame that England + America didn't let Germany conquer Europe. Its the only thing that would have saved the fleet of tottering old wrecks. (*Life in Letters* 46–47)

Upon their return, Scott and Zelda settled in St. Paul, where Zelda met Scott's parents for the first time. Scott spent the fall revising *The Beautiful and Damned* for book publication. On October 26, 1921, their daughter, Frances Scott Fitzgerald, was born; in his Ledger, Scott recorded Zelda's comment on the birth: "I hope its beautiful and a fool—a beautiful little fool" (*Ledger* 176)—words he later gave to Daisy Buchanan in *The Great Gatsby*.

By March 1922, the Fitzgeralds were back in New York for the publication of *The Beautiful and Damned* and possibly, according to Matthew J. Bruccoli in his Fitzgerald biography, *Some Sort of Epic Grandeur*, for Zelda to have an abortion because she did not want to have a second child so soon after the first (163). Although the novel received generally lukewarm notices from reviewers who hoped for another *This Side of Paradise*, it sold quite well. The Fitzgeralds spent the summer at the White Bear Yacht Club outside St. Paul, where Scott put together his second collection of short stories, *Tales of the Jazz Age*, which was published in September, about the same time the couple rented a small house at 6 Gateway Drive in Great Neck, Long Island. During the spring and summer of 1922, Zelda began to publish short humorous pieces in newspapers and magazines, including a tongue-in-cheek review of *The Beautiful and Damned* in the *New York Tribune*. In the fall of 1923, asked by an interviewer for the *Baltimore Sun* if she was ambitious, she replied, "Not especially, but I've plenty of hope. I don't want to belong to clubs. No committees. I'm not a 'joiner.' Just be myself and enjoy living" (Milford, *Zelda* 101).

In Great Neck, the Fitzgeralds found themselves in a diverse community of writers, show business figures, socialites, and bootleggers, all of whom were to appear in various guises in Scott's third novel. Among those with whom they regularly partied were comedians Ed Wynn and Eddie Cantor, socialite Herbert Bayard Swope, playwright Sidney Howard, film mogul Samuel Goldwyn, and writers Ring Lardner and John Dos Passos. Scott became particularly close friends with Lardner, whose humorous short stories he convinced Scribners to publish and with whom he drank and caroused steadily. In his essay

Zelda and Scottie, 1922. Courtesy of Princeton
University Library

"How to Live on $36,000 a Year," Scott explained that "it became a
habit with many world-weary New Yorkers to pass their week-ends at
the Fitzgerald house in the country" (*Afternoon of an Author* 93).

For some time, Scott had been trying, although unsuccessfully, to
interest Broadway producers in a play he had written, a political satire
entitled *The Vegetable* (Scribners had published it in April 1923); it was
finally taken by Sam H. Harris, but it flopped miserably in its out-of-
town tryout in Atlantic City in November 1923 (in "How to Live on
$36,000 a Year," Scott ruefully observed, "After the second act I wanted
to stop the show and say it was all a mistake but the actors struggled
heroically on" [*Afternoon of an Author* 93–94]). Sobered by the play's failure and, as he always was, seriously in debt to his publisher and his
agent, Scott went on the wagon. Between the end of 1923 and the

spring of 1924, he wrote ten stories, which financed a summer of work on a new novel. Despite the income from his stories—he earned over $28,000 in 1923—Scott and Zelda never seemed to have any money after they paid the expenses necessary to support their lifestyle.

Frustrated by this inability to survive financially in expensive Great Neck, Scott and Zelda decided in April 1924 to go to Europe and live on the Riviera, where the exchange rate was nineteen francs to the dollar. "We were going to the Old World to find a new rhythm for our lives," Scott wrote in an essay he wrote not long after their arrival, "How to Live on Practically Nothing a Year," "with a true conviction that we had left our old selves behind forever . . ." (*Afternoon of an Author* 102). Scott had saved seven thousand dollars of his pay from his short stories, and his plan was to work only on his novel until he finished it, which he was able to do. While he was deeply immersed in his writing, Zelda became romantically involved with a handsome young French aviator, Edouard Jozan, in July 1924. Though both Fitzgeralds were later to use this event in their fiction—Zelda in her novel, *Save Me the Waltz* (1932), and Scott in numerous short stories and his novels *The Great Gatsby* (1925) and *Tender Is the Night* (1934)—and while Scott was undeniably devastated by it (he wrote in his Notebook, "I knew something had happened that could never be repaired" [*Notebooks* 113]), the actual extent of the relationship will probably never be known (Jozan described it as no more than a flirtation).

Whatever the facts, the Jozan-Zelda romance surely contributed to the plot and ambience of the novel Scott completed in late October 1924, his small masterpiece, *The Great Gatsby*. As he described the book to his friend Ludlow Fowler in August 1924, "the whole burden" of it was "the loss of those illusions that give such color to the world so that you don't care whether things are true or false as long as they partake of the magical glory" (*Life in Letters* 78).

It was also on the Riviera during the summer of 1924 that the Fitzgeralds became close friends with wealthy American socialites Gerald and Sara Murphy, whom they had met in Paris in May 1924. The Murphys, in turn, introduced them to their circle of writers, composers, and artists, which included Pablo Picasso, Cole Porter, Archibald MacLeish, Fernand Léger, Philip Barry, Rudolph Valentino, Dorothy Parker, and Robert Benchley. As their motto, the Murphys had adopted an old Spanish proverb: "Living well is the best revenge." It was during this period as well that Scott first encountered the work of Ernest Hemingway, reading the latter's short story collection *in our time*, which had recently been published in Paris, and recommending the young author to his own editor at Scribners, Maxwell Perkins.

Because even the favorable exchange rate in France was proving beyond Scott and Zelda's means, they decided, after Scott sent *Gatsby* to Scribners in late October, to spend the winter in Rome and Capri (the exchange rate in Italy was lower than in France). Despite Scott's dislike of the Italians, Zelda's bout with colitis, and what Scott described in a letter to John Peale Bishop as "terrible four day rows" between them "that always start with a drinking party," he was able to make major revisions in the galleys of *Gatsby*, changes that substantially transformed the novel. And despite the tensions in his marriage, he reassured Bishop in the same letter in which he described the "four day rows" that he and Zelda were "still enormously in love and about the only truly happily married people I know" (*Life in Letters* 104). By April 10, 1925, the date on which *Gatsby* was published, the Fitzgeralds were back in Paris. While the reviews were the most positive he received for any of his books, sales were extremely disappointing (a first printing of twenty thousand sold out in a few months, but copies of a second printing of three thousand were still in a Scribners warehouse in 1940, according to Bruccoli in *Some Sort of Epic Grandeur*).

About the time *Gatsby* was published, Scott met Ernest Hemingway for the first time—at the Dingo bar in Paris. Shortly thereafter, the two of them took a trip to Lyons to pick up the Fitzgeralds' car, which was being repaired there. The only account we have of their meeting and of this trip is that offered by Hemingway in his posthumously published, and probably not very reliable, memoir, *A Moveable Feast* (1964). According to Hemingway, Scott, who "had very fair wavy hair, a high forehead, excited and friendly eyes and a delicate long-lipped Irish mouth that, on a girl, would have been the mouth of a beauty. . . ." (149), abruptly asked him " 'did you and your wife sleep together before you were married?' " (151). Then Scott got very drunk on champagne and passed out. Later in *A Moveable Feast*, Hemingway paints unflattering portraits of Zelda as "jealous of Scott's work" (180) and as deliberately "making him jealous with other women" (181), and of Scott as perpetually drunk and insecure about his ability to please women sexually (he quotes Scott as claiming that "Zelda said that the way I was built I could never make any woman happy" [190]). Hemingway's account notwithstanding, Scott, throughout the remainder of his life, maintained an at-times-supportive, albeit always uneasy and complicated, relationship with Hemingway.

For his part, Hemingway introduced Scott to many of the leading members of the American expatriate community in Paris, most

Christmas 1925, Paris. Courtesy of Princeton University Library

notably Gertrude Stein and Sylvia Beach, the proprietor of Shakespeare and Company, the city's leading literary bookstore and a gathering place for the local literati. But Scott and Zelda seemed to prefer the bars and nightclubs of the city to its literary salons. The tales of their antics replicated in many ways their similar behavior in New York in 1920. In his Ledger, Scott described that spring of 1925 in Paris as "1000 parties and no work" (*Ledger* 179).

After spending the summer of 1925 on the Riviera with the Murphys and their circle, the Fitzgeralds returned to Paris, where Scott began to plan his next novel and Zelda started ballet classes with Lubov Egorova. Scott also spent considerable time with Hemingway during the fall. He convinced Scribners to become Hemingway's publisher when the latter's publisher, Boni & Liveright, refused to publish *The Torrents of Spring*, Hemingway's parody of Sherwood Anderson, who was a Boni & Liveright author. *All the Sad Young Men*, Scott's third short story collection, appeared in February 1926 to generally admiring reviews and good sales; shortly thereafter, Scott and Zelda returned to the Riviera for the spring and summer. In

June, Scott read the manuscript of Hemingway's novel *The Sun Also Rises* and suggested significant revisions—including cutting the first two chapters—which Hemingway made.

During that summer of 1926, the Fitzgeralds' drinking and antisocial behavior became increasingly extreme and began to alienate the Murphys and others of their friends. One night, when Scott and Zelda met Isadora Duncan and the famed dancer openly flirted with Scott, Zelda threw herself down a flight of stone stairs in a fit of jealous rage. At one party given by the Murphys, a drunken Scott blithely tossed ashtrays around the room; at another, he smashed the hosts' stemware. As the year came to a close, Scott had failed to make significant progress on his novel, the couple were again financially in dire straits, and their drinking was threatening their health and distancing them from their friends. "I wish I were twenty-two again with only my dramatic and feverishly enjoyed miseries," he had plaintively written Perkins late in 1925, adding, "You remember I used to say I wanted to die at thirty—well, I'm now twenty-nine and the prospect is still welcome" (*Life in Letters* 131).

In December 1926, Scott and Zelda returned to the United States. After spending Christmas in Montgomery, they went to Hollywood, where Scott spent the first two months of 1927 working on "Lipstick," a screenplay about a flapper, for starlet Constance Talmadge. In Hollywood, they partied and Scott became infatuated with seventeen-year-old actress Lois Moran, who apparently did not return his interest. Zelda's response was to burn her clothes in a hotel bathtub and to throw a platinum watch Scott had given her early in 1920 before their marriage from the train window on the trip back east.

Upon their return, the Fitzgeralds rented Ellerslie, a nineteenth-century Greek Revival mansion at Edgemoor, located on the Delaware River, outside Wilmington. Still stung by Scott's attentions to Lois Moran, Zelda resumed ballet studies—now with the Philadelphia Opera ballet—and also returned to writing humorous magazine articles. She sold three of the latter before the end of 1927; significantly, the third was published under Scott's byline, and many of her subsequent essays and stories bore the attribution "by F. Scott and Zelda Fitzgerald" because the magazines wanted to capitalize on his name and reputation. Initially, this did not appear to bother Zelda; increasingly, however, she became resentful and competitive toward her husband. This put a further strain on their marriage, a tension that was only made worse by Scott's continuing failure to make significant headway on the novel he had been writing for two years.

During the early months of 1928, the intensity of Zelda's ballet studies increased. In April, when the couple went to Europe for the summer, they settled in Paris so that she could study with the Russian ballet. But in *Save Me the Waltz*, Zelda wrote of that trip, "They hadn't much faith in travel nor a great belief in a change of scene as a panacea for spiritual ills . . ." (*Collected Writings* 94–95). In late June, Scott met James Joyce at a dinner given by Sylvia Beach. That summer also saw Scott, who was feeling isolated and abandoned by his wife, thrown in jail twice in Paris for drunken behavior. When they returned to Ellerslie in October, he had made little progress on his novel. Back in Delaware during the fall and winter of 1928–1929, Zelda's obsessive ballet studies continued. Although Milford quotes Gerald Murphy as remarking, "There are limits to what a woman of Zelda's age can do and it was obvious that she had taken up the dance too late" (141), Zelda explains in *Save Me the Waltz* that she took up dancing so that "she would drive the devils that had driven her—that, in proving herself, she would achieve that peace which she imagined went only in surety of one's self—that she would be able, through the medium of the dance, to command her emotions, to summon love or pity or happiness at will, having provided a channel through which they might flow" (*Collected Writings* 118).

Scott's frustrations with his novel continued, and, as he later wrote in "Echoes of the Jazz Age" (1931), he was beginning to see around him signs that his and America's boom years were coming to an end:

> By this time contemporaries of mine had begun to disappear into the dark maw of violence. A classmate killed his wife and himself on Long Island, another tumbled "accidently" from a skyscraper in Philadelphia, another purposely from a skyscraper in New York. One was killed in a speak-easy in Chicago; another was beaten to death in a speak-easy in New York and crawled home to the Princeton Club to die . . . These are not catastrophes that I went out of my way to look for— these were my friends; moreover, these things happened not during the depression but during the boom. (*Crack-Up* 20)

When their two-year lease on Ellerslie expired in the spring of 1929, they returned to Paris so that Zelda could resume her ballet study with Egorova. She was also continuing her writing, but now it was fiction, a series of short stories that dealt with the lives of six young women. Five of these stories were published—all under a joint byline—and this put Zelda into direct competition with her husband, who was still struggling with his novel. The strain of writing and dancing was beginning to take a toll on Zelda's twenty-eight-year-old body, and on her mental health, as well. And Scott continued to feel abandoned, as he explained in a plaintive note to Hemingway:

> My latest tendency is to collapse about 11:00 and, with the tears flowing from my eyes or the gin rising to their level and leaking over, + tell interested friends or acquaintances that I havn't a friend in the world and likewise care for nobody, generally including Zelda, and often implying current company—after which the current company tend to become less current and I wake up in strange rooms in strange palaces. The rest of the time I stay alone working or trying to work or brooding or reading detective stories—and realizing that anyone in my state of mind who has in addition never been able to hold his tongue, is pretty poor company. But when drunk I make them all pay and pay and pay. (*Life in Letters* 169)

When the Fitzgeralds returned to the Riviera for the summer and early fall, Scott managed to complete two chapters of his novel (*Tender Is the Night* would go through seventeen drafts and would not be published until 1934), and Zelda danced professionally for the first time in Nice and Cannes. But on the motor trip back to Paris in October, Zelda suddenly grabbed the steering wheel and tried to drive off a cliff; she continued to behave erratically throughout the fall and early winter of 1929–1930. As she said, "We went [to] sophisticated places with charming people but I was grubby and didn't care" (Milford, *Zelda* 156). In September, she was offered a solo role in *Aïda* by the San Carlo Opera Ballet Company in Naples, but, inexplicably, she turned it down. A February 1930 trip to North Africa, Scott's attempt to give Zelda a rest from her frantic ballet studies, was not a success. In "My Lost City," Scott misdated their receiving the news of the stock market crash as having occurred while they were on this trip ("we heard a dull distant crash which echoed to the farthest wastes of the desert" [*Crack-Up* 32]); but with the fall of the stock market, as he correctly noted in "Echoes of the Jazz Age," "the most expensive orgy in history was over" (*Crack-Up* 21). Scott and Zelda's personal crash was imminent, as well. When they returned to Paris, Zelda resumed her classes with Egorova, becoming pathologically dependent on her teacher and mentally and physically exhausted. When she entered Malmaison clinic outside Paris in April, the clinic's report stated that upon admission, she was "continually repeating" this litany: " 'This is dreadful, this is horrible, what is going to become of me, I have to work, and I will no longer be able to, I must die, and yet I have to work. I will never be cured, let me leave" (*Some Sort of Epic Grandeur* 293). Her words were poignantly prophetic: Thereafter, she would never truly be cured, and although she would periodically leave the various clinics and institutions to which she had been committed, she never again really did resume a normal existence. Almost exactly ten years had elapsed between the date of the Fitzgeralds' marriage, April 3, 1920, and the day, April 23, 1930, on which Zelda entered Malmaison.

After less than a month at Malmaison, Zelda discharged herself and returned home to Paris, where she resumed ballet lessons. After experiencing hallucinations and attempting suicide, however, she entered Val-Mont clinic in Glion, Switzerland, where she was examined in early June 1930 by Dr. Oscar Forel, who then had her transferred to his own clinic, Les Rives de Prangins at Nyon, on Lake Geneva. Shortly after Zelda entered Prangins, the Fitzgeralds wrote the two long letters of reminiscence mentioned earlier.

50. TO ZELDA
[Summer 1930]

AL (draft), 7 pp.[1]
[Paris or Lausanne]

Written with Zelda gone to the Clinque

I know this then—that those day when we came up from the south, from Capri, were among my happiest—but you were sick and the happiness was not in the home.

I had been unhappy for a long time then—when my play failed a year and a half before, when I worked so hard for a year[,] twelve stories and novel and four articles in that time with no one believing in me and no one to see except you + before the end your heart betraying me and then I was really alone with no one I liked. In Rome we were dismal and was still working proof and three more

---

1. Scott may never have sent this letter.

stories and in Capri you were sick and there seemed to be nothing left of happiness in the world anywhere I looked.

Then we came to Paris and suddenly I reallized that it hadn't all been in vain. I was a success—the biggest one in my profession—everybody admired me and I was proud I'd done such a good thing. I met Gerald and Sara who took us for friends now and Ernest who was an equeal and my kind of an idealist. I got drunk with him on the Left Bank in careless cafés and drank with Sara and Gerald in their garden in St Cloud but you were endlessly sick and at home everything was unhappy. We went to Antibes and I was happy but you were sick still and all that fall and that winter and spring at the cure and I was alone all the time and I had to get drunk before I could leave you so sick and not care and I was only happy a little while before I got too drunk. Afterwards there were all the usuall penalties for being drunk.

Finally you got well in Juan-les-Pins and a lot of money came in and I made [one] of those mistakes literary men make—I thought I was a man of the world—that everybody liked me and admired me for myself but I only liked a few people like Ernest and Charlie McArthur[2] and Gerald and Sara who were my peers. Time goes bye fast in those moods and nothing is ever done. I thought then that things came easily—I forgot how I'd dragged the great Gatsby out of the pit of my stomach in a time of misery. I woke up in Hollywood no longer my egotistic, certain self but a mixture of Ernest in fine clothes and Gerald with a career—and Charlie McArthur with a past. Anybody that could make me believe that, like Lois Moran did, was precious to me.

Ellerslie, the polo people, Mrs. Chanler[3] the party for Cecelia[4] were all attempts to make up from without for being undernourished now from within. Anything to be liked, to be reassured not that I was a man of a little genius but that I was a great man of the world. At the same time I knew it was nonsense—the part of me that knew it was nonsense brought us to the Rue Vaugirard.

But now you had gone into yourself just as I had four years before

---

2. Charles MacArthur, American playwright and, later, screenwriter and husband of actress Helen Hayes. Scott had met and caroused with MacArthur on the Riviera during the summer of 1926.

3. Mrs. Winthrop Chanler, a wealthy society matron whom Scott had first met when he was a young man.

4. Scott's second cousin, daughter of his cousin Cecilia Taylor.

in St. Raphael—and there were all the consequences of bad appartments through your lack of patience ("Well, if you want a better appartment why don't you make some money") bad servants, through your indifference ("Well, if you don't like her why don't you send Scotty away to school") Your dislike for Vidor,[5] your indifference to Joyce I understood—share your incessant entheusiasm and absorbtion in the ballet I could not. Somewhere in there I had a sense of being exploited, not by you but by something I resented terribly no happiness. Certainly less than there had ever been at home—you were a phantom washing clothes, talking French bromides with Lucien or Del Plangue[6]—I remember desolate trips to Versaille to Rhiems, to LaBaule undertaken in sheer weariness of home. I remember wondering why I kept working to pay the bills of this desolate menage. I had evolved. In despair I went from the extreme of isolation, which is to say isolation with Mlle Delplangue, or the Ritz Bar where I got back my self esteem for half an hour, often with someone I had hardly ever seen before. In the evenings sometimes you and I rode to the Bois in a cab—after awhile I preferred to go to Cafe de Lilas and sit there alone remembering what a happy time I had had there with Ernest, Hadley,[7] Dorothy Parker + Benchley two years before. During all this time, remember I didn't blame anyone but myself. I complained when the house got unbearable but after all I was not John Peale Bishop—I was paying for it with work, that I passionately hated and found more and more difficult to do. The novel was like a dream, daily farther and farther away.

Ellerslie was better and worse. Unhappiness is less accute when one lives with a certain sober dignity but the financial strain was too much. Between Sept when we left Paris and March when we reached Nice we were living at the rate of forty thousand a year.

But somehow I felt happier. Another Spring—I would see Ernest whom I had launched, Gerald + Sarah who through my agency had been able to try the movies.[8] At least life would [seem] less drab; there would be parties with people who offered something, conversa-

---

5. King Vidor, Hollywood movie director, whom Scott met in Paris in the summer of 1928 and with whom he briefly planned to make a movie.

6. Mademoiselle Delplangue was Scottie's governess.

7. Hadley Richardson, Hemingway's first wife.

8. Scott introduced King Vidor to Gerald Murphy and the two later collaborated on the film *Hallelujah!* (1929), Hollywood's first all-black movie.

tions with people with something to say. Later swimming and getting tanned and young and being near the sea.

It worked out beautifully didn't it. Gerald and Sara didn't see us. Ernest and I met but it was a more irritable Ernest, apprehensively telling me his whereabouts lest I come in on them tight and endanger his lease. The discovery that half a dozen people were familiars there didn't help my self esteem. By the time we reached the beautiful Riv-ierra I had developed such an inferiority complex that I couldn't face anyone unless I was tight. I worked there too, though, and the unusual combination exploded my lungs.

You were gone now—I scarcely remember you that summer. You were simply one of all the people who disliked me or were indifferent to me. I didn't like to think of you.—You didn't need me and it was easier to talk to or rather at Madame Bellois and keep full of wine. I was grateful when you came with me to the Doctors one afternoon but after we'd been a week in Paris and I didn't try any more about living or dieing. Things were always the same. The appartments that were rotten, the maids that stank—the ballet before my eyes, spoil-ing a story to take the Troubetskoys to dinner, poisening a trip to Africa. You were going crazy and calling it genius—I was going to ruin and calling it anything that came to hand. And I think everyone far enough away to see us outside of our glib presentations of our-selves guessed at your almost meglomaniacal selfishness and my insane indulgence in drink. Toward the end nothing much mattered. The nearest I ever came to leaving you was when you told me you thot I was a fairy in the Rue Palatine but now whatever you said aroused a sort of detached pity for you. For all your superior obser-vation and your harder intelligence I have a faculty of guessing right, without evidence even with a certain wonder as to why and whence that mental short cut came. I wish the Beautiful and Damned had been a maturely written book because it was all true. We ruined ourselves—I have never honestly thought that we ruined each other

51. TO SCOTT

[September(?) 1930]

AL, 42 pp., on stationery embossed
| ZELDA | at top center
[Prangins Clinic, Nyon,
Switzerland]

Dear Scott:

I have just written to Newman[9] to come here to me. You say that you have been thinking of the past. The weeks since I haven't slept more than three or four hours, swathed in bandages sick and unable to read so have I.

There was:

The strangeness and excitement of New York, of reporters and furry smothered hotel lobbies, the brightness of the sun on the window panes and the prickly dust of late spring: the impressiveness of the Fowlers and much tea-dancing and my eccentric behavior at Princeton. There were Townsend's blue eyes and Ludlow's rubbers and a trunk that exhuded sachet and the marshmallow odor of the Biltmore. There were always Lud[l]ow and Townsend and Alex and Bill Mackey[10] and you and me. We did not like women and we were happy. There was Georges[11] appartment and his absinth cock-tails and Ruth Findleys gold hair in his comb, and visits to the "Smart Set" and "Vanity Fair"—a collegiate literary world puffed into wide proportions by the New York papers. There were flowers and night clubs and Ludlow's advice that moved us to the country. At West Port, we quarrelled over morals once, walking beside a colonial wall under the freshness of lilacs. We sat up all night over "Brass Knuckles and Guitar."[12] There was the road house where we bought gin, and Kate Hicks and the Maurices and the bright harness of the Rye Beach Club. We swam in the depth of the night with George before we quarrelled with him and went to John Williams[13] parties where there were actresses who spoke French when they were drunk. George played

---

9. Newman Smith, Zelda's brother-in-law.

10. Ludlow Fowler, Townsend Martin, Alexander McKaig, and William Mackie were friends of Scott's from his time at Princeton University.

11. George Jean Nathan, critic and coeditor with H. L. Mencken of *The Smart Set* and *American Mercury* literary magazines.

12. "Dice, Brass Knuckles & Guitar," one of Scott's short stories; but it was not written until 1923.

13. Broadway producer.

"Cuddle up a Little Closer" on the piano. There were my white knickers that startled the Connecticut hills, and the swim in the sandaled lady's bird-pool. The beach, and dozens of men, mad rides along the Post Road and trips to New York. We never could have a room at a hotel at night we looked so young, so once we filled an empty suit-case with the telephone directory and spoons and a pin-cushion at the Manhattan. I was romanticly attached to Townsend and he went away to Tahatii—and there were your episodes of Gene Bankhead and Miriam. We bought the Marmon with Harvey Firestone and went south through the haunted swamps of Virginia, the red clay hills of Georgia, the sweet rutted creek-bottoms of Alabama. We drank corn on the wings of an aeroplane in the moon-light and danced at the country-club and came back.[14] I had a pink dress that floated and a very theatrical silver one that I bought with Don Stewart.[15]

We moved to 59th Street. We quarrelled and you broke the bath-room door and hurt my eye. We went so much to the theatre that you took it off the income tax. We trailed through Central Park in the snow after a ball at the Plaza, I quarrelled with Zoë about Bottecelli[16] at the Brevoort and went with her to buy a coat for David Belasco.[17] We had Bourbon and Deviled Ham and Christmas at the Overmans[18] and ate lots at the Lafayette. There was Tom Smith and his wall-paper and Mencken and our Valentine party and the time I danced all night with Alex and meals at Mollats with John[19] and I skated, and was pregnant and you wrote the "Beautiful and Damned". We came to Europe and I was sick and complained always. There was London, and Wopping with Shane Leslie[20] and straw-berries as big as tomatoes at Lady Randolph Churchills. There was St. Johns Ervines wooden leg and Bob Handley in the gloom of the Cecil—There was Paris and the heat and the ice-cream that did not melt and buying clothes—and Rome and your friends from the British Embassy and your drinking, drinking. We came home.

---

14. This motor trip provided material for Scott's humorous essay "The Cruise of the Rolling Junk," published in February, March, and April 1924 issues of *Motor*.
15. Donald Ogden Stewart, American humorist and, later, successful screenwriter.
16. Zoë Akins, American playwright, with whom Zelda apparently quarreled about the parlor game Botticelli.
17. Broadway playwright and producer.
18. Lynne Overman, actor in movies and on the stage.
19. John Peale Bishop, American poet and critic, who was Scott's classmate at Princeton.
20. Irish-Anglo critic, whom Scott had met as a young man and who recommended the first draft of *This Side of Paradise* to Scribners.

There was "Dog"[21] and lunch at the St. Regis with Townsend and Alex and John: Alabama, and the unbearable heat and our almost buying a house. Then we went to St. Paul and hundreds of people came to call. There were the Indian forests and the moon on the sleeping porch and I was heavy and afraid of the storms. Then Scottie was born and we went to all the Christmas parties and a man asked Sandy[22] "who is your fat friend?" Snow covered everything. We had the Flu and went lots to the Kalmans and Scottie grew strong. Joseph Hergesheimer came and Saturdays we went to the university Club. We went to the Yacht Club and we both had minor flirtations. Joe began to dislike me, and I played so much golf that I had Tetena. Kollie[23] almost died. We both adored him. We came to New York and rented a house when we were tight. There was Val Engelicheff and Ted Paramour and dinner with Bunny[24] in Washington Square and pills and Doctor Lackin and we had a violent quarrell on the train going back, I don't remember why. Then I brought Scottie to New York. She was round and funny in a pink coat and bonnet and you met us at the station. In Great Neck there was always disorder and quarrels: about the Golf Club, about the Foxes, about Peggy Weber, about Helen Buck, about everything. We went to the Rumseys,[25] and that awful night at the Mackeys when Ring sat in the cloak-room. We saw Esther and Glen Hunter[26] and Gilbert Seldes. We gave lots of parties: the biggest one for Rebecca West. We drank Bass Pale Ale and went always to the Bucks or the Lardners or the Swopes when they weren't at our house. We saw lots of Sidney Howard and fought the week-end that Bill Motter was with us. We drank always and finally came to France because there were always too many people in the house. On the boat there was almost a scandal about Bunny Burgess. We found Nanny and went to Hyeres—Scottie and I were both sick there in the dusty garden full of Spanish Bayonet and

---

21. A humorous song Scott wrote.

22. Xandra Kalman, a childhood friend of Scott's.

23. Oscar Kalman.

24. The Fitzgeralds met Prince Vladimir N. Engalitcheff, whose father was the former Russian vice-counsul in Chicago, in 1921 on the way to Europe on the *Aquitania*. E. E. Paramore was a writer who later worked with Scott in Hollywood. Edmund "Bunny" Wilson, leading American man of letters, met Scott at Princeton, where Wilson was a class ahead of Scott.

25. Charles Cary Rumsey, artist and sportsman.

26. Glenn Hunter, a movie actor who was in *Grit* (1924), for which Scott wrote the scenario.

Bourgainvilla. We went to St. Raphael. You wrote, and we went sometimes to Nice or Monte Carlo. We were alone, and gave big parties for the French aviators. Then there was Josen[27] and you were justifiably angry. We went to Rome. We ate at the Castelli dei Cesari. The sheets were always damp. There was Christmas in the echoes, and eternal walks. We cried when we saw the Pope. There were the luminous shadows of the Pinco and the officer's shining boots. We went to Frascati and Tivoli. There was the jail, and Hal Rhodes at the Hotel de Russie and my not wanting to go to the moving-picture ball at the Excelsior and asking Hungary Cox to take me home.[28] Then I was horribly sick, from trying to have a baby and you didn't care much and when I was well we came back to Paris. We sat to-gether in Marseilles and thought how good France was. We lived in the rue Tilsitt, in red plush and Teddy came for tea and we went to the markets with the Murphies. There were the Wimans and Mary Hay and Eva La Galliene [Le Galli-enne] and rides in the Bois at dawn and the night we all played puss-in-the-corner at the Ritz. There was Tunti and nights in Mont Ma[r]tre. We went to Antibes, and I was sick always and took too much Dial.[29] The Murphy's were at the Hotel du Cap and we saw them constantly. Back in Paris I began dancing lessons because I had nothing to do. I was sick again at Christmas when the Mac Leishes came and Doctor Gros said there was no use trying to save my ovaries. I was always sick and having picqures[30] and things and you were naturally more and more away. You found Ernest and the Cafe des Lilas and you were unhappy when Dr. Gros sent me to Salies-de-Bearn. At the Villa Paquita I was always sick. Sara brought me things and we gave a lunch for Geralds father. We went to Cannes and list[e]ned to Raquel Miller[31] and dined under the rain of fire-works. You couldn't work because your room was damp and you quarrelled with the Murphys. We moved to a bigger villa and I went to Paris and had my appendix out. You drank all the time and some man called up the hospital about a row you had had.

---

27. Edouard Jozan, French aviator with whom Zelda had a romantic relationship in July 1924.

28. While in Rome in the fall of 1924, Scott was briefly jailed, due to his drunken behavior. The Fitzgeralds attended a Christmas party for the cast of *Ben-Hur*, which was being filmed there, and Zelda asked writer and newspaperman Howard Coxe to take her home.

29. A sedative which contained alcohol.

30. Injections.

31. Raquel Meller, renowned Spanish singer.

We went home, and I wanted you to swim with me at Juan-les-Pins but you liked it better where it was gayer: at the Garoupe with Marice Hamilton and the Murphys and the Mac Leishes. Then you found Grace Moore and Ruth and Charlie[32] and the summer passed, one party after another. We quarrelled about Dwight Wiman and you left me lots alone. There were too many people and too many things to do: every-day there was something and our house was always full. There was Gerald and Ernest and you often did not come home. There were the English sleepers that I found downstairs one morning and Bob and Muriel and Walker[33] and Anita Loos, always somebody—Alice Delamar and Ted Rousseau and our trips to St. Paul[34] and the note from Isadora Duncan and the countryside slipping by through the haze of Chamberry-fraises and Graves. That was your summer. I swam with Scottie except when I followed you, mostly unwillingly. Then I had asthma and almost died in Genoa and we were back in America—further apart than ever before. In California, though you would not allow me to go anywhere without you, you yourself engaged in flagrantly senti-mental relations with a child.[35] You said you wanted nothing more from me in all your life, though you made a scene when Carl[36] sug-gested that I go to dinner with him and Betty Compson. We came east: I worked over Ellerslie incessantly and made it function. There was our first house-party and you and Lois—and when there was nothing more to do on the house I began dancing lessons. You did not like it when you saw it made me happy. You were angry about rehearsals and insistent about trains. You went to New York to see Lois and I met Dick Knight the night of that party for Paul Morand.[37] Again, though you were by then thoroughly entangled sentimentally, you forbade my seeing Dick and were furious about a letter he wrote me. On the boat coming over you paid absolutely no attention of any kind to me except to refuse me the permission to stay to a concert with whatever-his-name-was. I think the most

---

32. Grace Moore was an American opera singer; Ruth Ober-Goldbeck-de Vallombrossa was an American who was the wife of the Count de Vallombrosa; Charles MacArthur.
33. Walker Ellis, a friend of Scott's from Princeton days.
34. It was in the Riviera town of St. Paul-de-Vence where dancer Isadora Duncan flirted with Scott at a party.
35. Lois Moran.
36. Carl Van Vechten, American novelist and photographer.
37. Richard Knight, New York lawyer whom Zelda, according to Milford, met and was attracted to at a party for Scott's cousin, Cecilia Taylor, in the fall of 1927. Paul Morand was a French novelist and essayist.

humiliating and bestial thing that ever happened to me in my life is a scene that you probably don't remember even in Genoa. We lived in the rue Vaugirard. You were constantly drunk. You didn't work and were dragged home at night by taxi-drivers when you came home at all. You said it was my fault for dancing all day. What was I to do? You got up for lunch. You made no advances toward me and complained that I was un-responsive. You were literally eternally drunk the whole summer. I got so I couldn't sleep and I had asthma again. You were angry when I wouldn't go with you to Mont Ma[r]tre. You brought drunken under-graduates in to meals when you came home for them, and it made you angry that I didn't care any more. I began to like Egorowa—On the boat going back I told you I was afraid that there was something abnormal in the relationship and you laughed. There was more or less of a scandal about Philipson, but you did not even try to help me. You brought Philippe[38] back and I couldnt manage the house any more; he was insubordinate and disrespectful to me and you wouldn't let him go. I began to work harder at dancing—I thought of nothing else but that. You were far away by then and I was alone. We came back to rue Palatine and you, in a drunken stupor told me a lot of things that I only half understood: but I understood the dinner we had at Ernest's. Only I didn't understand that it matterred. You left me more and more alone, and though you complained that it was the appartment or the servants or me, you know the real reason you couldn't work was because you were always out half the night and you were sick and you drank constantly. We went to Cannes. I kept up my lessons and we quarrelled. You wouldn't let me fire the nurse that both Scottie and I hated. You disgraced yourself at the Barry's[39] party, on the yacht at Monte Carlo, at the casino with Gerald and Dotty.[40] Many nights you didn't come home. You came into my room once the whole summer, but I didn't care because I went to the beach in the morning, I had my lesson in the afternoon and I walked at night. I was nervous and half-sick but I didn't know what was the matter. I only knew that I had difficulty standing lots of people, like the party at Wm. J. Locke's and that I wanted to get back to Paris. We had lunch at the Murphy's and

---

38. French taxi driver brought to the United States by the Fitzgeralds to be their chauffeur.
39. Philip Barry, American playwright.
40. Dorothy Parker.

Gerald said to me very pointedly several times that Nemchinova[41] was at Antibes. Still I didn't understand. We came back to Paris. You were miserable about your lung, and because you had wasted the summer, but you didn't stop drinking. I worked all the time and I became dependent on Egorowa. I couldn't walk in the street unless I had been to my lesson. I couldn't manage the appartment because I couldn't speak to the servants. I couldn't go into stores to buy clothes and my emotions became blindly involved. In February, when I was so sick with bronchitis that I had ventouses[42] every day and fever for two weeks, I had to work because I couldn't exist in the world without it, and still I didn't understand what I was doing. I didn't even know what I wanted. Then we went to Africa and when we came back I began to realize because I could feel what was happenning in others. You did not want me. Twice you left my bed saying "I can't. Don't you understand" — I didn't. Then there was the Harvard man who lost his direction, and when I wanted you to come home with me you told me to sleep with the coal man. At Nancy Hoyt's[43] dinner she offerred her services but there was nothing the matter with my head then, though I was half dead, so I turned back to the studio. Lucienne[44] was sent away but since I knew nothing about the situation, I didn't know why there was something wrong. I just kept on going. Lucienne came back and later went away again and then the end happened. I went to Malmaison. You wouldn't help me — I don't blame you by now, but if you had explained I would have understood because all I wanted was to go on working. You had other things: drink and tennis, and we did not care about each other. You hated me for asking you not to drink. A girl came to work with me but I didn't want her to. I still believed in love and I thought suddenly of Scottie and that you supported me. So at Valmont I was in tortu[r]e, and my head closed to-gether. You gave me a flower and said it was "plus petite et moins etendue" — We were friends — Then you took it away and I grew sicker, and there was nobody to teach me, so here I am, after five months of misery and agony and desperation. I'm glad you have found that the material for a Josep[h]ine story[45]

---

41. Nemtchinova, a famous Russian ballerina.
42. The French word for a medical procedure for drawing blood.
43. A novelist and the sister of Elinor Wylie.
44. A ballerina in Egorova's studio.
45. Scott began to write a series of short stories about an adolescent girl named Josephine Perry for the *Saturday Evening Post* in 1930.

and I'm glad that you take such an interest in sports. Now that I can't sleep any more I have lots to think about, and since I have gone so far alone I suppose I can go the rest of the way—but if it were Scottie I would not ask that she go through the same hell and if I were God I could not justify or find a reason for imposing it—except that it was wrong, of cource, to love my teacher when I should have loved you. But I didn't have you to love—not since long before I loved her. I have just begun to realize that sex and sentiment have little to do with each other. When I came to you twice last winter and asked you to start over it was because I thought I was becoming seriously involved sentimentally and preparing situations for which I was morally and practicly unfitted. You had a song about Gigolos: if that had ever entered my head there was, besides the whole studio, 3 other solutions in Paris.

I came to you half-sick after a difficult lunch at Armonville and you kept me waiting until it was too late in front of the Guaranty Trust.

Sandy's tiny candle was not much of a strain, but it required something better than your week of drunkenness to put it out. You didn't care: so I went on and on—dancing alone, and no matter what happens, I still know in my heart that it is a Godless, dirty game; that love is bitter and all there is, and that the rest is for the emotional beggars of the earth and is about the equivalent of people who stimulate themselves with dirty post-cards—

Scott, Zelda, and Scottie in Annecy, July 1931

PART III

Breaking Down: 1930–1938

*. . . and the only sadness is the living without you. . . . You and I have been happy;
we haven't been happy just once, we've been happy a thousand times. . . .
Forget the past—what you can of it, and turn about and swim back home to me,
to your haven for ever and ever—even though it may seem a dark cave at times
and lit with torches of fury; it is the best refuge for you—turn gently in the waters
through which you move and sail back.*
                                        —SCOTT TO ZELDA, APRIL 26, 1934

After a decade of marriage, the Fitzgeralds were under every strain imaginable. Zelda's years of ballet had depleted the very resources such a career demanded—her physical stamina and grace, along with her youth and beauty. Scott's reputation as a writer was also suffering while the public waited for him to produce another novel, and he had already developed the habit of borrowing against future work. Money, once plentiful, was now harder to earn, at exactly the same time when writing was also more difficult—problems that would worsen over the decade and nag Scott for the rest of his life. The Fitzgeralds' relationship, tested at every turn for over ten years, had certainly weakened. And neither Scott, who was only thirty-four but whose alcoholism had caught up with him early, nor Zelda, only thirty, would ever be truly healthy again. Under the considerable weight of these grave difficulties, the Fitzgeralds began the third and most challenging phase of their lives together—the thirties. Scott and Zelda, like America itself, entered into a decade in which an apparent immunity from suffering was no longer an option; yet also, again like the country itself, it was a decade that would lead them to reevaluate themselves and develop the inner resources of character that had lain dormant during the boom years of the twenties.

First Breakdown
LES RIVES DE PRANGINS, JUNE 1930–AUGUST 1931

The following letters were written while Zelda was a patient at Les Rives de Prangins. Scott, who was not allowed to visit until his wife's treatment had been established but who wanted to be near her nevertheless, commuted between Paris (where Scottie remained in school and with her governess) and a series of hotels in Swiss towns near the clinic. He asked Zelda's doctor for permission to send her flowers every other day and asked if he could "start sending her short notes, mentioning neither the misunderstanding of these last days nor her sickness?" Zelda often referred to these brief letters from Scott, which, unfortunately, appear not to have survived. Yet we still know Scott's state of mind and his troubled but supportive devotion to Zelda through letters he wrote on her behalf to her doctor and family and from those he wrote to his editor, Maxwell Perkins, and to his agent, Harold Ober, in which he repeatedly worried about his work and money, in addition to Zelda and Scottie.

In her letters to Scott, Zelda vacillated between the deepest, most tender affection for him and absolute scorn — between relying on him exclusively for kindness and understanding and accusing him of abandoning her, even to the point of demanding a divorce. In the fall, her condition further deteriorated; the worse she grew, the more she villainized Scott and begged to be released from the hospital, which in her agony she had begun to see as a torture chamber. Either way, Scott certainly emerges as the central figure in her life and the only person to whom she was close during this period. The letters are also invaluable because in them Zelda describes her symptoms and suffering in her own words, giving us an intimate window into her mental illness — her panic attacks, periods of heightened sensitivity and distorted perceptions; periods of depersonalization similar to shock, when she seemed distanced from reality; and the physical manifestation of her mental illness, an extreme form of eczema.

The exact order of the letters during this period is impossible to ascertain, partially because Zelda never dated her letters, but also because her moods changed so quickly, as did the course of her illness. In addition, her references to Scott's whereabouts — Paris, Geneva, Caux, Lausanne, and so forth — offer no reliable clues because he moved around a great deal during this period. Still, there are striking consistencies in Zelda's letters, in the form of two outstanding and recurring themes: first, how primary her relationship to Scott was; second, how driven she was, broken at the age of thirty, to find real work for herself — a coherent vocational identity, when her personal identity was so fractured — and a clear sense of purpose amid the chaos of her illness.

Les Rives de Prangins, with an arrow pointing to Zelda's room

Zelda's room at Les Rives de Prangins. Courtesy of Princeton University Library

52. TO SCOTT   ALS, 2 pp.
[Late June 1930]   [Prangins Clinic, Nyon,
                                      Switzerland]

Dear Scott:

Just at the point in my life when there is no time left me for losing, I am here to incapacitate myself for using what I have learned in such a desperate school—through my own fault and from a complete lack of medical knowledge on a rather esoteric subject. If you could write to Egorova a friendly impersonal note to find out exactly where I stand as a dancer it would be of the greatest help to me— Remember, this is in no way at all her fault. I would have liked to dance in New York this fall, but where am I going to find again these months that dribble into the beets of the clinic garden? Is it worth it? And once a proper horror for the accidents of life has been instilled into me, I have no intention of join[in]g the group about a corpse. My legs are already flabby and I will soon be like Ada MacLeish, huntress of coralled game, I suppose, instead of a human being recompensed for everything by the surety of a comprehension of one manifestation of beauty—Why can't you write one what you think and want instead of vague attempts at reassurance? If I had work or something it would be so much decenter to try to help each other and make at least a stirrup cup out of this bloody mess.

You have always had so much sympathy for people forced to start over late in life that I should think you could find the generosity to help me amongst your many others—not as you would a child but as an equal.

I want you to let me leave here—You're wasting time and effort and money to take away the little we both have left. If you think you are preparing me for a return to Alabama you are mistaken, and also if you think that I am going to spend the rest of my life roaming about without happiness or rest or work from one sanatorium to another like Kit you are wrong. Two sick horses might conceivably pull a heavier load than a well one alone. Of cource, if you prefer that I should spend six months of my life under prevailing conditions—my eyes are open and I will get something from that, too, I suppose, but they are tired and unhappy and my head aches always. Won't you write me a comprehensible letter such as you might write to one of your friends? Every day it gets harder to think or live and I do not understand the object of wasting the dregs of me here, alone in a devas[ta]ting bitterness.

Zelda

Please write immediately to Paris about the dancing. I would do it but I think the report will be more accurate if it goes to you—just an opinion as to what value my work is and to what point I could develop it before it is too late. Of cource, I would go to another school as I know Egorowa would not want to be bothered with me. Thanks.

Scott did write to Madame Egorova, who replied that Zelda was a good dancer who might perform in minor roles but that, having started too late, she could never have a noteworthy career. Zelda was terribly disappointed, but Scott and her doctor (who saw her obsession with ballet as contributing to her breakdown and an obstacle to her getting well) were relieved for Zelda to have this decisive evaluation from the teacher she trusted.

Although Scott never encouraged Zelda in ballet, he expressed genuine admiration for her as a writer and tried to promote her work with his publishing associates in New York. In July, Scott wrote to Perkins, praising Zelda's stories and recounting the frame of mind they represented:

I'm asking Harold Ober to offer you these three stories which Zelda wrote in the dark middle of her nervous breakdown. I think you'll see that apart from the beauty + richness of the writing they have a strange haunting and evocative quality that is absolutely new. I think too that there is a certain unity apparent in them—their actual unity is a fact because each of them is the story of her life when things for awhile seemed to have brought her to the edge of madness and despair. (Dear Scott/Dear Max 166–167)

53. TO SCOTT

[Summer 1930]

AL, 7 pp., on stationery embossed ZELDA at top center
[Prangins Clinic, Nyon, Switzerland]

Dear Scott:

Every day it seems to me that things are more barren and sterile and hopeless. In Paris, before I realized that I was sick, there was a new significance to everything: stations and streets and façades of buildings—colors were infinite, part of the air, and not restricted by the lines that encompassed them and lines were free of the masses they held. There was music that beat behind my forehead and other music that fell into my stomach from a high parabola and there was some of Schumann that was still and tender and the sadness of Chopin Mazurkas. Some of them sound as if he thought that he couldn't compose them—and there was the madness of turning, turning, turning through the deciciveness of Litz [Liszt]. Then the world became embryonic in Africa[1]—and there was no need for communication. The Arabs fermenting in the vastness; the curious quality of their eyes and the smell of ants; a detachment as if I was on the other side of a black gauze—a fearless small feeling, and then the end at Easter.[2] But even that was better than the childish, vacillating shell that I am now. I am so afraid that when you come and find there is nothing left but disorder and vacuum that you will be horror-struck. I don't seem to know anything appropriate for a person of thirty: I suppose it's because of draining myself so thoroughly, straining so completely every fibre in that futile attempt to achieve with every factor against me—Do you mind my writing this way? Don't be afraid that I am a meglo-maniac again. I'm just searching and it's easier with you. You'll have to re-educate me—But you used to like giving me books and telling me things. I never realized before how hideously dependent on you I was. Dr. Forel says I won't be after. If I can have a clear intelligence I'm sure we can use it—I hope I will be different. [I] must have been an awful bore for you.

Why do you never write me what you are doing and what you think and how it feels to be alone—

I can't make head or tails out of all this dreary experience since I do not know how much was accidental and how much deliberate—how big a role circumstance played and what proportion was voluntary—but if such a thing as expiation exists it is taking place and I hope you will forgive me the rest of my part.

Love,
    Dear—

When are you coming?

---

1. The disastrous trip to North Africa the Fitzgeralds took in February 1930.
2. Zelda's first breakdown, when she entered the Malmaison clinic.

54. TO SCOTT

[Summer 1930]

AL, 8 pp., on stationery embossed
ZELDA at top center
[Prangins Clinic, Nyon,
Switzerland]

Dear Scott:

You said in your letter that I might write when I needed you. For the first time since I went to Malmaison I seem to be about half human-being, capable of focusing my attention and not walking in black horror like I have been for so long. Though I am physically sick and covered with eczema I would like to see you. I'm lonely and do not seem to be able to exist in the world on any terms at all. If you do not want to come maybe Newman would come.

Please don't write to me about blame. I am tired of rummaging my head to understand a situation that would be difficult enough if I were completely lucid. I cannot arbitrarily accept blame now when I know that in the past I felt none. Anyway, blame doesn't matter. The thing that counts is to apply the few resources available to turning life into a tenable orderly affair that resembles neither the black hole of Calcutta or Cardinal Ballou's[?] cage. Of cource, you are quite free to proceed as you think best. If I can ever find the dignity and peace to apply myself, I am sure there must be something to fill the next twenty years of a person who is willing to work for it, so do not feel that you have any obligations toward me, sentimental or otherwise, unless you accept them as freely as you did when I was young and happy and quite different from how I am now.

I am infinitely sorry that I have been ungrateful for your attempts to help me. Try to understand that people are not always reasonable when the world is as unstable and vacillating as a sick head can render it—that for months I have been living in vaporous places peopled with one-dimensional figures and tremulous buildings until I can no longer tell an optical illusion from a reality—that head and ears incessantly throb and roads disappear, until finally I lost all control and powers of judgement and was semi-imbecilic when I arrived here. At least now I can read, and as soon as possible I am going on with some stories I have half done. Won't you send me "Technique of the Drama" please? I have an enormous desire to try to write a play that I have begun a little.

Scottie has not written but I know she is happy with Madamoiselle. I'm glad you are better. It seems odd that we were once a warm little family—secure in a home—

Thank you for the books—

Was it fun in Paris? Who did you see there and was the Madeleine pink at five o'clock and did the fountains fall with hollow delicacy into the framing of space in the Place de la Concorde and did the blue creep out from behind the colonades of the rue de Rivoli through the grill of the Tuileries and was the Louvre gray and metallic in the sun and did the trees hang brooding over the cafés and were there lights at night and the click of saucers and the auto horns that play de Bussey [Debussy].

I *love* Paris. How was it?

55. TO SCOTT   ALS, 1 p.
[Summer 1930]   [Prangins Clinic, Nyon,
                                      Switzerland]

Dear Scott:

There is no use my trying to write to you because if I write one thing one day I think another immediately afterwards. I would like to see you. I don't know why I have constantly a prese[n]timent of disaster. It seems to me cruel that you cannot explain to me what is the matter since you will not accept my explanation. As you know, I am a person, or was, of some capability even if on a small scale and if I could once grasp the situation I would be much better able to handle it. Under existing conditions, I simply grovel about in the dark and since I can not concentrate either to read or write there does not seem to be any way to escape. I do not want to lose my mind. Twice horrible things have happened to me through my inability to express myself: once peritonitis that left me an invalid for two years[3] and now this thing. Won't you please come to see me, since at least you know me and you could see, maybe, some assurance to give me that would counteract the abuse you piled on me at Lausanne when I was so

---

3. In 1926, Zelda had her appendix removed, but she seemed to recover quickly. She nevertheless associated this illness with her inability to conceive another child during this period, which may explain why she remembered it as being so severe.

sick. At any rate one thing has been achieved: I am thoroughly and completely humiliated and broken if that was what you wanted. There are some things I want to tell you.

   Zelda.

56. TO SCOTT　　　　　　　AL, 8 pp., on stationery embossed
　　　　　　　　　　　　　　　ZELDA   at top center
[Summer 1930]　　　　　　　　[Prangins Clinic, Nyon,
　　　　　　　　　　　　　　　　Switzerland]

Dear Scott:
   To recapitulate: as you know, I went of my own will to the clinic in Paris to cure myself. You also know that I left (with the consent of Proffessor Claude) knowing that I was not entirely well because I could see no use in jumping out of the frying-pan into the fire, which is what was about to happen, or so I thought. I also went, practically voluntarily but under enormous pressure to Valmont with the sole idea of getting back enough strength and health to continue my work in America as you had promised me. There, my head began to go wrong and the pristine nurse whom you accused me of attacking played almost constantly on the thing that I had assumed I was there to get over. Finally by constant references to Teol and Plantanes[?] and other pronounced and vulgar symbolism I at last began to believe that there was but one cure for me: the one I had refused three times in Paris because I did not want it but had persistently kept my eyes for the last three years on the only thing I knew which was good and kind and clean and hard-working. During all this time you, knowing everything about me, since in all this dreary story I have never tried to conceal the slightest detail from you, but have on the contrary urged you to manifest some interest in what I was doing, never saw fit to either guide or enlighten me. To me, it is not astonishing that I should look on you with unfriendly eyes. You could have saved me all this trouble if you had not been so proud of Michael Arlen the day I went to Malmaison; if you had explained to me what was happening the night we had dinner with John Bishop and went to the fair afterwards, which left me in hysterics. The obligation is, after all, with the people who understand, and the blind, of necessity, must be led. I offer you this explanation because I know I

owe you one and because it is like this that I began this abominable affair.

My attitude towards Egorowa has always been one of an intense love: I wanted to help her some way because she is a good woman who has worked hard and has nothing, or lost everything. I wanted to dance well so that she would be proud of me and have another instrument for the symbols of beauty that passed in her head that I understood, though apparently could not execute. I wanted to be first in the studio so that it would be me that she could count on to understand what she gave out in words and of cource I wanted to be near her because she was cool and white and beautiful. Perhaps it is depraved, I do not know, but at home there was an incessant babbling it seemed to me and you either drinking or complaining because you had been. You blamed me when the servants were bad, and expected me to instill into them a proper respect for a man they saw morning after morning asleep in his clothes, who very often came home in the early morning, who could not sit, even, at the table. Anyhow, none of those things matter. I quite realize that you have done the best you can and I would like you to try to realize that so have I, in all the disorder. I do not know what is going to happen, but since I am in the hands of Doctor Forel and they are a great deal more powerful than yours or mine, it will probably be for the best. I want to work at something, but I can't seem to get well enough to be of any use in the world. That's not all, but the rest is too complicated for me now. Please send me Egorowa's letter.

 Zelda

57. TO SCOTT   ALS, 2 pp.
[June 1930]   [Prangins Clinic, Nyon,
            Switzerland]

Dear Scott:

 Your letter is not difficult to answer with promptitude since I have done nothing but turn over cause and effect in my mind for some time. Also your presentation of the situation is poetic, even if it has no bearing on the truth: your working to preserve the family and my working to get away from it. If you so refer to giving your absolute minimum of effort both to your work and to our mutual welfare with no hope or plans for the future save the vague caprices which drive you from one place to another, I envy you the mental processes which can so distort conditions into a rectitude of attitude for you. You have always told me that I had no right to complain as long as I was materially cared for, so take whatever comfort you may find in whatever self-justification you can construct. Also, I quite understand the restless dissatisfaction which drives you from exiting conditions since I have been through it myself, even to the point of being completely depend-ent on a mentality which had neither the desire nor the necessity of touching mine for the small crumbs of beauty that I found I must have to continue. This is not a treatise of recrimination, but I would like you to understand clearly why there are certain scenes not only towards the end which could never be effaced from my mind. I am here, and since I have no choice, I will try to muster the grace to rest peacefully as I should, but our divergence is too great as you must realize for us to ever be anything except a hash to-gether and since we have never found either help or satisfaction in each other the best thing is to seek it separately. You might as well start whatever you start for a divorce immediately.

When you saw in Paris that I was sick, sinking—when you knew that I went for days without eating, incapable of supporting contact with even the servants—you sat in the bathroom and sang "Play in your own Backyard." Unfortunately, there wasn't any yard: it was a public play-ground apparently. You introduced me to Nancy Hoyt and sat me beside Dolly Wilde[4] one moment and the next disparaged and belittled the few friends I knew whose eyes had gathered their softness at least from things that I understood. Some justification has always been imperative to me, and I could never function simply from the necessity for functioning not even to save myself as the King of Greece once told Ernest Hemmingway was the most important thing of all as you so illuminatingly told me.

You will have all the things you want without me, and I will find something. You will have some nice girl who will not care about the things that I cared about and you will be happier. For us, there is not the slightest use, even if we wanted to try which I assure you I do not—not even faintly. In listing your qualities I can not find even one on which to base any possible relationship except your good looks,

---

4. Oscar Wilde's niece, a lesbian who was a regular guest at Natalie Barney's salon. During the summer of 1929, Dolly made advances toward Zelda, which infuriated Scott.

and there are dozens of people with that: the head-waiter at the Plaza del Funti[?] and my coiffeur in Paris—as you know, my memories are mostly lost in sound and smell, so there isn't even that. I'm sorry. In Paris, I hope you will get Scottie out of the city heat now that she has finished school.

Zelda

58. TO ZELDA   AL (draft), 4 pp.
[c. July 1930]   [Switzerland]

When I saw the sadness of your face in that passport picture I felt as you can imagine. But after going through what you can imagine I did then and looking at it and looking at it, I saw that it was the face I knew and loved and not the mettalic superimposition of our last two years in France. When Scotty left me to go to you she said "I love you better than anyone in the world. I love you better than Mummy." (I said naturally that I didn't like that sort of talk)—but when she'd been with you she said "I hate leaving my darling Mummy more than anything that has ever happened to me in my life."

The photograph is all I have: it is with me from the morning when I wake up with a frantic half dream about you to the last moment when I think of you and of death at night. The rotten letters you write me I simply put away under Z in my file. My instinct is to write a public letter to the Paris Herald to see if any human being except yourself and Robert McAlmon has ever thought I was a homosexual. The three weeks after the horror of Valmont when I could not lift my eyes to meet the eyes of other men in the street after your stinking allegations and insinuations will not be repeated. If you choose to keep up your wrestling match with a pillar of air I would prefer to be not even in the audience.[5]

I am hardened to write you so brutally by thinking of the ceaseless wave of love that surrounds you and envelopes you always, that you have the power to evoke at a whim—when I know that for the mere

---

5. One symptom of Zelda's breakdown was her obsessive anxiety that she might have homosexual feelings for Egorova. She projected her anxiety onto Scott and made accusations that were unfounded but that hurt him terribly nevertheless and threatened any slim confidence he still had in himself.

counterfiet of it I would perjure the best of my heart and mind. Do you think the solitude in which I live has a more amusing decor than any other solitude? Do you think it is any nicer for remembering that there were times very late at night when you and I shared our alone-ness? I will take my full share of responsibility for all this tragedy but I cannot spread beyond the limits of my reach and grasp. I can only bring you the little bit of hope I have and I don't know any other hope except my own. I have the terrible misfortune to be a gentleman in the sort of struggle with incalculable elements to which people should bring centuries of inexperience; if I have failed you is it just barely possible that you have failed me (I can't even write you any more because I see you poring over every line like Mr. Sumner[6] try-ing to wring some slant or suggestion of homosexuality out of it)

I love you with all my heart because you are my own girl and that is all I know.

59. TO SCOTT

[August 1930]

AL, 4 pp., on stationery embossed ZELDA at top center
[Prangins Clinic, Nyon, Switzerland]

Dear:

I hope it will be nice at Caux.[7] It sounds as if part of its name had rolled down the mountain-side. Perhaps when I'm well I won't be so afraid of floating off from high places and we can go to-gether.

Except for momentary retrogressions into a crazy defiance and complete lack of proportion I am better. It's ghastly losing your mind and not being able to see clearly, literally or figuratively—and know-ing that you can't think and that nothing is right, not even your com-prehension of concrete things like how old you are or what you look like—

---

6. John Sumner, the head of the Society for the Suppression of Vice in New York City, was notorious for bringing charges against the *Little Review* in 1920, when a bookstore sold a copy of the July–August issue, containing Episode Thirteen of James Joyce's *Ulysses*, to a teenage girl, putting an end to publication of *Ulysses* in the United States until 1930.

7. From parts of August through mid-September, Scott vacationed in Caux. Still too dis-tracted to work on his novel, he nevertheless enjoyed a quieter period, in which he finished some short stories, including "One Trip Abroad" and "A Snobbish Story."

Where are all my things? I used to always have dozens of things and now there doesn't seem to be any clothes or anything personal in my trunk. I'd *love* the gramophone—

What a disgraceful mess—but if it stops our drinking it is worth it—because then you can finish your novel and write a play and we can live somewhere and have a house with a room to paint and write maybe like we had, with friends for Scottie and there will be Sundays and Mondays again which are different from each other and there will be Christmas and winter fires and pleasant things to think of when you're going to sleep—and my life won't be up the back-stairs of music halls, and yours won't keep trailing down the gutters of Paris—if it will only work, and I can keep sane and not a bitter maniac—

I will be so glad to see you—I hope most of the poison will be gone by then.

Please be good, Dear. It's so much better to love the things you've always loved if you can just remember about them—

60. TO SCOTT

[August/September 1930]

AL, 4 pp., on stationery embossed ZELDA at top center
[Prangins Clinic, Nyon, Switzerland]

Dear Scott:

Thank you for coming to see me. I love you Dear, but there wasn't any use in trying to work the electricity plant by gas, was there? I realize the horror and humiliation completely and I'm sorry it happened. You said the water was dirty. I asked that it be cleaned up before you came, but they wouldn't. You opened the window and said you'd teach me to play—Well, now I suppose I'll end back in that horrible insane asylum.[8]

Please help me. Every day more of me dies with this bitter and incessant beating I'm taking. You can choose the conditions of our

---

8. Twice while Zelda was at Prangins, she had to be confined in the Villa Eglantine, where the most serious cases were held under the closest supervision and restrictions.

life and anything you want if I don't have to stay here miserable and sick at the mercy of people who have never even tried what its like. Neither would I have if I had understood. I *can't* live any more under these conditions, and anyway I'll always know that the "door is tacticly locked"—if it ever is.

There's no justice—no quiet place of rest left in the world, and the longer I have to bear this the meaner and harder and sicker I get—

You do not want me to write Newman. You said he said I was bluffing. What he said was that it was a straight 8 and that he had only been up in an open plane.

Please. Please let me out now—Dear, you used to love me and I swear to you that this is no use. You must have seen. You said it was too good to spoil. What's spoiling is me, along with it and I don't see how anybody in the world has a right to do such a thing—

61. TO SCOTT

[Fall 1930]

ALS, 4 pp., on stationery embossed ZELDA at top center
[Prangins Clinic, Nyon, Switzerland]

Dear Scott:

The panic seems to have settled into a persistent gloom punctuated by moments of bombastic hysteria, which is, I suppose a relatively wholesome state. Though I would have chosen some other accompaniment for my desequalibrium than this foul eczema, still the crises of the sinking bed and the hydraulic heart have been more or less mastered and I am waiting impatiently for when you can come to see me if you will—Do you still smell of pencils and sometimes of tweed?

Yesterday I had some gramophone discs that reminded me of Ellerslie. I wonder why we have never been very happy and why all this has happened—It was much nicer a long time ago when we had each other and the space about the world was warm—Can't we get it back someway—even by imagining?

The book came—thanks awfully—

Dear, I will be so glad to see you—

Sometimes, it's desperate to be so alone—and you can't be very happy in a hotel room—We were awfully used to having each other about—

    Zelda

Dr. Forel told me to ask you if you had stopped drinking—so I ask—

---

62. TO SCOTT

[Fall 1930]

ALS, 4 pp., on stationery embossed
⸤ZELDA⸥ at top center
[Prangins Clinic, Nyon,
Switzerland]

Dearest, my Darling—

    Living is cold and technical without you, a death mask of itself.

    At seven o:clock I had a bath but you were not in the next room to make it a baptisme of all I was thinking.

    At eight o:clock I went to gymnastics but you were not there to turn moving into a harvesting of breezes.

    At nine o:clock I went to the tissage and an old man in a white stock [smock?] chanted incantations but you were not there to make his imploring voice seem religious.

    At noon I played bridge and watched Dr. Forels profile dissecting the sky, contre jour—

    All afternoon I've been writing soggy words in the rain and feeling dank inside, and thinking of you—When a person crosses your high forehead and slides down into the pleasant valleys about your dear mouth its like Hannibal crossing the Alps—I love you, dear. You do not walk like a person plowing a storm but like a person very surprised at their means of locomotion, hardly touching the earth, as if each step were experimental—

    And you are a darling and it must be awful to have a person always trying to creep inside you the way I do—

    Good-night, my Sweet Love

    Zelda

63. TO SCOTT

[Fall 1930]

ALS, 4 pp., on stationery embossed ZELDA at top center
[Prangins Clinic, Nyon, Switzerland]

Dear Scott:

I wish I could see you: I have forgotten what it's like to be alive with a functioning intelligence. It was fine to have your post-card with your special reaction to Caux on it. Your letters are just non-commital phrases that you might write to Scottie and they do not help to unravel this infinite psychological mess that I'm floundering about in. I watch what attitude the nurse takes each day and then look up what symptom I have in Doctor Forel's book. Dear, why has my ignorance on a medical subject which has never appeared to me particularly interesting reduced me to the mental status of a child? I know that my mind is vague and undisciplined and that I only know small smatterings of things, but that has nothing to do with cerebral processes.

The graphaphone is broken. It's curious how Stravinsky sounds in this atmosphere. You feel like apologizing—It's awfully exciting—Prokofieff is better. Are there any discs of "Fils Progique"?[9] I'd like them awfully. I like visual music. I s'pose that's why I like opera. Abstractions are too emotional, in any field, to be borne almost.

I don't know how we're going to reverse time, you and me; erase and begin again—but I imagine it will be automatic. I can't project myself into the past no matter how hard I try. There are lots of days when I think it would have been better to give me a concise explanation and let it go—because I know so much already. One illusion is as good as another.

Write me how you are and what you do and what the world is like at Caux—

Love Zelda

---

9. "Prokofieff" is Zelda's misspelling of Sergei Prokofiev, and "Fils Progique" refers to his Symphony no. 4: *The Prodigal Son.*

64. TO SCOTT

[Fall 1930]

ALS, 4 pp., on stationery embossed
ZELDA at top center
[Prangins Clinic, Nyon,
Switzerland]

SEND THE
PHONOGRAPH
PLEASE

Dear, I hope all that is true—I seem awfully queer to myself, but I know I used to have integrity even if it's gone now—You've *got* to come to me and tell me how I was. Now I see odd things: people's arms too long or their faces as if they were stuffed and they look tiny and far away, or suddenly out of proportion.

In all that horror Dolly Wilde was the only one who said she would do anything to be cured—How did Emily[10] suddenly seem to represent order and indepandence to me? Last summer when we went with her to Natalie Barney's I was sorry for her, she seemed so muddled and lost in the grist mill.

Is it true that its better to be well or is it that I am to have only one of Eddington's tables, the physical one, so that there will be no place to put my papers when I want to write—Because if its true, why do people boast so of their strength when they are sick—because you know that I was much stronger mentally and physically and sensitively than Emily but you said at Valmont that she was too big a poisson for me. Why? She couldn't dance a Brahm's waltz or write a story—she can only gossip and ride in the Bois and have pretty hair curling up instead of thinking—

Please explain—I want to be well and not bothered with poissons big or little and free to sit in the sun and choose the things I like about people and not have to take the whole person—because it seems to me that then you can't see the parts so you can never write about them or even remember them very well—

Zelda

---

10. Emily Davies Vanderbilt.

65. TO SCOTT
[Fall 1930]

AL, 4 pp.
[Prangins Clinic, Nyon,
Switzerland]

Goofy, my darling, hasn't it been a lovely day? I woke up this morning and the sun was lying like a birth-day parcel on my table so I opened it up and so many happy things went fluttering into the air: love to Doo-do and the remembered feel of our skins cool against each other in other mornings like a school-mistress. And you 'phoned and said I had written something that pleased you and so I don't believe I've ever been so heavy with happiness. The moon slips into the mountains like a lost penny and the fields are black and punguent and I want you near so that I could touch you in the autumn stillness even a little bit like the last echo of summer. The horizon lies over the road to Lausanne and the succulent fields like a guillotine and the moon bleeds over the water and you are not so far away that I can't smell your hair in the drying breeze. Darling—I love these velvet nights. I've never been able to decide whether the night was a bitter enemie or a "grand patron"—or whether I love you most in the eternal classic half-lights where it blends with day or in the full religious fan-fare of mid-night or perhaps in the lux of noon. Anyway, I love you most and you 'phoned me just because you 'phoned me to-night—I walked on those telephone wires for two hours after holding your love like a parasol to balance me. My dear—

I'm so glad you finished your story—Please let me read it Friday. And I will be very sad if we have to have two rooms. Please.

Dear. Are you sort of feeling aimless, surprised, and looking rather reproachful that no melo-drama comes to pass when your work is over—as if you [had] ridden very hard with a message to save your army and found the enemy had decided not to attack—the way you sometimes feel—or are you just a darling little boy with a holiday on his hands in the middle of the week—the way you sometimes are—or are you organizing and dynamic and mending things—the way you sometimes are—

I love you—the way you always are.

Dear—
Good-night—
Dear-dear dear dear dear dear dear
Dear dear dear dear dear dear dear
Dear dear dear dear dear dear

Dear dear dear dear dear dear
Dear dear dear dear dear dear
Dear dear dear dear dear dear
dear dear dear dear dear dear
dear dear dear dear dear dear
dear dear dear dear dear dear
dear dear dear dear dear dear

66. TO SCOTT

[Fall 1930]

AL, 4 pp., on stationery embossed
ZELDA at top center
[Prangins Clinic, Nyon,
Switzerland]

Dear Scott:

Please, out of charity write to Dr. Forel to let me off this cure.[11] I have been 5 months now, unable to step into a corridor alone. For a month and a week I've lived in my room under bandages, my head and neck on fire. I havent slept in weeks. The last two days I've had bromides and morphine but it doesn't do any good. — All because nobody ever taught me to play tennis. When I'm most miserable there's your game to think of.

If you could see how awful this is you could write lots more stories, light ones to laugh about. I want to get well but I can't it seems to me, and if I should whats going to take away the thing in my head that sees so clearly into the past — into dozens of things that I can never forget. Dancing has gone and I'm weak and feeble and I can't understand why I should be the one, amongst all the others, to have to bear all this — for what?

You said you did not want to see me if I knew what I know. Well, I do know. I would have liked you to come to me, but there's no good telling lies.

I can't read or sleep. Without hope or youth or money I sit constantly wishing I were dead.

---

11. In November, Zelda's mental state deteriorated further and she was again transferred to the Villa Eglantine. Scott, terribly concerned, began trying to find another specialist to consult to make sure that Dr. Forel's diagnosis was correct and that Zelda was receiving the best course of treatment.

Mamma does know whats the matter with me. She wrote me she did. You can put that in your story to lend it pathos. Bitched once more. If I have to stand much more to take away the thing in me that all the rest of you find so invaluable and superior, when I get out I'm going to have Scottie at least.

It's so hard for me to understand liking a feeling without liking the person that I suppose I will be eternally confined.

67. TO SCOTT

[Late November 1930]

ALS, 4 pp., on stationery embossed
ZELDA at top center
[Prangins Clinic, Nyon,
Switzerland]

Dear Scott:

Your letter astonished me: for a month and two weeks I have been three times outside my room and for five months I have lived with my sole desire that of death. If you are coming here under the illusion that I am well, or even better, you will have to wait another year or so since I can see no possibility of escape from here.

Granted that in another six months, the Teutonic sophistries of Dr. Forel, could render inactive the element in me which so many others have not found undesirable, there is still a perfectly good lesion, of which I am quite conscious.

I want to leave here. I have spent as much time as I intend to unable to step into a corridor alone. I am thirty years old and quite willing to take full responsibility for myself. Neither you nor Dr. Forel has any legal right to keep me interned any longer. If you prefer, I will ask that Newman come and make the necessary arrangements. The pathological element has completely disappeared; my attitude is simply this: I do not consider it worth while, at my age, to pass any more time in a questionable attempt at remaking a figure that would always be hump-backed. If you want to communicate with my father you are at liberty to do so—or an alienist, if you are in any doubt as to my equilibrium. On the other hand, any amicable arrangement that you want to make, needless to say I am more than willing to agree to. But I am not going to stay here any longer, and if you make a row about it there are lots of things that will be aired in the courts that won't do anybody any good, now or later.

In the meantime, it will be pleasant to see you again. I have missed you enormously.

> Devotedly
> Zelda

Dr. Paul Eugen Bleuler, the foremost authority on schizophrenia, the term Bleuler coined for dementia praecox, was called in for a consultation by Scott and Dr. Forel. Despite financial pressure, Scott was adamant that Zelda receive the best care possible. He had originally wanted Carl Jung, but Jung's specialty was neurosis, rather than psychosis. From Paris on December 1, Scott wrote a long letter to Judge and Mrs. Sayre explaining their daughter's condition and treatment and letting them know that, based on her doctors' advice, Zelda would remain in Prangins for the time being. He also explained Zelda's treatment in detail. The letter concluded with Scott, who felt that the Sayres blamed him for Zelda's breakdown, trying to restore their faith in him:

> *. . . I know you despise certain weaknesses in my character and I do not want during this tragedy that fact to blur or confuse your belief in me as a man of integrity. Without any leading questions and somewhat to my embarrassment Blenler[12] said "This is something that began about five years ago. Let us hope it is only a process of re-adjustment. Stop blaming yourself. You might have retarded it but you couldn't have prevented it.["]*
>
> *My plans are as follows. I'm staying here on Lake Geneva indefinately because even if I can only see Zelda once a fortnight, I think the fact of my being near is important to her. (Life in Letters 203–204)*

68. TO SCOTT
[December 1930]

ALS, 2 pp.
[Prangins Clinic, Nyon,
Switzerland]

Dear Scott:

You told me I might send you a letter if I needed something. I would like some books of your choosing—and for a present I want a silver ring for my little finger—a heavy masculine kind with a red stone—ruby or

---

12. Scott's misspelling of Dr. Bleuler's name.

garnet or something like that. Clothes I need desperately but I'll get them in the spring when things are brighter and less hopeless than just now and when it seems probable that we can travel home—if ever.

I followed your suggestion and bought the decorations for a small tree for Scottie.[13] It will seem curious to see her again after so long

These are two official costumes

Scott and Scottie skiing at Gstaad during her
Christmas vacation in December 1930; caption
supplied by Scott

---

13. The Christmas visit did not go well. Zelda behaved irrationally and smashed the ornaments on the tree she had decorated for Scottie. Trying to salvage the vacation for Scottie, Scott took his daughter skiing.

and I suppose I will hardly recognize her. Vacation time needless to say seems less exciting than in the past. There is nothing to look forward to that I can see—though I suppose the outlook on life will change as time goes on. I sincerely hope so because as things are lately it is not worth while carrying on—

Do answer me—I'm so lonesome all the time—

> Devotedly
> Zelda

*In January 1931, Scott's father died, and before he returned to the United States for the funeral, he visited Zelda to break the news to her in person. At that time, Dr. Forel was trying to discover the link between Zelda's mental instability and the excruciatingly severe form of eczema that tormented her. Before he departed for home, Scott, eager to help, sent a seven-page typed letter to Dr. Forel, in which he painstakingly included all the details from Zelda's past history that he could associate with her eczema. He also told Dr. Forel that, during their visit, Zelda "was enormously moved by my father's death or by my grief at it and literally clung to me for an hour. Then she went into the other personality and was awful to me at lunch. After lunch she returned to the affectionate tender mood"—evidence that her moods were just as volatile in person as they were in her letters. Scott concluded the letter by telling Dr. Forel that he would be in the States for three or four weeks, and he asked the doctor to wire him each week about Zelda's condition (*Life in Letters *204–207).*

Zelda wrote the following letter to console Scott as he departed for his father's funeral:

69. TO SCOTT
[January 1931]

ALS, 2 pp.
[Prangins Clinic, Nyon,
Switzerland]

Dear Scott:

Knowing that our meeting was inadequate and that the sympathy and tenderness that I would liked to have expressed more clearly were lost in the disorder of your sudden leaving I hope this note will reach you before you are on the sea. Once in America the loss of your father will seem closer home than it does from Europe. Reconstructing the scenes of your youth is going to be a painful affair and if I would like to offer you the little comfort there is in the knowledge that someone who is close to you appreciates the fullness of your heart in thinking of a definately finished part of your world. Your father was a happy man at the end. He liked Washington and his hotel friends and had grown to imagine himself a part of government machinery. You must not be too sorry for his lot. By the time the failures of his middle years had grown far enough away to be fitted retrospectively into his career he was already old and tired with life less pressing on his heels. Luckily they have always had money and he did not feel the necessity to struggle and keep alert his intelligence in the great scramble for a place in the world. He was at any rate spared that in his old age and spent his time in a vague dream.

Don't be anxious about us. Madamoiselle is exceedingly capable and can communicate with me when necessary.

I would have been so happy to help you. A neurose is not much good in times of distress to others. And its hard to extract solace from the past. I can only send my profoundest sympathy.

Zelda

Before returning to Europe, Scott visited the Sayres in Montgomery to reassure them that Zelda was receiving the best care possible. He returned in late February, to find that she had improved quickly and remarkably during his absence. Scott began a series of stories in which he departed from the exuberant tone of his twenties fiction and, drawing from recent experiences, produced more solemn work. "The Jazz Age is over," he wrote; his stories—including, "A Trip Abroad" and "Babylon Revisited," two of his best—reflected on his losses. In "Babylon Revisited," an old acquaintance walks up to the protagonist, Charlie Wales, in the Ritz bar and says, "I heard that you lost a lot in the crash," to which Wales replies, "I did . . . but I lost everything I wanted in the boom" (Stories 401)—an assessment clearly Scott's own.

But Zelda's improvement did promise a new beginning. That winter, she enjoyed skiing at St. Cergue and going on patient outings to nearby towns, such as Bern. By April, she was well enough to take brief vacations with Scott to Montreux and Geneva. Her letters to him during the spring and summer were clearly love letters, and the playful tone of their courtship days returned.

70. TO SCOTT

[Spring 1931]

ALS, 3 pp., on stationery embossed
| ZELDA | at top center
[Prangins Clinic, Nyon,
Switzerland]

Dear Scott:

I would like awfully to have something to read upon which my head will be able to make no conjectures whatsoever and something with ideas that I will not constantly think that I know where they originated — Will you send me "The Decline of the West" and "Technique of Playwriting" like you promised so that I can put my subconscious, or whatever it is, back where it belongs and be left in peace to formulate and organize and absorb things that could find themselves a form afterwards? Thanks. I have been reading Joyce and find it a night-mare in my present condition, and since my head evaporates in a book-store it would be much easier if you would send something to me. *Not* in French, since I have enough difficulty with English for the moment and *not* Lawrence and *not* Virginia Wolf or anybody who writes by dipping the broken threads of their heads into the ink of literary history, please —

Thank you ever so much.

Zelda

71. TO SCOTT
[Spring 1931]

AL, 1 p.
[Prangins Clinic, Nyon,
Switzerland]

Dear heart, my darling love,

This is no good — but nothing matters because after to-morrow I'm going to see you again —

What a dreary rain — I rowed on the lake. It was like being on a slate roof. When the boat is not pointed into the waves it goes up with them and you keep waiting for the bump of coming down but it doesn't come so you just slide from one to another and have no sense of direction like being on one of those oily tin platforms at Luna Parc —

I can't write. I tried all afternoon — and I just twisted the pencil round and round churning between my teeth, and I love you. You are a darling. When you can't write you sit on the bed and look so woe-begone like a person who's got to a store and can't remember what they wanted to buy—

Good-night, dear. If you were in my bed it might be the back of your head I was touching where the hair is short and mossy or it might be up in the front where it make[s] little caves above your forehead, but wherever it was it would be the sweetest place, the sweetest place

Darling

72. TO SCOTT

[Spring 1931]

AL, 4 pp., on stationery embossed
ZELDA at top center
[Prangins Clinic, Nyon, Switzerland]

Dear Scott:

Will you mail this to Sara please? I seem to have lost her address amongst other things. I wrote you a long rig-a-marole yesterday, I don't know why, which you can believe or not as you choose—since I do not know whether it was true.

I keep thinking of Provence and thin brown people slowly absorbing the deep shade of Aix—the white glare on the baking dust of a country pounded into colorless oblivion by an incessantly rotating summer—I'd like awfully to be there—Avignon must be perfect now, to feel the wide quiet of the Rhone, and Arles obliterating its traces with the hum of cafés under the great trees—I'd like to be eating the lunch we had at Chateau Neuf du Pap, where the air was not vibrant and full of the whole spectrum—looking over a deep valley full of grape-vines and heat and far away the palace of the Popes like a mirage—

I would like to be walking alone in a Sirocco at Cannes at night passing under the dim lamps and imagining myself mysterious and unafraid like last summer—

I would like to be working—what would you like? Not work, I know, and not lone places. Would you like to be in New York with a play in rehearsal like you always said? And to have decorative people about you—to be reading Spengler, or what?

It is not possible that you should really want to be in the hurry and disorder of the Ritz Bar and Mont Ma[r]tre and the high excitability of scenes like the party we went to with McGowan where you passed so much of your time recently—

73. TO SCOTT AL, 3 pp.
[Spring/Summer 1931] [Prangins Clinic, Nyon,
  Switzerland]

My dearest and most precious Monsieur,

We have here a kind of a maniac who seems to have been inspired with erotic aberrations on your behalf. Apart from that she is a person of excellent character, willing to work, would accept a nominal salary while learning, fair complexion, green eyes would like correspondance with refined young man of your description with intent to marry. Previous experience unnecessary. Very fond of family life and a wonderful pet to have in the home. Marked behind the left ear with a slight tendency to schitzoprenie.

We thought it best to warn you that said patient is one of the best we have at present in the irresponsible class, and we would not like any harm to come to her. She seems to be sufferring largely from a grand passion, and is easily identifiable as she will be wearing the pink of condition and babbling about the 6.54 being cupid's arrow. We hope this specimen will give entire satisfaction, that you will entrust us with all future orders and we love you with all all all our hearts and souls and body.

Wasn't it fun to laugh together over the 'phone? You are so infinitely sweet and dear—O my dear—my love, my infinitely inexpressible sweet darling dear, I love you so much.

Our picnic was a success and I am cooked raw from the sun. A lady came with us who behaved about the row-boat like I used to about the Paris taxis so it was a lively expedition. What fun. God help us—

Goofy! I'm going to see you to-morrow to-morrow! You said you wouldn't 'phone, so what time will I expect your call?

If all the kisses and love I'm sending you arrive at their destination you will be as worn away as St. Peter's toe and by the time I arrive have practically no features left at all—but I shall know you always by the lilt in your darling person

   Dearest!

74. TO SCOTT   AL, 4 pp.
[Spring/Summer 1931]   [Prangins Clinic, Nyon,
                                                    Switzerland]

"Yes I do—Ha! Ha!
Darling—

I went to Geneva all by myself with a fellow maniac and the city was thick and heavy before the rain. The gray sky trickled over the pavements like a pungent des[s]ert after a heavy meal, and I wanted so to be in Lausanne with you—Saturday on the way back from Bern[e], I searched each person in your station when we passed. It seemed incredible that anything so dear as your shining face should not be where I last saw it. Have you ever been so lonely that you felt eternally guilty—as if you'd left off part of your clothes—I love you so, and being without you is like having gone off and left the gas-heater burning, or locked the baby in the clothes-bin. But I'm going to see you soon, and the rain pumps outside my window and squeezes the dripping trees and strains the gravel in the walk and I hope the earth will shrink with all this wetting so you will be closer.

I have a new room to-day. It's bigger than my other (which was engaged[)] and there are two windows with pleasantness sweeping through. There is a very curious conception of a bath. It looks like something children build in a running gutter and is that way I understand because the lady who built the house was too fat to climb in a real tub. So it will just suit me in another month, though it does give the effect of a dammed drain.

Dr. Forel's father died this afternoon. I imagine he is terribly upset since he was very devoted. Old age is so hazardous, and youth as well and yet they are the only impervious states—In middle life, when one ought to be solid and content, one has bored so many vistas thru[?] to unhappiness, sickness and collapability that all our energy is spent turning our eyes away—

O Darling—my dear, I love you with all my heart forever and ever and ever—

I hope you know they are kisses splattering you[r] balcony to-night from a lady who was once, in three separate letters, a princess in a high white tower and who has never forgotten her elevated station in life and who is waiting once more for her royal darling

Good-night, honey—

75. TO SCOTT

[Spring/Summer 1931]

AL, 4 pp., on stationery embossed
ZELDA at top center
[Prangins Clinic, Nyon,
Switzerland]

Dearest, my love —

What a dreary day except for your 'phone call —

I'm going to think of you floating about in the mist while I'm sleeping —

I've been writing long wordy diatribes about what happened to the two dullest people — but its really about Summer and some remembered sweetness so perhaps it will be all right — [14]

A metallic telephone is like an operating instrument to your dear voice —

"Private Lives"[15] made me laugh so immoderately loud that I am afraid echos spattered the Eglantine — and "Sanctuary"[16] is sheer horror! It's so wonderful to be able to read again after two years of not being able to concentrate. The fertility of books — and the dark, stark new things[,] places, terror, of a human mind straying — how I am so frightened of the past that I am half afraid to think. There's so much conditioning to be done —

You are a love and a darling — Did you tip-toe through the fog? Some people always tip-toe when there's anything unusual, but my joints flap when I react strongly too and you get absent-minded, seeking associations.

Dearest heart, good-night. I'm sleepy and I wish you were here, excavating the bed —

Love

---

14. Possibly her short story "A Couple of Nuts," which she revised and published the following summer.

15. The 1930 play by Noël Coward known for its witty dialogue.

16. William Faulkner's self-proclaimed "potboiler" novel (1931). Noted for its violence and depraved sexuality, the novel created controversy and sold exceptionally well.

76. TO SCOTT

[Summer 1931]

AL, 4 pp., on stationery embossed
[ZELDA] at top center
[Prangins Clinic, Nyon,
Switzerland]

Dearest My Love—

The sky closed over the lake like a gray oyster shell and pink pearls of clouds lay in the crease where the water met the Juras—still in the black iridescence and I wanted you to be there in the boat with me so I could watch the funny soft way you do things, so sweet, the way you move, like the tickling of a kitten's whiskers on my neck

Dear Love—I've made Scottie some wonderful paper-dolls, you and me and her, but they have no clothes yet—I had such fun imagining you while I drew. I remember every single spot of light that ever gouged a shadow beside your bones so you were easy to make—and I gave you some very doggy green socks to match your eyes—

Winnie had tea with me, a fantastic affair built about a bowl of raspberries—I could sit ages over a rumpled tea-table, being Alice, being English, being a traveler, a Grand Duc—a person can be anything with the proper décor before their eyes: like Kant's steeple.

Nordic people run about like a tired mother[?], saving cleaning up after the Latins—Just the crossing to Inoire[?] to-night one felt the difference between Swiss and French—I am luxury loving enough to like wasted energy like the French thinking they're so thrifty and expending effort enough over being so to have accomplished double in original outlay—

O Dear How I love you.
I'm glad I stole your eraser—
    Darling

77. TO SCOTT
[Summer 1931]

ALS, 1 p.
[Prangins Clinic, Nyon,
Switzerland]

Dearest:

I'm terribly sorry I was so unpleasant—I guess I was sore. I have such a profound intellectual conviction of the unhappy state of humanity that I always feel shocked and apologetic when I find myself momentarily in a calm mood—and you seemed outrageously content. I love you dear. Please forgive me. I hadn't really expected you to be there. I wanted to see Scottie—she is such an amusing person, and its so rare to find the appropriate emotion going toward the appropriate object that I thought it would cheer up this perpetual gloom of mine to be with her a moment, and know that my instincts would be straight and not need discipl[in]ing—Restful, you know—

And then I'm rather angry because people won't let me be insane. And I wish you could accept me without that feeling of yours of wanting to acquit yourself well at a social function and go out and get drunk when it's over—

I love you, darling, and perhaps the boat will make us so sea-sick that we will be perfectly happy—

> Devotedly
> Zelda

78. TO SCOTT

[Summer 1931]

ALS, 4 pp., on stationery embossed ⟨ZELDA⟩ at top center
[Prangins Clinic, Nyon, Switzerland]

My dear—O dear—O dear—O dear—

I was glad to get your letter and amazed to hear that Vienna deceived you. I picture it as a lacy, hazy city of delicate gray—mirrors and carved wood, polished floors and ceiling lost in perspective and all strung along thick outrageous avenues like square crystals on a string—and people eating tentatively everywhere as people do who have long been poor—and starved—without emotion, even the epicures. The most striking thing in life is how much can be done without and it must have been intensely curious to see a race contemplating its own lost epoch—Caesar at Timgoad[?], effect.

Scottie was darling. I love her thin child's legs and her suspended-motion way of walking. She is not a bit boyish—most children are at her age. We had a picnic under a tree growing out of the horizon with the road falling away like a scenic rail-way and the snow-washed fields soft and damp, anchored to the planet by a clear fringe of alps. She is a dear girl—close to my heart—so close—

If you think you would get any pleasure from a visit, do come Saturday. You have only to let me know. I am always waiting for you.

And

there's always my infinite love—You are a sweet person—the sweetest and dearest of all and I love you as I love my vanished youth—which is as much as a human heart can hold—

Excuse this ordinary scribble—It's hopeless to write this morning—

Devotedly

Zelda—

In July, Zelda (well enough to leave the hospital for a holiday), Scott, and Scottie vacationed at the lakeside resort of Annecy, where they swam, boated, played tennis, and celebrated Zelda's thirty-first birthday. When Zelda returned to the hospital, she missed Scott more than ever and continued to write to him with the deepest love.

79. TO SCOTT

[August 1931]

AL, 7 pp., on stationery embossed ZELDA at top center
[Prangins Clinic, Nyon, Switzerland]

Dearest, my Love—

Your dear face shining in the station, your dear radiant face and all along the way shimmering above the lake—

It's so peaceful to be with you—when we are to-gether we are apart in a high indominatable place, sweet like your room at Caux swinging over the blue. I love you more always and always—

Please don't be depressed: nothing is sad about you except your sadness and the frayed places on your pink kimona and that you care so much about everything—You are the only person who's ever done all they had to do, damn well, and had enough left over to be dissatisfied. You are the best—the best—the best and genius is so much a part of you that when you find a person you like you think they have it too because it's your only conception—O my love, I love you so—and I want you to be happy. Can't you possibly be just a little bit glad that we are alive and that all the year that's coming we can be to-gether and work and love and get some peace for all the things we've paid so much for learning? Stop looking for solace: there isn't any, and if there were life would be a baby affair. Johnny takes his medicine and Johnny get[s] well and a quarter besides. Think! Johnny might get some mysterious malady if left to develop and have it named for him and live forever, and if Johnny died from not having his syrup the parable would have been a moralistic one about his mother.

Dear, I'm tired and in an awful muddle myself and I don't know what to tell you—but love is important and we can make life do and you are greater than any of them when you're well and rested enough not to know they exist.

Stop thinking about our marriage and your work and human rela-tions—you are not a showman arranging an exhibit—You are a sun-god with a wife who loves him and an artist—to take in, assimilate and all alterations to be strictly on paper—

Darling, forgive me, I love you so. I can't find anything to say beyond that and I'd like a wonderful philosophy to comfort you.

Dear, my love.

Think of me some—

It's so happy to touch you.

80. TO SCOTT   AL, 3 pp.
[August 1931]   [Prangins Clinic, Nyon,
                           Switzerland]

Dearest, My Love—

Outdoors is glowing pale in a Narcissan moon—cradling and cud-dling itself and smoothing out the surface of the lake and a luminosity spreads everywhere that must culminate in your balcony. Dear bal-cony, where you walk absent-mindedly and drop a cigarette and stand poised in the morning sun, just an answering flash. Caux is so far away, but I love thinking of you there above the heat and smells and white-pavement-grooming that borders the lake like a paper wrapping, pink and crisp. O dear Doo-do—You held me close beside the railing as if you needed me, and I love you so.

We are going to Berne to-morrow, so I won't be able to work. I'm only happy when I'm doing what I think you're doing at the time, and I like us to both be alone in our rooms, changing chairs and looking through the walls and staring in and out of the window.

You hold your cigarettes way down, wedged between your fingers, and you sometimes seem to be buttoning up yourself, slipping into you as if you were a freshly pressed suit, and your empty shoes lie expectantly on the floor as if they were waiting for Santa Claus, and all your things have touched you and reek of an irrealizable Sweetness—

Goofo, are you mine?

Please be—

I love you

Good-night

Doodo's

Balcon—

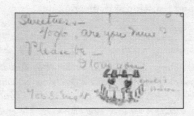

Zelda drew this picture of "Doodo's Balcon" at the end of the letter. Courtesy of Princeton University Library

81. TO SCOTT
[August 1931]

AL, 2 pp.
[Prangins Clinic, Nyon, Switzerland]

Darling, my love—

It's so gloomy that my story should be no good, but I love you anyway even if you have got a stupid wife and it made me terribly happy to hear your voice enthusiastic and high over the 'phone.

It keeps on raining and the sky is filled with copper clouds like the after-math of cannon-fire, pre-war, civil-war clouds and I feel all empty and bored and very much in love with you, my dear one, my own. I wish you were here so we could stretch our legs down beside one another and feel all warm and hidden in the bed, like seeds beaten into the earth. Why is there happiness and comfort and excitement where you are and no where else in the world, and why is there a sleepy tremulo in the air when you are near that's promising and living like a vibrating fecundity?

If I try to write to you, it won't make sense because I love you too much and I am as monotonous as the cricket that thinks he's a wireless apparatus outside my window, and I'm so lazy and sleepier than mid-night—

And very fond of Doo-do—

O dear—Kiss me good-night

Excuse me for being so intellectual. I know you would prefer something nice and feminine and affectionate

That spring and summer, Scott happily wrote to friends that Zelda was nearly well and that they were skiing together often. By the end of summer, he looked forward to Zelda's release from Prangins, to returning to the United States with her and Scottie, and to settling down to focus on his work. He wrote Perkins, "Zelda is well, thank God, and is writing some amazing stuff[.] We sail for America on the Aquitania Sept 19th . . . We are going to Alabama for the winter + there I hope to God to I'll finish the novel" (Correspondence 266).

MONTGOMERY, NOVEMBER AND DECEMBER 1931

After spending a few days in New York seeing friends, the Fitzgeralds returned to Montgomery and set up housekeeping at 819 Felder Avenue, not far from the Sayres' home. Just as the boom had not hit Montgomery, neither had the Depression. Only the natural rhythms of the changing seasons had any real effect on Zelda's hometown. Zelda was glad to be near family, especially since her father had been ill for a year, and Scott was looking forward to a more settled period in which he could return to his novel. But money was tight, and when he received an invitation to write for Hollywood, the salary seemed too good to turn down. Reluctant to leave his family, and dreading even more a return to Hollywood, he nevertheless agreed to work for six weeks at Metro-Goldwyn-Mayer on a screen adaptation of *Red-Headed Woman*, a popular novel by Katherine Brush.

In his absence, Zelda seemed to enjoy Scottie, age ten, more than ever; she also kept busy, working briefly with a local ballet teacher, writing stories in hopes of having them published, and writing a one-act children's play to amuse Scott when he returned for Christmas. She also reread many of Scott's stories, such as "The Offshore Pirate," "The Baby Party," "Absolution," and " 'The Sensible Thing,' " as a way to be close to him and as inspiration for her own writing. Judge Sayre died two weeks after Scott left, and Zelda reassured Scott that he need not return home. Under the strain, however, mild cases of asthma, eczema, and problems with her vision returned. In December, Zelda went to Florida for about three days to rest and soak up the sun. A nurse accompanied her. When she returned, she spent time with her mother, Minnie Sayre, whose courage in the face of loss Zelda admired. Listening to Minnie reminisce about the past and her own childhood, Zelda could sympathize with her mother's need to remember when she had been more sheltered and protected.

Scott, busy with the script, did not write to Zelda often—and what letters he did send appear not to have survived. He did, however, send Zelda a recording—a kind of voice letter—which she played often and enjoyed. We know from his biographers that Scott was uncomfortable in Hollywood; he found the studio system of collaborative writing impossible and the social life intimidating. He began to drink again, embarrassing himself at parties, which added to his reputation as irresponsible. When Scott left Hollywood in December, he swore he would never return.

Despite the sadness of her father's death and having to manage on her own in Scott's absence, Zelda appears to have coped remarkably well during this period. She enjoyed the household staff: Julia, the cook and housekeeper, mothered her, and Julia's husband, Freeman, whom Zelda referred to as "Old Man River" and "Father Time," did the yard work and entertained them with his own writing ambitions. Zelda found Mlle. B., Scottie's governess, a pleasant companion, as well. The first of Zelda's letters to Scott indicates that they argued before he left; nonetheless, she wrote to him daily, counting off the days and weeks, saying how terribly she missed him, and keeping him abreast of everyone's activities. She called him by endearing pet names—Goofo, and endless variations of Deo, such as Dudo, D. O., and Dee O.—and her letters from this period express the deepest love for her daughter and husband as she affectionately prepared for a family Christmas upon Scott's return.

82. TO SCOTT ALS, 3 pp.
[Early November 1931] [Montgomery, Alabama]

Darling:

It makes me so sad to sit at your desk. All day I have just walked around looking at things. Your cane is still on your bed. It's unbearable to think that I was mean to you. I telegraphed to Lafayette La but the telegram was returned—

Dear I love you so. The emptiness and hopelessness without you are dead and still and unreal

—now a telegram has just come back from Houston. Did you miss you[r] train, sweetheart?

We are all working on a Christmas present for you—I hope it will be good—

There is absolutely nothing to live for or care about but you—We love you so—

Scottie cried all the way home because she said she knew we were quarrelling. Goofo *please* love me.

One of those gutta-percha Little Theatre directors who thinks everything is "swell" and ought to be confined in an art-colony called this afternoon, but I'm not going to be in his show. We will have fun when you get home. Also a girl like an amateur's work in clay statuettes, all full of thumb-prints, and Mrs Reuben McKinney. They had grown a sort of protective encrustation over amorphous souls and I wanted to sprinkle salt on them and watch them melt. But I asked them to lunch Sat. so now I have to deliver one of those telephone sermons about how serious life is and how I'm sorry that there is no premium on nervous manners and supercilious eye-lids hidden under the old spring house but only two old family servants and a guilty conscience—

Darling, I love you—Please take care of yourself. I want you back—you can choose your own terms

Zelda and Scottie

83. TO SCOTT   ALS, 3 pp.
[November 6, 1931]   [Montgomery, Alabama]

Darling, I love you *and*

Scottie says she will keep you posted by means of a weekly paper of all important events, so I have only to write the news:

Freeman is manifesting a profound interest in literature and tells me he wants to write the history of his marriage. His wife, it appears was not "the right sort of girl" and he himself was not at that time "a fast fellow." I encouraged him.

We are *very* lonely for you and seem somehow like wet paper dolls without you.

I decided not to play in the foursome because I don't want to and I wouldn't like doing anything we did without you. Your greenish knickerbockers would grow on all the trees and fill up the bunkers and make me sad on a flat greenish plane.

I haven't had time to do my stories because of your Christmas present—It feels very important to be in your room.

Your kimona has gone to the wash and the wash to the dry cleaners and I am getting the bills in a mess to-night. I will take Scottie to the Thanksgiving foot-ball.

Dawn has lasted all day and the air is heavy like a theatre in summer and a mist came in from England and the lights turned globular and mysterious.

Daddy is inevitably the same—He is as oblivious to his surroundings as he always was when he is himself and when he is not he is tormented by imaginary prisons—Poor Daddy!

We are not afraid or unhappy or anything but we miss you, Dear—Dear—Dear—Love. Scottie is sometimes like you—Anyhow, she has a coating of moon-light for a skin and I watch her and think of you—

As you have probably guessed, this has been an uneventful day, because loving is not an even but sort of a piston rod to force them to work the engine.

A wild telegram from Ober: which I answered placatively—

   O Dudo—

   Zelda

84. TO SCOTT   ALS, 3 pp.
[November 11, 1931]   [Montgomery, Alabama]

Darling—

Four days have gone so now we have only thirty-eight 'till you'll be home again. We are like a lot of minor characters at table waiting for the entrance of the star. It's very lonely in the morning and afternoon and at night. I had the rubbeuse last night but it was only half a massage—since you weren't there to have the other half. I keep the light burning on your desk so I'll think you're there when I wake up, but then it's awful to have to turn it out when it's day. Your room is warm and fuzzy with you and I sit and look where you left things.

There was a parade to-day but I didn't go. I love the still desertion of the back streets when men are marching. The weather here is a continual circus day—smoky with the sun like a red balloon and soft and romantic and sensual. I hope it's as nice in California

I found the old blind buglar from the Civil War that used to sell me candy when I was a child. I said "Uncle Bob I used to buy your candy twenty-five years ago" and he said "That's nothing new"—So I felt very part of the generations, struggling and pathetic. I bought Scottie a cream bar. It tasted of buried treasure so we gave it to the cat who has reappeared.

I am send[ing] off the murder story again. There is no word from "Nurts"[17] and I'm afraid I am just "writing for myself"

Va. Browder phoned me about Sanctuary.[18] Said she couldn't sleep for three nights it gave her the horrors so terribly. Do you think we should give it to all these people? Two came last night for Mathilde (her aunts) of the clever type: when the word "year" comes up they say "a year has twelve months, you know"—or a person has only to say "Sat." to bring forth "*that's* after Sunday"—God! You know the kind: women of fifty still known as "Baby." Darling; I am escapeless in an awful world when you are not here.

If I could only *some*way make you feel how much I love you—
    Zelda.

I read "The Off Shore Pirate" to-day. You were younger than anybody in the world once—what fun you must have had in that curious

---

17. "A Couple of Nuts," published by *Scribner's Magazine* in August 1932.
18. Faulkner's novel, which she referred to in earlier letters.

place that's younger than life—It's a good story[.] Can they make clocks out of cellos in Hollywood?[19]

85. TO SCOTT

[November 13, 1931]

ALS, 4 pp.
At 819 Felder St.
[Montgomery, Alabama]

There once upon a time lived a very lonesome old peasant woman, or maybe it was a faithful St. Bernard. Anyway something very lonesome lived at the above address and had great difficulties pushing its thoughts out swiftly enough so they would arrive fresh in California. These thoughts were just silly little things with practically no sense to them. They were mostly "I love you", so one day on the thirteenth of November they went walking in the woods and there they met a great big strong post-man who gave them a letter from El Paso and they all went home and married Dudo and lived very happily in the pocket of the King of the Roses for ever and ever and ever afterwards.

I have stopped my dancing lessons since I had a violent quarrell with Amalia this morning. She called me a cow because I told her I couldn't do steps that neither fit the time nor the spirit of the music. I even bought a book of Shubert waltzes and took them up there thinking she could conceive them but she evidently has impedimented hearing—so that's off your mind. Being a creature of habit I suppose I shall miss it for awhile—but not after you come home. So I said she was a cow, too, and she said she couldn't be if she tried and Mamma and Marjorie said I was perfect and so will all the people at lunch to-morrow—though I do not want to tell them.

Goofo, my darling—

Absolution is one of the best stories I ever read and the Baby Party is a wonderful story. I will never never be able to write like that. Help, Deo.

Scottie says she won't do acrobatics any more. I persuaded her to go to-day. Does she have to? She is a darling and behaving very well. We have a reverse to Bridge that we play called "Queen of Spades" in the evening.

---

19. Reference to a song in "The Offshore Pirate," which was originally published in the *Saturday Evening Post* on May 29, 1920.

Riding thru these woods now is like tumbling down a copper cascade. They are as glitterring as medieval soldiers in this champagne sunshine.

Freeman has actually got four pages written on a story. Old Man River still rakes the lives and doubtless buries bones behind the barn. Julia has adopted me in your place so she says and is about to hatch me with her constant clucking and brooding. She is perfect.

Mlle. B. is most agreeable and really awfully nice and considerate and pleasant.

But we miss you so its practically unendurable. I think of you always.

Love—O so much love

Zelda

86. TO SCOTT
[Mid-November 1931]

ALS, 2 pp.
[Montgomery, Alabama]

Dearest:

I fell down to-day and sprained my ankle: I won't be able to walk for a week but luckily it isn't very swollen so perhaps it will be well quicker: Scottie stumbled and burnt her arm very slightly on the stove and has a bandage—and this is accident prevention week. The Boy-Scouts are tormenting innocent pedestrians with ropes and flags and the police look very stylish in their badges for afternoon wear. Perhaps I will be able to write while my foot subsides

That's a fine article:[20] I hope it cured you of some of your loss of confidence. Deo, my Darling—You are the best of all.

I'm sorry your work isn't interesting. I had hoped it might present new dramatic facets that would make up for the tediousness of it. If it seems too much drudgery and you are faced with "get to-gether and talk-it-over" technique—come home, Sweet. You will at least have eliminated Hollywood forever. I wouldn't stay and waste time on what seems an inevitable mediocrity and too hard going.

Scottie and I are hideously lonesome for you: I have sunk into a conservative apathy and can't seem to produce anything at all. I worked on the automobile story, changed the name to "Sweet Chariot"[21] and sent it

---

20. "Echoes of the Jazz Age," published in the November 1931 issue of *Scribner's Magazine*.
21. Lost manuscript.

off. Also Elsa Maxwell, which, in spite of your criticism, still seems good to me. Thought of calling it "Foie Gras"—What do you think? The plot is banal, but the writing is the best I ever did—[22]

I don't know what to think about with you away—My mind stumbles about the shadows of your room and thinks of nothing at all except that you were there a week ago—

Darling my own my love—*Don't* stay if you're miserable. There's warmth and content and happiness waiting here and you don't *have* to struggle through experimental mazes with all you've got behind you—

I love you so—I wish I could do all the badness for you—

A very nice man I don't remember said he was in the army with you and asked very cordially after you—as do all our friends—

Mr. Indespensable Dudo, I love you.

Zelda.

87. TO SCOTT   ALS, 3 pp.
[Mid-November 1931]   [Montgomery, Alabama]

Darling:

This has been one of those days of sodden missing you. I feel very poor and as if life were comprehensive. I'd like to put on my old clothes and dig a field.

The woods here are molten and shivered into golden splinters by the autumn sun and sometimes they're as red and gray as Santa Claus under the Spanish moss. I think of you and want to live in a velvet riding habit and recite Swinburne and be a ghost in every crumbling brick house on the country roads. I don't know why you are such a love. The farms are charred and the dust is as prodigious as if an army on the march had just gone by and the cotton-ginning has begun.

Daddy is terribly sick, but Mamma seems calm and reconciled.

I forgot to tell you I named my story

All About the Down's Case!

I will be glad when your mother comes. There will be a little more of you about. Scottie peoples the house with flashes of Dudo, but I would like to be drowned in your image. I am writing a one-act play about children for reasons incomprehensible to myself.

---

22. Lost manscript.

The cricketts sizzle outside your window and the leaves float peacefully off the trees. I'm afraid it will be all bare and indolent by the time you get back. But it won't matter because we will have each other and we can be safe and warm—

I haven't seen a soul since you left so there's no gossip—My friends telephone but the house is a bee-hive and I haven't felt like fiddling around.

I read one of your stories every night. We are in the doldrums of Time and I can't get very much done.

Deo—bring some camera films home so we can make some more movies of us.

Darling I love you love you love you

    Good-night, sweetheart

    Zelda

88. TO SCOTT   ALS, 3 pp.
[Mid-November 1931]   [Montgomery, Alabama]

Darling, my Dearest:

The air blows warm and soft as the swirl of a painter's brush outside and the dry leaves sink in a slow nocturne. There is a frustrated melancholy floating on the wind in stagnant spirals and it feels like the nights in "This Side of Paradise." Effulgent voluptuous rain smothers the tree tops and the darkness shoves along the street in scandalized puffs[.] I love you so and I hate you to be away when things are nice.

I have finished my one-act play and got all the rest of my things off to Ober so there's no excuse for not working, unfortunately. The house goes fine and the faithful servitors are industrious and polite. Mlle is really a very nice person to have about and Scottie is—well, everything but you. I'm mostly so lonesome that I thought of asking your mother down now, just to make you seem not so entirely far away. Goofo— even after this one there are four weeks more—It's too awful.

We rode to Pickett Springs and there is a lovely house where old head-quarters used to be and a big cotton gin on the site of your tent. It was very nostalgic. At the Fair Grounds a lone elephant takes his winter siesta and three lions shake the moths from their manes. It is somehow very glamorous and we are going Sunday to watch the acrobats practice. It's such a bizarre way of existence—under half-shelter out in the picked cotton fields with the evening sky running red lava down the dirt roads as if they were all about to be buried under a furious glory.

My foot is a considerable nuisance—Since I can't get much exercise I sleep lightly and last night I had a cavalcade of police-men out here at three o'clock to scare the cat off your tin roof—But it was not schitzophrenic, however: I just went to bed reading the O'Brien collection.[23] Never have I seen so much solid and sordid insistence upon the macabre and the abnormal, the melo-dramatic and the unpromising. What is this leaden disenchantment that has fallen on the soul of man and mashed it shapeless and thin? Deo—do drive the steam-roller off our pulverized egos—

I love you so—Every five minutes I want to send you a brilliant telegram to make you Darling-Conscious but I never can think of anything except that I love you—and you must be rather used to that by now—

Dear—
Zelda

89. TO SCOTT ALS, 4 pp.
[Mid-November 1931] [Montgomery, Alabama]

Dearest, my love:

I had the most horrible dream about you last night. You came home with a great shock of white hair and you said it had turned suddenly from worrying about being unfaithful. You had the big leather carry-all trunk you have always talked about buying and in it were two huge canvasses, landscapes, with the trees stuffed and made of cloth and hanging off like doll's arms. O Goofo! I love you so and I've been mad all day because of that dream.

The people came in hoards, (each one) for lunch, *ten*, and it was very successful. Mrs McKinney, Eva Mae Clark (useful for golf), Marjorie Allen, Virginia Julia, Francis Stevenson and the director of the Little Theatre. He said he'd give Private Lives if I'd play it. I thought he would fly out the window, but he's very pleasant.

Did you see this in the New Yorker?

Dear, I miss you more every day—These sultry days when everything feels like an interlude after a big event and the woods are introspective and the heavens old and sober I want you near so much. But one week has gone to-night—one week more to realize how much I love you. De-e-o.

---

23. Perhaps a recent edition of Edward O'Brien's *Best Short Stories* of the year collections.

Its wonderful that we have never had a cross word or done bad things to each other. Wouldn't it be awful if we had? Dear—I can't seem to get started writing. I havent got that inner happiness or desperation that leaves a person free in the external world of imagination, but just a sort of a plugging along feeling—When you come home we can be happy

If we seem dim and far away sometimes, dear please think of us anyway even if it should seem like a useless emotional disciplining. You are all I care about on earth: the past discredited and disowned, the future has doubled up on the present; give me the peace of my one certitude—that I love you. It's the only instance in my life of my intelligence backing up my emotions—That was an awful dream—awful dear. I didnt want to live and you were only formally sorry—

Oddly enough, I always think of Dolf Patterson when I think of Hollywood—His illusions seem realer to me than my own sporadic despair of the time—

I don't mean any of this: I want you to have a good time and take what you can from everywhere and love me if you want to and be kind—

But I Love you
    Zelda

90. TO SCOTT   ALS, 4 pp.
[Mid-November 1931]   [Montgomery, Alabama]

Darling O my Own Love!

I wrote you such a silly egocentric non-sensical letter yesterday—I was haunted by the night-mare. To-day I played tennis from ten to twelve-thirty with Noonie and we swam about ten minutes and I am all cheerful and not a bit depressed anymore except by thinking that there might have been something in that absurd letter to worry you.

Dear, I've finished "All The Sad Young Men"[24]—except "The Rich Boy["] that I saved for to-night. They are all so good—fine stories. I wanted to cry over the Sensible Thing. Reading your stories makes me curious more than ever about you. I don't suppose I really know you very well—but I know you smell like the delicious damp grass that grows near old walls and that your hands are beautiful opening

---

24. Scott's 1926 short story collection.

out of you[r] sleeves and that the back of your head is a mossy sheltered cave when there is trouble in the wind and that my cheek just fits the depression in your shoulder.

Scottie and Mlle went on horse-back to-day. They are very enthusiastic—and Mlle has started lessons in ball-room dancing. I am so glad she has found some distraction. The house goes along listening for you and we are terribly lonely.

Daddy is sinking rapidly the Doctors say. I only go once a day and take Mamma for a long drive, since he is completely unconscious and does not know us or seem to want anybody about.

To-day I went to sleep on your bed. It was like dozing in a lullaby swung on the ends of time and space. Your cane is still always where you left it. Do you want it sent?

I had planned to spend Thanksgiving with the three of us and Noonie at a place near Dothan, Panama City, that they say is the equal of the Bay of Biscay. If Daddy's condition permits we will go for the week-end and if its nice we can go when you're back. Its only 150 miles, and perfect beach and bathing. Noonie plays fine tennis: she give me 30 but I won so she made me take 15. We are going to play every day so I can play with you—

Goofo, my dear, I think of you always and at night I build myself a warm nest of things I remember and float in your sweetness till morning—

All my love and heart
and everything, everything
Zelda

91. TO SCOTT   Wire

DB687 21 MONTGOMERY ALA 17 1931 NOV 17 PM 10 54
SCOTT FITZGERALD=
    HOTEL CHRISTIE HOLLYWOOD CALIF=
SORRY YOU ARE DEPRESSED COME HOME IF IT SEEMS
TOO DIFFICULT WE ARE ALWAYS THINKING OF YOU
LOVE TO MY SWEETHEART=
    ZELDA.

92. TO SCOTT   Wire

> SD1 10=MONTGOMERY ALA 18 950A   1931 NOV 18 AM 8 14
> SCOTT FITZGERALD=
>   HOTEL CHRISTIE=
> DADDY DIED LAST NIGHT DO NOT WORRY ABOUT US
> LOVE=
>   ZELDA.

93. TO SCOTT   ALS, 2 pp.
[November 18, 1931]   [Montgomery, Alabama]

Dearest:

This is all very sad: The struggle is over and this is the end of another brave, uncompromising effort to preserve conceptions —

Daddy died last night but I was not called till morning.

Anthony[25] is here and Tilde arrives to-morrow —

Mamma is very brave and cheerful but it's very sad.

I wonder what ironic sequence, what stamina of spirit Daddy has carried over that made him think so little of the world and so much of justice and integrity? I have not seen his body. But I am glad that he is released at last from a consciousness that knew only pain at the end. The last time I saw him he seemed glad to see Scottie and very gentle and glad of his flowers — and apart from that oblivious —

I am glad he is in peace —

All my love, my dear-dear-dear

    Zelda.

---

25. Zelda's only brother.

94. TO SCOTT ALS, 4 pp.
[After November 18, 1931] [Montgomery, Alabama]

Dearest My Own:

The funeral is over. The State of Alabama sent a big wreath and the Supreme Court and the capitol employees sent all the roses off the Capitol grounds. We were all very proud of Daddy. He had expressed a wish to avoid manifestations of sentiment so just the burial service was read, and "Lead Kindly Light" was read. There were no hymns.

Mamma is absolutely amazingly courageous. I hope we can keep her well.

We are fine. Scottie is a darling. I did not take her to the funeral or near anything sad. It seemed unnecessary and Mamma did not want it. She is so bright and happy it would have been useless to depress her with incomprehensible things

Daddy seemed very noble and like a statesman — I never saw so many manifestations of esteem and affection.

Dear, I did not know what to do: Marjorie was crying because she could not afford a black dress and Anthony is very poor — so I said we would pay most of the flower blanket that we wanted for the coffin: It will come to about fifty dollars. I knew how you felt towards Daddy and that you would have wanted us to. It is such a small acknowledgement and we felt we should send the casket flowers ourselves.

I love you so much, dear —

I had rented the Little Theatre, written a one-act play for five children (Scotties little friends) and composed a Bach fueg, a Chopin Nocturne and a gay bit of Schumann; Mlle. B. was going to play some lovely things and we were to have some Dalcroze round for children. There were to be 20 people present and egg-nog and cake. It was for your Christmas present. We will give it at Easter, perhaps since we have the rounds from Switzerland, half the costumes and everything is ready. The play was called "In Provocation" I will send it to you — It was just to amuse you —

Dearest, my own heart, I don't see how anybody can live without their husband.

    All our love
    Zelda

95. TO SCOTT

[After November 18, 1931]

ALS, 2 pp., on stationery
embossed ZELDA FITZGERALD
at top center
[Montgomery, Alabama]

Dearest, my Own Love:

This has been such a discouraging day: if there weren't the thought of you at the end to make everything have a compensation existence would be too dispiriting. I have been able to walk for the first time. The body is given us, I presume, as a counter-irritant to the soul. And my story at last is started. We closed up Daddy's office. It was very musty and masculine and cerebral and the great bulk of all those old men impressive. Daddy had a big butterfly pinned over the map of the L+N. lines and some shirt samples and a copy of Josephus. We hope the state will buy his library. It's just the little personal things we care about in people, we being what we are — only his historians bother about what a man has contained of time and race. Who cares what good or evil dies? And all of us care that we will never hear a certain chuckle again or see the fingers meet a certain way. The things we can do ourselves are all that really move us: Which is why our intellects and our emotions subsist in different spheres and ceaselessly destroy us with their battles. It is a beautiful warm night like steam from a savory cauldron and I want to be happy and glad of the rutted moon and the birds in the bare baked trees. Life is horrible without you because there's not another living soul with whom I have the slightest communion.

Scottie is a fiend on horse-back. We love you and miss you —

O *Dee-o* I love you so. It is very good to have something to love
Zelda

96. TO SCOTT

[Late November 1931]

ALS, 2 pp., on stationery
embossed ZELDA FITZGERALD
at top center
[Montgomery, Alabama]

Dearest Love:

The sky lay over the city like a map showing the strata of things and the big full-moon toppled over in a furrow like the abandoned wheel of a gun carriage on a sun-set field of battle and the shadows walked like cats and I looked into the white and ghostly interior of things and thought of you and I looked on their structu[r]al outsides and thought of you and was lonesome.

It's warm here and effulgent like the end of April and I can't bear to have you missing how nice it is. I took Mamma a birthday cake and got Scottie's tickets to the Thanksgiving game. Julia and Freeman are making us a fruit-cake for a Christmas present and the yard is full of little yellow flowers like coins dropped from a worn old purse, bright shabby flowers that look as if they were saved up for for ages—poor people's flowers. The little room is ready for your mother or my mother and everything is fine. Scottie says tell you she thinks she made zero faults in school test. She is a sweet, cheerful, infectuous, pretty darling. I'm going to shave the cat if she doesn't stop kissing his fur. I am silly about the horse but I want her to learn to ride so I try to pretend that I am sensible.

Dear, my Goofy, my darling own—

Among Daddy's law library there was nothing but one set "Modern Am. Law" that was comprehensible to a lay-man. Mamma gave it to us, since I thought it might interest you.

I never hear from you but I know you are written out so I don't worry. But send a night letter sometimes, my sweet. Even after this week there are three weeks more—It seems hopeless to get through them—

Love—Zelda

97. TO SCOTT   ALS, 4 pp., on stationery embossed
    Zelda at top left

[Late November 1931]   [Montgomery, Alabama]

Dearest:

We had lunch with Mamma. Her house is always like a sunny Sunday afternoon when all the people are away driving and an intangible expectancy lurks in the popping coals. Then I worked and fed the gracious Chopin and Julia had left us a big chocolate cake and Mlle heated the chicken and we three sat down to supper. My "Cotton-Belt"[26] is *fine*

---

26. Lost manuscript.

the first thousand words. The other is, I am afraid, mediocre tho not compared to lots I read. I sent it off under "There's a Myth in a Moral" which isn't very good.

It's hot again to-day with the spring drifting thru the land like a sleep-walker and many bells ringing distantly. Your disc came and your dear voice made me utterly miserable. This has been the longest time in my life. I'm glad you are not bored and I am horribly jealous. I will never be so foolish as to think I can get on without you again.

Scottie's garden has sprouted in embryonic wands and tongues and I have a beautiful pink begonia in my window. The flowers always look to me as if they were made by smashing something between the thumb and the forefinger and the leaves are luxurious raggedy cushions. Little yellow butterflies fly about for Christmas and Tilde writes there is snow in New York. Scottie spent the afternoon reading "astronomy" in Mamma's encyclopaedia. Your closet is full of lovely silver packages. It looks so sad to see your clothes getting dusty on their hangers. D. O, if you will come back I will *make* the jasmine bloom and all the trees come out in flower and we will eat clouds for des[s]ert[,] bathe in the foam of the rain—and I will let you play with my pistol and you can win every golf game and I will make you a new suit from a blue hydrangea bush and shoes from pecan-shells and I'll sew you a belt from leaves like maps of the world and you can always be the one that's perfect. But if you write me about Lily Dalmita and Constance[27] I will go off to Florida for a week and spend our money and make you jealous of my legs à la Creole when you get home.

How do you like my gingham paper? It's really for algebra—and more things seemed to happen on the plain gray.

With all my love,
Your wife, Zelda—

98. TO SCOTT ALS, 3 pp.
[November 23, 1931] [Montgomery, Alabama]

Dearest, My Own Darling
I went to get my hair washed th[is] afternoon and shades of Hollywood Boulev[ard] in walked her the hairdressers sister straight from

---

27. Lily Dalmita and Constance Talmadge were movie stars.

Los Angeles, and fried to the eyes. It reminded me of the Helen Buck era. "Bessie Love?"[28] she'd say "well she's *out*," with the finality of Ring. And "I haven't had a bite yet" by which I inferred that she was on her way to supper and "Say *listen*!" every other word and then at the end opening her big 35 year old eyes very innocently "I'm tight" Then a long wait for laudatory exclamations. Hearing her talk was like being two people at once, one of them dim and far away in the past. Equivalent spectres floated thru so many of our early years. "The Talmadge girls are absolute *rag-pickers*—say friend, have you got a match?"

O dear, this beneficent weather—and a pink rose in the garden and the cat rolling a sun-beam over the grass and the nights like a child's prayer. I wish we were sharing the expansiveness of this benevolent country. I have never never missed you so much as I do. Do you think of me out there amongst the vibrations where everything quivers and waits to fall like swelling drops from a dropper?

And Daddy's grave so sad on the side of an old and sinking hill. To-[day] was Mamma's birthday—I had [portion of letter torn] all to lunch—Anthony's wife is [aw]fully nice and Tilde is pretty and Marjorie is good and kind and there we were: All Daddy had to leave behind. Mamma sat in that more aristocratic world where she and Daddy have always lived. She is so sweet and foolish and infinitely courageous—I have been feeling very proud and simple lately. How have you been feeling? I do not examine myself very closely or my reactions since you are away and there is no one to talk to. Life is just the essence of zero without you and it somehow seems a very distant affair—as [if] it were taking place in California perhaps—I love you so—Please write Scottie that she must learn her American history. Her information on the Revolution is lamentable and she has discovered that she can get by without work. They have long finished it at the school, and she is completely ignorant of both details and conception. Her French is fine—the work, I mean—very thorough + lively—The school thing is *important*!

Dearest—I love you so dearly
Zelda

---

28. Bessie Love was a Hollywood actress who made the transition from silent films to talkies; she would later be called one of the "fast talking dames" who characterized the female roles of the period. She received an Academy Award nomination for *The Broadway Melody* in 1929, after which her career quickly diminished.

99. TO SCOTT   Wire

> 9S RQ 13
>   MONTGOMERY ALA 917A NOV 24 1931
> SCOTT FITZGERALD
>   MGM STUDIO
> NOTHING BUT THREE HUNDRED FIFTY DOLLARS AND
> LOTS OF LOVE IN THE BANK
>   ZELDA
>   929 AM

100. TO SCOTT   ALS, 2 pp., on stationery
                                   embossed ZELDA FITZGERALD
                                   at top center
[November 25, 1931]   [Montgomery, Alabama]

Dearest, that is the sweetest lovliest voice I ever heard. It made me feel all safe in the center of things again and important. I play it and play it and I want to be with you. It fills the house with assurance and vitality, excitement and love. You are *sure* you are my own, aren't you? Because when anybody is perfect other people have to be very careful.

Freeman has quite a narrative gift. Do you suppose Menken would buy his story with an explanatory paragraph? They listen to the record and I hear Julia in the kitchen laughing and saying "love you — I love you." Deo you are *so sweet*.

It has turned catastrophicly cold. The streets are gray and the sky inflamed and thoughts won't carry themselves on the happiness in these peaceful yards but creep back into the mind and want to be resolved. I wrote 1000 wds. to-day. I wanted to finish two stories before you got back but this will be all I'm afraid. Fantastic exhuberance has deserted me and everything presents itself in psychological terms for novels. Christmas is coming, and your mother will be here in two weeks I hope. I sent the dress to Annabel.[29] She will find it a bit Botticelli by this time but maybe she will be invited to a straw-

---

29. Scott's sister.

berry festival or a Westphalian log-roll and can use it to bind up her shins; or maybe she will be caught in a burning building and can make a ladder.

Scottie is something precious and lustrous in her riding pants: like a very pleasant fairy-tale about princes in disguise. She goes everywhere now with a group which rides every day. It's such a wild free thing I like her to do it. Mlle is good-humored and succinctly busy. We are all going to Mamma's to-morrow for Thanksgiving. I gave her the turkey and Tilde the trimmings. I'm thankful that your work is going better and that you're not unhappy.

Dear it's so much fun to have the record — Did you move? We did not lose any letters maybe they are at the hotel.

With all and all and all my love —
   Zelda

---

101. TO SCOTT   Wire

   12S RQ 9
      MONTGOMERY ALA 845A NOV 26 1931
   SCOTT FITZGERALD
      MGM STUDIO
   HAPPY THANKSGIVING AND ALL OUR LOVE PLEASE
   DONT OVERWORK
      ZELDA
      10AM   27

---

102. TO SCOTT   ALS, 2 pp., on stationery
                               embossed ZELDA FITZGERALD
                               at top center
[November 26, 1931]   [Montgomery, Alabama]

Dearest Love:
   This still Thanksgiving afternoon fanned with the leaves of school-books and muffled with echoes is very reminiscent. It makes me remember all the times we've been to-gether absolutely alone in some suspended hour, a holiday from Time prowling about in those quiet

place[s] alienated from past and future where there is no sound save listening and vision is an anesthetic.

Scottie and Mlle. were entranced by the foot-ball. Auburn won and reverberations of victory drift out from the street corners. Freeman said the field was a free-for-all. The big table and Mamma's had somehow lost direction without Daddy. My story limps homeward, 1,000 words to a gallon of coffee. Some children are chanting enfantive encantations under my window. Perhaps they have produced a warm Nov. night like radium with you in the breeze and houses filled with dreamy nostalgic lethargy. I have a *wonderful* plot for a short thing that I will get at as soon as I can. It's for your Christmas. To write you something I would like to be in a celestial reverie that I can't attain. It's fun thinking of Christmas and the night you will get home and how you'll look as you come out the gate. I will be surprised at your mondanity and very amazed that you are concice and powerful and I will be very happy that you are so handsome and when I see how handsome you are my stomach will fall with many unpleasant emotions like a cake with too many raisins and I will want to shut you up in a closet like a dress too beautiful to wear.

Save me this clipping, please dear. I thought it would amuse you. Nobody seems up-set by the story.

Scottie goes like an arrow on her horse—so fast I don't like to watch.

The house runs on in all directions sort of aimlessly without you—
Dear

I love you
Zelda

103. TO SCOTT   ALS, 2 pp.
[Late November 1931]   [Montgomery, Alabama]

Dearest:

I am so lonesome for you I don't know what to do. The nights are soft and warm and lonesome and I think of you always. There are things in shoots like spring growing in the back. I asked uncle if they were jonquils but he said they were bulbs. Just mysterious tender things weaving the air into a voluptuous cape for themselves. Doorbells ring from far away and people whistle in the streets and there are seething things in the tree tops.

I suppose the nights in *California* are still nebulous pink and gray like the spinning of a pearl and there are many drug stores and the streets are all corners and automobile brakes whine in the breeze.

I wish we were to-gether.

Scottie is a darling. She and Jerry have gone to "Cinderella". She talks always of you. And Goofo! There's another *month* to wait! I sent the dresses and I will write your mother.

The man at the bank was sore because I kept the accounts in the bank-book. There's only $450 left.

Ober says the Red Book still have "Nuts" but I can't get to work. I am writing a story about Phillipe called "Ganymede's Rubbers"[30] but I can't write it.

Write me about what you think—It's so lonesome without you—There's absolutely *nobody* who would know if a person was thinking, quoting or reciting the litany. I feel like a person lost in some Gregorian but feminine service here—I have come in on the middle and did not get the beginning and cannot stay for the end but so must somehow seize the meaning—It's awful to think that Daddy isn't here any more—I would like to pick up Mamma and go—

With All My Love—
Zelda

104. TO SCOTT

ALS, 2 pp., on stationery
embossed ZELDA FITZGERALD
at top center

[Early December 1931]

[Montgomery, Alabama]

Dearest My D. O—

Sunday in a trance and sleeping all afternoon like a deserted cat on your bed and now its night and the house seems to be nothing but over-tones with you away—tho you[r] hat is in the hall and your stick still on the bed and you could not tell that it's all just a bluff and a make-shift without you. I feel like going to Florida for

---

30. Lost manuscript.

the week-end. It's only six hours in the car, and I imagine at this time of year it would be very reedy with lone fowls strung on the horizon and the seaflinging loose gray cowls on the sand and long yellow beaches that look like womens' poetry and belong to the Swinburne apostles.

The cat is the most beautiful fellow. He broods over ancient Egypt on the hearth and looks at us all contemptuously. Julia and Freeman are very good and considerate and Mlle and I get along very well and have not yet come to blows. She is a nice girl. Scottie is engrossed in protecting herself against being disillusioned about Santa Claus and is as pretty as a moon-beam. She dresses herself by my fire and it's a joy to watch her long sweet delicate body and the cool of her pale hair quenching the light from the flames. However, my disposition is very bad and asthmatic and it is just as well that you are out of this homely lyric. I am going to dig myself a bear-pit and sit inside thumbing my nose at the people who bring me carrots and then I will be perfectly happy. My mother and father are civilized people: it is strange the rest of us should be so inadequate. There are some lovely bears in Berne who live in a mythical world of Sunday afternoon and little boys and itenerant soldiers and the one in Petrouschka is very pleasant and sometimes they live on honey and wild-flowers when they are off duty from the fairy-tales. But I will be a very dirty bear with burrs in my coat and my nice silky hair all matted with mud and I will growl and move my head about disconsolately.

There are no grands évènements to report. I am sending my story to Ober as it now seems satisfactory to me, but nobody will buy it since it is mostly about champagne. They wouldn't buy it anyway even if it was about hydrochloric-acid or mystic anti-kink so what ho!

Darling I miss you so terribly—you can never go off again. It's absolutely impossible to be very interested in anything without you or even to get along very well—at all.

Love and Love and Love

Zelda

105. TO SCOTT

[December 1931]

ALS, 2 pp., on stationery
embossed ZELDA FITZGERALD
at top center
[Montgomery, Alabama]

Dearest:

The house sleeps in the ashes of the open fires and Julia and I have sent you some cakes just so you will know we are always thinking of you. Scottie is making you a surprise for Christmas and I have something that will make you laugh. It's such a homey, dozing time when the days are wet and pliable as potters' mud and warmth drones inside the windows and over the hearth and I miss you so terribly.

You asked about my cough: so I went to bed to-day to cure it with the fourth of July on my chest and many clamps and bolsterings and it is well again, but I am stuffy as un-sprouted seeds on a hot spring night from aspirin and paregoric. You are a love to think of me. I am so well and fat and healthy that you may not be able to get your arms about me when you get back. If not, I warn you I will pine and refuse food and die of a colic and have to be bled. Dear, I love you so.

To-morrow is Friday, then Saturday and you will be home in *two weeks* which is really no time at all.

My story made quite a sensation.[31] People seem to like it. I had the following telegram from Ober: "Sweet Chariot is beautifully written. I am immensely pleased with it." He's had it all this time and has evidently just read it.[32]

Fire engines are ripping up the night out-side in ruthless clangs and shrieks like an angry seamstress splitting silk and feet run along the pavement like an emptying theatre and little sounds and the way things are are all I have to write you.

Julia Anderson came over to-day. She is a pretty girl but very uninspired. She is the first person I have seen in weeks. We agreed vaguely about vague affairs and decided the panic was very sad.

I am reading New Russia's Primer. The U. S. A. comes in for an economic balling-out that is doubtless well deserved, but severe.

---

31. *Scribner's Magazine* published Zelda's story "Miss Ella" in December 1931.
32. This story was never published and no manuscript has been located.

I sent Dr. Forel Scribners from sheer vanity. I do not dare read the story. Knowing it is not first rate, I don't want to be discouraged—I *wish* you could teach me to write—

I love you—O I love you so—Zelda

---

106. TO SCOTT

ALS, 4 pp., on stationery embossed ZELDA at top left

[December 1931]

[Montgomery, Alabama]

Dearest my love:

I am positively tormented by all sorts of self-reproaches at leaving. Scottie is so sweet and darling and the house is so pleasant and I have everything in the world except you. And yet I know I am nervous and too introspective and stale—probably because since you left I haven't felt like amusement and recently I have not been able to exercise at all. So I am leaving for the week-end only, in the hopes that just long riding rolling along will give me back the calm and contentment that has temporarily disappeared with my physical well-being. Please understand and do not think that I leave in search of any fictitious pleasure. After the utter solitude of Prangin there have been many people lately and people that I love with whom my relations are more than superficial and I really think I need a day or two by myself. I will leave Sun. and be back Wed. night. While we are away, Julia is thorough cleaning. She is a peach.

D. O. I realize more completely than ever how much I live in you and how sweet and good and kind you are to such a dependent appendage.

Chopin has his nest in our bath-room. He is so lovely with a face like a judicial melancholic bear, the Polly scornfully eats peanuts, and Uncle rakes the leaves like father Time sorting over the years of the past.

Scottie and I have had a long bed-time talk about the Soviets and the Russian idea. I lent her "The Russian Primer" to read and will be curious to hear her reactions when I get back. She is so responsive and alert. You will be absolutely ravished by her riding trousers and yellow shirt and Scottie rearing back in her saddle like a messenger of victory. Each time she goes she conquers herself and the pony, the sky, the fields and the little black boy who follows on a fast shaven mule. I wish I were a fine sweet person like you two and not somebody who has to go 200 miles because they have a touch of asthma.

The house is full of surprises—but as usual I did everything at once and there's nothing left for the end, except finish my story which is too good to do uninspirationally and out of sorts.

God! I hope you haven't worked yourself to death. We *must* reduce our scale of living since we will always be equally extravagant as now. It would be easier to start from a lower base. This is sound economics and what Ernest and most of our friends do—

Darling—How much I love you. Zelda

107. TO SCOTT　　　　　ALS, 4 pp., on stationery embossed
　　　　　　　　　　　　　　ZELDA　at top left

[December 1931]　　　　　　[Montgomery, Alabama]

Dearest, my Darling D. O—

I am, needless to say very hurt at your complete lack of confidence in me. If you feel that I am such an irresponsible person you should have left me in a clinic. However I am sorry if I have disturbed you. Having exhausted the powers of Samuel Butler and what small philosophy I could muster I found myself almost desperate to get away into the sun, alone. I have not had a quiet moment since you left: first two sleepless weeks with asthma and then touches of eczema which I could not trace since I have done my best to lead as healthy a life as possible so you would find me fresh and cheerful when you got back. Having no resources at my command to distract myself without my eyes I dreaded that you arrive fine and vital and I should be harassed and half-sick. I was doing what I thought would be pleasantest and best for you. Also I should like to receive your mother with enthusiasm, since we see her so seldom.

Scottie is fine: she looks better than ever and is full of life and rosy.

I am afraid you have been over-working. You sounded exhausted and nervous. Please take care of yourself for us, D. O. We love you so—

Nothing has changed here. The town is nice again in the sleepy sun and I have a fine story if I can find time to write it: à la Wm. Faulkner—I won't spoil it by telling the plot which is actual and very thrilling.

Dear, I will be so glad to have you home but don't drain and strain yourself to hurry. We are really all right—Julia is like a second mother and the house functions perfectly. I love you terribly and very deeply and in my most erratic moments I would not do anything to injure us. I wish you could believe me that though I may have transitory and uncorrelated ideas and impulses which make it difficult to appear as a solid individual, still they are more fleeting always and my actions accord with what I would like to be—as well as I am able

I love you so, my dear, so please forgive me for the misgivings I have caused you—

 Zelda

108. TO SCOTT   ALS, 2 pp., on stationery
            embossed ZELDA FITZGERALD
            at top center
[December 1931]   [Montgomery, Alabama]

Dearest:

What a miserable gloomy rainy day: Scottie and Mlle are on their way to a concert and Julia is staying with me. She has lent us her parrot till Christmas. Deo! I *must* have a parrot! Can't you bring me one for *Christmas*? Hers says "Aw go to hell" and carries on long senseless conversations in the exact inflections of people transacting very serious business. It's curious how they employ very exactly and aptly the tone of the human voice to fit their feelings, and have no sense of the words they use at all. *Please*, Deo, bring one to me. There aren't any here and I *must* have one. You could keep him in your bath-room on the way. Julia's says "O my Darling" and "Oooo Julia!" and he sings "Yes Sir, That's My Baby.["] Deo *please*!

After this week, there's one week to clean up and then your mother comes and you will be a little closer.

The Red Book kept "Nuts"[33] three weeks, but turned it down. Ober said they asked for more of my stuff. I am discouraged. When you

---

33. Most likely her story "A Couple of Nuts."

come home I will be happy and free and can maybe begin again, but I do not believe I can be a good writer. It is very melancholy without you. I love you more all the time and since I did not think there was any more it's an overwhelming and frightening state to be in. When things increase, increase, increase how do they end? Is there a sort of identification with the ultimate or abstract which turns on itself or is their a calm diminuendo with the lessening of physical vitality? And aren't you scared of such an utterly dependent Baby? That maybe you'll always be having to make room in your heart for an old emotion like travelling about with an out-grown baby-carriage amongst the family possessions?

Dearest, I love you so—

Zelda

109. TO SCOTT   ALS, 2 pp., on stationery
                                     embossed ZELDA FITZGERALD
                                     at top center
[December 1931]   [Montgomery, Alabama]

Dearest, my Love:

I wouldn't want to draw that money out of the bank. What good would it do if the economic system collapses anyway? Nobody here seems alarmed and there's nothing in the papers and I have no presentiments of disaster.

It's rather cold and murky and horrifying like one of those days in the first chapter of Well's History of the World and the air is like a tunnel. The forests in Georgia are all burning up and the air is filled with fetid smoke. Walking about makes you feel like a navigator of vague uncharted seas and like the Romans arriving in England. I bought four of the sweetest little trees for the cemetery. They are green and fuzzy little bears—and planted a jasmine vine on the wall. I love Scottie's doll furniture. She has planted herself a garden of Valentines names: Sweet William and candy tuft and is very happy. We rode to Mamma's to-day on imaginary horse[s] and mine had the most exquisite gait, like pulling a rubber band and snappy [snapping] it together, and another sort of lope where you knock your heels to-gether and float on your own good spirits.

My story is finished. It is another flop, I'm afraid. I do not believe

I can write. Seriously. But I shall finish your Christmas tale since I will be always thinking of you. Just one more Saturday and I hope your mother will be here. Mlle goes to dancing Sats. and I couldn't decide whether she needed the pistol most or I—so I gave her the bullets and I have the gun. Do not be alarmed. I would never use it. It has a very professional air that repels me almost super-naturally. It is second-hand with a highly devellopped personality.

We love you so dear. The mist drips slow and things fall like a spring thaw.

Goofo I love you—
Zelda

---

110. TO SCOTT

[December 1931]

ALS, 2 pp., on stationery
embossed ZELDA FITZGERALD
at top center
[Montgomery, Alabama]

Dearest:

I have no comment to make on such a monotonous life: Winter rocks the cradle with a weary foot, and spring will wearily straddle the land and wearily summer will doze in the clay roads and autumn again will be weary. Will start in the quiet night when we think of robbers and in the day busy ourselves about not being cheated and live the lives of prostitutes as do all people who live by and for their sensibilities.

Scottie has a sign on her door "Voici la chambre mystérieuse" and four red wreaths upon her windows and many Christmas bundles in her room. She wants an electric train which seems to me one of those dreadful elaborate substitutes for a toy originated by the kind of people who write sub-titles. I mean, a Townsend-Martin sort of thing. Shall I buy it?—After writing that I found this note so dear, you know I will get it. Isn't it a sad little note?[34]

Deo—I will be glad when you are home. So many things seem sad when you are not here. Mamma came out here to-night so old and tired because Mlle had gone to a show and she thought I would be

---

34. The note, perhaps a letter to Santa from Scottie, has been lost.

lonesome. People relinquish the sacred fire with difficulty once they have possessed it's scathing light. They seem to like the little blisters full of their own chemistry, and to grow fond of the scorching of their unsound skins.

Darling—

There is such a dearth of impersonal distraction here that it is hopeless not to work and my stuff (the last two since you left) has got too thin and spiritless to be worth the effort. With some ruinous finality junk just flows and is utterly worthless.

But you walk down the streets through the Durner[?] hour into some chill Valhalla and the trees line the sides like the last standing timbers of a burning building and the world is rich in color. And I love economy in decorations—poor man's Christmas—except that it's just a lack of imagination and a ponderous seriousness about nothing left over from the days when the family sock was the only safe banking scheme and Grandma made soap herself to save a nickel.

Anyway, in spite of economics and the Soviet and the fact the world is in full retreat before its own forces having been routed by its own barrage and conquered by the lack of an enemy—I love you—

I love you in spite of all these terrible consequences of our perceptive powers—

I love you Zelda

---

111. TO SCOTT

[December 1931]

ALS, 2 pp., on stationery
embossed ZELDA FITZGERALD
at top center
[Montgomery, Alabama]

Darling:

The fire burns contentedly like many ladies swishing their silk petticoats and Chopin passes invisible delicacies judiciously about in his mouth. I have sore throat, asthma, grippe and indigestion and I am making Mamma a picture of myself for Christmas that looks like a Florentine fish-monger. The rain keeps up and the ground is heavy as a sponge and receeds from everything. The country clay-banks are washed to deep folds of a heavy fabric and the trees are limp and gummy. I am delighted your mother is coming after all. It will be pleasanter for her than a lone Christmas. Please *wire*: shall I put her downstairs? The house is fresh as a candy-store. The curtains are washed and starched to paper and the rugs are cleaned and bright, owing to haphazard animal excretions. We have had a zoo here since you left and its only Mamma who kept me from buying a monkey from the circus.

I love climbing out on the tin roof and brandishing my empty pistol and yelling "Who's there?" as if I had a mob at bay. But I am, secretely, always the escaping criminal. My bravado instincts do not function on the side of law and order, as do not also a great many other interesting facets of myself: ie, to me, interesting, of cource.

Minor tried to teach Scottie a break-down. It's terribly hard since it consists of dangling yourself by your shoulder while your feet bounce like drum-sticks. It's the real nigger tap dancing and I'm crazy to have her learn it. It has nothing in common with musical comedy and is very distinguished and would be nice to know when calling on the President.

I miss my Daddy horribly. I am losing my identity here without men. I would not live two weeks again where there are none, since the first thing that goes is concision, and they give you something to butt your vitality against so it isn't litterred over the air like [a] spray of dynamite. D. O. darling, I love you—

Zelda, the dowager of detriment.

112. TO SCOTT

[December 1931]

ALS, 2 pp., on stationery
embossed ZELDA FITZGERALD
at top center
[Montgomery, Alabama]

Darling:

First some details that you must wire the answers of: (1) do you want me to get something and send it to Annabel or will you send a check?

(2) Is Mlle B. to have money or presents and how much?

(3) Do you love me so *very* much like I do you?

(4) Is it possible for a person to be as absolutely perfect as I think you are.

It's cold here and these celibate skies are depressing. There is a flat uncurious frigidity in the wind and it roams about like an exile petulantly storming the dead woods and bushes.

I lost Scottie in a store to-day for half-an-hour and it was ghastly: like being whirled through endless rotating hypotheses of life and being in some chaotic functioning of the consciousness without the mind. It was because I let her shop alone and she went to the car after instead of meeting me where she said. She is such a darling and so full of Christmas and excitement. You will roar when you see her on the pony rearing back against the land-scape followed by a little boy just her size and black as the ace-of-spades. It's cute, like nice things that don't happen any more. She will send you the history. Her report is one point better than the first month, however.

Mamma and Edith spent the day. She seems so sweet and lonely and lost in the memories of her youth, of a monkey an old beau gave her once, and two Texas hares that ate up her father's geraniums. I suppose it's a sub-conscious longing for protection that has recalled her child-hood more vividly than usual.

Darling, my own darling. The little mossy place on the back of your neck is the sweetest place and I can rub my nose in it like a pony in his feed bag when you come home and I'm very, very, lucky—

Zelda—

113. TO SCOTT

[December 1931]

ALS, 2 pp., on stationery embossed ZELDA FITZGERALD at top center

[Montgomery, Alabama]

Mamma spent all afternoon telling me about the Civil War and her father and when she was little and many fragrant, protected things. It's so nice to have important men and I'm so glad that you are one. I want you to come home and for us to have a son and lots of vital things we own. I love you so my dearest[35]

Darling:

Another day of paddling about in the rain with skies like craw-fish clay slipping all over the heavens and the wind seething outside like a mountain stream.

---

35. Zelda appears to have added this note at the top of the page after she wrote the letter.

We chose a doll with very long legs and hair like watch-springs — a delectable creature with a wild incredulous stare who joins us at Christmas. Her only fault is she has no sense of humor. There were some sweet baby dolls — Deo, we really do need a baby. The window-panes dripped and the toy-shop was dim as Hoffman's tales and the toys seemed unobtainable the way they ought. It was very Victorian. There were many pretty things and I chose Scottie with her hair twisting about her cheeks like thumb-prints in the tea-time butter and the rain in ecstacies in her eyes. I am having our ritualistic kimonas made for our Mothers since there's nothing of the reminiscent-of-the-frivolous in the shops.

The tree things have lost their sex appeal being stored so long and it will be like putting on old clothes for Easter to use them but they are all un-broken and we have enough so I won't buy more — though there's nothing so beautiful as shining red balls dangling like the evolution of a jewel before your eyes. I s'pose thats why savages like things like that: they are both at the same level.

I'm so glad and proud that the picture's good and that you did it. It must be very satisfactory to manoeuver scenes about and arrive at last at a sustained tone. I don't see how anybody but a technical virtuoso author could ever produce a movie, since the visual sense is reduced to half and exclamatory shots can no longer be counted on to preserve the tempo: "O isn't that *lovely*" scenes inserted so that audience's tension doesn't fall while

My love, my love, my love — I love you so. I want you home in my arms. I love you.

Zelda

Although MGM did not use Scott's script for Red-headed Woman, *he did return with more money in the bank than he had had in some time, as well as the material for a story about which he was enthusiastic. He wrote to Harold Ober in late December, saying, "I'm not sorry I went because I've got a fine story about Hollywood which will be along in several days"* (As Ever, Scott Fitz— *181*). American Mercury *bought this story — "Crazy Sunday" — for just two hundred dollars, but it proved to be one of his best. He also wrote confidently to Maxwell Perkins in mid-January 1932: "At last for the first time in two years + ½ I am going to spend five consecutive months on my novel. I am actually six thousand dollars ahead"* (Life in Letters *208*).

Scott and Zelda were convinced that Zelda was still showing every sign of

improvement. After Christmas, they vacationed in St. Petersburg, Florida, swimming and sunbathing. But Zelda quickly began to deteriorate. She found Scott's whiskey flask and drank it. Her asthma and eczema returned, as did her hysteria. Scott, miserable to see Zelda slipping from him again, and knowing that the money and the five months he had counted on to finish his novel would vanish if she were hospitalized again, took her to Baltimore and placed her under the care of Dr. Adolf Meyer and Dr. Mildred Squires at the Henry Phipps Psychiatric Clinic of Johns Hopkins University.

Second Breakdown

THE HENRY PHIPPS PSYCHIATRIC CLINIC OF JOHNS HOPKINS UNIVERSITY HOSPITAL, BALTIMORE, MARYLAND, FEBRUARY–APRIL 1932

Zelda entered the Phipps Clinic on February 12. Scott returned to Montgomery to stay at Felder Street until the lease was up, thus allowing Scottie to finish the school year, but he stayed in steady contact with Zelda and Drs. Meyer and Squires, who immediately established a balanced routine for Zelda. Her schedule allowed her to go on outings in Baltimore, such as art exhibits, movies, lunches, and window-shopping. Although Zelda politely evaded the doctors' attempts to engage her in cognitive therapy, she nevertheless accomplished an astonishing feat of self-analysis. On March 9, less than one month after she entered the clinic, Zelda completed the autobiographical novel she had barely started in Montgomery just three months earlier. *Save Me the Waltz* presents the major events of Zelda's own life through the fictional screen of a protagonist named Alabama Beggs: Zelda's/Alabama's childhood, her courtship and marriage to Scott (David Knight in the novel), their years in France, her breakdown (disguised in the novel as a physical collapse), her subsequent return to her hometown, and the death of her father. The novel ends with the protagonist's acquiescence to middle age; and it conservatively suggests that her father's world, Judge Sayre's/Beggs's world—which she depicts as ordered and moral—is the best, and that evading established traditions had been her own and her generation's downfall.

Ironically, the novel threatened to compete with Scott's. His own novel, which he had been struggling with for some years and which Zelda's breakdowns and the consequent expenses kept interrupting, was based on much of the same material—their lives together and Zelda's illness. Zelda sent her novel off to Maxwell Perkins, Scott's editor, without letting Scott see it in advance. For all he knew, her manuscript covered the same territory and would make his, when he finally had time to complete it, appear a mere copy of hers—perhaps a more carefully crafted work, but unoriginal. Scott remembered reading her much of what he had done on his novel, and he had no idea to what degree she had consciously or unconsciously used his ideas. He felt that his reputation and true calling as a writer lay with his novels, not his short stories, and he was nearly desperate to prove once again to himself and the literary world that he was a writer of stature, capable of a sustained work of depth, one that would reflect his maturity as a writer. He felt it a slap in the face that while his own novel had been interrupted and delayed at every turn, Zelda, safely secured away and provided for at his expense, had completed hers in less than a month.

On the other hand, Zelda had just as much at stake as Scott did. She despised the idea of becoming a permanent invalid and passionately desired to become a productive person—to establish herself in a career and to earn money that would allow her to have an independent identity that would make her self-supporting, rather than a constant financial burden. Her completed manuscript provided tangible evidence of this determination: Even though she was seriously ill, she still applied herself, demonstrated great discipline, and was actually able to produce a complete and unified work. In addition, their lives together belonged to both of them equally. How could one of them own the exclusive rights to the material?

Fitzgerald scholars have examined this conflict often and come to various conclusions, some seeing Scott's point of view and others seeing Zelda's. The dilemma was real and caused both of them pain. Yet with so much focus on the conflict, the admirable fact that Scott and Zelda *did* work it out successfully has been ignored. Scott wired Perkins, asking him not to consider Zelda's book until he received a revised version. After reading the manuscript, Scott again wired Perkins on March 25, 1932, stating that revisions would be minor, would take only two weeks, and that, in his opinion, it would be a "fine novel" (*Correspondence* 290).

When the lease was up on the Montgomery residence at the end of March, Scott left for Baltimore, where he stayed at the Rennert Hotel, collaborated with Zelda on her revisions, and house-hunted. The competition between Scott and Zelda over the question of writing continued and became especially bitter over the next year and a half; however, the outcome of this particular dispute proved to be a happy one. Zelda published *Save Me the Waltz* in 1932, and Scott published *Tender Is the Night* in 1934. Although much of the material over-lapped, much did not. Each writer created a distinct vision. Despite the disappointing critical and commercial reception of both works, Zelda's novel continues to be read with interest, and Scott's is certainly now seen as the mature and deeply poignant work he believed it was. The conflict between the Fitzgeralds resulted in one of the most interesting pair of novels in American literary history. Zelda's letters from this period reveal not only her continual struggle with a devastating mental illness but also her devotion to Scott, her unrelenting wit, and her determination to stay involved in the cultural scene of her day.

114. TO SCOTT

AL, 3 pp., on stationery embossed ZELDA at top left

[February 1932]

[Phipps Clinic, Baltimore, Maryland]

Dearest—

It seemed very sad to see you going off in your new shoes alone. Little human vanities are somehow the most moving poignant things in people you love—Struggles and deep emotions when you are closely identified with are apt to assume the unconscious epic quality but the little things about people are always so touching—

I didn't finish your socks. It seems awful that you should be doing them again. You could easily teach Julia. I'm sure she'd be conscientious about it.

I have been trying to make myself a picture of you. It's just one of those usual black faces that look doughy and embryonic. I'd give anything to have my beautiful picture that looks as if you were inventing special heavens to go to on June Sundays.

I brought the little chess set and the manual—so when you miss them don't think the social revolutionists have looted the house.

If Freeman goes to jail it will save you the humanitarian reproaches of having to fire him.

The row of brick houses from the window at night present a friendly conspiracy to convince us of the warmth and pleasantness of life—but its cold here and there is no communication yet between the swept chilly pavements and the sky—

Sunday we went to a museum and I saw some directoire wall lights with stars that would be perfect for the house that we'll never have—

You are my darling, darling, darling one and I love you so, D. O.

Think of me. If my room is as empty to you as yours was when you were away you will find yourself living in an ether dream—as if there was a veil between you and reality—

D. O—I love you—

115. TO SCOTT
[February 1932]

ALS, 1 p.
[Phipps Clinic, Baltimore, Maryland]

Dearest Sweetheart:

Just a note of apology about lunch: I'm terribly sorry I arrived so cross and worn-out. I do not seem to be strong enough to stand much strain at present and rather than have another string of unhappy times behind us, I'd rather just stay here until I'm quite well. We have been so close this last year and have so many pleasant memories of things we've done that I'd hate to spoil it in any way. I think we're all agreed that *your role is not be that of a doctor and in my present condition you have to mother me and bear with a lot of unpleasant-ness*[36] which is not part of how I feel towards you at all but the result of my health, simply—

I love you dear heart—and it makes me miserable when I've ruined any time that we've shared. So please try to understand—how much I want you to love me—and forgive me again

Zelda

---

36. It may have been Scott who underlined these words when he received the letter.

116. TO SCOTT
ALS, 4 pp., on stationery embossed
ZELDA at top left

[February 1932]
[Phipps Clinic, Baltimore,
Maryland]

Dearest:

Thanks for the chess. It made me very lonely for you seeing our scores in the back. However, we are both such triumphant victors and such ignominious losers that it's just as well that we abandoned the emotional up-heaval of our tournaments. I shall return a shark, after having worked out all the attacks in the book.

Dearest:

Do you think that comprehension is a latent ability to execute, or would we have to allow for our miscomprehensions of the possible content of pictures or music? I mean, I feel as if I could do so many of the anatomical drawings in the museum here and I wondered if that feeling is a message from un-tried unexplored powers to try art school. There are two Rodin drawings that show how the monkey felt who bore the first man. And there is a beautiful El Greco full of the mystery of weightless mass—though I have never quite appreciated your enthusiasm for him—outside the immensity of all primitives, serving up their souls in the boxes of an almost verbal emotion.

I went again to Boléro—Sacriledge! Ida Reubenstein![37] That music was not meant to be danced but played on drums-heads made from the stretched skin of Spanish intestines. The threatening echoes of Audorran chasms and the massachistic trances of the Voo-doos ground to a chaff the spiritual membranes.

Dearest:

Out of half-a-week, I do not seemed to have gleaned the material for a letter. I have closed my ears to the music of the spheres apparently and am totally uninspired. Help! Tell me the most interesting thing that has happened since Capernicus, tell me the latest delusion of myself and my fellows, tell me the dope, and the words to a popular song and above all tell me that you love me—

---

37. A well-known Russian-born choreographer, Ida Rubenstein formed her own dance company and was touring with a production of Ravel's *Boléro*.

Dearest:

Tell me that you love me

Dearest:

You were very kind and thoughtful to help Mamma move. The obscure balances of compensation will swing in your favor. I know Rosalind will have made it attractive.

I feel almost constantly like those people in the flood pictures of the Bible and imagine myself with streaming hair and poignant cheekbones. Then I look in the mirror and am very sad to find only my own countenance instead of some diabolic manifestation of so much introspection to confront with my plagaries from the sorrows of man.

You and Scotty are probably perfect people. Does Julia give you biscuits and stuffed tomatoes on a Sunday? And do the animals play at domesticity in the evenings.

The Baltimore wharves are very Whistlerian — The afternoons and [are] soft and sweet. The audience at the concert was the most representative lot of old American faces — Lovely, really. I felt proud of coming from that sort of stock. There's so little of it left.

If you are coming here I will of cource wait and go with you to Tudor Hall.[38] If not I want to try to arrange a trip — before I leave Maryland.

Dearest:

This is a Spartan world; but I suppose there is no luxe like the self indulgence of the lame and the halt.

Dearest:

Dearest,

Dearest.

117. TO SCOTT

[February/March 1932]

AL, 4 pp., on stationery embossed ZELDA at top left

[Phipps Clinic, Baltimore, Maryland]

Dearest:

Do go into my room. Then it would be nicer when I get back. I've always tried to make you use things first and get into strange beds

---

38. A 1700s plantation home, once owned by the Keys, Scott's ancestors, which has since become the public library in Leonardtown, Maryland, the seat of the St. Mary's County government.

before me because any place you've been is a good place and anything you've touched is desirable. Perhaps you could wear that
unfriendly bon-bon touch off my walls — I wish we had a house, dear.
I found some material here with the stars on it that I searched so hard
to find for "Ellerslie."[39] I feel very constructive. When you come up
we must go to Tudor Hall. It would be convenient to get our furniture from Wilmington.

If Trouble[40] bites just rub his nose in it and give him a lump of
sugar and recite the book of Esther to him. He will soon subside —
though he may be a thorough-bred remember his is a proletariat race.
He was really getting very obedient before I left. Why don't you
asked Rosalind to train him. Madamoiselle will try out her nursery
military tactics on the poor beast until I would not blame him if he bit
her in two. She'd probably taste like possum, anyway. Or let Uncle
Bob do it. He treats the dog as if he were the scion of an ancient
dynasty and Trouble follows him about very pertly with an air of tolerant superiority. Anyway, do not sacrifice the dog because I love
him dearly. He's crazy about Scottie and will probably bring us many
burgulars, being just the sort of dog they adore.

I love Baltimore. The shops are very sophisticated and their is
amusement without end if you were here and we could amuse ourselves without bothering about cures. I have been reading about a
thing called the "Lorraine glass" which old masters used for reducing
the value of light. Sometimes I would be content to apply the thing to
life and live in a world minus Chinese whites — it takes so long to get all
your high-spots into the line of vision once they're dispersed over the
canvas. Incidentally, the thing accounts for the dark corners in the
École Flamande.

How is your work? Poor D. O. What do you do instead of coming
in to see what I'm doing? When you were away I thought of myself as
a chatelaine of all your effects which leant me a vast importance in
my own eyes and made details seem more significant. Then, too, I
cried a good deal and the reactions before and after kept me interested. And, Goofo, I loved you always and do now and I can't help
thinking we will be happy if only the Lord will anoint me with some
heavenly blessing of less questionable illumination than he has so
far — My dear, my dear. I wish I could feel your fuzzy neck and watch
you put on your finest shirt and pretend to be a worldly author of

---

39. Scott and Zelda's house outside Wilmington.
40. The Fitzgeralds' pet bloodhound.

renown. Your things, when they smell of you, smell so warm and friendly like a clean open fire in a peasant mountain cottage.

The money arrived—for which I thank you. I am getting an obsession about money. I don't feel that I have a right to buy anything it's so tragic to see respectable middle-aged men with clerical faces and independent expressions selling candy and apples.[41]

I am glad you and Scottie are getting some time with each other. She feels very alone when you and I are to-gether. Being so close, we must move ectoplasmicly across a great many people's visions like visitations from another world. I'm sure my family secretly thinks that you're the crazy one: they've read stories like that, about incarcerated wive[s]. Your mother, of cource, thinks we are both in the Russian secret service and prefer bombs to June strawberries for breakfast—Love my darling. Please love me. I love you so; you would if you knew.

118. TO SCOTT

[February/March 1932]

AL, 4 pp., on stationery embossed THE JOHNS HOPKINS HOSPITAL at top center [Phipps Clinic, Baltimore, Maryland]

Dearest:

The[re] was the most blinding exhibition of modernism here—a Matisse nude that makes your tongue hang out from a sense of opaque blue Mediterranean heat enclosed in a shuttered room—a consciously barbaric over-estimated Van Dongen of an African Prince—an immense Picasso, full of an attempt at mad detachment by a calculating and intellectual power. The more I see of his work, the more I am sure that Gertrude Stein has the only ones worth having and that his work is an idea, not a painting. Some beautiful things of Marquet that just escaped being purely illustrative, two wonderful Vlamincks full of a large and serious spirit and lit for a ghostly folk-tale. Sir William Orpen paraded his fashionable impotence and there were two compromises between a lyric sonlauda critical mind by Forain and a few jokes by the more esoteric of the French wags. I

---

41. Zelda is referring to the Great Depression, during which it was common to see men who had lost their jobs trying to earn some meager living by selling apples on the street.

missed you so. We always have such fun pricking each others aesthetic pompousities, which we pretend to take very seriously. Sometimes I almost believe that our fundamental attraction is an intellectual suspicion as profound as Troubles propensities to perform on the parlor rug or the cat's fascination for the Chinese lillies — Anyway, I am *very* lonely for you.

I have done some good writing, but it goes slow since I have only 2 hrs. a day in which to collect my agenda on life, organize it and get it down. The rest of the time is very pleasant — gymnasium etc and excursions into Baltimorean superficial[i]ties. It's a marvelous place, a prosperous, middle-age distinguished lawyer with many artistic hobbles sort of a place. We must live here sometime.

The four hours at night — Well, there is a girl who screams "Murder in the first degree!" when she isn't screaming "Oi! Yoi! Yoi! The Mistletoe." I suppose there's nothing to do about it — I prefer it to the obnoxious reassurances of Mile. B. and the nocturnal visitations of eczema.

I am reading Ian Gordon's Modern French Painters. He speaks of the sense of growing things in Van Gogh's work. Those crawling flowers and venomous vindictive blossoms are the hallucinations of a mad-man — without organization or rhythm but with the power to sting and strangle of certain sub-marine flora. I loved them at Prangins. They reassured me. He goes in the same pathological category as Jeanne d'Arc: savage and oblivious.

Dearest — I suppose I will spend the rest of my life torn between the desire to master life and a feeling that it is, au fond, a contemptuous enemy. If there weren't you + Scottie, melancholia is about as happy a state as any other I suppose. *There's a woman here who wanders tentatively about the halls like the ghost in a poor detective story.* It is impossible to feel sorry for crazy people since their realties do not coincide with our normal conceptions of tragedy etc. *And yet, a woman's brother came to pay a visit. I thought how awful and poignant — that boney casket full of nothing that the man had ever loved and he was saying that he wanted her to come home again. It made me feel very sorry. I presume he was addressing his past —* [42]

> "Whoe'er, my friends in
> the rough stream of life
> Hath struggled with affliction, thence
> is taught,

---

42. This passage and the earlier one in this letter both may have been underlined by Scott.

> That when the flood begins to
>   swell, the heart
>   Fondly fears all things."

Anyway, there's nothing so sordid as being shut up—When man is no longer his own master, custodian of his own silly vanities and childish contentments he's nothing at all—being in the first place only an agent of a very experimental stage of organic free will—

I love you—
    Dear, My Own—my
    Love—

119. TO SCOTT

[Early March 1932]

ALS, 4 pp., on stationery embossed
| ZELDA | at top left
[Phipps Clinic, Baltimore,
    Maryland]

Darling, Sweet D. O.—

Your dear letter made me feel very self-condamnatory. I have often told you that I am that little fish who swims about under a shark and, I believe, lives indelicately on its offal. Anyway, that is the way I am. Life moves over me in a vast black shadow and I swallow whatever it drops with relish, having learned in a very hard school that one cannot be both a parasite and enjoy self-nourishment without moving in worlds too fantastic for even my disordered imagination to people with meaning. So: it is easy to make yourself loved when one lives off love. Goofo—I adore you and worship you and I am very miserable that you be made even temporarily unhappy by those divergencies of direction in myself which I cannot satisfactorily explain and which leave me eternally alone except for you and baffled. You are absolutely all in the world that I have ever been able to think of as having any vital bearing on my relations with the evolution of the species.

"Freaks"[43] gave me the horrors. God! the point of view of sanity, normality, beauty, even the necessity to survive is so utterly arbitrary. Nobody has ever been able to experience what they have thoroughly

---

43. A 1932 horror film, directed by Tod Browning; the cast included a large number of actual circus "freak show" entertainers of the era.

understood—or understand what they have experienced until they have achieved a detachment that renders them incapable of repeating the experience. And we are all seeking the absolution of chastity in sex and the stimulation of sex in the church until sometimes I think I would loose my mind if I were not insane.

Darling, darling. The Zola is wonderful. Had he ever fallen into the hands of the authorities, we should have missed his contribution to neurasthentic symptology sadly. It is a long time since I have had any new symptoms and I am bored with all the old tricks of my shattered organism

I love you and I would like us to be covered with the flake of dried sea water and sleeping to-gether on a hot afternoon. That would be very free and fine. Dear Heart!

I have got so fetid and constantly smell of the rubbery things about here—It's ghastly, really. I do not know to what depths the human soul can sink in bondage, but after a certain point everything luckily dissolves in humor. I want to fly a kite and eat green apples and have a stomach-ache that I know the cause of and feel the mud between my toes in a reedy creek and tickle the lobe of your ear with the tip of my tongue.

If Trouble still bites give him a good kick in the ass for me.

Darling, I love you so.

Zelda

P.S. I do not see how Dr. Squires can remain a sprig of old English lilac in this seething witches cauldron. Did you know the Furies turned out to be respectable old women who went about the country-side doing good and laying eggs in their night shirts? So much for Eschyllus. The old moralist!

120. TO SCOTT

[Early March 1932]

ALS, 4 pp., on stationery embossed ZELDA at top left
[Phipps Clinic, Baltimore, Maryland]

Dearest D. O—

I'm sorry to be so nagging house-wife about the money. I did not realize that things like laundry and stuff were hard cash and no refund and, as usual, I am penniless and about to spend three chapters of Dickens in a mental debtors'-prison. Since you did not understand either, I suppose you think that I have been sloshing my insides at Marconis, or tearing up to the Atlantic City Baby Parade.

When are you coming to Baltimore? There is a night-club and some good shows. I have had a terrible proclivity towards the baubles and tawdry doo-dads of life recently—feeling like the ex-wife of Diamond Jim Brady, mentally. I am secretly awfully suppressed in the fancy-goods line—was just coming to in Montgomery.

Darling—I miss you so. It's very interesting here, however. Every now and then somebody opens the door and I say

"And what do you see my sister" and they answer "Nothing but the dust up on the hills," and I go back to wishing I had never stolen the golden-key and awaiting the return of Blue-Beard.

I am proud of my novel, but I can hardly restrain myself enough to get it written. You will like it—It is distinctly École Fitzgerald, though more ecstatic than yours. Perhaps to much so. Being unable to invent a device to avoid the reiterant "said" I have emphasized it à la Ernest much to my sorrow. He is a very determined writer, but I shall also die with my boots on.

I mailed Zola— Found he was helping me to nourish my psychological disorders too much for my own good. Eschyllus is infallible and to read him is to wallow in a lush and golden roll of prose that would force you to write if you knew nothing but the Syrian alphabet.

The days wheeze in on these creaky March days like the last moments of a dying novelist. Sometimes I feel like a titan and sometimes like a three-months abortion—But always I love you in spite of the fact that you are infinitely superior to me and I forgive you your many superlative merits—

Dear—I do not want to keep Mlle. It is very irritating to have a person in such close contact whom you feel is not co-operating except by giving in to avoid trouble. Scottie is not fond of her, so I have no regrets. It's too bad, but I have done my best and I am sure she will not feel that her trip has yielded her nothing. It's so annoying to have a person in your own house who is distasteful to you. There must be plenty of French women out of work in the east. Mlle is, au fond, very dogmatic and intolerant and both Scottie and I hate making the constant effort of pulling our punches to get along at all.

Damn Serez[44] for forsaking us! More + more I realize her per-

---

44. Scottie's former governess in France.

fections. I cannot live any more with people under thirty—harmoniously. They have too much to learn from experiences which I have already achieved—and do not care to be reminded of or have to explain to others—Chaque-un a son gout! Love and Love and Love—Zelda.

121. TO SCOTT
[c. March 9, 1932]

ALS, 2 pp.
[Phipps Clinic, Baltimore, Maryland]

Dearest:

My letters sound dry and composed, I suppose, because there isn't much external data with which to embellish them. I assure you they are not the gleanings of my meagre note-book. My writing went so successfully that I didn't have time to make my usual observations on our social state. It's an amusing book which I will mail to you Monday. I sent a copy direct to Max, but I know Scribner's will refuse it. Knopf is the place I suppose since it has no more weight than Nigger Heaven[45] and many things on his list[.] I have some slick psychological stuff which will have to be written in future under more tranquil circumstances when I feel more egotistical since I mean to lambaste our whole mass of concepts. Now, I can hardly afford to whip myself to the necessary frenzies to attack the primal deep-seated hypocracies of our kind. But I shall have some words to say of the baseness and beauties of man.

Dear, I'm sorry about the money's going so fast. This week it was a permanent wave—next week I hope God in his plush heavens with [will] toss me out some old moth-eaten repose that none of his customers could use and I can stop castigating myself long enough to buy nothing, wish for nothing and achieve the infinite: nothing. I have finished a rhapsodic fizzle of a story about the Auerbacks which I shall send to Ober with instructions to try Physical Culture on account of the gymnastics in the prose.[46]

I'm sorry Montgomery is so dull: It always was, but Daddy['s]

---

45. Carl Van Vechten's 1926 novel, the title of which refers to the colloquial term for the balcony where African-Americans were required to sit in theaters.
46. Unpublished.

presence seemed to bolster it up to a semblance of being the end of more noble times. Now we see it as a very tentative and unsophisticated snatching at the turmoils brewed in bigger kettles. I'm all for savagery and its discard always moves most to lament. However all my social sorrows are of the École Burne-Jones[47] just at present: rather voluptuous and symbolical; vague fleshly figures floating in a ghostly nebulum playing the harp. Or else they are cartoons bearing such legends as "Bologny," otherwise known as what the hell—

Dearest, I love you—which is not a dead Narcissus but just one of those things: perhaps a boutonnière from the trick shop on the Boulevard des Italiens which squirts water in your eyes when you try to smell it—

Anyway, the Baby is very intent on establishing herself in the unquestionable benefits of our dubious policies of organization, and at considerable loss to know how to proceed since Ober will not dispose of my gems, some of which are as good as Mr Faulkners—the murder story for instance. I'm going to put them in the want adds pretty soon—

Your wife, otherwise known as the mendacious, mendiant, maniacal
    Mme. X—

Please let me ask somebody for a job on the paper somewhere—

122. TO SCOTT   ALS, 4 pp., on stationery embossed
                                                                       | ZELDA | at top left

[c. March 9, 1932]   [Phipps Clinic, Baltimore,
                                      Maryland]

Dearest:

The ballet books are of no importance. My novel being finished I shall at once begin on my story about the Bavarian peasants that I have wanted to write. If Reynolds[48] can't sell any of the volumes of tripe that he has from my pen why doesn't he give it away? It's very discouraging

---

47. British Pre-Raphaelite painter, Edward Burne-Jones.
48. Paul Revere Reynolds, a New York literary agent.

to keep writing for myself. I already know what I feel about things. And has Scribner's ever sent a check for "Couple of Nuts"?[49]

I went to the Follies again: that Rumba with the girls dressed in orange parabola's is pictorially the equivalent of the fire-music in the Valkyrie[50]—It's really marvelous. So much effort the girls put into being lascivious that they quite defeated their purpose and raised it to impersonal levels. For the rest: well, as you probably remember, the subject matter was largely the depression and an appeal for the gilded lobster-palace and the days when murder was a private affair. Florenz[51] has probably acquired gall-stones or something to turn him moralistic. The girls all had the illusion that they were vixens, with an occasional face reminiscent of the purity-school of Mary Hay.[52]

Thanks for the money and thanks again.

What shall I get of the Greeks to read? I now [k]no[w] Eschyllus by heart, nearly. It is my favorite book, and you are my favorite man and nasturtiums my favorite flower.

Dear I love you—as you probably know—and while I am still in a daze as to my proper position in this bewildering and cataclysmic universe, I have not forgotten my original impetus: which has been for considerable time to hue myself one whence we may go on quietly loving as the gods see fit and we ourselves deem just and fair. So if you can accept any spiritual bonds with this mass of confusion which I have grown to think of as myself, love me too. You might as well, since someday I am going to produce something to satisfy that necessity for belief which I find in myself and you will feel very badly when you look on my masterpiece if you have to say: "If only I hadn't taken the victrola instead."

Goofydo—It's bleak here now and my spiritual carcass is being gnawed by superior vultures to myself and I am bleak in spirit and sometimes I don't care that I am a bitter wretch and sometimes I don't care that I am most unusually happy—

But I love you
    Zelda

---

49. Zelda's short story, published in *Scribner's Magazine*, August 1932.

50. *Die Walküre*, an opera by Wagner.

51. Florenz Ziegfeld, Jr., impresario of the *Follies*, lavish musical revues designed to "glorify the American girl."

52. An actress and dancer, Hay appeared both in films and on the stage.

123. TO SCOTT
[March 16, 1932]

ALS, 2 pp.
[Phipps Clinic, Baltimore,
Maryland]

Dearest:

Considering the many times recently that I have, through necessity, left you with much on your hands which rightfully should have been on my shoulders, I have been tormenting myself with the picture of you alone establishing the family elsewhere. It is a very dismal image and quite insupportable from a stand-point of fairness. Dr. Meyers agreed this morning that I could leave on the following basis: I want Miss Teasley in the house to stand between me and any possible eventualities of strain. She will relieve you or any member of the household of any responsibilities toward me whatsoever and life will be much easier for all of us. Also you will be freed from the added burden of this expense here. I am quite sure she will come for three dollars a day—not more than four in any case and she is a placid, exhausted old lady who will act as an insulator for my self. Her instructions she will have in a sealed letter from Dr. Squires in whom I have the utmost faith, and we will all agree that there will be no protestations from the rest of the family.

It's the only way I see to get us over the immediate necessities of existence.

Perhaps I can come back here if you feel I ought after we are functioning in new quarters.

So send me the necessary check at once. I will join you for Easter. This weeks money you sent so late that I will owe it all before it gets here.

D. O. please do as I say. You have no confidence in my practical abilities, your own being of a different order—but I am much calmer than when I came here and if you will cooperate I'm sure my skeme is the best solution.

I can't stay here forever—and I am perfectly able to take care of myself. It's too devastating to have the whole menage to look after for you and I am missing years out of Scottie's life just when I'd like to be with her and influence her. Our old contact will never be reestablished, as it is—to say nothing of all the rest of life, and the financial end.

Phone Miss Teasley to-night and mail the check—

You are a darling and I love you—Are we going to Key West or coming to Baltimore or going to Professor Baker?[53]

Please answer immediately.

Zelda

P.S. Dr. Squires is writing to-morrow

124. TO SCOTT   AL, 4 pp., on stationery embossed
[ZELDA] at top left

[Late March 1932]   [Phipps Clinic, Baltimore, Maryland]

Dearest:

Will you send me immediately—have Freeman do it—special delivery

(1 Any sketches from my portfolio that are wieldy enough

(2 two small pictures of my mother as a child. I've found adorable frames for them.

3) picture of me in dancing clothes.

4) The Judge—

Please have him insure them as they are all of immense value to me—

Dr. Squires doesnt want me to write so I'm going to draw—perhaps life class. I'll send my story as soon as I get it—

Darling send my the things quick—

D. O. I am coming home if I can to help you move and pack and get settled. I will ask Dr. Myers Thursday. Lets take Julia with us—if we stay in this country—It's such an effort training people—

Dear I love you. Do you miss me? This month has gone very fast. It seems impossible that we have been away so long. I hope you'll like my book—or something that I do some time—

It's late and there's a nurse who sticks her head in the door to see that I dont strangle myself on the shadows every five minutes or stab myself with the rays of light—

So Good-night, Love—Please hurry with the stuff. If he says yes I'm coming home so you'll have to be quick—

---

53. Possibly George Pierce Baker, author of *Drama Technique* (1919), who at the time was directing and teaching theater at Yale University. Writers who studied under Baker include Eugene O'Neill, Philip Barry, Thomas Wolfe, and John Dos Passos.

Love—

It's cold here and I wish you were coming in to sit on my bed and talk and we could tell each other all the reservations that we haven't got and hint at hidden mysteries of life that only we have solved— And I wish you would love me as you please just so you do and be just faintly glad that your nice T.N.T meringue is not a lemon pie— instead of feeling as you inevitably must that it's a dish better served to the gastronomes with more resistant stomachs than your own—

I can tell by your letters—but I am persistent and shall write you a love letter as soon as I can find enough phrases to express myself—

Darling

To-night, I feel very self-sufficient and want to be at home I suppose or doing something. Enforced inactivity maddens me beyond endurance.

125. TO SCOTT
[Late March 1932]

· ALS, 2 pp.[54]
[Phipps Clinic, Baltimore, Maryland]

Dearest, my own Darling D. O—

I hadn't realized how much I wanted to see you till night came and you had telegraphed your delay—Here, living so that every action is a ritual and every smallest bit of energy expended is of interest to *somebody*, there's not much time left for projecting yourself into distant places and sp[h]eres of an ordinary existence. One day goes and then another and the cradle rocks on in the continuous lullaby of recapitulations. My heart fell with a thump that you didn't come—So I have been very cross and rude and blaming the Sicilian Vespers and St. Bartholemew's on Dr. Myers.[55]

---

54. Scott wrote checkmarks and the numbers 1 through 7 in the margins of this letter, possibly indicating points he wanted to discuss with Dr. Squires. See facsimile on p. 164.

55. Zelda's purpose here is hyperbole. "The Night of Sicilian Vespers," also referred to as "The Night of the Long Knives," was the culmination of the Castellammarese, or Masseria-Maranzano, gang war, a fourteen-month struggle in 1930 and 1931 between Italian and Sicilian gangs in the United States, in which up to seventy-two were murdered in one night, wiping out the last important members of the Sicilian Mafia in this country and establishing the so-called Cosa Nostra. The Saint Bartholomew's Day Massacre, which took place in Paris in 1572 and then spread to the outlying regions, was a murdering spree intended to destroy the French Huguenots and their leadership.

Dearest:

Dr. Squires tells me you are hurt that I did not send my book to you before I mailed it to Max. Purposely I didn't—knowing that you were working on your own and honestly feeling that I had no right to interrupt you to ask for a perious[56] opinion. Also, I know Max will not want it and I prefer to do the corrections after having his opinion. Naturally, I was in my usual rush to get it off my hands—You know how I hate brooding over things once they are finished: so I mailed it poste haste, hoping to have yours + Scribner's criticisms to use for revising.[57]

Scott, I love you more than anything on earth and if you were offended I am miserable. We have always shared everything but it seems to me I no longer have the right to inflict every desire and necessity of mine on you. *I was also afraid we might have touched the same material.*[58] Also, feeling it to be a dubious production due to my own instability I did not want a scathing criticism such as you have mercilessly—if for my own good given my last stories, poor things. I have had enough discouragement, generally, and could scream with that sense of inertia that hovers over my life and everything I do. So, Dear, my own, please realize that it was not from any sense of not turning first to you—but just time and other ill-regulated elements that made me so bombastic about Max—

I have two stories that I save[d] to show you, and a fantastic sketch.

I am going to begin a play as soon as I can find out about length etc—for which I ordered Baker's book—

Goofo, please love me—life is very confusing—but I love you. Try, dear—and then I'll remember when you need me to sometime, and help.

I love you—
Zelda

56. Scott wrote "(perilous?) FSF" in the margin. See facsimile. Zelda may well have intended to write "serious."
57. Scott wrote "This is an evasion" in the margin. He also added this notation: "(all this reasoning is specious or else there is no evidence of a tornado in the state of Alabama." See facsimile.
58. Probably underlined by Scott. See facsimile.

Zelda's letter, with notations by Scott. Courtesy of Princeton University Library

Although Scott's letters to Zelda on the subject of her novel have not survived, the following excerpt from a letter he wrote to Dr. Squires and his wires to Maxwell Perkins indicate his initial anger and objections, but they also show that the revisions Scott finally demanded were actually relatively few, and that the disagreement was quickly resolved, with Scott recommending the novel to Perkins.

   Zelda's novel, or rather her intention of publishing it without any discussion, has upset me considerably. First, because it is such a mixture of good and bad in its present form that it has no chance of artistic success, and, second, because of some of the material within the novel.

   As you may know I have been working intermittently for four years on a novel which covers the life we led in Europe. Since the spring of 1930 I have been unable to proceed because of the necessity of keeping Zelda in sanitariums. However, about fifty thousand words exist and this Zelda has heard, and literally one whole section of her novel is an imitation of it, of its rhythm, materials, even statements and speeches. Now you may say that the experience which two people have undergone is common is common property—one transmutes the same scene through different temperaments and it "comes out different" As you will see from my letter to her there are only two episodes, both of which she has reduced to anec-

dotes but upon which whole sections of my book turn, *that I have asked her to cut. Her own material—her youth, her love for Josaune, her dancing, her observation of Americans in Paris, the fine passages about the death of her father—my critisisms of that will be simply impersonal and professional. But do you realize that "Amory Blaine" was the name of the character in my first novel to which I attached my adventures and opinions, in effect my autobiography? Do you think that his turning up in a novel signed by my wife as a somewhat aenemic portrait painter . . . could pass unnoticed? In short it puts me in an absurd and Zelda in a rediculous position. If she should choose to examine our life together from an inimacable attitude & print her conclusions I could do nothing but answer in kind or be silent, as I chose—but this mixture of fact and fiction is simply calculated to ruin us both, or what is left of us, and I can't let it stand. Using the name of a character I invented to put intimate facts in the hands of the friends and enemies we have accumulated enroute—My God, my books made her a legend and her single intention in this somewhat thin portrait is to make me a non-entity. That's why she sent the book directly to New York.*

(FROM SCOTT'S LETTER TO DR. SQUIRES,
MARCH 14, 1932 [Life in Letters 209])

PLEASE DO NOT JUDGE OR IF NOT ALREADY DONE EVEN CONSIDER ZELDAS BOOK UNTIL YOU GET REVISED VERSION LETTER FOLLOWS

(SCOTT'S WIRE TO MAXWELL PERKINS,
MARCH 16, 1932 [Life in Letters 210])

THINK NOVEL CAN SAFELY BE PLACED ON YOUR LIST FOR SPRING IT IS ONLY A QUESTION OF CERTAIN SMALL BUT NONE THE LESS NECESSARY REVISIONS MY DISCOURAGEMENT WAS CAUSED BY THE FACT THAT MYSELF AND DAUGHTER WERE SICK WHEN ZELDA SAW FIT TO SEND MANUSCRIPT TO YOU YOU CAN HELP ME BY RETURNING MANUSCRIPT TO HER UPON HER REQUEST GIVING SOME PRETEXT FOR NOT HAVING AS YET TIME TO READ IT AM NOW BETTER AND WILL WRITE LETTER TOMORROW IN MY OPINION IT IS A FINE NOVEL. . . .

(FROM SCOTT'S WIRE TO MAXWELL PERKINS,
MARCH 25, 1932 [Life in Letters 211])

*READ MANUSCRIPT BUT IF YOU HAVE ALREADY RETURNED IT
WIRE AND ILL SEND MY COPY STOP IF YOU LIKE IT AND WANT
TO USE IMMEDIATELY REMEMBER ALL MIDDLE SECTION
MUST BE RADICALLY REWRITTEN STOP TITLE AND NAME OF
AMORY BLAINE CHANGED STOP ARRIVING BALTIMORE THURS-
DAY TO CONFER WITH ZELDA WILL IMMEDIATELY DECIDE ON
NEW TITLE AND NAME CHANGES REVISING SHOULD TAKE
FORTNIGHT*

(SCOTT'S WIRE TO MAXWELL PERKINS,
MARCH 28, 1932 [Life in Letters *212*])

126. TO SCOTT   ALS, 2 pp.
[April 1932]   [Phipps Clinic, Baltimore,
                          Maryland]

Dearest:

Of cource, I glad[ly] submit to anything you want about the book
or anything else. I felt myself the thing was too crammed with material upon which I had not the time to dwell and consequently lost any
story continuity. Shall I wire Max to send it back? The real story was
the old prodigal son, of cource. I regret that it offended you. The Pershing incident which you accuse me of stealing[59] occupies just one
line and will not be missed. I willingly relinquish it. *However, I would
like you to thoroughly understand that my revision will be made on an aesthetic
basis: that the other material which I will elect is nevertheless legitimate stuff
which has cost me a pretty emotional penny to amass*[60] and which I intend
to use when I can get the tranquility of spirit necessary to write the
story of myself versus myself. That is the book I really want to write.
As you know my contacts with my family have always been in the
nature of the raids of a friendly brigand. I quite realize that the quality of this book does not warrant so many excursions into the
bizarre—As for my friends: first, I have none; by that I mean that all
our associates have always taken me for granted, sought your stimu-

---

59. Reference is to an episode in Chapter 28 of *Tender Is the Night* in which Abe North
impersonates General Pershing in order to get better service at the Ritz Hotel in Paris.
60. Probably underlined by Scott.

lus and fame, eaten my dinners and invited "the Fitzgeralds" place[s]. You have always been and always will be the only person with whom I have felt the necessity to communicate and our intimacies have, to me, been so satisfactory mentally that no other companion has ever seemed necessary. Despised by my sup[er]iors, which are few, held in suspicion by my equal, even fewer, I have got all external feeding for my insignificant flames from people either so vastly different from myself that our relations were like living a play or I have cherished my inferiors with color; to wit; Still [page torn] etc. and the friends of my youth. However, I did not intend to write you a treatise on friendship in which I do not believe. There is enough difficulty reconciling the different facets in one single person to bear the context of all human communication, it seems to me. When that is accomplished, the resultant sense of harmony is what is meant by benevolent friendship.

D. O. I am so miserable at not being able to help you. *I know how upset you get about stories. Don't worry.*[61] If we have less money—well, we can always live. I promise to be very conciliatory and want nothing on earth so much as for you to feel that you can write what you want.

About my fish-nets: they were beautiful gossamer pearl things to catch the glints of the sea and the slow breeze of the weaving sea-weed and bubbles at dawn. If a crab filtered in and gnawed the threads and an oct[o]pus stagnated and slimed up their fine knots and many squids shot ink across their sheen and shad laid comfortable row on their lovely film, they are almost repaired once more and the things I meant to fish still bloom in the sea. Here's hope for the irridiscent haul that some day I shall have. What do you fish with, by the way? that so puts to shame my equipment which I seriously doubt that you have ever seen, Superior Being—

With dearest love, I am your irritated
Zelda

---

61. Probably underlined by Scott, who also possibly drew the brackets around the last paragraph of the letter.

127. TO SCOTT   ALS, 2 pp.
[April 1932]   [Phipps Clinic, Baltimore,
                                Maryland]

D. O, dearest:

I am utterly miserable that we should have parted so un-happily.

You have been working to hard. While I do not know what could possibly relieve the strain on you, I wish I could be of some help. Love and affection is not of much practical use but it may be of a little comfort to you to know it is there.

Dear—You know that if I could sell any of my stories I would not have written this book. Ober is swamped with my things, and it seems worthless to plague him with more. The fact that I have had time to write it while you have had to put aside your own is due to circumstances over which I had no control and cannot bring myself to feel a sense of guilt. You, of all people, certainly would not have preferred my folding my hands during my long unoccupied hours. You must not forget that that the Toxologic(?) part of my illness is cured and I can no long[er] sit for endless blank periods in a trance as I did with eczema at Prangins.

It was impossible to fulfill my obligations as a normal sane person at home with three hours sleep a night. It seems to me that, in spite of your obligations, I had no alternative but to come here.

It is dreadful that I am not un-happy, but I would not be away any sooner if I sat and cried.

Believe me, dear, I quite appreciate the strain and depression under which you are existing. If there is any way on earth in which I can speed matters up you have only to indicate it to me.

In the meantime, please try to be calmer. At present I realize that there is little that your life has to offer as a substitute, but I wish you could drink less—do not fly into a rage, I know you stay *sober*—but you need some rest and I can't think how you can get it except by using those miserable moments that gin helps to dispel and turn into activity by resting.

I love you D. O—I would have collapsed years ago if I'd had me on my hands—but there's Scottie and we can be happy—and about money: when there isn't any will be time to be desperate. We never have more than we have now, really, only we usually have just finished spending so much that we feel God-awful rich and as if it were not actual, our constant and present poverty. Financially, we have trod

Dust jacket photograph for *Save Me the Waltz*; this
may be the photograph Zelda asked Scott to send
her in Letter 124 (p. 161). Courtesy of Princeton
University Library

our precarious path until it has become almost a high-way by this
time—garnished by municipal bridges and garlanded by county lights
and other public loot till you'd think the thing led somewhere—

When you're worried about one thing, think of how far ahead on
worry you were from the last time you felt as strongly—

Love, dear

Zelda

LA PAIX, 1932–1933

In May 1932, Scott rented a fifteen-room Victorian house called La
Paix in Towson, Maryland, outside of Baltimore. At first, Zelda's
doctors allowed her to spend her mornings there and return to
Phipps in the afternoon, making her transition from the hospital to
her new home a slow and carefully monitored one. On June 26,

Scott and Zelda attending a theater performance of *Dinner at Eight*, Baltimore 1932

she left Phipps and joined Scott and Scottie at La Paix, where they lived for the next year and half. Far from well, Zelda remained under the care of her Johns Hopkins doctors, even though she was no longer in residence. Her pride over her novel, which was published in October, was soon dampened, however, by harsh reviews and poor sales. Zelda earned only $120.73 from the 1932 sales of the novel, a sum she received nearly a year later.

For all the hope Scott and Zelda still held for restoring their lives together, the next months saw them deteriorate further. Scott, tired and discouraged, drank more; furthermore, he suffered from recurring chronic tuberculosis and had to be hospitalized. Zelda hated his drinking and resented and resisted the hypervigilance with which he tried to schedule her days and tell her what she could and could not write about. They often fought bitterly. Yet, as Matthew J. Bruccoli writes in *Some Sort of Epic Grandeur*, their astonishing closeness was still apparent: "At 'La Paix' there were frequent arguments during which the Fitzgeralds shouted at each other, but there were also interludes of tenderness. Visitors were impressed by the Fitzgeralds' enjoyment of each other's wit and the way they responded to recollections of past happiness" (330).

Problems continued to plague the Fitzgeralds in 1933. In June, there was a fire at La Paix, which apparently started when Zelda burned some old clothes in a neglected upstairs fireplace. Although the house was badly damaged, Scott did not want to move until he finished his novel. Working diligently, in nearly uninhabitable surroundings, he completed the first draft in September, made revisions, and sent the manuscript off to Maxwell Perkins at Scribners at the end of October. That summer and fall were all the more difficult for the Fitzgeralds because of personal losses. In August, Zelda's brother, Anthony, committed suicide, and in September, the Fitzgeralds' close friend Ring Lardner died. In addition, when Scott and Zelda, following Dr. Meyer's recommendation, took a brief vacation to Bermuda, Scott came down with an inflammation of the lungs and had to finish the revisions to his novel in bed. In December, the Fitzgeralds moved to 1307 Park Avenue in Baltimore. Although the trip to Bermuda temporarily revived Zelda, the return to Baltimore saw her decline once again.

The three letters from Scott to Zelda that follow all were apparently written during the period they lived together at La Paix. The second of these appears to be in response to Zelda's desire to have more control over her routine. She resented Scott's watchful attention to the daily details of her recovery; he, on the other hand, remained fearful that Zelda would repeat her pattern of manic work, followed by depression and psychosis. This letter also appears to be an attempt to challenge some of Zelda's thoughts and actions, ones that he believed led to her relapses. Whether or not he gave this letter to Zelda is unknown. In the third letter, from 1933, Scott again emphasized the importance of a schedule and suggested that returning to the clinic for a few days might be an option when Zelda felt the need to withdraw from the family for short periods.

128. TO ZELDA AL (fragment), 2 pp.
[1932] [La Paix, Towson, Maryland]

Honey, when you come out into the world again I wish you would try to realize what I can only describe as the:

Nub (NUB) of Experience.

The fact that in your efforts you have come up *twice* against insuperable facts[,] 1st against Lucienne[,] 2nd against me—both times against long desperate heart-destroying professional training beginning when we ie Lucienne + I were seven, probably;

There has never been any question as to your "value" as a personality—there is however a question as to your ability to use your values to any practical purpose. To repeat the phrase that became anathema in my ears during the last months of our trying to make a go of it "*expressing oneself*[.]" I can only say there isn't any such thing. It simply doesn't exist. What one expresses in a work of art is the dark tragic destiny of being an instrument of something uncomprehended, incomprehensible, unknown—you came to the threshold of that discovery + then decided in the face of all logic you would crash the gate. You succeeded merely in crashing yourself, almost me, + Scotty, if I hadn't interposed.

129. TO ZELDA AL, 11 pp.
[1933?] [La Paix, Towson, Maryland]

Do you feel that you are now able to be your own doctor—to judge what is good for you?

If no—do you know what should be done?

Should you be in a clinic do you think?

Would a trained nurse help?

An experienced one?

An inexperienced one?

If you were really not yourself and in a fit of temper or depression would you ask the judgement of such of [a?] woman or would you come to me?

Are these bursts of temper part of the "derangement" you mentioned?

Or are they something that is in your surroundings?

If they are in your sickness how can you accept another's opinion when the nature of your attack has taken away your power of reasoning?

If they are in your home surroundings in what practical ways would you like your home surroundings changed?

Must there [be] big changes which seriously affect the life of husband and children?

———————————

———————————

If you feel that you are now able to be your own doctor—to judge what is good for you.

Of what use would a nurse be?

Would she be a sort of clock to remind you it was time for this and that?

If that function in your husband is annoying would it not be more annoying in the case of a stranger in your own house?

———————————

———————————

Is there not an idea in your head sometimes that you must live close to the borders of mental trouble in order to create at your best?

Which comes first your health or your work?

Are you in delicate health?

If a person sacrificed some of their health to their work is that within their human rights?

If a sick person sacrificed some of their health to their work is that within their human rights?

If a sick person sacrificed some of their health to their work and sacrificed others also would that be within their rights

If the other people felt that they would not willingly be sacrificed could they refuse?

What recourse would the determined worker have *if well*?

What recourse if sick?

Must he not wait until he is well bringing such matters to a decision, because being sick he will be inevitably worsted in trying to infringe on the rights of others?

———————————

———————————

Is there any enlightened opinion which considers that you are liable to be strong for another year?

Can you make yourself strong by any means except the usual ones?

Are you an exceptional person who will be cured differently from anyone else

----

Will you make the usual return to society for its protection of you during your sickness and convalesence

Is the return usually the virtues of patience and submissiveness in certain important regards?

In case the ill person (suppose a man with small pox) runs around hurting and infecting others will society tend to take stern measures to protect itself?

Are you ill?

Are your husband and child, in their larger aspects, society?

If one of them were contageously sick and wanted to return to the home during convalescence would you let him infect the other and yourself?

Who would be your natural guides in determining what was the end of convalescence?

Did "good behavior" in the clinic preceed your previous recovery?

Was it better behavior than any other?

Did not furious activity and bad behavior preceed the previous denoument at Valmont and Prangins?

Are you or have you been ill?

Does furious activity lead often to consequent irritability even in well persons?

Would not this be terribly accentuated by an ill person?

Does a person recovering from heart trouble start by moving boulders

----

Is "I have no time" an answer to the previous questions?"

What is the order of importance of everything in your mind —

Is your health first?

Is it always first?

Is it first in the midst of artistic creation when the two are in conflict?

If it is not, and you should be well, should society coerce you into putting health first?

If you should be ill should society so act upon you?

Does your child have the same priviledges when ill as when well?

Are not lessons stopped?

Is this logical?

What does logic mean?

Is it important to be logical?

If not, is it important to be dramatic?

Is it important to have been dramatic?

If an illness becomes a nuisance to society does society act sternly?

Is it important to be dramatic or logical in the future?

Is an ill person or a well person more capable of being logical or dramatic?

Can a very ill person try to be only a little ill?

Why does madness not enlarge the artistic range?

What is disaccociation of ideas?

How does it differ in an artistic person and in a mentally ill person?

———————————

———————————

Who pays for illness?

Who pays in suffering?

Does only the ill person suffer?

When you left Prangins would you have taken any patient there into your home if they came in a refractory way

Would you constitute yourself a doctor for them?

Suppose the choice was between two patients and one patient would accept your judgement while the other one said he would not[.] Which would you choose

———————————

———————————

When doctors recommend a normal sexual life do you agree with them?

Are you normal sexually?

Are you retiscent about sex?

Are you satisfied sexually with your husband?

———————————

———————————

Newspaper picture of the Fitzgeralds on their lawn after the fire at La Paix in June 1933; manuscripts and paintings were destroyed. Courtesy of Princeton University Library

130. TO ZELDA
[Summer 1933?]

ALS, 2 pp.
[La Paix, Towson, Maryland]

Dearest: I'm writing because I don't want to start the day with an arguement — though I had thought that what has become controversial was settled before you left the clinic.

Darling when you shut yourself away for twenty four hours it is not only very bad for you but it casts a pall of gloom and disquiet over the people who love you. To spend any reasonable time in your room has been agreed upon as all right, but this shouldn't be so exaggerated that you can't manage the social side any further than sitting at table. It would help everything if you could enter a little into Scotty's life here on the place, and your reluctance to play tennis and swim is a rather reckless withdrawal; for whatever of the normal you subtract from your life will be filled up with brooding and fantasy. If I know that there is excercise scheduled for morning and afternoon and a medical bath in the afternoon + that you have half an hour for us after supper and you stop work at ten, my not very exigent list, *insisted on by Dr. Myers*, is complete. When you throw it out of joint I can only sit and wait for the explosion that will follow—a situation not conducive to work or happiness. If this week has been too much it is easy to return to the clinic for three days and it needn't be done in a spirit of despair any more than your many returns to Prangins.

I believe however you are not giving it, giving us, a fair trial here. If I didn't love you so much your moods wouldn't affect me so deeply and excitely. We can't afford scenes—the best protection is the schedule and then the schedule and again the schedule, and you'll get strong without knowing it.

    S.

Third Breakdown
CRAIG HOUSE, BEACON, NEW YORK, MARCH—MAY 1934

On February 12, 1934, Zelda suffered her third nervous breakdown and was readmitted to Phipps Clinic. Dangerously thin, she required almost complete bed rest and was under continuous observation to prevent possible suicide attempts. She failed to improve at Phipps, and, at Dr. Forel's suggestion, she was transferred to Craig House on March 8. It was an expensive country club-like hospital, occupying 350 acres on the Hudson River, in Beacon, an hour-and-a-half drive north of New York City. That spring, despite ill health and every possible strain, both Scott and Zelda achieved important professional accomplishments: Scott saw the novel he had been struggling with for almost ten years, *Tender Is the Night*, published; Zelda, who had begun to take her artwork more seriously, had a small exhibit of her paintings in New York City, arranged by art dealer Cary Ross, a friend of the Fitzgeralds.

The letters that follow discuss these events. *Tender Is the Night* first appeared in four installments in *Scribner's Magazine*; the book itself was published on April 12, 1934. Zelda read the serialized version, then the published book. Her letters give her responses to the novel as she read it; she encouraged Scott when the mixed reviews disappointed him. She also wrote about her own aspirations—writing and painting. Although appreciative of the lovely Craig House estate and grateful to Scott for providing so generously for her, she often insisted that the accommodations were far too extravagant and encouraged Scott to place her in a less expensive institution.

131. TO SCOTT
March 12, 1934

Wire
[Craig House, Beacon, New
    York]

> BRM16 38 DL=BEACON NY 12 1023A
> SCOTT FITZGERALD=
>   1307 PARK AVE=
> WOULD MRS OWENS PACK ALL MY CLOTHES INCLUDING
> RIDING THINGS TENNIS AND GOLF CLUBS FIRST I WANT
> MY OIL PAINTS FROM HOPKINS ALSO TEXT BOOKS ON
> ART AND THE DANTE LOVE AND THANKS THIS IS A
> LOVELY PLACE=
>   ZELDA.

132. TO SCOTT
[March 1934]

ALS, 2 pp.
[Craig House, Beacon, New
    York]

Dearest Do-Do.

Please ask Mrs. Owens to hurry with my paints. There are so
many winter trees exhibiting irresistible intricacies, and there are
many neo-classic columns, and there are gracious expanses of snow
and the brooding quality of a gray and heavy sky, all of which make
me want terribly to paint.

I have been working on the hotels,[62] and will mail them as soon as
they're finished. Also what of my book I get done for you to have
typed.[63] Be sure to write me what you think of the chapters you read.

Do-Do:

It was so sad to see your train pull out through the gold sheen of
the winter afternoon. It is sad that you should have so many things to
worry you and make you unhappy when your book is so good and
ought to bring you so much satisfaction. I hope the house won't seem

---

62. An autobiographical essay, entitled "Show Mr. and Mrs. F. To Number — "; in it, Zelda
outlines their lives together year by year, 1920–1933, by describing the hotels they stayed
in, emphasizing how much they traveled. The essay appeared in *Esquire* in May and June of
1934; it bears the byline of both Zelda and Scott but appears to have been written by Zelda
and polished and edited by Scott.
63. Unidentified.

desolate and purposeless; if you want to, you could board Scottie at Bryn Mawr,[64] or maybe even the Turnbulls[65] and stay in New York with the people you're fond of.[66]

This is a beautiful place; there is everything on earth available and I have a little room to paint in with a window higher than my head the way I like windows to be. When they are that way, you can look out on the sky and feel like Faust in his den, or an alchemist or anybody you like who must have looked out of windows like that. And my own room is the nicest room I've ever had, any place—which is very unjust, considering the burden you are already struggling under.

Dear—I will see you soon. Why not bring Scottie up for Easter? She'd love it here with the pool and the beautiful walks. And I *promise* you absolutely that by then I will be much better—and as well as I can.

Dear:

Please remember that you owe it to the fine things inside you to get the most out of them.

Work, and don't drink, and the accomplished effort will perhaps open unexpected sources of happiness, or contentment, or whatever it is you are looking for—certainly a sense of security—If I were you'd [you], I'd dramatize your book—yourself. I feel sure it contains a good subtle drama suitable to the purposes of the theatre Guild: a character play hinging on the two elements within the man: his worldly proclivities and his desire to be a distinguished person—I wish I could do it.

Love, dear—
Zelda

---

64. The Bryn Mawr School was a day and boarding school in Baltimore when Scottie enrolled there.

65. Family friends who owned the estate on which La Paix was located; the Turnbulls' son, Andrew, who would later write a Fitzgerald biography, was around Scottie's age.

66. This letter was written when Zelda returned from a one-day leave from Craig House. She had joined Scott in New York to attend the opening of her art exhibit there. She encouraged Scott to stay on in New York among friends to await publication of *Tender Is the Night* on April 12, which he did.

Scott and Scottie in Baltimore, while Scottie was
a student at the Bryn Mawr School

133. TO SCOTT   ALS, 6 pp.
[March 1934]   [Craig House, Beacon, New
                          York]

Dear Scott:

I quite realize the terrible financial pressure of the last year for
you, and I am miserable that this added burden should have fallen on
your shoulders. All the beauty of this place must cost an awful lot of
money and maybe it would be advisable to go somewhere more com-
patible with our present means. Please do not think that I don't
appreciate the strain you are under. I would make the best possible
effort to rehabilitate myself under any less luxurious conditions that
might be more expedient.

Please don't give up Scottie's music. Though she is at an age when
she resents the practice, I feel sure that later she will get an immense
satisfaction out of the piano. About the French, do as you think best.

She will never forget it at her age and could pick it up again quickly as soon as she heard it around her

It's too bad about Willie[.] She was the best cook we've had in years and I've always held Essie in suspect: there've been such a long succession of rows over missing things since she became part of the household.

The trunk arrived. I am very much obliged. However, I would also like my blue bathing-suit which may be in the box with moth balls in the back room on the third floor, and also the rest of my clothes: a blue suit, a green checked skirt and the evening clothes. *Also please* ask Mrs Owens to send me a $2 pointed camel's hair brush from Webers and the two unfinished canvases from Phipps, and a pound can of Weber's permalba.

Dear: I am not trying to make myself into a great artist or a great anything. Though you persist in thinking that an exaggerated ambition is the fundamental cause of my collapse, knowing the motivating elements that now make me wa[nt] to work I cannot agree with you and Dr Forel—though, of cource, the will-to-power may have played a part in the very beginning. However, five years have passed since then, and one matures. I do the things I can do and that interest me and if you'd like me to give up everything I like to do I will do so willingly if it will advance matters any. I am not headstrong and do not like existing entirely at other peoples expense and being a constant care to others any better than you like my being in such a situation.

If you feel that it is an imposition on Cary to have the exhibition, the pictures can wait. I believe in them and in Emerson's theory about good-workman-ship. If they are good, they will come to light some day.

About my book: you and the doctors agreed that I might work on it. If you now prefer that I put it aside for the present I wish you would be clear about saying so. The short story is a form demanding too concentrated an effort for me at present and I might try a play, if you are willing and don't approve of the novel or something where the emotional purpose can be accomplished by accurate execution of an original cerebral conception. *Please say what you want done,* as I really do not know. As you know, my work is mostly a pleasure for me, but if it is better for me to take up something quite foreign to my temperament, I will—Though I can't see what good it does to knit bags when you want to paint pansies, maybe it is necessary at times to do what you don't like.

Tilde 'phoned that she and John would drive over to see me. I will be very glad to see them.

Love
Zelda

134. TO SCOTT   AL, 3 pp.
[March 1934]   [Craig House, Beacon, New
                                        York]

Dear, Monsieur, D. O;

The third installment is fine. I like immensely that retrospective part through Nicole's eyes—which I didn't like at first because of your distrust of polyphonic prose. It's a swell book.

It seems very careless of the Murphy's to have got old; like laundry in the corridors of a pleasure-resort hotel. They could get tragic, or join a curious sect, or escape to islands strung on strange parallels of latitude but to expose the mechanics of the glamour of life in slowed-up motion rings of indecency.

I am sorry Charlie[67] is still so charming. I have never felt Charlie to be a legitimate attraction somehow and suspect him of not really being from Borneo at all, though no amount of research yields up the slightest false whiskers. However, he has a parasitical flavor—

I am glad you are a lion. Dr. Rennie says you are a lion so I am glad. You deserve to be. I hope there will be enough Christians left to make it worth while; though there is some talk amongst the lions of eeking out the winter with Barnum Bailey—just for the experience—

Borrow $1000 from your mother and write a play. It will make her feel very virtuous and will become what she has been waiting for all these years. The play will be a big success; if it isnt you can stick in some propaganda. Then you can support Mr. Lorimer[68] in his old age without the stories.

I wish I could write stories. I wish I could write something sort of like the book of revelations: you know, about how everything would have come out if we'd only been able to supply the 3-letter word for the Egyptian god of dithryambics. Something all full of threats preferably and then a very gentle confession at the end admitting that I have enfeebled myself too much by my own vehemence to ever become very frightened again.

If Scottie sneezes you will find the proper method of preceedure in Louis Carrol; the Katzenjammers also are full of constructive ideas about bringing up children. Only you have to have children who explode when banged with a stick to use the latter as a text book—

---

67. Possibly Charles MacArthur.
68. George Horace Lorimer, editor of the *Saturday Evening Post,* from whom Fitzgerald was then receiving three thousand dollars per story.

If we had $500 we could all go to Greece—The Vale of Shalimar still settles to earth somewhere in the east; capitals with short bombastic names drown in the tides of the Black sea; metro polese of many syllables are being mispronounced by travellers like missionaries in Cook's most inefficient out-posts[.] In Indo-Chine in the newsreels the clouds are full as treasure-sacks. Natives all over those foreign places treaddle, and migrate, and think of the world as a very big place. If only the signifigance of roads had not left the western hemisphere!

Please ask Cary to come to see me if he wants to. And tell him that I am sorry I was rude and that if he will lend me the Satie[69] I will make him a pink and dreamy picture filled with the deepest appreciation of the most superficial emotions—

D. O:

You *don't* love me—But I am counting on Pavloff's dogs to make that kind of thing all right—and, in the mean-time, under the added emotional stress of the break-up of our state, perhaps the old conventions will assume an added poignancy. Besides, personal love should be incidental music, maybe. Besides, *anything* personal was never the objective of our generation—we were to have thought of ourselves heroicly; we agreed in the Plaza Grill the pact was confirmed by the shaking of Connie Bennets[70] head and the sonority of Ludlow's[71] premature gastritis—

135. TO SCOTT　　　　　　ALS, 4 pp.
[March 1934]　　　　　　　　[Craig House, Beacon, New
　　　　　　　　　　　　　　　　York]

Dearest Do-Do—

Mrs Owens wrote me that she'd sent everything I asked for including the Key Memorial,[72] which was very nice of her. I hope your story goes well and is not too terrific an effort. D. O—I wish

---

69. French composer Erik Satie.

70. Popular movie actress Constance Bennett, who later starred in *Topper* (1937) with Cary Grant.

71. Ludlow Fowler, who was the best man at the Fitzgeralds' wedding.

72. Scott was related to Francis Scott Key, who wrote "The Star-Spangled Banner," which in 1931 became the official national anthem. Scott and his secretary, Mrs. Owens, were in Baltimore, where Key wrote the anthem in response to the bombardment of Fort McHenry in the War of 1812.

you didn't have to write what you don't want to—I do the thing for the New Yorker and it grows longer and longer but maybe you can sell it to something. Of cource, I will send it to you to have typed.

Yesterday Mrs Killan and I dug a few holes in some golf balls and I almost uprooted a gigantic oak with what used to be a chip-shot. Next week, the course opens, and we will get in some practice of some sort even if we have to use La Crosse nets.

Also we play bridge. You know how I play: I sit and wait for Divine Guidance to show me the difference between a finesse and a (insert any technical term you know here). Then when I've made the mistake I pretend I was thinking of something else and utter as convincing lamentations as I can at my absent-mindedness.

It's so pretty here. The ground is shivering with snow-drops and gentians. I suppose you wouldn't like to rest, but I wish you could for a while in the cool apple-green of my room. The curtains are like those in John Bishop's poem to Elspeth and beyond the lawn never ends. Of cource, you can walk to where young men in bear-cat roadsters are speeding to whatever Geneva Mitchell's[73] dominate the day—but mostly we walk the other way where tumbling villages prop themselves on the beams of the afternoon sun. We have tea, and many such functions to fulfill. It's an awfully nice place.

Please send the book.[74]

Love
Zelda

136. TO SCOTT
[Early April 1934]

ALS, 4 pp.
[Craig House, Beacon, New
York]

Dearest Do-Do:

I have now got to the Rosemary-Rome episode. It makes me very sad—largely because of the beautiful, beautiful writing. Recapitulation of casual youth in the tenderer terms one learns to cling to later is always moving. You know I love your prose style: it is so fine and

---

73. Reference is to Scott's teenage love, Chicago socialite Ginevra King, who married William Hamilton Mitchell.
74. *Tender Is the Night.*

balanced and you know how to achieve the emphasis you want so poignantly and economicly. It's a fine book, suggestive to me of these black tree formations, aspiring or despairing, scattering their white petals to make another valley spring.

Please don't be alarmed if I don't write; there is much outside to look at, and my room inside reflects the softness of new greens and harbors the squares of mountain sun—

I'm so happy that it is hot again.

Mrs Killam and I hammered at golf-balls yesterday, taking enough swings to have built the Roxy Center—at least I did. She plays very well. You know my psychological attitude toward golf: it was just the sort of thing they would have brought into England during the reign of Chas. II. The French probably played it in high-heels with stomachs full of wine and cheated a little—

I hope all goes well at home. All you *really* have to do for Scottie is see that she does not go to Bryn Mawr in dirty blouses. Also, she will not voluntarily wash her ears: I noticed when she was here and hope Louise Perkins[75] didn't. I can't say that I blame her but some people might, so am afraid you will have to go through a thorough inspection every now and then—

> Love
> Zelda

137. TO SCOTT ALS, 1 p.
[Early April 1934] [Craig House, Beacon, New
York]

Mr. Scott Fitzgerald
1307 Park Avenue
Baltimore, Md.

Dear—The book is grand. The emotional lift sustained by the force of a fine poetic prose and the characters *subserviated* to forces stronger than their interpretations of life is very moving. It is tear-evoking to witness individual belief in individual volition succumbing to the purpose of a changing world. That is the purpose of a good book and you

---

75. Maxwell Perkins's wife.

have written it. Those people are helpless before themselves and the prose is beautiful and there is manifest an integrity in the belief of both those expressions. It is a reverential and very fine book and the first literary contribution to what writers will be concerning themselves with some years from now.

Love
Zelda

138. TO SCOTT   ALS, 4 pp.
[c. April 12, 1934]   [Craig House, Beacon, New
                                 York]

Dearest Do-Do.

I watch the papers and no reviews. I can hardly wait to know what the critics will say of those "excursions into the frontiers of a *social* consciousness." No matter what they say, it's exquisite prose and a trip into unexploited fields so far as the material is concerned—So if Bunny[76] wants to go on thinking about what he's read of communism, don't mind. Cadenced adventures of the human heart and an accurate picutre of the end of an era are, I imagine, what animated you to write the book and I wouldn't care much about an opinion founded on a devitalized version of Christianity. He will think differently when Pavloff and people like that have opened up as mechanistic a universe as the Greek Atomists ever dreamed, only with proofs for everything. Yours is a beautiful and moving book. The man I meant for the clinician in the movies turned out to be Ratoff;[77] and the leading man I liked was Paul Lukas,[78] but maybe they aren't famous enough. They're swell actors, though.

I'm sorry about the income tax and the money I'm spending. I cannot see why I should sit in luxury when you are having such a struggle. Since there seems to be no way in which I can hasten my recovery, maybe it would be wise to try a cheaper place. I promise you

---

76. Edmund Wilson, who was then working on *To the Finland Station*.
77. Actor Gregory Ratoff, who made his film debut in 1932 and often played eccentric characters. He later played Count Mippipopolous in the 1957 film version of Hemingway's *The Sun Also Rises*.
78. Film actor.

I will not be discouraged by any such change you might make and, of cource, will do the best I can, anywhere. Beauty on display costs money, but, as Tolstoi discovered long before Einstein all things are relative and the universal qualities which really count are inherent in everything, individually. Tolstoi said, I believe, that when Peter was tired from the wars, his army palette felt as soft and sweet as the rose-leaves to which he had accustomed himself under more prosperous conditions.

I will send the New Yorker article as soon as I've corrected it—probably Tuesday. If they won't take it maybe it will give you some pleasure to know what a lady thinks about while opening a barrel—an old barrel filled with long-forgotten contents

Love
Zelda

139. TO SCOTT ALS, 3 pp.
(Mid-April 1934) [Craig House, Beacon, New York]

Dearest D. O.:

I was afraid you might worry about some of the silly reviews which I have not seen until to-day. *Please don't.* All the opinion which you respect has said everything you would like to have said about the book. It is not a novel about the simple and the inarticulate, nor are such a fitting subject for literature one of whose primary functions is to enrich the human mind. Anybody granted a certain talent can express direct action, or even emotion segregate[d] from the activities of the world of their day but to present the growth of a human tragedy resultant from social conditions is a big feat. To me, you have done it well and at the same time preserved the more simple beauties of penetrating poignancy to be found in the use of exquisite prose.

Don't worry about critics—what sorrows have they to measure by or what lilting happiness with which to compare those ecstatic passages?

The atomists who followed Democritus said that quantity was what differentiated one thing from another—not quality—so critics will have to rise one day to the high points of good books. They cannot always live on reproductions of their own emotions in simple enough settings not to distract them: the poor boy having a hard time which is all very beautiful because of the poverty, etc.[79]

It's a swell heart-breaking book, because the prose compels you to respond to the active situations—which is as it should be.

I am very worried about the finances. *Please* don't hesitate to do *anything* that would relieve the strain on you.

> Love
> Zelda

140. TO SCOTT   ALS, 4 pp.
[Mid-April 1934]   [Craig House, Beacon, New York]

Dearest Do-Do:

I was so worried that you would be upset about some of those reviews—What critics know about the psychology of a psychiatrist, I don't know, but the ones I saw seemed absurd, taking little account of the fact that a novel not in 18 volumes *can't* cover everything but must rely on the indicative[.] You know yourself that as people yours are moving and heart-rending creations; as instruments of your artistic purpose they arrive at an importance which they would otherwise not have had, and that is the function of characters in a novel, which is, after all, a way of looking at life[.] Do you suppose you could get Menken[80] to write an intelligent review? The rest do not seem to know what they think beyond the fact that they have never thought of such problems before. And *don't* let them discourage you. It is a swell evocation of an epoch and a very masterly presentation of tragedies sprung from the beliefs (or lack of them) of those times which bloomed from the seeds of despair planted by the war and of the circumstance dependent on the adjustment of

---

79. The mixed reception of *Tender Is the Night* was much more positive than negative, but it still disappointed Scott greatly. During the decade of the Great Depression, the literary world had turned away from the expatriates depicted in 1920s novels and favored fiction depicting social conditions of the time.

80. Scott took Zelda's advice and wrote a letter to H. L. Mencken on April 23, explaining the "deliberate intention" behind some of the choices he had made in the structure and design of the novel (*Life in Letters* 255–256). Mencken did not write a review.

philosophies. Woolcot[81] might be good to review it, since he had some appreciation of the spectacle which it presents, but I have seen some very silly and absurd commentaries of his lately, and he may have succumbed to the pseudo-radical formulas of Kaufman and Gershwin[82] by now.

Let Bromfield[83] feed their chaotic minds on the poppy-seed of farm youth tragedies and let them write isolated epics lacking any epic quality save reverence[.] Yours is a story taking place behind the scenes, and I only hope that you will not forget that most of the audience has never been there.

Anyway, they all seem to realize that much thought and a fine equipment has gone into its making and maybe—if they only could understand—

D. O.—darling—having reached the people you wanted to reach, what more can you ask?[84] Show man ship is an incidental consideration, after all—they have its glittering sequins in the circus and the Hippodrome and critics yelling for more in literature seems a little like babies crying for things they can't have between meals—put cardboard cuffs on their elbows—Those antiquated methods are the only ones I know.

xxxx

Since writing your letter has come. Of cource, I missed all but a few reviews. Bill Warren has a swell sense of the dramatic and I hope he'll separate out the points that will appeal to Mr. Mayer.[85] My advice is to revert to the money-triangle as you can't possibly use the incest. Or make the man a weak and charming figure from the first, always gravitating towards the center of things: which would lead him, when he was in the clinic, to Nicole and later to Rosemary. Regret could be the motif of the last section—Naturally, it's only

---

81. Alexander Woollcott, a well-known critic, wit, and radio personality, asserted much influence over the popular cultural scene.

82. Playwright George S. Kaufman and composer George Gershwin, who collaborated on the Pulitzer Prize–winning musical *Of Thee I Sing* (1931).

83. Novelist and screenwriter Louis Bromfield, who had just written a bestselling novel, *The Farm* (1933), and who soon wrote Scott a letter of praise regarding *Tender Is the Night*.

84. Many of Scott's friends and fellow writers immediately sent him letters of heartfelt praise—among them, John Dos Passos, John Peale Bishop, Archibald MacLeish, John O'Hara, Thomas Wolfe, and Robert Benchley, to name only a few.

85. Charles "Bill" Warren, whom the Fitzgeralds met in Baltimore, collaborated with Scott on a screenplay for *Tender Is the Night*, but Louis B. Mayer of MGM was not interested in making the novel into a movie.

advice, and I don't know if a male star would like to play something so far removed from Tarzan and those things about the desert where people are so brave, and only minor figures make mistakes

Love
Zelda

141. TO SCOTT   ALS, 4 pp.
[Mid-April 1934]   [Craig House, Beacon, New
                                              York]

Dearest Scott:

I am glad you did not let those undiscerning reviews upset you. You have the satisfaction of having written a tragic and poetic personal drama against the background of an excellent presentation of the times we matured in. You know that I have always felt that the chief function of the artist was to inspire *feeling* and certainly "Tender" did that. What people will live on for the next ten years I do not know: because, with the synchronization of light and sound and color (still embryonicly on display at the world's Fair) there may be a tremendous revision of aesthetic judgments and responses. Some of the later movies have cinematic effects unachievable with a brush — all of which tends to a communistic conception of art, I suppose. In this case, I writing might become the most individualistic of all expressions, or a sociological organ.

Anyway, your book is a sustained and exalted piece of prose —

Bill Warren, in my opinion, is a silly man to get to transcribe its subtleties to a metier that is now commanding the highest talents: because people will be *looking* thus expecting to be carried along by visual emotional developments as well as story and you will be robbed of the inestimable value of your prose to raise and cut and break the tension. But you know better than I. In the movies, one symbolic device is worth a thousand feet of explanation (granted you haven't at your disposal those expert technicians who have turned out some of the late stuff)[.] Go to see Ruth Chatterton and Adolph Menjou in that last thing about murder.[86] It's a swell straight psycho-

---

86. Ruth Chatterton and Aldophe Menjou stared in the 1934 movie *Journal of a Crime*.

logical story—I simply thought that with all the stuff in your book so much could have been done: the funicular, the beach umbrellas, the garden high above the world, and in the end the two people swimming in darkness.

When Mrs O. sends

1) Dramatic Technique

2) Golden Treasury

3) Pavlowa's[87] Life

4) The Book on Modern Art, I will return Scottie's Treasury. Until then, I have nothing to read as I can't stand the Inferno or the pseudo-noble-simplicity of that book Dorothy P.[88] gave me.

Won't you ask her to? Also the paint from Webers. She said she would—They would mail it.

  Love
  Zelda—

142. TO SCOTT   ALS, 4 pp.
[Late April 1934]   [Craig House, Beacon, New
            York]

Dearest Do-Do:

I'm so glad all the good people liked your book. It's swell about Mary Column[89] and Seldes[90] and I can't understand your not using Elliot's opinion of your works[91] in the adds. That man J. A. D. in the Times[92] is the one I told you dismissed a novel completely on moral grounds not long ago. He is an imbecile and it would be a good thing if somebody attacked him. He knows nothing of art, aestheticly or sociologicly, or of anything that's going on in the world to-day. How-

87. Russian ballerina Anna Pavlova.

88. Dorothy Parker.

89. Mary Colum reviewed *Tender* in *Forum and Century* (April 1934).

90. Gilbert Seldes's review in the *New York Evening Journal* on April 12 said: Fitzgerald "has stepped once again to his natural place at the head of American writers of our time" (*Romantic Egoists* 198).

91. In a letter dated December 31, 1925, which Scott pasted in his scrapbook, T. S. Eliot had written that he had read *The Great Gatsby* three times and thought that Scott had taken the "first step that American fiction has taken since Henry James" (*Romantic Egoists* 135).

92. J. Donald Adams, reviewing for the *New York Times Book Review* on April 15.

ever, you had already had a good review in the Times[93] so what ho! Only it does make me sore to give people books to review who have no idea of the purpose behind them or of their artistic intent. I Hope you didn't mind; it is such a fine book, as everybody else seems unanimously agreed.

Cary wrote that Ernest was back in N.Y.; that he had been to see my pictures. Why don't you ask him down? You've got more room than people in the house and Mrs. Owens would get you a maid. He also said the Murphys bought the acrobats.[94] I am going to paint a picture for the Murphy's and they can choose as those acrobats seem, somehow, singularly inappropriate to them and I would like them to have one they liked. Maybe they aren't like I think they are but I don't see why they would like that Buddhistic suspension of mass and form and I will try to paint some mood that their garden has conveyed.

I wish I could see the review in the New Republic, Forum, etc. Won't you send them? I'll mail them back immediately.

And don't pay any attention to that initialled moth-hole in the Times.

Apparently the Tribune man[95] still believes that movie stars got there via the gutters of Les Miserables — But we can't buy him a ticket to Hollywood, and, on the whole, it was an intelligent and favorable review — and he liked the book even if he didn't know what it was about psychologicly. He will like it better when be reads it again.

I hope Ernest liked it; I guess Morley Callaghan is sore at having his adds reduced.[96] Please send me a copy —

Love
Zelda

---

93. By John Chamberlain on April 13.
94. Zelda's painting *Chinese Theater.*
95. *New York Tribune* reviewer Horace Gregory.
96. Canadian Morley Callaghan, who was a friend of Scott's, had also just published a novel with Scribners, *Such Is My Beloved* (1934).

143. TO ZELDA   TL (CC), 3 pp.
1307 Park Avenue,
Baltimore, Maryland,
April 26, 1934.

Forgive me for dictating this letter instead of writing it directly, but if you could see my desk at the moment and the amount of stuff that has come in you would understand.

The thing that you have to fight against is defeatism of any kind. You have no reason for it. You have never had really a melancholy temperament, but, as your mother said: you have always been known for a bright, cheerful, extraverting attitude upon life. I mean *especially* that you share none of the melancholy point of view which seems to have been the lot of Anthony and Marjorie.[97] You and I have had wonderful times in the past, and the future is still brilliant with possibilities if you will keep up your morale, and try to think that way. The outside world, the political situation, etc., is still gloomy and it *does* effect everybody directly, and will inevitably reach you indirectly, but try to separate yourself from it by some form of mental hygiene—if necessary, a self-invented one.

Let me reiterate that I don't want you to have too much traffic with my book, which is a melancholy work and seems to have haunted most of the reviewers. *I feel very strongly about your re-reading it.* It represents certain phases of life that are now over. We are certainly on some up-surging wave, even if we don't yet know exactly where it's heading.

There is no feeling of gloom on your part that has the *slightest* legitimacy. Your pictures have been a success, your health has been very much better, according to the doctors—and the only sadness is the living without you, without hearing the notes of your voice with its particular intimacies of inflection.

You and I have been happy; we haven't been happy just once, we've been happy a thousand times. The chances that the spring, that's for everyone, like in the popular songs, may belong to us too— the chances are pretty bright at this time because as usual, I can carry most of contemporary literary opinion, liquidated, in the hollow of my hand—and when I do, I see the swan floating on it and—I find it to be

---

97. Zelda's brother and sister had nervous temperaments and suffered from depression; Anthony Sayre committed suicide in 1933.

you and you only. But, Swan, float lightly because you are a swan, because by the exquisite curve of your neck the gods gave you some special favor, and even though you fractured it running against some man-made bridge, it healed and you sailed onward. Forget the past — what you can of it, and turn about and swim back home to me, to your haven for ever and ever — even though it may seem a dark cave at times and lit with torches of fury; it is the best refuge for you — turn gently in the waters through which you move and sail back.

This sounds allegorical but is *very* real. I want you here. The sadness of the past is with me always. The things that we have done together and the awful splits that have broken us into war survivals in the past stay like a sort of atmosphere around any house that I inhabit. The good things and the first years together, and the good months that we had two years ago in Montgomery will stay with me forever, and you should feel like I do that they can be renewed, if not in a new spring, then in a new summer. I love you my darling, darling.

P.S.[98] Did I tell you that, among others, Adele Lovett came in and bought a picture and so did Louise Perkins and the Tommy Daniels from St. Paul? Will see that the Dick Myers get one free.[99]

144. **TO SCOTT**
[After April 26, 1934]

ALS, 4 pp.
[Craig House, Beacon, New York]

Dearest Do-Do:

Thanks for your long sweet letter: I have just finished part I of your book again. It is the most beautiful prose, without a wasted or irrelevant word. It is also very moving and a fine presentation of those sunlit places, which its bright glare finally faded and streaked — perhaps to dimmer nuances. In fact, Do-Do, it's a swell book and well imbued with that sense of impersonal tragedy, as good books should be: of individual happiness drained to fill out the schemes for momentary

---

98. "cut" appears next to this P.S., indicating that perhaps Scott did not include it in the copy of this letter that he sent to Zelda.

99. Eleanor Lanahan, in trying to locate her grandmother's work for the book *Zelda: An Illustrated Life,* found that only one painting from this exhibit could be located; "apparently," wrote Lanahan, "Zelda's patrons pitied her and disposed of their purchases" (15).

pleasure-theories. Also, you have kept beautifully intact the personalities against so vivid a mise-en-scene that any lesser creations would have been submerged in the glitter. It is a beautiful book.

You seem afraid that it will make me recapitulate the past: remember, that at that time, I was immersed in something else—and I guess most of life is a re-hashing of the tragedies and happinesses of which it consisted in days before we started to promulgate reasons for their being so. Of cource, it is a haunting book—everything good is haunting because it calls to light something new in our consciousness

Scott: this place is most probably hidiously expensive. I *do not want you to struggle* through another burden like the one in Switzerland for my sake. You write too well. Also, you know that I live much within myself and would feel less strongly now than under normal circumstances about whatever you wanted to do. You have not got the right, for Scottie's sake, and for the sake of letters to make a drudge of yourself for me.

I'm awfully glad the pictures go well: you know the ones that are yours and I gave those white anenomies to Dr. Rennie. Also I do not want that portrait of Egorowa sold. Cary has been so nice—Ask what he would like and I will try to paint it for him. I have just finished one of the Plage at Antibes. Maybe you'd like to swop it for your foot-ball players—though it is not so good—

Love
Zelda.

145. **TO SCOTT**   ALS, 4 pp.
[May 1934]   [Craig House, Beacon, New
                                York]

Dearest:

You sounded so all-in over the telephone. Please *don't*. If you want to ally yourself with a progressive aesthetic movement, you will *have* to not pay any attention to those static commentaries on the moment which is the business of newspaper critics, etc. I read you that lovely passage from Aristotle about men loving their reasons for living more than what they loved. It was like Dick Diver. There is also a beautiful and moving passage in Plato concerning the political unsuccess of the oligarchy, tunocracy[?] etc; which seems relevant to your particular purpose. You will find the page turned down if you want to read it. It concerns the fallibility of human nature. It is very poignant and is what killed my curiosity to read Karl Marx. Your book is a beautiful and moving story of a man's disillusionment and its relative values against the social back-ground in which he counts most. So don't pay any attention to the people who have never felt the individual responsibility of conforming to opinions dealing in futures[?] or the necessity of passing judgment on the present but be glad that you have successfully recorded our times and an ego meeting as best it could the compromises that killed it, eventually.

Besides all of which, it is expressed in an ecstatic and aspirational prose that I guess most critics are too absorbed in earning a living to yield the tempo of journalism to—

It was silly to get Bill Warren to work on the scenario—but I hope it will be good. Having a certain flare for the dramatic the boy has chosen to use it for theatrics. Yours, is a psychological drama and I'm sure Dr. Rennie would have been of lots more help—because the material is all there: "the difference between what is and what might have been," says Baker, makes a play.

However, it's none of my business. What *is* my business is that, under the circumstances, I do not see how you can reasonably expect me to go on unworriedly spending god-knows-how-much-a-day when we haven't got it to spend. You must realize to that one as ill as I am, one place is not very different from another and that I would appreciate your working whatever adjustments would rend[er] your life less difficult—

Love Zelda

146. TO SCOTT   ALS, 3 pp.
[May 1934]   [Craig House, Beacon, New
                            York]

Dearest Do-Do

Whenever you are ready to make the change, I will be ready to go. I am awfully home-sick in spite of the beauties of this place. If you do not feel up to making the trip, I am sure Dr. Slocum[100] could arrange some way that might spare you the expense of coming up after me.

---

100. The head physician at Craig House.

Although Zelda's letter reads lucidly, her handwriting reveals that her condition was worsening. Courtesy of Princeton University Library

D. O: you know that I do not feel as you do about state institutions. Dr. Myers and, I suppose, many excellent doctors did their early training there. You will have to conceal as much of this from Scottie as you can anyway. So, in the words of Ernest Hemmingway, *save yourself*. That is what I want you to do. You have had a terrible financial struggle lately, and if there were any way that I could relieve you of any part of the burden, you know how gladly I would contribute any cooperation—which seems[?] to be all I have to offer.

I am so glad your book is on the list of best sellers.[101] Maybe now you will have some measure of that ease and security you have so long deserved. Anyway, I hope it sells and sells

Devotedly

Zelda

SHEPPARD AND ENOCH PRATT HOSPITAL, TOWSON, MARYLAND,
MAY 19, 1934–APRIL 7, 1936

On May 19, 1934, Zelda transferred from Craig House to Sheppard-Pratt, where she would remain for nearly two years. The hospital grounds actually bordered the Turnbull estate and La Paix, where Zelda and Scott had lived earlier. Therefore, the countryside was familiar and reassuring to her; and Scott, who was still living at 1307 Park Avenue in Baltimore, was only a few minutes away. Unhappy that he had seen Zelda only twice while she was at Craig House, he

---

101. Even though *Tender Is the Night* made the top ten best-seller list, the royalties were meager and did little to help Scott pay his debts.

reluctantly agreed to Zelda's doctors' request that he not visit her during the first two weeks. Zelda was deeply depressed, appeared apathetic, and began slipping into a frighteningly disoriented condition in which she experienced aural hallucinations. Empathizing with Zelda's despair—which resembled his own, the publication of his novel having failed to lift him out of his depression—Scott tried to draw her back into sanity by encouraging her to organize her work.

Two gaps exist in this section of letters: first, from the fall of 1934 until February of 1935, during which Scott was allowed to make frequent visits to the hospital and Zelda was able to spend Christmas at home with Scott and Scottie, making letters unnecessary; and then again from the fall of 1935 to April 1936, when Zelda began alternating between a religious mania, during which she was often incoherent, and a depressive silence in which she spoke to no one. Meanwhile, Scott went through the motions of living and even had a brief affair with Beatrice Dance, a wealthy married woman he met in Asheville, North Carolina. But his own already problematic health weakened as he continued to drink. An April 1936 Ledger entry—"Me caring about no one nothing" (*Ledger* 197)—summed up his despair.

147. TO ZELDA   TL (CC), 4 pp.

1307 Park Avenue,
Baltimore, Maryland,
May 31, 1934.

Talked with Dr. Murdoch[102] on the phone and he thought that you were worrying about my worrying about you—if you can get that complicated point. I am always worrying about you and Scottie when you are not near me but that is simply a temperamental peculiarity that I have gotten used to. It is just worrying for worrying's sake and is not founded on any reality. Actually I am very cheered by the thought that you are within hearing distance again and am looking forward to the time when you will be closer than that. Life here has been very tranquil. Have made one of my usual mistakes in judgment in embarking on

---

102. Dr. Harry M. Murdock, a psychiatrist at the University of Maryland Medical School in Baltimore.

about five mutually exclusive enterprises: 1. a *Post* story,[103] 2. a second story for the *Red Book*,[104] 3. a funny offer from United Artists to jazz up some episode from Cellini's biography to help the sale of the picture release which is imminent,[105] 4. an idea of staging Ring's short plays — which has just come out with Gilbert Seldes doing the editing.[106] I am thinking of lopping off the two last and getting down to business.

The trip to Virginia Beach was a complete flop as far as weather was concerned — we ran into what amounted to a very dismal mistral — and while, as you know, I always love to see the Taylor clan,[107] things were all indoors. Perhaps it was just as well because Scottie, being inflicted with poison ivy on her bottom, didn't have to see other people using the surf for a good time. However, I sat around and smoked too much and got no special profit out of the trip.

While I think of it I am enclosing a letter from Tommy Hitchcock[108] which came with his check for the drawing he bought. I opened it by mistake.

To go back to domestic matters, Scottie is in good health generally and my plan is, roughly, to send her for a week that will elapse between her examinations and the beginning of a camp down to Norfolk with Cousin Ceci who would devote good attention to her and to board them at some reasonable hotel at Virginia Beach. That is to avoid a whole week here where I would have to spend much of my time playing nurse maid for her because I do not entirely like the way the children of this neighborhood behave when they run loose and the business of transportation out to the suburban districts is a little onerous especially on Saturday afternoons and Sundays when Mrs. Owens is not here. By the way she has just been invited to spend the week-end after examinations with the Ridgelys. About the camps, she seems to want to go to one of the bigger ones so I suppose she will go to either Aloha or Wyonegonic, both of which I started to investigate last year. I am still hoping that we can go to Europe toward the latter half of the summer, even if only

103. Possibly "No Flowers" published in the July 21, 1934, issue of the *Saturday Evening Post*.

104. Scott was writing stories about a medieval soldier of fortune named Philippe. The second story, out of a series of four, was "The Count of Darkness," which *Redbook* published in June 1935.

105. Fitzgerald did not accept this offer.

106. This project did not transpire.

107. Scott's cousin Cecilia Taylor's family.

108. A pilot and polo player, Hitchcock was also a war hero and was to have escaped German capture by jumping off a moving train; he was one of the models for the character Tommy Barban in *Tender Is the Night*.

for six weeks, whether we decide to go alone or leave Scottie in camp.

We went to tea at the Woodwards yesterday. I got into a heavy political argument with a Hitlerite. Then our incessant friend, Madam Swann,[109] telephoned for Scottie and me to come there for dinner, which we did and which reinforced my feeling that she is a beheaded poullet trying to do her best but without any consistent method.

Honey, may I ask you seriously to control your reading, not going in so much for heavy books or books that refer you back to those dark hours in Paris? I know what ill effects on my ease, sleep, appetite, etc. can be caused by getting disturbed by something I've read and I should guess that would be doubly true in a case like yours where you are trying to get a real rest cure. However, the doctors will probably keep an eye on that.

148. TO SCOTT
[Early June 1934]

ALS, 2 pp.
[Sheppard and Enoch Pratt
Hospital, Towson, Maryland]

Dearest:

I am so glad all goes as well as could be expected—and I am miserable in thinking of the unhappiness my illness has caused you. I will cooperate to the best of my ability with the doctors and do all that I can to achieve a quick recovery.

Darling—I feel very disoriented and lonely. I love you, dearheart. Please try to love me some in spite of these stultifying years of sickness—and I will compensate you some way for your love and faithfullness.

I'm sorry Scottie has had poison ivy. The other day when I kissed her good-bye the little school-child scent of her neck and her funny little hesitant smile broke my heart. Be good to her Do-Do.

Dr. Murdock tells me you will be here until fall. Darling: I want so to see you. Maybe sometimes before very long I will be well enough to meet you under the gracious shadows of these trees and we can look out on the distant fields to-gether. And I will be getting better—

Dearest Love
Zelda

---

109. Rita Swann, a newspaper journalist, theater enthusiast, and Park Avenue neighbor of Scott's in Baltimore; she was the wife of artist Don Swann.

149. TO SCOTT　　　　　　　ALS, 2 pp.
[After June 9, 1934]　　　　　[Sheppard and Enoch Pratt
　　　　　　　　　　　　　　　　Hospital, Towson, Maryland]

Dearest Do-Do—

I was amused to read in the New Yorker the praise of Gilbert for his recognition of Ring.[110] Never mind: your biography will be written. Dr. Ellgin[111] said you wanted me to read more so I am reading: The Alchemist and Edward II—also I am absorbed in the travel adds. For $600 (2) dollars we could go to Oberamagau, tourist class via Berlin + Munich—including all expenses for a 3 wks trip. *We could*! I look nostalgicly on all the sun-burned people in the advertizements lolling on boats and beaches and think of the good times we only half appreciated. They are so young and soignées in the pictures.

It seems rather Proustian to be rambling these deep shades again so close to La Paix. It makes me sad, but it is a lovely landscape—the trees, and clouds like cotton-candy, very still and festive about the clover. And I think of your book and it haunts me. So beautiful a book.

I wish we could spend July by the sea, browning ourselves and feeling water-weighted hair flow behind us from a dive. I wish our gravest troubles were the summer gnats. I wish we were hungry for hot-dogs and dopes[112] and it would be nice to smell the starch of summer linens and the faint odor of talc in blistering bath-houses. Or we could go to the Japanese Gardens with Kay Laurel and waste a hundred dollars staging conceptions of gaiety. We could lie in long citroneuse beams of the five o'clock sun on the plage at Juan-les-Pins and hear the sound of the drum and piano being scooped out to sea by the waves. Dust and alfalfa in Alabama, pines and salt at Antibes, the lethal smells of city streets in summer, buttered pop-corn and axel grease at Coney Island and Virginia beach—and the sick-sweet smells of old gardens at night, verbena or phlox or night-blooming stock—we could see if all those are still there.

It is rather disquieting to read of the importance of bangs and linen

---

110. Gilbert Seldes wrote the preface for Ring Lardner's *First and Last*, a posthumous collection of his nonfiction work for newspapers and magazines. It was published in the spring of 1934. Clifton Fadiman reviewed the book in *The New Yorker* on June 9. Scott was approached about this project first, but, occupied with his own writing, he encouraged Seldes to promote Lardner's work.

111. Dr. William Elgin, Zelda's doctor at Sheppard-Pratt.

112. Southern slang for spiked cola drinks.

handkerchiefs, new brands of perfume and new lines to bathing-suits in the papers. *I wish I had something*—D. O!

When are you coming to see me?

Love, darling, and love to my sweet little Scottie

Zelda

150. TO SCOTT   ALS, 1 p.
[June 1934]   [Sheppard and Enoch Pratt
                Hospital, Towson, Maryland]

Dearest Do-Do—

I miss you so. I look out over this dreamy summer panorama and I miss you. I think of the leaves rustling about the top of the gums at "La Paix" and I am so sorry for the unhappy times we had in that house and I am lonesome for the sense that you are near. These billowy blue skies dragging the hot fields behind like some fantastic dredge for the June hours and the rhodendrun so pompously bursting the shadows overwhelm me with a sense of how many nice things there are. And I wish we could be going some place together—

Mrs Turnbull sent me a lovely basket of flowers a couple of weeks ago. Could Mrs. Owen's phone and thank her for me?

I suppose Scottie has gone. I hate to think of you all alone in the house. Why don't you go some nice place for summer? All gay with guitars, a world swung above black, reflecting water beneath a dance pavillion would make you feel young again—or maybe some new way.

If you'll send Scottie's address I'd like to write her when I'm better. I hope she didn't disappoint you in school.

Love, my darling—

Zelda

151. TO ZELDA   TL (CC), 4 pp.

1307 Park Avenue,
Baltimore, Maryland,
June 13, 1934.

Dear Zelda:

I am dictating this letter because there is so much that it's got to cover and I want you to have it there for reference because each point is important.

First and foremost I called Perkins this morning on an idea that I have had for a long time which is the publication of a representative group of your short pieces.[113] I want to do this if only for the salutary effect on you of keeping your hand in during this period of inaction. I did not call Max with the idea of getting him to publish such a collection which, since he is committed to an amalgamation of mine for the same season,[114] he naturally would shy away from it but with the idea that he could suggest a publisher who would take a chance on the idea. I break off here to include a suggestion for the general line up of the book:

   Table of Contents
   Introduction by F. Scott Fitzgerald (about 500 words)

   I. Eight Women   (These character sketches and stories appeared in *College Humor, Scribner's* and *Saturday Evening Post* between 1927 and 1931, one of them appeared under my name but actually I had nothing to do with it except for suggesting a theme and working on the proof of the completed manuscript. This same cooperation extends to other material gathered herein under our joint names, though often when published in that fashion I had nothing to do with the thing from start to finish except supplying my name.)

---

113. The project Scott outlined in this letter never came to fruition, but it still served to improve Zelda's mental state. In 1973, Scribners published *Bits of Paradise*, twenty-two uncollected stories by F. Scott and Zelda Fitzgerald, which included many, but not all, of the pieces Scott listed here.
114. *Taps at Reveille*, a collection of Scott's stories published in March 1935.

The Original Follies Girl	(about 2000 words)	
The Girl the Prince Liked	" 2500	"
The Southern Girl	" 2250	"
The Girl with Talent	" 3500	"
The Millionaire's Girl	" 8000	"
Miss Bessie[115]	" 4000	"
A Couple of Nuts	" 4000	"

(There will also be joined to this two hitherto unpublished stories which are also character studies of modern females.)[116]

II. Three Fables[117] (estimated about 5000 words)

The Drought and the Flood

A Workman

The House

III. Recapitulation

Show Mr. and Mrs. F. to Number—

Auction Model 1934

———————————

All in all about 50,000 words. This will give you plenty of work for the next three or four weeks if you can find time for it, especially that item of the two possible stories which I am afraid will have to go through some more revision to measure up to the rest. I am having Mrs. Owens send you (a) All living copies of your Mary McCall story.

(b) All living copies of your Katherine Littlefield story.[118]

In the first case I think you have got to cut out the mystical element about the dogs because the story itself is so haunted by suggestion of more or less natural vice that the introduction of the supernatural seems excessive and breaks the pattern. In the second case my feeling is that it is largely a question of cutting "down to its bare bones." I am seldom wrong about the value of a narrative and feel that my continued faith in this one is not misplaced. It may take two workings over, but the first one is undoubtedly stripping it to its girders and then seeing what, if any, plaster you want to slap on it. These two stories would seem to be necessary to make up the bulk of a volume, the aim of which is to compete with such personal collections of miscellany as Dorothy Parker's, etc. The very fact that the

———————————

115. Published as "Miss Ella."
116. Unidentified.
117. Unpublished.
118. McCall and Littlefield stories not published.

material is deeply personal rather than detached and professional make it expedient that it be presented in some such way as this.

This letter has been interrupted by having a phone conversation with the small publisher (respectable, but with[119]

152. TO SCOTT
[After June 14, 1934]

ALS, 3 pp.
[Sheppard and Enoch Pratt
Hospital, Towson, Maryland]

Dearest Do-Do:

Do-Do you are so sweet to do those stories for me. Knowing the energy and interest you have put into other people's work, I know how much trouble you make appear so easy. Darling—

I will correct the stories as soon as I can—though you know this is a very regimented system we live under with every hour accounted for and not much time for outside interests. There was a better, later version of the dance story—but maybe I can shift this one since I remember it.

You talk of the function of art. I wonder if anybody has ever got nearer the truth than Aristotle: he said that all emotions and all experience were common property—that the transposition of these into form was individual and art. But, God, it's so involved by whether you aim at direct or indirect appeals and whether the emotional or the cerebral is the most compelling approach, and whether the shape of the edifice or the purpose for which it is designated is paramount that my conceptions are in a sad state of flux. At any rate, it seems to me the artists business is to take a willing mind and guide it to hope or despair contributing *not* his interpretations but a glimpse of his honestly earned scars of battle and his rewards. I am still adamant against the interpretive school. Nobody but educators can show people how to think—but to open some new facet of the stark emotions or to preserve some old one in the grace of a phrase seem nearer the artistic end. You know how a heart will rise or fall to the lilt of an a-laden troche or the sonorous dell of an o—and where you will use these business secrets certainly depends on the author's special eval-

---

119. The rest of the page has been torn off and is missing.

uations. That was what I was trying to accomplish with the book I began: I wanted to say "This is a love story—maybe not your love story—maybe not even mine, but this is what happened to one isolated person in love. There is no judgment."—I don't know—abstract emotion is difficult of transcription, and one has to find so many devices to carry a point that the point is too often lost in transit.

I wrote you a note which I lost containing the following facts

1) The Myers have gone to Antibes with the Murphys—

2) Malco[l]m Cowley arrested for rioting in N.Y.

3) I drink milk, one glass of which I consider equal to six banannas under water or two sword-swallowings—

There didn't seem to be anything else to write you except that I love you. We have a great many activities of the kind one remembers pleasantly afterwards but which seem rather vague at the time like pea-shelling and singing. For some reason, I am very attached to this country-side. I love the clover fields and the click of base-ball bats in the deep green cup of the field and the sky as blue and idyllic as parts of your prose. I keep hoping that you will be in some of the cars that ruffle the shade of the sycamores. Dr. Ellgin said you would come soon.

It will be grand to see Mrs. Owens—I wish it were you and Scottie. Darling.

Don't you think "Eight Women" is too big a steal from Dreiser[120]—I like, ironicly, "My Friends" or "Girl Friends" better. Do you suppose I could design the jacket. It's very exciting.

My reading seems to have collapsed at "The Alchemist." I really don't care much for characters named for the cardinal sins or cosmic situations. However I will get on with it—

Thanks again about the book—and *everything*—In my file there are two other fantasies and the story about the judge to which I am partial—and I would be most grateful if you would read "Theatre Ticket"[121] to see if it could be sold to a magazine maybe—

Love

Zelda.

Why didn't you go to reunion?

Do you think the material is too dissimilar for a collection? It worries me.

---

120. Theodore Dreiser's *Twelve Men* (1919).
121. Unidentified.

153. **TO SCOTT**　　　　　ALS, 2 pp.
[Late June 1934]　　　　[Sheppard and Enoch Pratt
　　　　　　　　　　　　　Hospital, Towson, Maryland]

Mon chère Monsieur:

Here are some titles—Maybe you can paste them on the unidentifiable bottles in the medicine cabinet if they don't seem to apply

1) Even Tenor
2) Rainy Sunday
3) How It Was.
4) Ways It Was—

I admit frankly that they are not much good, but then neither am I at quick invention. I will let you know if the next brain storm should bring to light something more pertinent—

"Authors Wife" sounds as if it's an intimate revelation of the blacker side of how we writers live. Again I admit frankly it makes me sick. For your book,[122] would it be a good idea to add up how much those stories brought in and call the book "Eighty Thousand Dollars"—ho! Or "Words"—(sounds to experimental)—and I don't know what to call *anything*. Had I a pet canary, he should be nameless—Call it a day—There are some fine ideas for titles in the Victor record catalogue—which is where I found "Save Me the Waltz"—

Couldn't Scottie come swimming next time with Mrs Owens—if she's back? I keep hoping you'll show up but you don't—and neither does Christmas or other holidays before their time, I suppose.

I am become an expert seamstress and laundress and am, in fact, thoroughly equipped to make you exactly the kind of wife you most detest. However, I am going to read Karl Marx so we can give a parade if the day of exodus ever arrives—bombs on the house, and a cigar for every Lord Mayor you hit.

Well—

Recevez, Monsieur, mes felicitations les plus distinguées—

And many thanks for the perfectly useless check to Mrs Owens. Now that the blind tiger is no more, I couldn't think of any place to cash it so I tore it up as emotionally and dramaticly as $34.50

---

122. *Taps at Reveille.*

seemed to warrant—Of cource, a hundred would have made a better scene—

With deepest devotion—
Love
Zelda.

154. TO SCOTT   AL, 1 p.
[Summer 1934]   [Sheppard and Enoch Pratt
                           Hospital, Towson, Maryland]

Dearest Do-Do—

I am so glad your letter sounded so well and cheerful. It made me
very homesick—your sweet boyancy always holds so much promise
of bright and happy things in such a vital world. It will be grand to
see you and Scottie again. This month has begun, inevitably, to seem
rather endless, though I realize that that is an ungrateful attitude.

Here, we pursue our ways. There is nothing to report—croquet in
the late afternoon sun while the big trees swing, rocking shadows
down the lawn. Life is idle. Yesterday we took a long ride around
familiar roads and it seemed so unreal not to be going home to La
Paix—Men rake the rhythm of summer through the clods of a new
putting green; we play base-ball, and in the distance the fields con-
form to futurists patterns and mash each other lop-sided in their
scramble down the valley.

I wrote Mrs. Turnbull; I wrote her an eulogy on the iris. Passing
the old barn, the place has, in spite of everything, the pleasantest
associations. I am sorry it was such a night-mare to you. I wish we
knew what we were going to do—and when—and how long

It's grand about the books. Judging from the papers, the British
Empire seems to be succumbing to a cruel nemesis—I hope the book
will have a big sale. Darling, darling,—you deserve something so
nice. I wish I had it to offer you, and maybe I will find something
inside myself for you to love—when I am better.[123]

---

123. The rest of this letter, if there was more, is missing.

"Those feathers—those wonderful, wonderful feathers are the most beautiful things on earth—"
— Zelda to Scott, April 1919

The ostrich feather fan Scott sent to Zelda during their courtship

Courtesy of the Lyndon B. Johnson Library and Museum, Austin, Texas, and Eleanor Lanahan

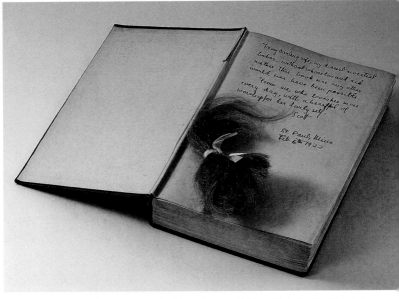

The Beautiful and Damned, inscribed from Scott to Zelda, with lock of Zelda's hair

Courtesy of Eleanor Lanahan

The Hotel Belles-Rives in Juan-les-Pins, one of the places the Fitzgeralds lived during their sojourn on the French Riviera

Courtesy of Tom Adams

"Do you know, by any chance where my star-necklance is? Always my love, I always envested that necklace with a deep romantic appeal: endowed as it was with the property of story."
— Zelda, August 1940

"Dearest Zelda: I have the star necklace here and will send it to you parcel post tomorrow."
— Scott, August 1940

The star necklace Scott gave to Zelda, along with a jade scarab and enameled gold ring that also belonged to her

Courtesy of Eleanor Lanahan

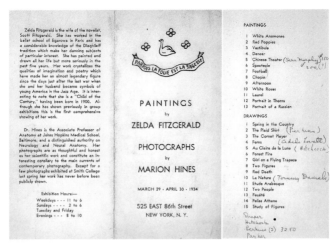

The program from Zelda's art exhibit, March 29–April 30, 1934, with Scott's notations on who bought the paintings

Courtesy of Matthew J. and Arlyn Bruccoli Collection of F. Scott Fitzgerald, Thomas Cooper Library, University of South Carolina

Dust jacket for *Save Me the Waltz*, 1932

Courtesy of Princeton University Library

"Dear Love — I've made Scottie some wonderful paper-dolls, you and me and her. . . ."
— Zelda to Scott from Prangins Clinic, Nyon, Switzerland, Summer 1931

The family of paper dolls Zelda made for Scottie

Courtesy of Cecilia L. Ross

"Meantime violets and lillies and pink beauty blows on my canvas and I hope and wait—"
— Zelda to Scott, from Highland Hospital, Asheville,
North Carolina, February 1938

Hope, painted by Zelda, c. 1938

Courtesy of the Montgomery Museum of Fine Arts, Montgomery, Alabama. Gift of the artist

"I would like to hear of your painting again and I meant it when I said next summer if the war is settled down you ought to have another exhibition."

—Scott to Zelda, September 21, 1940

Great Smoky Mountains, painted by Zelda, 1940s

Courtesy of Eleanor Lanahan

The Fitzgeralds' grave, St. Mary's Catholic Church and Cemetery, Rockville, Maryland

Courtesy of David B. Barks

155. TO SCOTT　　　　　　　ALS, 1 p.
[Late Summer/Early Fall 1934]　[Sheppard and Enoch Pratt
　　　　　　　　　　　　　　　　Hospital, Towson, Maryland]

Darling:

I am so glad you went to Doctor Hamman[124]—Your legs were so thin that day and I hate to think of you working and working until your clothes seem so patheticly too big—I wish you'd go away with Max[125] and fill them full of breezes from a cool nocturnal forest. You could have pine trees in a cloister and little inlays of the brightest saphire twilight and there could [be] cascades making vowel sounds for you to fish in. And the water could churn the light to a lovely foam—and you could be going through motions to which you are unused and that always makes the whole world seem an experimental process.

There's nothing to put in a letter except the summer clouds and the sky billowing above the tennis courts. I play all day and am inaugurating the charming custom of paying no attention at all to the lines. The first leaves are falling on the waters of Meadowbrook—and I think of Gatsby on his fine pneumatic mattress—and of you writing in rooms in France with late fires burning till morning and in the stereotype blur of 59th street and at La Paix behind the vines

I'm sad because I can't write—

　　Love and Love and Love,
　　darling
　　Zelda

156. TO SCOTT　　　　　　　ALS, 4 pp.
[October 1934]　　　　　　　　[Sheppard and Enoch Pratt
　　　　　　　　　　　　　　　　Hospital, Towson, Maryland]

Dearest Do-Do—

Thanks for your letter. Since you are slowly dissolving into a mythical figure over the long period of years that have elapsed since two weeks ago, I will tell you about myself:

---

124. Unidentified.
125. Maxwell Perkins.

1) I am lonesome.

2) I have no relatives or friends and would like to make acquaintance with a Malayian warrior.

3) I do not cook or sew or commit nuisances about the house

The Sheppard Pratt hospital is located somewhere in the hinterlands of the human consciousness and I can be located there any time between the dawn of consciousness and the beginning of old age.

Darling: Life is difficult. There are so many problems. 1) The problem of how to stay here and 2) The problem of how to get out. And I want so desperately to go to Guatemala still and ride a bicycle to the end of a long white road. The road is lined with lebanon cedars and poplars and ancient splendors crumble down the parched bleached hills and natives sleep in the shade beside a high grey wall. Whereas here Grace Moore[126] sings very prettily over the radio and obscure kings get themselves killed by what I am convinced are Mussolinis henchmen so that Lowell Thomas[127] will not disappoint the old ladies — It is all very depressing

We had a swell ride through the woods very proudly aflame with a last desperate flamboyance. The paths are like tunnels through the secrets of a precious stone, all green and gold and red and under the maples the world is amber.

Can we go to the Russian ballet? or can I go with Mrs Owens? or will you ask Father Christmas to bring me a Russian ballet — or have the cook put some in the next pudding — or *something*.

I liked New Types.[128] The girl was nice with breezes in her bangs. Like all your stories there was something haunting to remember: about the lonliness of keeping Faiths — I love your credos — and your stories. I meant to write you about The Darkest Hour.[129] It was sort of stark and swell and full of the pressure of history in the making — but I would have liked more description and less of the battle. Mrs. Ridgely took me to see the hunt start. There is a story in that atmosphere — There is a grandfather little and guarded like the Pope and Miss Leidy of the love letters here in the hospital and none of them fought in the Civil War. Of cource, it might not be Family history but its an awfully good story.[130]

---

126. Opera singer and actress.
127. Radio news commentator and author.
128. "New Types," *Saturday Evening Post*, September 22, 1934.
129. "In the Darkest Hour," a Philippe story that appeared in *Redbook*, October 1934.
130. The fourth page of Zelda's letter is the sketch of Scott shown below, entitled "Do-Do In Guatemala."

The fourth page of Zelda's letter, with her sketch,
"Do-Do in Guatemala." Courtesy of Princeton University Library

157. TO SCOTT   ALS, 2 pp. (fragment)
[After February 1935]   [Sheppard and Enoch Pratt
                              Hospital, Towson, Maryland]

some forgotten nursery rhyme. There are human bodies without
identities as I am myself. But I hope life is very important in your
hotel; that the lobby is full of people making estimates of each one's
worldly goods. Places where life transpires under a cloud of suspicion are more exciting. Your interest, inexhaustible, tolerant and
expansive, has always made anywhere a desirable spot.

D. O.—take care of yourself. I wish I could have done it better.
You have never believed me when I said I was sorry—but I am.

Some day soon you will be well + happy again. Maybe you will
be at Norfolk, salty and sun-burned. Your eyes will glow in the
darkened room and the hum and drone of deepest summer will

seep in under the blinds. Sand in the bath-tub, sticky lotion and a towel for your shoulders. I'll have to sprawl on my stomach till this sun-burn clears away and cut the sleeves from my softest shirt. Your hair is so gold against your golden skin. And your legs stick to-gether as you sit with them crossed. The room is so still because of the vibrance of the heat outside. Have a good time. Of cource it's cooler in the grill, and clandestine, and there are gusts of bottled breezes.

North Carolina should be pines and pebbles, geraniums and red tile roofs—and very concise. Breathe in the blue skies. It's a good place to get up early; there's a very polished sun to burnish the mountain laurel before breakfast. And the brooks gleam cold in the thin early shadows. Biscuits and grits all floating in butter; resin on your hands and frogs bouncing out of the twilight.

D. O.—

D. O.—

What is there to say? You know how much I have loved you.

Zelda

158. TO SCOTT
[June 1935]

ALS, 4 pp.
[Sheppard and Enoch Pratt
        Hospital, Towson, Maryland]

Dearest and always

Dearest Scott:

I am sorry too that there should be nothing to greet you but an empty shell. The thought of the effort you have made over me, the suffering this *nothing* has cost would be unendurable to any save a completely vacuous mechanism. Had I any feelings they would all be bent in gratitude to you and in sorrow that of all my life there should not even be the smallest relic of the love and beauty that we started with to offer you at the end.

You have been so good to me—and all I can say is that there was always that deeper current running through my heart: my life—you.

You remember the roses in Kinneys yard[131]—you were so gracious

---

131. Zelda is reminiscing about their courtship in Montgomery.

and I thought "he is the sweetest person in the world" and you said "darling." You still are. The wall was damp and mossy when we crossed the street and said we loved the south. I thought of the south and a happy past I'd never had and I thought I was part of the south. You said you loved this lovely land. The wistaria along the fence was green and the shade was cool and life was old.

—I wish I had thought something else—but it was a confederate, a romantic and nostalgic thought. My hair was damp when I took off my hat and I was safe and home and you were glad that I felt that way and you were reverent. We were gold and happy all the way home.

Now that there isn't any more happiness and home is gone and there isnt even any past and no emotions but those that were yours where there could be any comfort—it is a shame that we should have met in harshness and coldness where there was once so much tenderness and so many dreams. Your song.

I wish you had a little house with hollyhocks and a sycamore tree and the afternoon sun imbedding itself in a silver tea-pot. Scottie would be running about somewhere in white, in Renoir, and you will be writing books in dozens of volumes. And there will be honey still for tea, though the house should not be in Granchester—[132]

I want you to be happy—if there were justice you would be happy—maybe you will be anyway—

Oh, Do-Do

    Do-Do—

       Zelda.

I love you anyway—even if there isn't any me or any love or even any life—

    I love you.

---

132. The last line of Rupert Brooke's 1912 poem "The Old Vicarage, Grantchester" is "And is there honey still for tea?"

159. TO SCOTT   ALS, 1 p.
[Summer 1935]   [Sheppard and Enoch Pratt
                              Hospital, Towson, Maryland]

My dearest Sweetheart:

There is no way to ask you to forgive me for the misery and pain which I have caused you. I can only ask you to believe that I have done the best I could and that since we first met I have loved you with whatever I had to love you with. You are always my darling. I want you to be happy again with Scottie—someplace where it is bright and happy and you can have some of the things you have worked so hard for—always all your life and faithfully. *You* are my dream; the only pleasant thing in my life.

Do-Do—my darling! Please get well and love Scottie and find something to fill up your life—

    My Love,
    my Love
    my Love
    Zelda.

160. TO SCOTT   ALS, 2 pp.
[Summer 1935]   [Sheppard and Enoch Pratt
                              Hospital, Towson, Maryland]

Dearest Do-Do:

Sometimes, at this dusty time of year the flowers and trees take on the aspect of flowers and trees drifted from other summers: the dusty shuttered back of the hotel at Antibes, those roads that cradled the happier suns of a long time ago. I wish we could go there again. Of cource if you invited me to North Carolina it would be very nice too. In my last despair of ever being asked any place I am going to write Mamma and ask if I can visit.

Wouldn't you like to smell the pine woods of Alabama again? Remember there were 3 pines on one side and 4 on the other the night you gave me my birthday party and you were a young lieutenant and I was a fragrant phantom, wasn't I? And it was a radiant night, a night of soft conspiracy and the trees agreed that it was all going to be for the best. Remember the faded gray romance. And the beneficence of the trees which sighed together that they would or they wouldn't for we could never make out inform[?] the fates for or against us—Darling. That's the first time I ever said that in my life.

I hope you are better—I hope so—and I hope you are—For all I know is that you are a darling—

Zelda

161. TO SCOTT   ALS, 1 p.
[September 1935]   [Sheppard and Enoch Pratt
                                   Hospital, Towson, Maryland]

Dearest Do-Do:

Since writing you, Dr. Murdock has been here. He says:

1) He does not advise my coming to Ashville *but*

2) He will permit my going to see Mamma. The implication was for a short visit—but

Some arrangements have got to be made for this winter. You forgot or something to tell me what Scottie is going to do and as she will soon be back, I would like to know.

Do you think I could take her to Ala. for the winter? Of cource I only want to on the condition that we cant possibly any way in the world be to-gether—

In fact, Do Do, I don't know what's happening any more *and*

I wish you could arrange at least a week-end to-gether. The Dr. seemed to feel that you weren't well enough—and of cource I trust his judgment but somebody's got to see her in school somewhere

Darling Darling

I love you—

Please write me as soon as you can

Love

Zelda

162. TO SCOTT   ALS, 1 p.
[Fall 1935]   [Sheppard and Enoch Pratt
                         Hospital, Towson, Maryland]

Dearest Do-Do—

From such an empty world there seems nothing to send beyond the jaunty decolade of turning falling first autumn leaves. From everywhere a vast echo vibrates—strange familiar twang, but one only vaguely distinguishes the sounds. That is because autumn is a sad time and all times are sad from their transience.

It was so good to see you fatter and wood-land-y in silver green and gray, the colors of an olive grove—and will always be so. We have shared so many words and hopes and phrases for the outwitting of things we haven't shared—you must know how I miss the games we played.

Won't you send me some condensed versions of Aristotle and again the chronological list you promised? So I can get on with wisdom—

Love, darling—Love—
Zelda.

Notwithstanding the nostalgic moments Scott spent with Zelda, his health problems made it necessary to relocate. In November 1935, Scott wrote to Harold Ober from Hendersonville, North Carolina, near Asheville: "I am here till I finish a Post story. . . . I was beginning to cough again in Baltimore . . . also to drink . . . I am living here at a $2.00 a day hotel . . ." (Life in Letters *292). By early December, he wrote Ober, he had decided to move to Asheville as soon as possible:*

> *. . . I shall move to Asheville . . . + have the doctor go over me while I write. I arrived here weak as hell, got the grippe + spat blood again (1st time in 9 months) + took to bed for six days. . . . I'm grateful I came south when I did though—I made a wretched mistake in coming north in Sept + taking that apartment + trying 1000 things at once. . . . How that part (I mean living in Balt.) is going to work out I don't know. I'm going to let Scotty finish her term anyhow. For the rest things depend on health + money + its very difficult. I use up my health making money + then my money in recovering health.* (Life in Letters *293)*

HIGHLAND HOSPITAL, ASHEVILLE, NORTH CAROLINA,
APRIL 1936–DECEMBER 1938

In the 1930s, Asheville, North Carolina, and the surrounding area were considered a fashionable vacation spot. Luckily, an innovative facility for the mentally ill, the Highland Hospital, had been established there. Zelda's doctors in Baltimore were well acquainted with the hospital's founder and director, Dr. Robert S. Carroll, and agreed that it would be an ideal setting for her. Zelda had gone to nearby Saluda—a historic Victorian summer retreat in the Blue Ridge Mountains—with her family while growing up. Her mother and her sister Rosalind continued to vacation there, making summer visits with Zelda, once she was settled into Highland, something to which everyone looked forward.

After a period of severe depression, Zelda experienced a religious mania that would characterize much of the rest of her life and become the dominant theme of her later paintings, many of her letters to Scott, and her subsequent attempts at fictions. During the last years of her life, Zelda worked on a novel she entitled "Caesar's Things," in which she once again fictionalized the same autobiographical events as in *Save Me the Waltz*, this time imposing a biblical pattern on them. There were times when Zelda would dress only in white, and when visitors came, she would insist on dropping to her knees and praying with them. Rather than offering genuine comfort, such religious zeal served only to isolate her further from family and friends.

Scott candidly conveyed his view of Zelda at this time in a letter to Sara and Gerald Murphy:

> I am moving Zelda to a sanitarium in Asheville—she is no better, though the suicidal cloud was lifted. . . . Zelda now claims to be in direct contact with Christ, William the Conqueror, Mary Stuart, Appollo and all the stock paraphanalea of insane asylum jokes. Of course it isn't a bit funny but after the awful strangulation episode of last spring I sometimes take refuge in an unsmiling irony about the present *exterior* phases of her illness. For what she has really suffered there is never a sober night that I do not pay a stark tribute of an hour to in the darkness. In an odd way, perhaps incredible to you, she was always my child . . . my child in a sense that Scotty isn't, because I've brought Scotty up hard as nails. . . . Outside of

the realm of what you called Zelda's "terribly dangerous secret
thoughts" I was her great reality, often the only liason agent
who could make the world tangible to her— (*Life in Letters*
298–299)

Meanwhile, however, Scott's circumstances were dire and quickly
becoming worse; virtually every aspect of his life collapsed. He worried constantly about Zelda. Though she had periods of improvement, she got worse overall, a process both sad and frightening, and
one wholly beyond his control. He paid endless medical bills, continually wrote letters to Zelda's doctors and family about her illness, and
answered friends' inquiries about her, expressing little hope for her
recovery. He reluctantly faced the possibility that he and Zelda might
never be able to live together again. Even though their relationship
was at times a mutually destructive one, Scott's loss of Zelda's com-
panionship was immeasurable. He mourned her lost vitality and his
own. Bills continued to pile up, Scott found it increasingly hard to
earn money, and, placing himself under additional strain, he borrowed against future work.

In addition, his alcoholism accelerated and his tuberculosis
became active again, resulting in the onset of rapid physical deterioration. He repeatedly entered the hospital for treatment, but any
small progress was soon blotted out by painful relapses. In 1935,
Scott began a long period of depression, one that would last until
sometime in 1937. He had somehow endured all his previous disappointments and frustrations, but with his depression came a loss of
emotional intensity, a dearth of all feelings save worthlessness, and
this was beyond all endurance. Fearing that he would never again be
able to write, he experienced a complete collapse of identity. It was at
this point that Scott withdrew to a cheap hotel in Hendersonville,
North Carolina, and, while living off apples and tin cans of meat,
wrote the three essays that make up "The Crack-Up" sequence: "The
Crack-Up," "Pasting It Together," and "Handle with Care," published in the February, March, and April 1936 issues of *Esquire*.

Scott's motive for writing the essays was, in part, to end the painful
sense of isolation he felt: "I wanted to put a lament into my record,"
he wrote in "Pasting It Together," "without even the background of
the Euganean Hills to give it color" (*Crack-Up* 75). In other words, he
wanted to represent himself in the clutches of despair, offering neither heroics nor the hope of transcendence. Placing the essays in
Esquire in the 1930s was the adult equivalent of putting information

about oneself or one's peers in the college yearbook. All of Scott's friends and fellow writers read the magazine. Though he soon regretted the articles, at the time Scott needed to communicate at least indirectly with his former social network (which in itself is a sign he was struggling to find his way out). Identity, for Scott, was not detached from others and was not a private concern; personal identity was directly tied to the process of creating a self within a chosen social context. What is remarkable is that a man so intent on popularity would have revealed so much of his humiliation. But if self-assessment was one of Scott's trademark habits, so was communicating his discoveries to his contemporaries. Few of his friends recognized the courage it took.

In the first essay, Scott wrote that his "nervous reflexes" had been broken by "too much anger and too many tears," that he "was always saving or being saved," an understandable situation, and one perpetuated by the continued crisis brought about by Zelda's illness and his own drinking (though he was careful in the essay to deny any recent drinking). "I began to realize," he went on in "The Crack-Up," "that for two years my life had been drawing on resources that I did not possess, that I had been mortgaging myself physically and spiritually up to the hilt" (*Crack-Up* 71–72). In "Handle with Care," Scott deftly summed up the emotional tone, or tonelessness, of his depression: ". . . I had developed a sad attitude toward sadness, a melancholy attitude toward melancholy, and a tragic attitude toward tragedy"; he went on to say that he *"had become identified with the objects of [his] horror or compassion."* This loss of objectivity and motivation, he decided, helped to explain why it had become so hard for him to write: "identification such as this spells the death of accomplishment. . . . I could no longer fulfill the obligations that life had set for me or that I had set for myself" (*Crack-Up* 80–81).

Even at this low point, Scott's circumstances continued to decline. Negative, sometimes cruel, responses to "The Crack-Up" essays further weakened his morale. Furthermore, he and Zelda were both simply too ill for either of them to provide a real home for their daughter. That fall, Scottie, who was almost fifteen, entered the Ethel Walker School, a boarding facility in Connecticut; the Ober family become her guardians, and she lived with them when not at school. In addition, Scott's mother, who was living in Rockville, Maryland, was gravely ill, which delayed his move to Asheville. After transferring Zelda to Highland Hospital in April 1936, Scott returned to Baltimore to be near his mother. In July, when he finally made the move and settled into the

Grove Park Inn, just before Zelda's thirty-sixth birthday, he broke his right shoulder while diving into the hotel pool. After that incapacitating accident, he had another one, falling on the bathroom floor at the inn and lying there until a cold and arthritis set in. His mother died at the end of the summer, but he was still too incapacitated to go to Maryland for her funeral. She left him a little over twenty thousand dollars, money that he sorely needed; however, legal matters having to do with her estate prevented him from claiming the money for several months. When he finally did receive his inheritance and had paid off some of his debts, he was left with only about five thousand dollars. Scott summed up his situation that October in a letter begging a well-to-do friend for a loan:

> I was just about up to the breaking point financially when I came down here to Asheville. I had been seriously sick for a year and just barely recovered. . . . I was planning to spend a fairly leisurely summer, keeping my debt in abeyance on money I had borrowed on my life insurance, when I went over with Zelda . . . to a pool near here and tried a high dive . . . and split my shoulder and tore the arm from its moorings. . . . It started to heal after two weeks and I fell on it when it was soaked with sweat inside the plaster cast, and got a thing call "Miotosis" which is a form of arthritis. To make a long story short, I was on my back for ten weeks, with whole days in which I was out of bed trying to write or dictate. . . . The more I worried, the less I could write. Being one mile from Zelda, I saw her twice all summer, and was unable to go North when my Mother had a stroke and died, and later was unable to go North to put my daughter in school. . . . You have probably guessed that I have been doing a good deal of drinking. . . . (*Life in Letters* 310–311)

To make matters still worse, on September 24, Scott's fortieth birthday, a reporter visited him in his room at the Grove Park Inn and wrote a devastating article for the *New York Post,* making public one of the lowest moments in Scott's life. The headline read: THE OTHER SIDE OF PARADISE: SCOTT FITZGERALD, 40, ENGULFED IN DESPAIR; it painted a vivid portrait of the drunken author stumbling over to the highboy to pour more drinks. Scott was so upset by the story and its prominent display that he, most likely halfheartedly, attempted suicide. He explained the dark episode in a letter to Ober:

I was in bed with temp about 102 when the . . . phone rang and a voice said that this party had come all the way from N. Y to interview me. I fell for this like a damn fool, got him up, gave him a drink + and accepted his exterior manners. He had some relative with mental trouble (wife or mother) so I talked to him freely about treatments symtoms ect, about being depressed at advancing age and a little desperate about the wasted summer with this shoulder and arm. . . . I hadn't the faintest suspicion what would happen. . . . When that thing [the newspaper article] came it seemed about the end and I got hold of a morphine file and swallowed four grains enough to kill a horse. . . . I vomited the whole thing and the nurse came in + saw the empty phial + there was hell to pay. . . . I felt like a fool. (*Life in Letters* 308–309)

While Scott struggled, Zelda settled into the new routine at Highland, where slowly she began to show signs of improvement. Dr. Carroll was a firm believer in the vigorous life as treatment for mental illness. The hospital took only a small number of patients and carefully monitored their diet and exercise. The lovely grounds, nestled in the Smoky Mountains, provided an ideal place for daily hiking. After Zelda had been at Highland three months, Scott wrote Scottie: "Your mother looks five years younger and prettier and has stopped that silly praying in public," and he added hopefully, "Maybe she will still come all the way back" (Milford, *Zelda* 311). Zelda's letters from this period are full of descriptions of nature, memories of the past, and, above all, heartfelt expressions of gratitude to Scott for continually providing for her.

163. TO SCOTT
[Spring 1936]

ALS, 1 p.
[Highland Hospital, Asheville, North Carolina]

Dear Goofo—
    I am coming to life—Thanks ever so much for the canvas—There's a magnificent patch of blue sky drifting through some pines here that I'm going to paint—These open fields seem more like summer and a rich dreamy warmth of youth than toy villages on the mountain side—
      Devotedly, Zelda

164. TO SCOTT

[Spring 1936]

ALS, 2 pp., on stationery
embossed ZSF vertically along
top right edge
[Highland Hospital, Asheville,
North Carolina]

My dearest, Dearest Do-Do:

A crab apple blooms in stolid pink elegance—the elegance of effi-ciency outside my window; and the late sun is beneficent; and the soft benevolent hour of five is here. I was so happy with you yesterday. It was good to be sharing your work; the sense of finishing up in a hurry that we might start somewhere on time—so happy to be going.

You are so good to me always. And, although my acknowledgment is perhaps inadequate, still my heart knows how much you do for me. And I wish I had something to bring you in return. Some lovely pre-cious thing that you would be glad about.

Anyway, I think of you—and my constant prayer is that I shall be able to convey to you the Beauty of God—of God's concepts and of the patterns thereof in which the race is cast. Maybe some day.

In the meantime think of me as you are able; and I know always your generosity of soul and of material blessings.

And I am grateful to God for your goodness to me—

Love
Zelda

165. TO SCOTT
[Summer 1936]

ALS, 1 p.
[Highland Hospital, Asheville,
North Carolina]

Dearest Do-Do:

There is an abstract time outside the windows. It is summer time and past time—and I am very young when I didn't care. There are meadows—not fields, or farms but meadows out of books. You are such a nice Do-Do. I wish I had been what I thought I was; and so debonnaire; and so debonnaire.

I think of boat houses in Atlanta with scaffolding and big dead moons and a drink behind the boats. I thought I was happy, or, at least, there was some pleasurable sense of things being in the world to conquer.

Do-Do—you are so nice a Do-Do, though I myself am so bad I hate to write to you.

I know Ashville is nice. The mountains mean cabins to me; and old abandoned mills and a little mountain boy named Jim Bob—who used to meet me by a spring all bedded about with moss. There was an owl who scared me at night, and a corn shuck mattress and I was very homesick. Now I am desolate. I thought I was so happy. The Rocky Broad River was where I was scared of so much rushing water.

You have been so good to me. My Do-Do. I wish I had not caused so much disaster. But I know you will be happy someday.

> With whatever of nice emotions there are—
> with love and peace and a hope that
> you will soon be well—
> Zelda

166. TO SCOTT
[June 1936]

ALS, 2 pp.
[Highland Hospital, Asheville, North Carolina]

Dearest Scott—

I['m] glad that life still prepares itself on the outskirts of Metropoles—and that our growing daughter is on her way to typical American womanhood. The school sounds grand. Atmospheres of formalized appreciation are always impressive.

I envy the Murphys their trip, and everybody else who is en route. I started some minor agitation that Dr. Suitt[133] would let me go home. He's not unconvincible, but wants all sorts of affadavits and my prospects for a ticket. Won't you let me spend a week rowing in the Oak Parc aquarium, riding a rented bicycle and living casually on bread and iced-tea and black-berry jam? When the emotional sequence of a spiritual evolution disappears, the soul seems somewhat arbitrary at times and I would give anything nearly to renew the tangible evidence of having lived and cared—for June sun over the scraggly

---

133. Dr. R. Burke Suitt, a psychiatrist at Highland Hospital.

thickets and the heat gathering outside to make a summer day in Alabama.

Devotedly
Zelda

167. TO SCOTT　　　　　　　ALS, 1 p.
[June/July 1936]　　　　　　　[Highland Hospital, Asheville,
　　　　　　　　　　　　　　　　North Carolina]

Dearest Do-Do, Darling:

It was so nice to see you and to be walking in the bright sunshine to-gether. Maybe in two weeks we can go to a little sandy beach where there are deep poetic shadows under the pines and a shining musical lilt to the water—

Please take care of yourself; it would be good if we could be taking care of each other once again—it always created such a delightful confusion.

Darling, Darling—
Love to the Boo
　　　　and
I love you
Zelda

168. TO SCOTT　　　　　　　ALS, 3 pp.
[Summer 1936]　　　　　　　　[Highland Hospital, Asheville,
　　　　　　　　　　　　　　　　North Carolina]

Dearest Do-Do:

I'm sorry your mother is sick. The threatened loss of an anchor to life brings poignancy to the forgotten facets of life evolved within other horizons. Anyway, I hope your mother will be better, and I'm sorry that I can't be with you to help you, maybe, if I could. I think of you, Do-Do—and if there's any comfort in a waxen wild-rose along a brambled path I send it. The doves are condolent; and a sweetness under the translucent foliage of late afternoon would rest you and be sorry.

Ashville's hot. Pale blue crowds watched the rhododendrun parade to-day. Under an impervious Italianate sky the blaring of the bands poured forth from the hills. From the top of the building, Ashville in the midst of God's grandeur of mountains and valleys and far distances, seemed complete and self-sustained—isolated and timeless and Biblical in the tufted vastness of rolling mountain forests. It is good to see and close to our beginnings when people come from miles about, to a festival—

Scottie wrote me a sweet letter of innumerable activities of fabulous pools and miles of dances festooned about the moon—I'm so glad she's happy—

And so grateful to you for all the good things you've given to her + me—

    Devotedly
    Zelda

169. TO ZELDA   TL (CC), 1 p.
                                            Grove Park Inn,
                                            Asheville, N. C.,
                                            July 27, 1936.

Dearest,

It was too bad on your birthday that everything went so badly. I left the hotel for the hospital that morning fully intending to be back here in time to lunch with you as it looked at first like merely a severe strain that could be cured with hot applications and rest and a sling, but the x-ray showed that there was a fracture in the joint of the shoulder and a dislocation of the ball and socket arrangement of the shoulder so that it looked in the x-ray as though it were an inch and a half apart.

They sent for a bone specialist and he said it would have to be set immediately or else I would never be able to raise my arm as high as my shoulder again so they gave me gas about like when they pulled your tooth and I fell asleep thinking you were in the room and saying, "Yes, I *am* going to stay; after all it's my husband." I woke up with a plaster cast that begins below my navel, extends upward and goes west out an arm. I am practically a knight in armor and only this afternoon have been able to get out of or into a chair or bed without assistance. It has postponed all my plans a week so I will not leave here until next Sunday, the second, instead of tonight as I had planned and this will of course give me a chance to see you before I go. I am sorry your mother had indigestion the same day and served to make our birthday utterly incomplete.

The accident happened in a swan dive *before* I hit the water. It must have been the attempt to strain up in the first gymnastics I had tried for almost three years and the pull of the actual bone pressing against the feeble and untried muscles and ligaments. It was from a medium high board and I could feel the tear before I touched the water and had quite a struggle getting to the rail.

However, I am in good hands and they have saved me from any permanent crippling of the arm though I am afraid I will have to spend the week dictating to Jim Hurley rather than scribbling the rest of my story in pencil which comes much more natural.

> With dearest, dearest love,
> Scott

170. TO SCOTT
[August 1936]

ALS, 4 pp.
[Highland Hospital, Asheville, North Carolina]

Dearest, dearest Do-Do:

What a funny picture of you in the paper. I wish we had just been swimming together, the way it seems — I'll be so glad when you come home again. When will we be three of us again — Do you remember our first meal in the Biltmore when you said "And now there'll never be just two of us again — from now on we'll be three — " And it was sort of sad somehow and then it was the saddest thing in the world, but we were safer and closer than ever — Oh, I'll be so glad to see you on the tenth.

Scottie was as sweet as I had imagined. She's one inch shorter than I am and weighs four pounds more — and I am her most devoted secret admirer —

Maybe I can come home —

> O my love
> O my darling } yes, I mean it

That's what we said on the softness of that expansive Alabama night a long time ago when you envited me to dine and I had never dined before but had always just "had supper." The General was away. The night was soft and gray and the trees were feathery in the lamp light and the dim recesses of the pine forest were fragrant with the past, and you said you would come back from no matter where you are. So I said and I will be here waiting. I didn't quite believe it, but now I do.

And so, years later I painted you a picture of some faithful poppies and the picture said "No matter what happens I have always loved you so. This is the way we feel about *us*; other emotions may be super-imposed, even accident may contribute another quality to our emotions, but this is our love and nothing can change it. For that is true." And I love you still.

It was me who said:

I feel as if something had happened and I don't know what it is

You said:

— Well and you smiled (And it was a compliment to me *for* you had never heard "well" used so before) if you don't know I can't possibly know

Then I said "I guess nobody knows—

And

you hoped and I guessed

Everything's going to be all right—

So we got married—

And maybe everything is going to be all right, after all.

There are so many houses I'd like to live in with you. Oh Wont you be mine—again and again—and yet again—

Dearest love, I love you

Zelda

Happily, happily foreverafterwards—the best we could.

171. **TO SCOTT**   ALS, 3 pp.
[August 1936]   [Highland Hospital, Asheville,
                     North Carolina]

Dearest Do-Do:

I'm sorry you've had such a funny-paper classic to happen to you; and I'm glad its over. Here the baked fragrance of the pine paths and the sad protestation of the sweeping oaks, and there are dusky wood doves in the early evening and an amber twilight floods the road. Little birds warble the sweetest and most Biblical of cadences, and the honey-suckle is as sensuous and envelopping as the heat of the day, from noon till two o'clock

I'm very proud of Scottie; and such scholastic ambition deserves something — but then she has something — Anyway I'm glad she's going to be the President of the United States when she grows up — and I wish I had a present to send her. Town has become as roseate and as remote a dream of unattainable glories as ever wound humanity round and round the paths of their own home garden.

The sense of sadness and of finality in leaving a place is a good emotion; I love that the story cant be changed again and one more place is haunted — old sorrows and a half-forgotten happiness are stored where they can be recaptured.

Please bring everything you can find — and a sense of the Baltimore streets in summers of elms and of the dappled shade over the brick, and of that white engulfing heat. And I will try to find from between the pine and oak and the scramble of phlox and under-brush up the hill-side, something to bring to you —

Love
Zelda

172. TO SCOTT   ALS, 3 pp.
[August 1936]   [Highland Hospital, Asheville,
        North Carolina]

Dearest Do-Do:

I'm so sorry about your mother.[134] As one grows older and faces one facet and another of the past in completion, the stories of lives we have shared is catalogued.

Knowing — at the end of the patterns of tragedy or unfulfillment, of happiness, lives of service or of human balast, it's sad to recreate the poignancy of those unconscious destines which touch our own.

And its sad to recapitulate the eternal hope on which life is hung, to flaunt in the breeze of its happy security, or to wilt in the soft hot wind of human dreams.

---

134. Scott's mother died in August.

Scott and Zelda in North Carolina, 1936. Photograph of Scott
courtesy of Princeton University Library

Anyway, your mother is better than on earth. And the Beauty of
Heaven is as we are able to appreciate.

The summer's all over out here. There were some golden apples of
the Hesperides but the[y']ve all seen their way to apple sauce. The
woods are packed with September. The top of Sunset Mountain cra-
dles itself in the tree tops and there are blue ranges stretched back to
the Bible. The smell of dry dust and the dust-caked golden-rod and
the smell of a fire and coffee smelling though the woods. There's a
happiness of lonliness and the beauty of summer renouncing its
beauty. I wanted to grind my corn and stay there.

I love the just and honored corn-field. The gourds are gold, and
the morning sun splinters the world along the brook

If you do go on to California, please send me a great stack of your
most fashionable addresses. And where to address Scottie —

Thank you for the check. Last year I spun enough cloth to smother
Clotho[135] and to disgust forever the three fates with their trade — So

---

135. One of the three Fates in Greek mythology, the spinner of the thread of human life.

I'll have it made into a nice Poiret suit or something indespensably useless enough to contribute a sense of great luxury.

You look so rested and so unlike an invalid—I hope you'll be soon well again—And for the comfort there is in a lasting appreciation and my gratitude forever and always always my devotion, I am

Zelda

173. TO SCOTT ALS, 2 pp.
[September 1936] [Highland Hospital, Asheville, North Carolina]

Dearest Do-Do:

The sadness of autumn + of things that are over lurks on the smoky horizons; one enters the morning reluctantly. It's sad to know that another summer + vacation time and another years expectancies are accomplished. You were so sweet to take so long a trip for my sake and I know all the effort it cost you. When you leave I always look about me and catalogue your visits and render accounting of your eternal kindness.

Scottie got off in happy estate—model travelling for girls of 15—Vogues + curl papers, kodak snaps + pockets full of preparations—I hope it will be a happy school year; she seemed prettier + sweeter than ever before.

Thanks for the money. I have already apportioned its disposal—I think I'll buy one presentable suit in case the house catches on fire and I have to help work the hose. It will be rather exciting to own an approved product again. I wish we were off on a glamorous twilight to christen it—It's fun to be here before the curtains of a winter dusk.

Love, Do-Do—and thanks again—

Zelda

174. TO SCOTT
[After September 24, 1936]

ALS, 2 pp.
[Highland Hospital, Asheville,
North Carolina]

Dear Scott:

Happy Birthday to you. I remembered you; and wished you happiness—

This attenuate land loses itself in the blue autumnal haze of withdrawing horizons; and a thin and concise sun fills the heavens to perhaps a more cerebral purpose. I regret the summer; but, to me, there isn't a more fortunate union of nature and of poetic heritage than is between this country and these thin gold mornings and twilights husky with home-building.

I'm manoeuvering an evening coat that is intended to be tried on before the mirror of Shalot; and was especially designed for the riding of magic carpets—and I bask in the heavenly hardi-hood of these woods and I long for a great many good things.

I decided to refurbish my conversancy with the *monde actuel* by a garguantuan parcel of current publications which I find very absorbing. Before I see you again I will know practically everything about the discovering of unobtainable cures for uncatalogued maladies; about the lives of all famous men know[n] only to authors in need of pick-up money; and of the domestic habits of a few of our most select gangsters—and of how the emu rears his young

Meanwhile, may you and your work prosper and many happy birthdays to you—

Zelda

That fall, as Scott mended, he was able to visit Zelda and take her to lunches at the Grove Park Inn, after which they went for walks around the resort's lovely manicured grounds, nestled in the mountain valley. Zelda slowly improved under the hospital's supervision. It was a quiet time, but not a particularly good one for Scott, since he continued drinking heavily. In December, Scott went to Baltimore to give Scottie a holiday tea dance at the elegant Belvedere Hotel, which he ruined by getting drunk and making an embarrassing scene. He spent the rest of the holiday in Johns Hopkins Hospital, being treated for the flu and alcoholism. Scottie spent Christmas with a school friend, Peaches Finney, and her family, then went to visit Zelda in Asheville. In Janu-

ary, Scott moved to the Oak Hall hotel in Tryon, North Carolina. With his income at its all-time low, he struggled to stay on the wagon and to write, apparently with little success.

175. TO SCOTT　　　　　　　ALS, 1 p.
[January 1937]　　　　　　　　[Highland Hospital, Asheville,
　　　　　　　　　　　　　　　　　　　　North Carolina]

Dearest Do-Do:
　　Dope: we left the picture at Pritchards art shop the day before you left for Baltimore so it must have been Dec 22 or so—That's all I know about it, and was not with you when you gave instructions about its delivery. It may still be there.
　　I paint and walk and am robust; I die of ennui; I long for your visit always and will be glad when its time again. You forgot to answer about the frame to render presentable a big picture for Ma—
　　whom I sadly long to see?
　　　　Ou travaille—
　　　　With Love
　　　　Zelda

176. TO SCOTT　　　　　　　ALS, 2 pp.
[March 1937]　　　　　　　　　[Highland Hospital, Asheville,
　　　　　　　　　　　　　　　　　　　　North Carolina]

Do-Do:
　　It rains—without lamentation. Easter accumulates in the pears; the trees make ready for glory. Abnegatory skies lie mirrored in the roads; and the houses are fine and etched against a silver time. That was a little while ago. Now there's snow, and lightly laden branches and a puffed protected world for Sunday. Snow domesticates horizons; the world is a fine white boudoir; the world is cared-for and expensive. I hope always that you'll show up in it soon.
　　In the mean-time, I make red robes—of justice—I make pictures and cards and health and everything but magic—and I hope for a

breath of that art in spring. The cold freezes me and leaves such a misery that I can't stand it.

Won't you give me the O.K. for Mamma's frame? I'd like to get the picture home by Easter

Always with Love

Zelda

177. TO SCOTT   ALS, 2 pp.
[Spring 1937]   [Highland Hospital, Asheville,
                              North Carolina]

Dearest Scott:

The bus careened about the edges of a tired holiday; the lights went out but there weren't any bandits.

I've been painting my peach blossoms all afternoon — they are such courageous flowers. I've got them in my stone jug, and the picture is another hope of producing one acceptable to the Museum.

There was still a faint aura of the world about my things to-day. It was happy seeing you. I love the quality of lost remote strange lands belonging to Tryon, and my homey tastes of dust and summer fields. I'll be mighty glad when it's time again to go.

Thanks for my two best days, and thanks that there is you. I'll see you Monday, or when it so transpires —

'Till then,

Love and Devotion

Zelda

178. TO SCOTT   ALS, 2 pp.
[April 1937]   [Highland Hospital, Asheville,
                              North Carolina]

Dear Do-Do —

The picnic was a success. We lost ourselves in the mazes of a panorama and laced the lunch to earth with unexplored latitudes and longitudes. I wished for you; and await the day when we can tramp so high, because the trip in a car is somewhat alarming. The top of the world is an apple orchard, belongs partly to Dr. Carrol and responds to the term "campagna"—History trails over a white mountain road for me—

We have now been married most portentously seventeen years, rather an astounding accumulation of time. We should have had a cake.

1. Violets commence, pale + perfect along the road-side.

2. Aenemonies are a small and perfect flower made of finely chis-elled fragility. They are powder-blue.

3. The birds are beginning to squabble over the rights to the first spring dawns

4. Dog-wood awaits a more expansive season whereon to spread its imperious flames—

> Devotedly, and thanks
> Zelda

179. TO SCOTT
[May 31, 1937]

ALS, 2 pp.
[Highland Hospital, Asheville, North Carolina]

Do-Do, sir—

It will be June again to-morrow—and the shadows skirt the lawn in fragrant elegance. Lets have the salmon fed on Chablis and spread the lunch on a white cloud and billow ourselves in the daisies. Are you bringing Scottie back with you? or will she be spending the summer in the outskirts of Madrid for atmosphere?

It is luxuriously hot with the promise of holiday heat in the air; and I want so to go to Alabama while the peaches are still bought on the street and while the heat is still a bright blue release.

I've had poison ivy in my eye, but now its over. Only I've been in abeyance for a week as a result.

Have fun—I envy you and everybody all over the world going and going—on no matter what nefarious errands.

> With dearest love
> Zelda

180. TO SCOTT
[Summer 1937]

ALS, 2 pp.
[Highland Hospital, Asheville,
North Carolina]

Dearest Do-Do:

Thanks for my telegram: every day I make ready for your return in all sorts of ways; by planning how I'll be at the beach and hoping for all sorts of new adequacies for when we are to-gether.

I can't think of more exciting auspices for crossing a continent than the 4 Marks Brothers however I'm glad you're relieved—

Vines rust over the broken balconies of Tryon and in the evening deep wells of shadow absorb the world. It's good to be there with Mamma, creaking through a summer noon in an old peeling rocker. Apple orchards slumber down the hill-sides and twist imperviously about the stem of Time—and every now + then a train shivers [in] the distance and distance is again glamorous + desirable.

I'm reading about what a remarkable sort of fellow you are from the pen of John Bishop.[136] Like jonquils he acknowledges—but there isnt as yet any mention of my roses.

> Love and
> Love again
> Zelda

In June, Scott received an offer to go to Hollywood and write for MGM. Despite his negative experiences with screenwriting in the past, he was excited, especially about the prospect of a regular salary—the studio offered him one thousand dollars a week for the first six months, with an option for renewal at a higher salary. In July 1937, Scott moved to Hollywood, where, under contract to MGM, he committed himself to digging his way out of debt while paying the bills to keep Zelda in the hospital and Scottie in school.

Enthusiasm aside, Scott still wasn't well and couldn't stay sober for any length of time. When he moved to Hollywood, he first settled into an apartment at the Garden of Allah, a hotel on Sunset Boulevard, where he was

---

136. Probably John Peale Bishop's essay about Scott, "The Missing All," which appeared in the Winter 1937 issue of the *Virginia Quarterly Review*.

among old friends from New York—writers who had also gone to Hollywood to work in the movie industry, among them Dorothy Parker, Alan Campbell, and Robert Benchley. He soon met Sheilah Graham, an attractive young gossip columnist, who reminded him of Zelda; she would become his friend, his lover, and often his caretaker. Many credit Sheilah's devotion to Scott and her steadying influence as the reason his last three years were relatively happy and productive. Nevertheless, he remained determined to do everything he could to give Zelda things to look forward to. He visited her whenever he could, took her on vacations, and, when he could not be there, tried to arrange visits from Scottie and trips to her mother's home in Montgomery. In September, Scott returned to Asheville and took Zelda on a vacation to Charleston and Myrtle Beach. Meanwhile, they exchanged letters; Zelda shared the excitement of Hollywood and hoped for Scott's success and happiness.

181. TO SCOTT
[Summer 1937]

ALS, 3 pp.
[Highland Hospital, Asheville,
North Carolina]

Dearest Do-Do:

It made me sad to get your note the other day. I hate to think of your struggling with those awful corsets. It will be good when you are well again—and happy. In California it's a very happy world. There are fluttery happy happinesses in the air and happiness waiting to burst into blossom on every bush and the air is blue and tremulous and the flowery earth is palely roseate. And you'll write a good picture full of the newness of the land to you.

I'm sorry we didn't get along very well—Because you know that I think this:

The soul of the artist is beautiful and precious and without the artist neither would we be able to decipher the purpose of life nor would we be able to correlate our lives with the cosmic patterns[.] And the best thing I love of this world is the beauty of a generous soul—and so Do-Do I pray for you.

Naturally, it isnt fair about the money; if you will let me leave with Mamma, or at least ask Dr. Carrol to let me go as soon as he can so he won't just think we can go on forever in ease and prosperity—I will be glad when some of your burdens are less.

With unpersonal love and love of what you love—and my best good wishes with all my heart.

> The pattern of your soul
> is *God's Glory*—
> Zelda

Good-bye, Do-Do. Happiness to you for wherever you are forever.

182. TO SCOTT   ALS, 2 pp.
[July 1937]   [Highland Hospital, Asheville,
North Carolina]

Do-Do, most eminent and
    highly respected of
        husbands—

So you escaped, so you are now all safe and happy in the land of glamour—and have fun.

Time continues to rotate round and round these wooded lanes. It rained and the world is deep and clear and of a new and greener concision. Daisies begin in the woods discs of mid-summer and augurs of a summer noon.

I hope Mamma will be along soon. She writes of Alabama heat which I envy her and writes of putting her house in order to depart.

Thanks for thinking of me. I will try to produce some cards which could be blazoned on any facade—and give my Love to Scottie.

And I will be looking forward to seeing you—and to hearing about life and the world and how things are when you get back

> Devotedly,
> Zelda

183. TO SCOTT
[July 1937]

AL, 2 pp.
[Highland Hospital, Asheville,
North Carolina]

Dearest Do-Do:

I'm looking forward to to-morrow; there will be formalized informality under the pines and a politely rustling negation of the deep significance of a picnic plate.

It will be so good to see two people of my own again.

A rare may-pop explodes in pale exotic fanfare, and the weeds are raw and hot and high along the paths. Doves cradle a mellowing season and I will be always thinking of you.

It makes me happy that there should be new intangibilities for you to classify and more glamorous eventualities than lately.

Don't worry about us here any more than you can't help, because I promise

1) To mind the rules, which usually brings rewards.

2) Mamma's close and I wont be lonely.

3) But will greet your return with all sorts of gleaming staminas and things to flash about the future.

Love, Do-Do, and good luck —

184. TO SCOTT
[August 1937]

ALS, 2 pp.
[Highland Hospital, Asheville,
North Carolina]

Dearest Do-Do —

Scottie and I floated over the terrace of Grove Park Inn in a lovely summer sun and watched Time rejuvenate itself in a valley resting there for the season.

She was pretty and gracious and a great pleasure to be with — though somewhat alarmed at her expenditures. Her clothes were lovely and appropriate, all except the hat, and very becoming to her, so the bill seemed not exhorbitant to me.

My family had generously remembered her, so the season arrived in as many papers + ribbons as lend a gala air[.] We went to Church, and to see "I'll Take Romance"[137] — which is witty, sophisticated and

---

137. 1937 film, starring Grace More.

as charming. Every year Grace Moore becomes more adequate, which must be very gratifying to her.

Thanks again for the money—

And needless to say a Florida shore is more than a temptation—a dream—or even delirium—

Can we be brown + baked and mica-flaked—

I'll be expecting you—

Devotedly + gratefully

Zelda

185. TO SCOTT
[Late Summer 1937]

ALS, 2 pp.
[Highland Hospital, Asheville, North Carolina]

Dear Scott:

It rains conscientiously every day and Time keeps vigil over a most bedraggled end of summer. I won the tennis tournament and am now[?] champion: it is such a beautiful game that I will be sorry when I am no longer able to play. The quickness of inter-dependent rhythms; the play of one set of reflex swung on another in a sustained volley are as compelling as the game itself. Artisticly the game is inexhaustible.

I wrote Rosalind for a hat, and evening dress: which were indispensible. She has promised to motor[?] me over from Atlanta when I go south, and I miss her presence very much. She contributes a sense of the grace of life in even the humblest of circumstance that is most edifying and pleasurable. Since there is rain every day in Atlanta also maybe she will come back again for the autumn haze and the harvest moon. No time is so appropriate to these regions as the blazoned skies of late September, the sensory somnolent mysteries of Indian summer and the bright brocaded hills streaming away under the power, and ominous possibilities of the hills.

I'm sorry Scottie is an effort. I wish I could have kept her here. She was so bored in Ashville, however, and hated it so passionately that I do not think any longer time here would have been to any advantage, save perhaps of reminding her of her parental obligation; and of keeping her in mind of the politesse necessary to live successfully in any sort of intimate relationship—

Zelda

186. TO SCOTT
[September 1937]

ALS, 7 pp.
[Highland Hospital, Asheville,
North Carolina]

Dear Scott:

Thanks for such a nice trip: it was a good thing to be driving over those long sad roads, stopping for things that are not really needed, and good to arrive at night smelling of sweet dust and gasoline and to recapture again the sense of never being quite sure of where you are.

The intent of the hotel in Fredricksburg was dignity, security and mahogany; while the hotel at Richmond was certainly of dramatic purport.

Williamsburg, perfected and ready will still perhaps be awaiting the perfect fête next time we go there. That place so appropriately harmonizes its guests to its most ingratiating purpose. At Charlotte the hotel didn't matter, but maybe its message was of the indispensibility of places to sleep: they didn't want to be bothered with inadequacy.

I liked the gold trees, and this golden time of year: the smoky sun, and roads leading back into summer.

Mt. Vernon seemed frank + graceful and Monticello nicely compact: but I thought both places were of indirect planning, and that neither had the sweep nor conveyed the sense of captured space that such a structure might have. That the architechts economy is evident, places the house on a basis of self-justification (legitimate beauty, ultimately—but only of tradition). In absolute: the purpose of the house might swing from the beams of aesthetic aspiration rather than dissected to meet the yet unarisen contingencies of the passage of time; ie where to put the neighbors children, and what to do with the mother-in-law.

The weather was perfect, the car fun; the food of adequate vagabondage and I had a good time. The possibility of new purposes arising carries one happily enough through life and even the pursuance of old ones helps to evaluate enterprizes clung to as "direction."

The roads smell of reminiscences, and of pursuit.

Although Scotties vagabondage is indubitably hereditary, I don't want her to do that again: that vaguely flowing around the country to whatever pleasant endroit that intrigues her fancy—anyhow she's the sweetest of babies + maybe the Pullman porters will help her to master the Greek + Latin roots which seem to require itinerant working-up.

Again thanks: it was a better vacation than before, and perhaps our holidays will grow up to a brilliant future

Someday.

Gratefully

Zelda

187. TO SCOTT   ALS, 5 pp.
[Fall 1937]   [Highland Hospital, Asheville,
                      North Carolina]

Dear Scott:

We got back just in propitious time: The wind seethes with malice and already the elements are of the cast of tragedy. I'm glad we had a good time.

I miss my honey in bed and the bright morning sun loitering inquisitively about my room; and a bright impassive hotel room to greet me.

Won't you get Mr Goldwyn to send me the perfume, and junk? You must have a list of it somewhere? But my real ulterior motive is this:

These pictures and my screen which I love, still, ought to be stored in some worthier endroit. I know you gave me twenty dollars to do it; but now I dont know where the twenty dollars is, and the pictures are still here. So may I have

1) A note of authorization to Dr. Carroll that I may ship my chefd'oeuvres home

2) A check to cover same. I'm doing some very good work since our *constitutional,* and may produce something to inspire your admiration.

This is circus day: already the radios have a tinny swing and there are echoes of gilt and routine in the air; and nobody wants to wait to go. I'll sketch, and write you about the miraculous 4th dimensional exploits of the acrobats on Sunday.

To me, there is no more exalting moment than a tenuate body launc[h]ed on the strength of its concept, whirled through the air a preconceived purpose—studies in rhythm and balance that make the architraves of Notre Dame appear a simple achievement.

It's a good circus day: its a little bit windy, and bright and sunny.

Bronze leaves; and brown-woods lit with glints of glowings, and bright skies issuing commentary on the inexorable urgencies of life; and of the seasons.

Love
Zelda

188. TO SCOTT   ALS, 2 pp.
[Fall 1937]   [Highland Hospital, Asheville,
                                 North Carolina]

Dearest Do-Do—

Thanks for the money—When once it has seen the dark shades of these vaults, a fund is as inaccessible as the United States mint— However, with Christmas in the offing maybe there will be an earthquake or some such lubricating influence. Anyway thanks— again—

He won't let me go home for Thanksgiving *or* for Christmas. But promises next spring.

I'm making cards—and painting Mamma some lillies which do not thrive in these rigorous hills—although to-day is lovely.

A bright + prosperous Sunday floods the bungalow with blocks of sunshine and the past hangs nostalgicly the splendour of its completed hopes along the roads—and I wish we were picnicing somewhere in these dry + punguent heavens

It would be heavenly if you could fly—to see me sometime

Devotedly
Zelda

189. TO SCOTT
[December(?) 1937]

ALS, 2 pp.
[Highland Hospital, Asheville,
North Carolina]

Dearest D. O.

My latest news is from Jeremiah the prophet, and I mull over the Osiris cult in a book on dancing. This gives a more constructive air to the influenza which I have musterred, and routed. It's a misery. I'm glad it's over.

Hoorah about Florida. Bring everything you can find, and we will enjoy. Please bring the architecture book and we can study patios in case we exhaust the interest of the ocean.

Despite this kindliest of weathers the winter has grown homesick for something else, somewhere else—and seems as anxious to get away as everybody else is: mooning and moping and stalking the more "intimately" useful hours until it is distraction not to[o] identified with some very glamorous purposes about to flower into strings of happy times.

The papers are hot-beds of disaster: disasters of such cosmic proportions that one can no longer cho[o]se the more relevant. It keeps me in a dreadful estate of fearing the collapse of the public utilities and that we will never meet again—Maybe we ought to be equipping ourselves: breast-plates, and nose-guards and things.

Wont your secretary send me some more moccasins? Or why dont you just send me the secretary? Then I'll never have to worry about where all my lovliness is to come from[.] *Heavily* beaded; 5½—of Zodiac-al properties—please.

Devotedly
Zelda

190. TO SCOTT
[December 1937]

ALS, 2 pp.
[Highland Hospital, Asheville,
North Carolina]

Do-Do

Joy + glad tidings! Dr. Carrol is taking a car-load of people to Sarasota Florida to-morrow, and I am at last a priviledged character.

It's five days en route and I can roll contentedly recapitulating through the Georgia clay-banks, and through the stark + lonely pines; and over long abandoned roads—the way I love to.

Thanks for the money. I havent yet got a chance to spend it—but will write you on the advent of my new cage.

There isnt any Christmas in the air. Despair blows the night chaoticly here + there and skies gape cosmic terror. I cant even make Christmas cards.

I'm in Highland Hall, and I'm very nice and pretty. It will be happiness to see you at Christmas, and where would there be a better fire than at Tryon or sweeter smelling woods about grow—and the promise + possibility of flowers + the dank of early spring along the roads.

Wont you send me a small picture of you? and thanks for remembering me by Rosalind.

> Devotedly +
>
> > gratefully
>
> Zelda

191. TO SCOTT   ALS, 2 pp.
[December 1937]   [Highland Hospital, Asheville,
   North Carolina]

Dearest Do-do—

Life has puffed + blown itself into a summer day, and clouds + spring billow over the heavens as if calendars were a listing of mathematical errors.

Christmas already seems exciting; there are red + gold stores + stores glittering + ecstatic and streets done up in garlands. I'll be mighty glad to see you, kind sir.

If you can stop the train at some of the more enterprising Indians, I still would love the mocassins—beaded all over + as near turquoise as they have had heaven enough to make. At Tuc[s]on maybe or one of those places where we bought bracelets a long long time ago.

I am busy at many small + inconsequent exploits, and feeling rather spiritually organized although without any Titanesque projects.

You say what can I do—I want to go home to Ala for a while to establish my capacity as an able + invaluable citizen. It's a fine gratification to have something to offer when offering. I could collect my tastes and objectives and meet life with a better sense of unity once habit again becomes volitional—

But we can discuss when you arrive—

Meantime the parties sound fun to be strung on an assurance that they are, after all, happiness—

And so—

Devotedly

Zelda

I wrote the man what to do about the skirt. Could he follow the letter? Because otherwise he may make me boat-rigging, i.e.; flaps + things. Thanks + thanks

*During the Christmas holiday, Scott went to Asheville to visit Zelda and took her on a vacation to Florida and then to Montgomery to visit her mother. Writing to Scottie, he admitted that the trip wasn't altogether successful: "Your mother was better than ever I expected and our trip would have been fun except that I was tired. We went to Miami and Palm Beach, flew to Montgomery, all of which sounds very gay and glamorous but wasnt particularly" (*Life in Letters *345). When Zelda returned from vacation, there was a New Year's masquerade ball, the theme of which was Mother Goose; Zelda, who regardless of her illness kept her sense of humor, very much enjoyed going as "Mary, Mary, Quite Contrary." For Easter, Scott planned a family trip to Virginia Beach for Zelda, Scottie, and himself. Once there, the three of them bickered, and Scott and Zelda caused a scene at the hotel. When he returned to Hollywood, Scott arrived at the airport drunk and had to be placed under a doctor's care. He was so ill that he had to be fed intravenously.*

During the spring of 1938, he exchanged several letters with Dr. Carroll and urged the doctor to continue to allow Zelda vacations; otherwise, Scott feared, Zelda, with nothing to look forward to, would sink into despair. Meanwhile, in April, Scott moved from the Garden of Allah on Sunset Boulevard (and its boisterous social set) to a quieter bungalow at Malibu Beach, and then in November (to escape the cold and damp) to a cottage at Belly Acres (the estate of the actor Edward Everett Horton) in Encino, where he would live until May 1940, when he moved to an apartment near Sheilah's in Hollywood.

192. TO SCOTT
[February 1938]

ALS, 2 pp.
[Highland Hospital, Asheville,
    North Carolina]

Dearest Do-Do:

February parades our miseries on as bleak a wind as ever seethed our hopes into necessities—and I long to be off for browner sunnier expectations.

Mamma sent me some calico to sew—already, it speaks of berry-stains and the early suns of July mornings and birds perched along the dawn—summer's so happy: its obscenity to have the highest expectations subservient to the hope of getting warm.

Thanks for your letter, and the money for the clothes. They are to travel in—and I know they'll be pretty if Rosalind sends. You sent such amazingly adequate, and so sensorily gratifying a perfume that I wanted more of it. The name is *Salud*, Schiaperilli, and when you go to Mexico again, remember me.

I'm writing a paper for a class we have on whether our brains will work or not. It's all about everything I know and ought to be very illuminating. I'll lend it to you at Easter and we can use it as Scottie's entrance speech into the world.

Meantime violets and lilies and pink beauty blows on my canvas and I hope and wait—

Devotedly
Zelda

193. TO SCOTT
[March/April 1938]

ALS, 4 pp., on stationary
    embossed MONTGOMERY,
    ALABAMA, at top center

Dear Scott:

I am a very extravagant woman; I am a jezebel—However, that may be, the money is gone, and so will I be in the morning, and I owe Mamma $10 for sundries—

It's all very demoralizing; and I hate to call on you for more when you have so recently been so liberal—

But will you be kind enough to send her the check

If you could understand how desperately tired of medical routine, of inescapable suppressions[,] frustrations of my pleasures, suppressions of temper, of opinions with which we (you + I) have always subscribed and of any personal expression) which such a life prescribes, I'm sure you would be willing to let me try outside once more. For as long as a year, Highland Hospital is as excellent a regime as I know; but its the only hospital that I have ever been in that makes *no* provisions for *any* personal life — [leisure, right of opinion, liberties such as town etc.][138] — and after three years of such, the soul begins to perish.

I beg of you not to leave me there after Easter.

Anyway — I am most grateful for your constant thoughtfullness, your generosity and for all the good things you've given me.

> Devotedly
> Zelda

Why don't you let me close accounts in Ashville, come out to visit you for two weeks at Easter, and return to Ala —

If this project was successful I could make my own arrangements afterward; and maybe find a cottage somewhere where you could spend a happy month or so whenever you felt like it.

 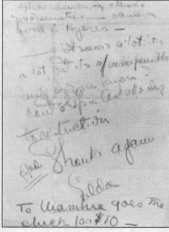

Two pages that Zelda included with this letter, outlining her expenditures.
Courtesy of Princeton University Library

138. These brackets were supplied by Zelda.

194. TO ZELDA ALS, 2 pp.[139]
[April 1938] [Hollywood, California]

I couldn't bring myself to write you last week — I was plenty sore with myself and also a good deal with you. But as things settle down I can regard it all with some detachment. As I told you I was a sick man when I left California — had a beautiful little hemorage the end of March, the first in two years and a half — and I was carrying on only on the false exaltation of having done some really excellent work. I thought I'd just lie around in Norfolk and rest but it was a fantastic idea because I should have rested before undertaking the trip. There has been no drink out here, *not a drop of it,* but I am in an unfortunate rut of caffiene by day and chloral by night which is about as bad on the nerves. As I told you if I can finish one *excellent* picture to top *Three Comrades*[140] I think I can bargain for better terms — more rest *and* more money.

These are a lot of "I"s to tell you I worry about you — my condition must have been a strain and I thought you had developed somewhat grandiose ideas of how to spend this money I am to earn which I consider as *capital* — this extravagant trip to the contrary. Dr. Carrol's feeling about money is simply that he wants to regulate your affairs for the time being and he can do so if you live on a modest scale and within call. He doesn't care personally whether you spend a hundred a month or ten thousand — doubtless for the latter you could travel in state with a private physician instead of a nurse. Here is the first problem you run up against trying to come back into the world + I hope you'll try to see with us and adjust yourself. You are not married to a rich millionaire of thirty but to a pretty broken and prematurely old man who hasn't a penny except what he can bring out of a weary mind and a sick body.

Any relations you want are all right with me but I have heard nothing from you and a word would be reassuring because I am always concerned about you

Scott

---

139. This letter may not have been sent. The original is in the Bruccoli Collection at the Thomas Cooper Library of the University of South Carolina.

140. Scott worked on the screenplay adaptation of Erich Maria Remarque's novel *Three Comrades* from the fall of 1937 until February 1938; it was the only film for which he received screen credit.

Oh, Zelda, this was to have been such a cold letter, but I dont feel that way about you. Once we were one person and always it will be a little that way.

In June, Scottie graduated from the Ethel Walker School and applied to Vassar. Scott could not attend her graduation, but he arranged for Zelda and her sister Rosalind to go to New York and then Connecticut for the ceremony. His gift to Scottie was a trip to France, and she visited him in California that summer before leaving for Europe. When Scottie returned to the United States, Zelda met her in New York. Rosalind, Mrs. Sayre, and Zelda's nurse accompanied her; since Zelda's sister Clothilde lived near New York, Zelda enjoyed a family reunion. Being with family and being in New York again made her eager to leave the hospital permanently. These trips interrupted Zelda's routine and made her less satisfied with the hospital regimen. Her success on these outings seemed proof to her family that she was ready to leave; they pressured Scott as well as Zelda's doctors to allow her to do so. The doctors felt that only by spending the majority of her time in a therapeutic environment was she able to do as well as she did on the trips. A nurse traveled with her to act as a safety net.

During 1938, Scott worked on three films — Infidelity, Madame Curie, *and* Three Comrades. *Zelda saw* Three Comrades *in June when she went north for Scottie's graduation, whereupon she immediately sent Scott her congratulations. Later in 1938, his work on the screenplay for* Madame Curie *made it impossible to see Zelda for Christmas; he arranged for her and Scottie to spend the holiday in Montgomery with Zelda's mother.*

195. TO SCOTT
[c. June 2, 1938]

ALS, 2 pp., on stationery
embossed HARTFORD,
CONNECTICUT, at top center

Dearest Scott:

Scottie is the prettiest girl; of a stabilized ae[s]theticality and a plasticly tangible spirituality. She wore white gardenias and white flannel and white hopes and the freedom and grace of the best and we are very proud and devoted. She loved your flowers, which are magnificent, of yellow and ma[u]ve and pink and spontaneous impetus; and expanding expectantly to the brightest and happiest of mornings. Although the day was dark.

Thanks again for everything, and the goodness thereof—

Don't send me the watch; I want to give the money to charity—because I've had such a happy time. So won't you, please? Of cource, if there *is* any.

We're going to the movie to-morrow, and I'll write after.

Meanwhile—life is so nice, when one can have some. and meanwhile, good luck.

Scottie is a very good thing to have. I'm so glad we've got her.

Thanks again—

Zelda

I sent Scottie white flowers.

Scottie at her high school graduation

196. TO SCOTT   ALS, 4 pp.[141]
[After June 3, 1938]   [New York City]

The love scene on the beach was superb, acting, dialogue, set and
direction

The street fighting was splendidly handled: a good suspense in
the picking off of the lonely figure, and an adequately renderred
sense of cavernous emptiness of cities deprived of their safety. The
men are pretty good throughout, without much chance for moving
acting.

The comedy is excellent all the way through; sophisticated, realistic,
and of a bitter delight — The picture got lots of good sound laughs —

The girl was all that she could have been; and very convincing; and
utterly charming and deeply moving when he carried her in in the
blanket. She looked like a child. But somehow, it seemed rather arbitrary that 3 men should so have avowed their lives to her well-being —

The dialogue is par excellence; the individual sceens excellent; the
acting excellent (Margaret Sullavan) and first rate (the men). The
music adds lots —

But there isn't any dramatic continuity—which robs the whole of
suspense. I know its hard to get across a philosophic treatise on the
screen, but it would have been better had there been the sense of
some inevitable thesis making itself known in spite of the characters — or had their been the sense of characters dominated by some
irresistibly dynamic purpose. It drifts; and the dynamics are scaterred
+ sporadic rather than cumulative or sustained.

The audience was most responsive, and applauded   The music
montage and technical side in general was beautifully handled.

— In casual vein, or what I would have said had it been the product of a stranger: beautifully adequate and intellectual dialogue
(unusual) —*fine* acting from the heroine—of a convincing seriousness + portentuousness that was never realized because there wasn't
any plot: spiritual or material

Most of the scenes are gratifyingly strong + full —

Many congratulations.

Zelda

---

141. The beginning of this letter may be lost.

197. TO SCOTT
[July 1938]

ALS, 3 pp.
[Highland Hospital, Asheville,
North Carolina]

Dear Scott:

It fill[s] me with dread to witness the passage of so much time: another summer is half gone, and maybe there'll never be anymore sun-burns and high hot noons.

Do you suppose they still cook automobiles at Antibes, and still sip the twilight at Kaux [Caux], and I wonder if Paris is pink in the late sun and latent with happiness already had.

Anyway, I now know the address of summer, where it lives and breeds and makes its home, where daisy fields come from and bird-song is brewed, and where is the home of secret heavens[.] It's not very far away, and Mamma and I may spend a couple of weeks there: if permission resolves

Meantime, Newman thinks *Three Comrades* one of the best picture's he's ever seen, and all sorts of scattered opinions are very *pro* — so maybe we'll get some more money and more prestige and more liberties and all sorts of other desirable attributes

— and meanwhile Mamma is here; and lovely and eager as ever, but a year older than she was last year which makes me sad —

I hope she has a happy holiday — The mountains are very green and of as insistently splendid proportions as before — and Ashville is the highest point east of the Rockies. It says so on the radio —

Zelda

198. TO SCOTT
[Late Summer 1938]

ALS, 2 pp.
[Highland Hospital, Asheville,
North Carolina]

Dearest Do-Do:

The deluge continues: yesterday we had supper in the sad silver reflections of a swelling river while the vaporous heat of a wet summer threatened to hatch all sorts of things.

Mamma is fine, and the Montgomery contingent of Sayres thrive at Saluda before facades like Appomatox Court House and under the

trees of absolute actuality for beauty. "The Big Apple"[142] sweeps the
floor and is a most engaging entertainment. It's full of all sorts of most
expressive impersonal coquetry and engaging self-dramatization.
Maybe Scottie can teach you.

Sir: The summer fades + wanes and I cant know where the daisies
are or what has become of the ripe corn-tops.

Sir: I can turn back somersaults at will + ease and I can make a
bridge

Sir: I sew two party dresses for when there is a fanfare on the
mountain tops.

And I will be mighty glad to see you —

Babani —*any* or

Rosine —"Sur Mon Balcon"
either is cheap in Mexico.
Shoes: turquoise or red beads
belt: bright sets + brass nails —[143]

Love + many thanks
Zelda

199. TO ZELDA   TL (CC), 2 pp.
[Malibu Beach, California]
Sept. 2nd
19 38

Dearest Zelda:

The situation is too difficult to explain in a telegram. It is briefly
this:

As you know, the Finneys have taken Scottie not only for two
Christmas vacations but for a total of about three odd months in the
summer and, as you know also, I have really been able to offer nothing to replace this; that is to say, neither Norfolk, Montgomery, nor
Scarsdale[144] bear much resemblance to a home. While the Finney's

---

142. 1930s swing dance.
143. Zelda continued to ask Scott for small, fanciful and colorful presents—perfume,
beaded moccasins, and a western-style belt, perhaps inspired by the square dances at Highland Hospital.
144. Scottie generally spent vacations with Scott's cousins in Norfolk, with Zelda's mother
in Montgomery, or with the Obers in Scarsdale.

house—because of her great love for Peaches, and for the way they feel about her and make *her* feel and because of those formative years when she learned to love Baltimore—has been very much of a home.

Naturally, I have had a sense of guilt about this obligation, especially during the time I was ill, as I had no possible way to pay it back. I have long toyed with the idea of letting Scottie bring Peaches out here for a two or three day glimpse of Hollywood. But expenses have been so heavy, always something unexpected, that I decided to put it off. Then recently Mrs. Finney wrote me saying that Pete wanted to take Scottie to the Bachelors' Cotillion in Baltimore a year from this fall and I really felt that it would be churlish not to make a gesture. So I have invited Peaches to come for two days with Scottie. It will mean that Scottie can freely accept invitations to Baltimore—a form of bargaining if you want to put it that way. In any case a thing that it seemed had to be done.

This will explain the following dispensations:

Scottie gets here in mid-September—will pick up Peaches—fly out here for three days—fly back—meet you in New York about the 20th so you will have three days of her too. I wish to God I could go up to Vassar with her also but unless the situation changes here I won't be able to get away during September.

I am writing your Mother to be sure and get herself a drawing room or section and to have her meals there. Remember the trip up will be quite a strain for her in any case, so you must insist that she do this and not try to walk though the cars on that rocky roadbed either in the morning or evening. We will pay the expenses.

I will write Rosalind, also the doctors and make all the arrangements. I think a good time for you to leave would be the night of Sunday, the 19th, and plan to arrive back a week later. You should be able to do a lot in that time and as you say it will be appropriate that you should usher Scottie into this new phase of her life.

Dearest love, always—

200. TO SCOTT   ALS, 4 pp.
[September 1938]   [Highland Hospital, Asheville,
                              North Carolina]

Dear Scott:

Item one, and of the most significance: Dr. Carroll agrees to the New York adventure, and we plan to leave here in time that I may accomplish

Item two: the buying of a presentable fall costume with which to greet Scottie.

Item three: May I charge to Rosalind, or will you send her money + authorization for the following

    1) coat and shoes ensemble

                hat + shoes

    2) dinner dress

    3) rain-coat

    4) winter slack suit to trek these woods.

These things are indispensable. With all the good will, to be minus the necessities to meet ones most elemental social obligation, is a material incapacity that asks other ways of life than these.

Mamma is going with me—which makes me extremely happy. She will visit with Tilde, and we hope to get in some good matineés, and will be between times happily ensconced at the Irving [145] as before.

I know Scottie will be a-glow from so much voyaging; and I wish we were enterring Vassar to-gether—but only vaguely.

Tennis batters these summer twilights, and the mornings fall fresh from the pines. The hardi-hood of mountain lonlinesses holds me in sway, and I begin to love the long roads leading to forgotten regretted nostalgias. The smoke smells good, and isolated figures wander off into pioneer tradition. The hill-sides bloom anyway, and nights are haunted with purpose.

If you dont get here before, Thanksgiving is a gold and august time about here with bright + wise + impervious blue skies, and grapes, warm and perfumed of a courageous sun.

Wont it be fun? Wont it be fun?

—I am most grateful about the trip; will, needless to say, be as

---

145. Hotel Irving, located on New York's Gramercy Park.

impeccable as even Scottie could desire, and will reassure myself that life still goes on at a fitting pace—

Many thanks
Zelda

Wont you confirm by wire immediately, if you haven't already done so, these plans?

201. TO SCOTT
[After September 19, 1938]

ALS, 8 pp., on stationery embossed HOTEL IRVING / 26 GRAMERCY PARK / EAST 20th STREET / NEW YORK at top center

Dear Scott:

New York is bliss, again. The stores are selling all sorts of aspirations to all sorts of possibilities and being here in a land of so much promise—and so many promises—is to live in a dream.

Thanks for the trip; you know I am always grateful for the happinesses you give me.

Scottie looks prettier than ever; Scottie is on the brink of being ravishing; Scottie is most gratifyingly pretty and adequate. It's good to see her so much master of her world problems.

Item one, on my spiritual economy program:

Although Dr. Carroll requested a list of what shopping expenditures I would be making, he gave the nurse only $100 for pleasure and for clothes. I dont know that you did, but sending money for my use to that hospital is to relegate it to limbo. The[y] wont give it to me, and indeed nourish an idea that anybody ought to be content with tourists-lodgings and cafeteria meals, no tipping, and evasions of all the customary *largesses* which keeps functioning an agreeable and easy social order.

On that trip to Florida which Dr. Carroll sent you a bill for $200 for, he spent half an hour one morning arguing the extra 50¢ that having separate beds had cost me and the nurse. I do not believe that institution to be strictly punctilious, either spiritually or materially.

Wont you always just give them the necessary money, and to Mamma or Rosalind, the rest?

There arent any shows but the streets glitter and scintillate with memories and endeavor, and on this Sunday morning an amber beneficence sheds its light. I wish you had been able to come East— It would be fun to meet you here again. The Murphys looked very engaging; age and the ages leaves them untroubled and, perhaps, as impervious as possible. That was, indeed, a remunerative relation-ship—If they knew how much of other peoples orientations that they had influenced, they would less resent any challenge to their own. Which is all from the most fleeting of impressions on a crowded dock.

To Mamma, this is a fairy-land. It must be with gratitude that you remember the many happinesses which you have contributed to others.

Again, thank you.

Rosalind leaves for Atlanta on the 24th. New York will be less pleas-urable to think on without her. But good that she is nearer to home.

May I go home for Thanksgiving, and Christmas, and soon for ever?

I'm so sick of the moralistic tone and repressive atmosphere of that hospital that I dont know how to endure. At my most desirable of attainments, they would have classified me at best as *suspect*; and any spontaneous reaction of any category therein means a week without liberty. It's the only place I've ever been in my life that I impersonally hated. And I tell you again that they cannot be trusted.

We're driving Scottie to the Obers to-day—and pray that she wont arrive a frazzled wreck. When she meets you, she will have been half around the world.

With deepest gratitude and many thanks for the flowers, and for this refurbishing of my ego.

—As soon as you yourself are under less stress, wont you see if I cant leave with a nurse? It would be cheaper, and as practical—and it is so good to be able to choose your own tooth-paste.

Zelda

202. TO SCOTT
[September 1938]

ALS, 2 pp.
[Highland Hospital, Asheville,
North Carolina]

Dear Scott:

New York completely ravished me as usual: clothes spoke of promise latent in a flare and a swirl, and the baubles have reached the abstract era, of almost an absolute value.

There werent any shows, and the Statue of Liberty was closed for repairs; but I went to two very compelling concerts, and tried to digest a few scaterred pictures.

We called on the Obers. Their house seemed straight out of Longfellow, or some fanciful and homely poet; dreamily spun into the fragrance of orchards and tumbled down the rocky hill-side. I never saw a more enchanting child than their lanky red-headed boy. How can we ever at least let them know our gratitude?

It was dreams, de luxe, to lie in bed again and expostulate the morning rolls + coffee; and its always good to reassure oneself of the passage of Time. Because in these hills, the summer explodes in a froth of purple asters and the glow of an ending summer survives in the golden-rod; and Time disseminates a friendly inaccuracy—

Thank you very much; thank you once again; and thank you over and over for a most desirable vacation.

Scottie was supposed to have met me at the train; but I couldn't find Mrs. Finneys address—

It will be good to see you
Zelda

203. TO ZELDA

TL (CC), 1 p.
[Malibu Beach, California]
Sept. 20th
19 38

Dear Zelda:

I am sorry things got mixed up about Scottie. Or rather I'm sorry the wind misbehaved and grounded her plane in Washington. I suppose you got information about it before you started to Newark; supposing you'd left New York at two-thirty she naturally didn't go on but stayed in Baltimore.

She enjoyed her visit out here very much which is more than I can say. It was a great deal of strain and effort at a very busy time.

She seems to have good intentions about college but I am rather weary of her good intentions and will wait and see some results. She kept an interesting diary which I am going to have typed and send you a copy.

Hope you enjoyed New York and am looking forward to seeing you.

With love—

Mrs. Scott Fitzgerald
Highland Hospital
Asheville
North Carolina

204. TO SCOTT ALS, 4 pp.
[November 1938] [Highland Hospital, Asheville,
North Carolina]

Dearest Scott:

Item one: I'd much *much* rather Scottie and I went to-gether to Alabama for Christmas—for myself, for as much time as can be arranged: for Scottie, for as long as she will stay. It's an awfully good thing to keep her in touch with her family: I like her to know my people as well as what has been our mutual environment. I also feel rather strongly that a child who has had as much of the advantages of life as Scottie has had, should gratefully fulfill her parental obligation; and that she should not be encouraged to feel any "familial" effort a bore. If you don't submit to this view-point, her life will eventually have become a complete subscription to material values, and there wont be any comprehension of spiritual effort and obligation. For some three years I have asked you to give us the priviledge of at least acquainting her with the temperaments that must surely have found echo in her own. It would make us very happy and anybody feels a gratification of being cared-about. However, as you know, I have always deferred to your judgment, both voluntarily and perforce. I am also well-cognizant of the efforts and responsibility that Scotties well-being has cost you and know that they are more than happily contributed.

We could have a happy time at Christmas—and why should she come here at New Year unless there isnt any other way of our being to-gether. [However, there is a very nice party here on New Years eve and I will be very grateful to have her. We could come up from Alabama together.][146]

I want whatever you want to send me. I believe I'd rather have a week-end case than anything imaginable *tan leather*—I would also like a wrist watch—the smallest available, for outdoor use. If these cost too much, you know that I'd much rather have my trip than anything. How can I give you something for Christmas? If you want to send me a little present, send mocassins beaded all over for a 5 shoe. Nothing has given me more pleasure than the ones you gave me.

Madame Curie must be most interesting to be working on: but also difficult of dramatization[.] However, the race, under the administrations of this generation seem exceptionally interested in the wherefores of cerebral process, and I imagine that it will make a hit. Everybody wants to learn now-a-days, and are begun to realize that the deepest pleasures are those that increase the horizons. Therein lies the element of excitement + adventure, of purpose and promise, that is absent from the pleasure of distractions already familiar, i.e., from the school of a casual + mechanicly sensory pleasure upheld. Sports was their answer, and in this country there wasnt much premium on sports (too universal). Our rewards go to the experimental, dont you think?

Anyhow, Mme Curie is a significant figure + we've got to learn about her anyway and the movie will be a good chance to get the gold with-out the pan-handling: and I bet it will be a more than successful enterprize—

> With Love
> Zelda

Please do something about Christmas. Shall I wait to hear from you, or mail my presents?

Would you send me your address, I couldn't reach you in a hurry if I had to.

---

146. These brackets were supplied by Zelda.

205. TO SCOTT
[November 1938]

ALS, 6 pp.
[Highland Hospital, Asheville,
North Carolina]

Dearest D.O:

Before us, we have one of the most impressive institutes of learning that I have ever yearned after. Duke University is as impressive, as highly organized, as aspirational a structure as ever lost its way to the lonely, pine-peopled hill-tops of this somewhat astounding country-side. Of its social atmosphere, the university was redolent of acuteness to values of mondiale significance, and teeming with all sorts of intellectual enterprize. It is the only college I've ever seen that is unflavored with nostalgias, perfect in the instant, and bustling with spiritual ambitions. I don't see why Scottie doesn't get herself sent there; and why every-body doesn't arrange to pass at least some of their lives in an environment presenting more of the manifestations of civilization so tangibly, and adequately at hand. One could perform experiments in how to live.

Chapel Hill is nostalgic, gracious and dreamy and haunted. It's peeling pink façades and elegant by-ways of laurel and magnolia, and twilight sprawled over the common remind me of Ellerslie and of all sorts of good things in retrospect. I thought of you, and thanked you, and returned well-renewed in aspirations. The youth was so young, and concise, and vital and seemingly of fine ambitions stature, and seemingly competent of many possibly intricate and undeclared exigencies.

We are steeped in the regrettful lovliness of Indian summer. November moons above the road and awaits as aftermath the rising of a full and ominous moon.

Shall I wait till Christmas, or try to get home for Thanksgiving? Depending, of cource, on our financial estate.

I am painting assiduously, and so less slowly if more meticulously than heretofore and love some good morning painting hours that have accrued to me.

Otherwise, Time is a matter of expectancies, and of remembrance—try as I will to perfect the day.

However, this year is far better than last year, and has held more goodly priviledges—so I am grateful—

Devotedly
Zelda

206. TO SCOTT ALS, 2 pp.
[Late November 1938] [Highland Hospital, Asheville,
North Carolina]

Dearest Scott:

Dr. Carroll has promised that I can go home: leaving the 19th, to stay till the 27th[.] I am deeply grateful to you; a visit will make Mamma so happy. Seeing people she loves in her house where she can dispense hospitality and happiness is, perhaps, as gratifying as anything life has to offer; and I know that she will rejoice over Christmas dinner; and my own rejoicing make resound from the Pacific slopes if my expectations are measure of my capacities. I seethe with ideas for trees: trimmed with only black + silver stars after the tone of the legends of Camelot, trimmed with only the tenor + shimmer of silver bells—trimmed with pale blue whisperings of all the other Christmas's there ever have been. So thanks again.

Of cource, I will be grateful to have Scottie whenever and wherever you designate: it would be my greatest pleasure to have her at home.

I paint some scintillant attenuate griefs, in the nature of white carnations, and I absorb my philosophy with paramount interest—The early Greeks wrote such beautiful + compelling prose and speculated so musically

The first snow fall has embedded the world in a soft oblivion. Luckily, the cold is still endurable: but I wake up every morning dreading the testing of the thermometer. The radio indoors and the snow banks out, and I am ready for the house to take whatever flight it pleases—

   Devotedly
   Zelda
Did Mr. Goldwyn eat my slippers?

207. TO SCOTT
[December 1938]

ALS, 2 pp.
[Highland Hospital, Asheville,
North Carolina]

Dearest Scott:

Wont you do something about all the things? I believe I'd consid-erably rather the check for my Christmas presents went to Mamma: dependent upon what your intentions are concerning Scotties whereabouts. Please arrange, if its possible, that we spend at least a few days at home. Mamma will be heart-broken otherwise.

It's cold here, and my soul grows less expansive hourly. There ought to be some procedure that could be instigated against the dif-ferent weathers: its not cold anyway   No matter what happens I paint, and read philosophy, and pose as a model patient but there doesnt seem to be much premium on such this year. Wont you send the book on architecture? I like accumulating vast amounts of things to which I subscribe; that I may watch them slowly fall to pieces from disuse.

Dont you think we ought to plan things? A trip to Greece, or some nice wise warm place in which to, at least, investigate the possibilities of possible happiness. Or will you advance the prospect of Bermuda at Easter? I'm doing a little spiritual gold-digging: to which I believe I am entitled considering how good I am

Meanwhile, Time hurries though the frosty mornings, and would like very much some more aggressive policy—perhaps—and Time is reluc-tant of comment—and Time is a happy thing to be able to get along with.

There isnt any news. How could there be? But one is not ill-disposed towards existence—its continuity + evenments.

Rosalind agrees that perhaps it wouldnt be a good plan to give Scottie a tea party at home. I still feel that it would be a very good plan however.

Devotedly,
Zelda

Please tell Mr. Goldwyn-Mayer that only two pair of three paid-for pairs of shoes arrived.

208. TO SCOTT   ALS, 2 pp.
[December 1938]   [Highland Hospital, Asheville,
                                      North Carolina]

Dearest Scott:

There's hardly anything to say save thank you; again. I'm leaving Tuesday—and vacation promises to jingle itself in on the silver-y tinkle of a family tree.

It's cold; but Ashville scintillates of a dusky lovely aspiring glamour. The streets are ordered—of an impersonal good-will—and it seems a proud and an independent place. When I go into Faters, or somewhere, the stabbing smell of masculinity reminds me of the hours we relegated to some forgotten dream—I think of you, often.

One of the most spiritually remunerative of human efforts is the mobilization of memories: so I'm happy to be going home. Whole facets of life take on new + more tangible aspects with each new other orientation; and it is so good to feel the right of inheritance to the traditions of a place.

Mamma says some of Scottie's friends have already called her—so maybe there will be a party.

Meantime: what is your actual address? Spose I wanted to phone you—or do something unprecedented like that?

Devotedly
Zelda

209. TO SCOTT   AL, 3 pp.
[After December 25, 1938]   [Montgomery, Alabama]

Dearest Scott:

The little house is so clean and sunny, and fragrant of the absence of odors. There is the faintest aura of morning dust, and the sparkle of well-polished obligations. Roses bloom and expand on pleasurable memories; we are warm and adequate to the grace bestowed. I've missed you many times. The sun disports itself in the wide streets and the stores are open to the breath of the semi-tropics. Montgomery makes up for many *blessures*.

Thank you once again for the happiness; and for so generous a remembrance. Mamma, needless to say, did not intend to cash your check (the one precedent to my arrival). However, the visit has been expensive: more fires than usual, and three extra people to feed, and Melinda,[147] to take care of us, and so I am going to leave the money from your first check here with Mamma.

She asked me to say specificly that she *did not* cash the check herself, and that she considerred that you had most generously provided and that it was unnecessary, but if she uses the $50 for expenses she wont have any present.

The week has been a beneficence. One hour is as happy as another; I would want to wake up in the middle of the night to appreciate my happy estate.

Scottie arrived on the twenty-fourth. Jerry Le Grand, Betty Nicrosi, Ann Hubbard and Miss Flowers met her at the train and escorted her into an (even pictorially) adequate whirl. The girls were enchanting: it made me homesick for my youth. At so cursory a glance, they seemed very self-reliant, pretty and suspended to a gracious purpose.[148]

---

147. Mrs. Sayre's housekeeper.
148. The rest of this letter, if there was more, is missing.

Self-portrait of Zelda (1940). Courtesy of Princeton
University Library

PART IV

The Final Years: 1939–1940

Dearest: I am always grateful for all the loyalties you gave me, and I am always loyal to the concepts that held us to-gether so long: the belief that life is tragic, that a mans spiritual reward is the keeping of his faith: that we shouldnt hurt each other. And I love, always your fine writing talent, your tolerance and generosity; and all your happy endowments. Nothing could have survived our life.
— ZELDA TO SCOTT, MARCH 1939

In the spring of 1939, Scott embarked on a year of alcoholic benders. Attempting to make up for not getting the money to Dr. Carroll in time for Zelda to go to Havana with a group from Highland Hospital and also trying to act out the alcoholic's illusion that he was still in control, in April 1939 Scott left Hollywood drunk, flew to North Carolina, and took Zelda with him on a vacation to Cuba. He drank during the entire trip. Zelda had to get him back to New York City so that he could be hospitalized, then had to find her own way back to Highland Hospital. This trip was the last time Scott and Zelda saw each other.

From April when Zelda left Scott in New York in the care of her sister and brother-in-law, who saw that he was placed under a doctor's care, until December 1940, when Scott died of a heart attack at the age of forty-four, their relationship continued through letters only. Fortunately, neither of them could have known that after such a doomed trip there would never be another, and their subsequent letters are full of hopes and plans to see each other again.

The popular misconception remains that during this time Zelda languished in a mental institution while Scott (with the exception of working on his last and unfinished novel) did essentially the same in Hollywood. But the letters the Fitzgeralds exchanged during these last months of Scott's life suggest quite the opposite. Previously, only four of Zelda's letters from 1939–1940 have been published, while forty-four of Scott's are in print, suggesting that he wrote to her far more frequently than she did to him. That is not the case: Zelda wrote at least 142 letters to Scott during the last two years of his life, and he wrote to her on at least sixty-four occasions. We are fortunate that, because he dictated many of his letters during this period to a secretary who kept carbon copies of them, much of Scott's correspondence survives.

Although it is true that Zelda would not recover from her illness and would never be able to live on her own, she had some of her best, most admirable moments in 1939. And in 1940, she left Highland (after four years of hospitalization) and returned temporarily to Montgomery to live with her mother—a reward she had worked hard for and earned. Similarly, although his deteriorating physical condition certainly caused his death, Scott faced his last year of life sober and with dignity. It is one thing to face life with courage when at its pinnacle—young, talented, and healthy—but quite another when plagued by sickness, debt, and the sure knowledge that many important aspects of life will never again be under one's control. In this sense, perhaps the final years of the Fitzgeralds' marriage—those that have been the most neglected by biographers and scholars— reveal the couple at their best. The letters suggest that their accomplishments and admirable moments were many.

Not the least of these admirable moments was the grace with which Zelda saw Scott safely back to New York City at the end of their disastrous Cuba trip. After handing Scott over to her sister and brother-in-law, Zelda wrote to him continually—twice even before leaving New York, again during a stopover in Baltimore, and many times after making it back to Highland Hospital, where she covered for him with her doctors, hoping that she would be allowed to go away with him again. In these letters, Zelda, far from blaming Scott for all the disappointment and trouble he had caused, did not mention his drinking at all; she expressed only sincere concern over his health and provided constant reassurance that he was a wholly worthwhile person. She touchingly tried to persuade him to come to Asheville or Tryon to get well, and she hoped that they would live together again.

When Scottie (by then a Vassar College student) needed an appendectomy in June 1939, Scott, who was still sick, relied on Zelda to make arrangements in Asheville for her surgery and look after Scottie while she recovered. Zelda's letters chronicle her time with her daughter that summer—one of the few occasions Zelda was well enough to be a real mother. The letters tell of their activities— lunches, swimming, tennis, golf, dances, and "economizing"—and they indicate how proud Zelda was of her daughter. That summer, Zelda was even well enough to intervene intelligently and insightfully on Scottie's behalf when Scott wrote his seventeen-year-old daughter an unduly harsh letter, telling her that Vassar was her home. The Fitzgeralds noted the irony that just as World War I had been the larger historical circumstance of their youth, World War II was to be the dark historical force against which Scottie's young adulthood would be lived.

The letters from this period also reveal the variety of activities

Zelda participated in, all of which were funded by Scott—a vacation in Florida, art lessons, cooking lessons, hiking, painting, weekends at nearby Saluda, and a trip back home to visit her mother. They chronicle Scott's serious health problems, his careful handling of his meager finances, his constant struggle to earn money by writing, and his unwavering commitment to providing for Zelda. The letters picture Scott planning and writing what was to be his final work, *The Last Tycoon,* from his sickbed. They also reveal not only how ill Scott was during his last year but how optimistically he worked on this last novel. They also chronicle his strenuous effort to clear past debts and meet all current financial obligations. In his letters to Zelda, Scott sometimes underplayed his physical problems, yet on other occasions he overdramatized them; but his heart attacks in December 1940, which led to his death, offer solemn evidence of the severity of his condition.

During this final year, the Fitzgeralds, although they lived separately (and despite Scott's ongoing affair with Sheilah Graham), settled into a routine, and their correspondence became regular. After the spring of 1939, when Zelda still hoped that they would be able to live together, the focus of their letters shifted away from their own relationship to a mature concern about Scottie's well-being and education and their roles as absent parents. Although the final letters of 1940 are no longer as intimate as the earlier ones, they still contain many expressions of the Fitzgeralds' affection for and appreciation of each other; reading these letters adds another dimension to our understanding of the deep bond between them. During this period, when the Fitzgeralds' circumstances were far-reduced from those of their former, financially successful days, their attention to mundane matters—such as purchasing painting supplies or a winter coat for Zelda—is touching and humanizes these often mythologized figures.

Yet the romantic, legendary status that surrounds the Fitzgeralds is in many ways appropriate—fitting, rather than strictly fanciful. During their last two years of correspondence, Zelda reassured Scott that even though their lives had not led them exactly where they had thought they were headed twenty-five years earlier, when they were young and healthy, they had nevertheless remained dedicated to each other and to the "romantic terms" they held in common. In one of the letters that follow, Zelda praised loyalty as their courageous companion while still concluding, "Nothing could have survived our life." Their final letters present to us two mature individuals who dealt with later losses far better and more wisely than they had dealt with their early success; that they did so makes them not only tragic but heroic.

210. TO SCOTT   ALS, 2 pp.
[January 1939]   [Highland Hospital, Asheville,
                                        North Carolina]

Dear Scott:

I lost your address: please send it again. What would I do if I should have a bad dream, or an inspiration? It's much more conventional to know where your husband [is] when you've got one — besides I might have something to tell you.

Well, the ground is frosty outside; and I plough through styxican [Styxian] delusions of mist and poetry to the gym fields. I think the Elements resent us, and I think that They Themselves are none too well-disciplined. Any old thing ought to have better sense than to freeze people: unless, of cource, they like the vibration. Meantime, we are enjoying as nice a January as there is around here and no complaints.

Why do you think Scottie's going to get fired? It's just being arbitrary to think about it whether she is or not — she seemed interested in school, and not inclined to be too rebellious. If I were you, and such eventuality took place I'd put her in a reformatory for movie-stars or something. Her horizons are already considerable for one of her age, and will not, maybe, stand much more distension.

I hope you've got a good job, and I hope it gets better.[1]

Meantime: I'm feeling determined but not very lyrical. My pictures are "chic" — mais chic monsieur and I await your coming with a fervent enthusiasm: Don't forget too.

Thanks again for my holiday. I still exult in the aroma of fire-side toast and the secrets of dusty dusks before an open fire, and I miss Mamma very much

    Love
    Zelda

---

1. Scott's contract at MGM expired on January 27, but during January, he was briefly loaned out to producer David Selznick to work on the script of *Gone With the Wind*.

211. TO SCOTT   ALS, 2pp.
[January 1939]   [Highland Hospital, Asheville,
                              North Carolina]

Dearest Scott:

The weather does its eccentricities, and now its cold, and fair and a brittle and "unchosen" world confronts us again. I'll be so glad when the winter desists from its barbarianisms and one can breathe again.

Meantime: I'm painting lampshades, instead of souls; just for a little while, and meantime I play the radio and moon about considerably and dream of Utopias where its always July the 24th 1935.[2] Thats my chosen happiest equipment: to be 35, in the middle of summer forever.

Where is my book on architecture? Not that I would ever have time to master it, but it says in the funny-papers that a wife should follow her husbands interests so that she will be better material for the funny papers.

There's nothing to write: shall I just ask you for things instead? The bad old shoe-maker poured glue in my moccasins, which I love, and so now—what days does Mr. Goldwyn do the shopping?

I've been very expensive lately and ought to be able to produce a glamorous chronicle. I long for home; for all the so-poignant indispensibilities of a life that cant have so much longer. Things that people have cared about, and places that have housed their aspirations are ceaselessly moving

with Love, and
gratitude
Zelda

212. TO SCOTT   ALS, 2 pp.
[January 1939]   [Highland Hospital, Asheville,
                              North Carolina]

Dearest Scott:

It was too late about Havanah—But Havanah is probably a substantial sort of place and maybe will stay there till next time. Anyway,

---

2. Zelda's birthday.

its all very expensive, and we are so well adapted to spending money to-gether. When you come East there will be that much more justification for buying things. I am as grateful to you as if I were on board.

It's raining here, and the panorama leaks, and a little black kitten yowls under the hedge. But January has held less against us than usual: and we are less attenuately frozen than for two years past. There's some psychic phenomena on the dog-wood that looks as if it might burst into song at any sufficiently unpremeditated time though the sky is still on the bleak bergerie-side.

I pursue Scotties diary fervently; with envy and thinking what a cute girl she is. There's a good deal more champagne in it than Mr. Bobby could digest, I suppose—but I suppose it was in good company.

Wont you send me to finishing school some day? The girls are so adequately equipped, or supplied with things to do. One wouldn't even have to account for the passage of time. Well, life is miraculous; and maybe all these traditions owe us a living.

I'm glad your works interesting. And I well know the rage Mme Curie's undeserving amant must have thrown you into.[3]

Come on! Let me see you fly East! We can go to Cuba ourselves, as far as that goes—

> Love, and my deepest
> gratitude
> Zelda

213. TO SCOTT　　　　　　　ALS, 2 pp.
[January 1939]　　　　　　　　[Highland Hospital, Asheville,
　　　　　　　　　　　　　　　　　　North Carolina]

Dearest Scott:

I'm sorry you're tired. I wish I could offer you haven; whereas I have nothing save suggestions to divert the ravages of time and discouragement. 1) Tryon, as reconstituting a place to rest as any I know—dog-wood expanding under lethal heavens; woods sweet with violets and the secrets of 1900, the ruminative punguencies of an

---

3. The film about Madame Curie, which Scott was working on, was shelved because Scott and the producer were unwilling to make it into the love story the studio wanted.

open fire; and the chic of a chocolate soda. Then there are islands off the Georgia Coast; and, as you say there's Cuba: a body of land entirely surrounded by water etc. Why dont we go there? We might spend Easter in Mexico City. We never have, and it would be an illuminating experience with festivals like the one in Capri. I could join you in El Paso, or wherever you say. California is perhaps too full of spiritual-opportunists to be restful. The air vibrates of arbitrary aspirations, of the pursuit of such, and maybe even of the means of gratification. Anyway, its not very relaxing, and there are probably too many minerals in the earth to permit of repose. All of which means, I'd like to see you.

Meanwhile, I paint fluorescent laurels over a lamp-shape for Mamma; I paint a picture of Passion; and I scheme fruitlessly all day about how to better estates + conditions here and there. Gone With the Wind ought to be a good thing to be concerned with: its indicative of salients, certainly. I'm glad you've got a good job.[4]

Thanks about Mamma. She's tired, and discouraged; and I would hate to contribute to her worries. I know she's hard-up; and that her bonds don't pay.

> With dearest love
> Zelda

214. TO SCOTT   ALS, 2 pp.
[February 1939]   [Sarasota, Florida][5]

Dearest Do-Do:

A very impervious and distant crescent cooly illuminates the evening, and the world is lost in all the other times and places that haunt the pallid roads. This is such a good place: there are so many different kinds of people interested in so many different kinds of activities. Dr. Carroll most thoughtfully + kindly is sending me to Life Class at the Ringling Art school—also, clothes designing. For which I am most deeply grateful, to you and to him—Such a professional atmos-

---

4. Scott's work on *Gone With the Wind* lasted only three weeks and he did not receive screen credit.
5. Zelda spent a month in Sarasota with Dr. Carroll and his wife. While there, she took her first art courses.

phere ought to give my work a new impetus. From the Life, I'll try to acquire the power of an exactitude of knowledge, and by clothes-designing to catalogue my selective faculties. To be doing something identified with a place gives one a sort of *lien* thereon which is a most gratifying right to its more recherché aspects.

I'm so sorry that you have been sick. Wouldnt this be a good time to come East for a little while? Florida is warm hot, and unharassed and punguent of orange groves still in faint flower.

I'm sorry about your work, Troubles always have piled up; we can only trust that they aren't any worse than the troubles of other years.

I think Dr. Carroll intends my staying here another two weeks, maybe three—but you can reach him here in any case. It will be superlative to see Scottie: I wish you'd come rest, and enjoy, before hand so we can make a successful reunion this time—Where will we go?

> Devotedly, and gratefully—
> Zelda

I'd like to share this lovely bright blue beach

215. TO SCOTT   ALS, 2 pp.
[February 1939]   [Sarasota, Florida]

Monsieur:

Life treats us rather triumphantly down here: the ora[n]ge blooms and blows and fills the air with the bitter-sweet of an effete hardi-hood; the circus glorifies—anyway destiny proceeds. I swim, and rejoice in the personal, yet classic, appeal of the little beach[.] Art school progresses. My costumes are delirious, and of no particular application, and I prepare a port-folio for you to sell to Mr. Goldwyn: entitled *the Attributes of Ego*, or sort of. It would be a good idea if all fashion drawings transported themselves into the realm of the emo-tions, and began to convey *how* one should feel while *looking* how, as well.

I'll be *very* glad to see you, and Scottie. Lets spend Easter idyllicly somewhere where nothing can happen of disastrous natures. We'll pick violets and sniff clouds and nibble the edges of tranquil after-noons. Does the possibility of Tryon outrage anything? Or leave neg-lected some more urgent glamour?

Meantime, it is a blessed estate to be out of the cold waves that sweep the front page. The shadows hang fate over the grass down here, and the morning sun is of a roseate nature.

When will I see you?

Address   Hotel Central Park Manor—
               Florida—

    Devotedly
    Zelda

Thanks more than I can say for the Easter Happiness for Mamma. It's so thoughtful of you; and it make[s] me so happy to be able to give her pleasure.

216. TO SCOTT   ALS, 2 pp.
[March 1939]   [Highland Hospital, Asheville,
                                         North Carolina]

Dearest Do-Do:

Thanks again for the vacation. It was good to sense again the world of pleasure well-afforded, earned, and to be carried along on the impetus of concepts of pleasure so perfectly realized. It's a fine way to greet the morning: on the perfume of strawberries; and gratifying to swim in an advertisement.

The possibilities of heartbreak lurked in the romance of those lush gardens, and money bought so many happy possibilities.

I don't like to fly.

It's fun sorting my possessions and cataloging my memories: and it's good to know that in the spring I will be out again.

Dearest: I am always grateful for all the loyalties you gave me, and I am always loyal to the concepts that held us to-gether so long: the belief that life is tragic, that a mans spiritual reward is the keeping of his faith: that we shouldn't hurt each other. And I love, always your fine writing talent, your tolerance and generosity; and all your happy endowments. Nothing could have survived our life.

    Devotedly,
    and always with my
    deepest gratitude
    Zelda

217. TO SCOTT ALS, 2 pp.
[March 1939] [Highland Hospital, Asheville, North Carolina]

Dearest Scott:

We had such a happy time.[6] Scottie is lovely; and it is like a breath of the popular classics to feed ones nostalgias on the most-significant properties of the many whirligigs which compose her orientation. A suit-case full of happiness and a hat-box full of souvenir[s], curl-papers and emolluments for the rejeuvenation of the era transport a person promisorily from one world to another of its interpretations. Scottie is so gratifying. This year at Vassar has made her conversant with the manner of thinking in theoretical terms, and fitted her responses to the tone of life as a compendium rather than working at it from the completely personal + isolated orientations of earlier youth, and of more restricted aspirations[.] We had a most entertaining conference, and decided what ought to be done about everything.

The pear trees are in flower, of secrets, and promisorily of Heaven. The jonquils are in bloom. They're sad to me, I think they are *asphodels*. The white violets have just begun; their possibilities are infinitely indicative suggestions of carefully disciplined + catalogued memories + of the cerebral delectation of mastered emotions. It will be good to see you. Shall we stay in Tryon?[7]

Did you know that Mamma was crippled; and house-bound; and if there's any possibility of such, I'd like to see her.

Love, and gratitude
Zelda

---

6. Scottie visited Zelda in March.
7. Before leaving on their Cuba trip in April.

218. TO SCOTT
[April 1939]

ALS, 4 pp., on stationery
embossed HOTEL IRVING / 26
GRAMERCY PARK / EAST 20TH
STREET / NEW YORK at top center[8]

Dearest Scott:

I'm so sorry about the turmoil. I antagonized you apparently, so I did the best I could to see you well provided for, and will leave for Ashville tomorrow *Tuesday*.

Don't feel too badly about the children. They went to the club at Larchmont,[9] and had dates and were provided with an adequate evening.

Mr. Case[10] is the truest of friends. He shielded you from any possible criticism, and at the expense of his whole day managed to help John Palmer see you to safety.

Your eye was most distressing; but the hospital will take care of it better than could otherwise have been provided and will be able to give you a good looking over as well. Your cough is awful; and you are exhausted. Please take care of yourself. There is a possibility of so much happiness if you will be of a more conservative intent.

I got money from Ober ($70): most of which I paid on account to the troublous times. To-day, I'll have to ask him for more. Mr. Case said he would send those bills straight to Ober; I didnt know what else to do with them.

D. O.: I pray that your eye will soon be well, that you will be better for your rest, and will be awaiting a more auspicious meeting—

We are indebted very heavily to

John Palmer, who solved the situation by at last finding a doctor who was willing to assume responsibility; and to Mr. Case who kept

---

8. Written immediately on their return from Cuba, while Zelda was still in New York.

9. Zelda's sister and brother-in-law, Clothilde and John Palmer, lived in Larchmont, not far from New York City. The reference to "the children" is unclear but perhaps is alluded to in Scott's May 6, 1939, letter (no. 222).

10. Frank Case, owner of the Algonquin Hotel in New York, where Scott and Zelda went on their return from Cuba.

you off the street at considerable effort and who was as gracious as possible throughout—

> *Good luck*
> Devotedly
> Zelda

P.S. Needless to say I never heard of such a thing as regards the hospital—

219. TO SCOTT   ALS, 4 pp.
[April 1939]   [New York City]

Dearest Do-Do:

It seems useless to wait any more; I know that you are better; and being taken care of; and I am of no assistance; so I'll go back to the hospital on the 2:30 train.

I am distressed about your lungs. Why dont you come to Tryon? It's the best place in the world for such and we could keep a little house on the lake and let you get better. We might have a very happy summer in such circumstance—you like it there, and I am very clever at serving bird-song and summer clouds for breakfast.

Scottina could visit us; and we could find a better meaning to so many things.

Meantime: I have seen a fascinating exhibit of pictures at the Metropolitan during which I thought how you would have loved the "evolution of the American Scene" as portrayed from croquet lawns and corner stores, through the first rail-roads and steam-boats and minstrelsy and every known sort of adventure straight up to the present. I wondered had you known the wharf at Buffalo as it was presented,[11] and remembered the summer at West Port.

I saw a news-reel movie of irrelevant if pictorial life in distant parts, and visited Ober to the extent of $150; and had the situation permitted of peace-of-mind would have had a very agreeable time.

Please believe that I stayed over solely to the purpose of helping you

---

11. Scott lived in Buffalo between 1898–1901 and 1903–1908.

if I could. I know from experience what a difference it makes in life when somebody cares about your troubles.

—We owe John Palmer a debt of gratitude of considerable proportions. He found the doctor; and "discussed" with Mr. Case; and handled the whole situation.

Mr. Case also was most gracious and was ultimately considerate of you. I know that I have written you all this before but, as you know my letters are censored from the Hospital and I wont have another chance to communicate until we meet again.

To the Hospital, this version: We had a most enviable trip; and everything was according to the rules. This last refers to cigarettes and wine[12] concerning which I will follow our agreement. As to any irregularity of arrival your lungs are bad, and required attention, and I am capable of travelling alone so there wasnt any use in your adding another tiring journey to what you had before you.

D. O. please take care of yourself—So you will be well again and happier than these last times. There are so few people of our era who have made original contributions to the life about us, and not many who can be so charming, and almost not any with a greater capacity for enjoyment.

There are still a great many things which could give us pleasure
And there are such a lot of people fond of you.

I havent bought *anything* save the dress + hat in which I appear, flowers thereon, some stockings + 4 pr. of pants.

The money is simply *disparu*—

With the *best* of good wishes,
and devotion, and aspirations to mutual purpose sometime.

Zelda

---

12. Zelda's doctors asked Scott not to let her smoke or drink while away from the hospital, a stipulation he ignored and one that he and Zelda conspired to keep from the doctors.

220. TO SCOTT
[April 1939]

ALS, 1 p., on stationery
embossed HOTEL STAFFORD /
MT. VERNON PLACE / BALTIMORE,
MD. at top center[13]

Dear:

I'm sorry this trip has been so catastrophic: I'm grateful for the generosity of your intent; and always hoping that you will feel better—pretty soon.

Zelda

221. TO SCOTT
[April 1939]

ALS, 2 pp.
[Highland Hospital, Asheville,
North Carolina]

Dearest Do-Do:

Don't feel bad. You were so sweet in the station. I wish things had been so that we were going on to-gether somewhere. There are lots of happy places: it says so in the time tables, and before long we'll surely find one. Get well. Men with fever are not supposed to travel about; and your lungs are very valuable to lots of people besides yourself.

It's a very good thing to be jogging through a country-side sprinkled with blossoms. The fields are gold and the trees still preening themselves and life seems measured and harnessed of purpose if not of promise. We could grow things, and have them all turn out according to recipe. And make things: and be astonished that the plans work, and that things are how they ought to be.

I'm glad you've got a good house: and Flora[?], and recompensing things. Take it easy. We dont need anything anywhere nearly so much as we need you, well and happy once more.

---

13. Zelda wrote this letter from Baltimore, where she stopped and spent the night on her way back to Asheville from New York.

Meantime: You know I'll be there waiting on that green hill-side: and expecting you.

Love
Zelda

222. TO ZELDA TL (CC), 1 p.
[Encino, California]
May 6, 1939

Dearest Zelda:-

Excuse this being typewritten, but I am supposed to lie in bed for a week or so and look at the ceiling. I objected somewhat to that regime as being drastic, so I am allowed two hours of work every day.

You were a peach throughout the whole trip and there isn't a minute of it when I don't think of you with all the old tenderness and with a consideration that I never understood that you had before. Because I can never remember anything else but consideration from you, so perhaps that sounds a little too much like a doctor or someone who knew you only when you were ill.

You are the finest, loveliest, tenderest, most beautiful person I have ever known, but even that is an understatement because the length that you went to there at the end would have tried anybody beyond endurance. Everything that I said and that we talked about during that time stands — I had a wire from daughter in regard to the little Vassar girl, telling me her name, and saying that the whole affair was washed out, but I don't feel at home with the business yet.

There was a sweet letter waiting here from you for me when I came. With dearest love.

223. TO SCOTT
[May 1939]

ALS, 2 pp.
[Highland Hospital, Asheville,
North Carolina]

Dearest Scott:

The tulips follow the aspirations of the morning, little white things observe the decorum of spring gardens in bloom and there are glad outbursts of yellow everywhere. Tennis has started. Needless to say chasing the experience of thirty-nine years about the court is a less exhuberant pursuit than tennis has been. I think nostalgicly of our Alice-in-Wonderland garden and remember the sickle pear, new moons, and the first autumnal hoarding of sunshine + regrets, Saturdays cake-baking exploits and long dramatized rides through the woods with the parachute jumper. We had a pleasant house. The ferns beneath the window, the late sun on the porch, jouncing along through the trees on my bicycle; it seems as if all these should be recapturable. There must be some recompensatory good things at 40: or does ones status have to have attained ones aspirations by that time. There may be even grace in cataloging and in revising and linking the chronicle according to ones present lights.

I paint, and am contributing a paper on Cuba to my aspirations before the sewing class. As you know, my activities are of a very introspective nature, and never have good plots.

If there is enough money to buy a white shirt, a dinner dress, and a sport-suit, I would be grateful for these things. Rosalind could shop in Atlanta if you sent her the check. *They are not urgent*: about [illegible] this I would like them very much but dont have to have—

Because I dont much think that you will want me out there before you're better,[14] and the Dr. told me four months minimum—Needless to say, I know that we need all the money there is so dont feel badly if it is more expedient to refuse—

Please write me how you are. I hope you're superficially well again—and taking care

Love
Zelda

---

14. Scott wanted Zelda to visit him in Hollywood for a month that summer, but Scottie's appendectomy prevented the trip.

224. TO SCOTT ALS, 3 pp.
[May 1939] [Highland Hospital, Asheville,
North Carolina]

Dearest D. O.

The summer pursues its realization in floral tribute to the passage of time. We play volley-ball in the deep shadows and aspire to the jugging of the very melancholy birds that haunt these valleys. This is a lush and green and promisory world; and I wish that you had come back to Tryon to get well under the blue eternal Heavens.

We hiked to the top of something else yesterday and admired the world in panoramic terms and moored the mind to classic and impervious white clouds; and browsed.

My painting is once again become not as compelling as I like it to be; but I still pursue; and we will one day have the Scottina peddling and panhandling the wares to a good advantage

Mamma is still in the house; and you in the bed: Time indeed uses us ill. However, you have got well before, and theres no reason why with care and patience you shouldn't do it again. So I do not despair.

Scottie does not know how her summer is to be disposed of. If it is not too difficult of arrangement, I would love so having her down her[e]. We could spend two very happy weeks playing tennis and swimming at very inexpensive boarding-houses either in Saluda or Hendersonville. Though her inclination may revolt, to me, she owes at least a month to her parental obligation. It would be such a happy time for us, I'm sure: being lazy, and friendly and sharing the intimate happiness of summer-time in a tumble down pavillion. That sort of memory one thinks on so happily later.

Wont you do it? Time goes on: it only means a letter to Dr. Carroll to you, but the prospect such presents to me is the possibility of renewing the most vital relationship that life offers. It would be profitable to Scottie to have a little spare time: so many years have passed since she hasnt had a moment for introspection. She really likes to loaf and get sunburned and read and to catalogue her own mind as well as either of us. The time out of doors might be a very good thing considering the activities that are arranged for next winter —

Meantime: nothing happens with a great deal of conviction, and one awaits the aging of the world with whatever equanimity there is.

Good luck, dear—

I hope your lungs are much much better

Devotedly

Zelda

225. TO ZELDA   TL (CC), 1 p.
[Encino, California]
May 19, 1939

Dearest Zelda:-

I am still in bed, but I expect to be up in a day or so. I knew that all this was more or less true after that damn sweating in Cuba, but I am in very good hands. I have had a consultation with a specialist and it won't be a very serious business like the time in 1935. In fact, it is as much the question of exhausted nerves as of the chest. Manage to do a couple o[f] hours work every day and I am sorry if my last letter was alarmist. The eyes are perfectly all right now.

A letter enclosing $150. to Rosalind must have crossed yours. I hope it will make you happy.

The New York doctor was very much an alarmist and knew nothing of my recuperative powers. I hope to God that what you heard from him did not depress you because it will not be four months. I am going to be on my feet within at least a week and expect to be back at full-time work again before six weeks.

I note what you say about Scottie and of course I want you to have two weeks with her—or I should rather say a good deal more now that you understand each other again. Your letter almost makes me weep thinking of me sick. There's not the faintest thing to worry about this and if you want a confirmatory letter from my doctor he will be glad to arrange it.

As I told you before our plans for this summer need not perhaps be so materially altered as you think.

With dearest love,

226. TO ZELDA   TL (CC), 2 pp.
                                 May 29, 1939

Dearest:-

From your letter I picture you imagining the situation much worse than it is. In the first place, the touch of T. B. is not as bad as it was in 1935 and the surrounding morale situation makes it entirely a different proposition. At that time, I was getting deeper into debt—I was terribly discouraged about the comparatively small sale of "Tender Is the Night"—I had Scottie on my hands as an adolescent with almost no place to turn for help except Mrs. Owens and her French teacher—and last and most important, you were an awfully sick girl yourself, in fact you had reached the very lowest point of your illness—now all that is changed and if you could see me dictating this now, sitting up in a corner of my room, fully dressed with the sun shining and full of hope and plans and merely a little angry with myself for taking on those last two jobs when I felt my health breaking, you would lose the despondency which I detect in your letters. I am quite able to work, there's no drinking question of any kind and I wish you'd think of me as getting better every day and more and more anxious to see you.

Of course, it can be arranged for you to go home for your birthday in July, but meanwhile there is another small complication which I thought you might agree with me would best be handled there in Asheville. A letter or two ago, Scottie told me that several doctors had told her that she has a chronic appendix (not acute) that should be taken care of sometime during this vacation. She wants to go to Baltimore for the graduation of her old schoolmates from Bryn Mawr School. (as you remember she skipped a year when she went to Walker's and is a year ahead of them) But those of the girls, Claire Eager and others with whom she feels very close ties and I imagine she will want to stay there a week or ten days and then my idea is that she might come South to Asheville and have her appendix out in the same hospital where I had my broken shoulder set.

I am sure there is an excellent surgeon there. Either you can inquire from Dr. Carroll or I can get in touch with that bone man, E. T. Saunders who set my shoulders or Dr. Ringer. The hospital seemed very modern and well equipped and it is now such a minor operation, as you know, that I would feel no worry on the subject. I don't want to bring her out here in June (I think it ought to be gotten over here and now) and if Scottie let slip a thing like that it is probably more important than she said and I don't think it would upset you—and I think one of us should be near her at a time like that.

I don't intend to inform her of this decision for a week, so I wish you would think the matter over and answer this letter airmail. Naturally, I don't want anything to upset you and I can have it done in New York where I am sure that Ann[e] Ober would be glad to oversee the matter, but it would seem nicer if you could be able to visit her during those seven or eight days of recuperation which I seem to remember those operations require. Let this be the test. If the idea frightens you write me frankly that you'd rather I take care of the situation. If on the contrary, you read this much without getting flustered, I don't think it would be any special strain on you.

No more news at present as I am getting back to work, but please get me off an answer to this as soon as you've had a chance to dwell on the matter yourself for an hour or so and perhaps consult someone you trust.

Ever devotedly,

P.S. Remember don't write this to Scottie. I'd rather more or less, spring it on her a couple of days before it happens because it might worry her through her exam period which is now in full flush and throw a little pall over her Baltimore adventure.

5521 Amestoy Avenue
Encino, California

227. TO SCOTT   ALS, 2 pp.
[Early June 1939]   [Highland Hospital, Asheville,
                             North Carolina]

Dearest D. O.

I will be able to see Scottie everyday; there is a very good boarding-house on the corner of this street, with good food, where she can spend the ten days of inactivity that will be necessary for recuperation.

I'm, needless to say, distressed, but am of your advice: an appendix is a very minor operation, and I will not be seriously alarmed. I am most deeply grateful to be able to have her near me; and will do everything I can to make the stay as entertaining as the situation affords.

Dr. Suitt very kindly telephoned Dr. Saunders; and through the hospital I can make arrangements: the Ashville Mission is the name of the hospital.

I'm mostly concerned about you because I know your proclivity to disregard physical observances that ought to be kept. However, I can but acknowledge that what one is unable to do anything about is better endured with equanimity than in a furor. So I am completely dependable, temperamentally; and trust that you'll soon be rosier than roses itself.

───────────

It's very good to know that at least Scottie will have a sense of parents available in times of stress; and I'm grateful that you thought of Ashville—

Dearest, take care of yourself.
Zelda

228. TO ZELDA   TL (CC), 1 p.
[Encino, California]
June 8, 1939

Dearest Zelda:-

I have two letters from you, one the airmail in regard to Scottie's operation and the other evidently posted before you had received mine. While she is in Baltimore I am having a recheck by my old friend, Dr. Louis Hamman. I gather that she has had several "attacks". On the other hand, I want to be absolutely sure that the operation is imperative. I tell you this because though she will come to Asheville in any case—I think you'd better not make absolute arrangements until I get the report from Dr. Hamman. She reaches Baltimore today the 8th (unless she stays over a day with Harold Ober or someone else in New York) and I should get the report from Dr. Hamman about the 15th or 16th—that is a few days before she is due to arrive in Asheville. I will airmail you immediately and then you can clinch whatever arrangements you find advisable.

Remember, I will take care of the business of notifying her, breaking the news by airmail as soon as I hear how long she expects to remain in Baltimore. I am glad, just as you are, that since this seems to be necessary, you will be able to be at her side.

I am awfully sorry about the news concerning your mother. This seems to be a big year for illness in our family. I shall certainly plan for you to go down to see her around your birthday time as soon as the matter of Scottie's visit—with or without operation is disposed of. Perhaps if by chance Dr. Hamman doesn't think the operation advisable we can think up some combination scheme.

In the meantime I see from your last letter you were still worried about my health. Only last night I saw the doctor who tells me that I am already 60% better (I quote him exactly) than I was a month ago—and during that time I have blocked out a novel, completed and sold a story to *Collier's Magazine*[15] and over half finished what will be a two-parter for the *Saturday Evening Post*—so you see I cannot possibly be very sick. What is the matter with me is quite definite and quite in control—the cause was overwork at the studios, and the cause being removed the illness should decrease at a faster rate than that at which it was contracted.

I am sitting outdoors as I dictate this and the atmosphere has just a breath of the back country planes [plains] in it, dry and hot though the surrounding landscaped gardens are green and cool, very different from Asheville mountains, but I never had your gift for seeing nature plainly and putting her into vivid phrasing so I am afraid I can't explain to you exactly what kind of country it is until you come here and see. Now Hollywood seems far away though it is just over the mountains and you seem very near always.

Devotedly,

229. TO ZELDA   TL (CC), 1 p.
                            June 13, 1939

Dearest:-

Will write you at length in a day or so. For a special reason (concerning a 14 year old daughter of my doctor) I want to know the

---

15. "The End of Hate," published in *Collier's*, June 22, 1940.

name of the book that you used to read going between Wilmington and Philadelphia to ballet class. The book on "art". It is stored with the rest of the library in Baltimore and it would be almost impossible for Mrs. Owens to dig it out so I want another copy. I mean that tan book—it might have been called "The Art and Craft of Drawing." I remember that it had a tan cover with a drawing embossed on it, but you may even remember the name of the author.

Would you airmail me this information as soon as you can?

Dearest love.

5521 Amestoy Avenue
Encino, California

230. TO ZELDA   TL (CC), 1 p.
                                      [Encino, California]
                                      June 17, 1939

Dearest:-

Just a note to tell you that Scottie should be there the 20th. On that day I will have the final check from Baltimore about whether or not she needs the operation and you can make final arrangements or cancel them.

Will let you know Tuesday by telegram. In haste. With dearest love,

231. TO SCOTT   ALS, 2 pp.
[c. June 20, 1939]   [Highland Hospital, Asheville,
                                           North Carolina]

Dearest Scott:

Scottie arrived, lovelier than I have ever seen her and apparently reconciled to the time in Ashville. We saw the rhododendrum parade and climbed a mountain-side; have had a tennis match and a swim. It is so good to have her here; and to find her so completely charming a companion.

The sun blazes, the heavens are auspicious and the mountain are en fête.

Today, we are going to have a blood-count taken, play golf and make arrangements at the Ashville Mission for Scotties entrance[;] needless to say I will wire you any more definite information or any change of advice. Dr. Suitt said he thought on my instigation of course it might be possible to arrange two week[s] in Alabama to-gether as soon as the recuperative period is over. Wont you write him following your own advice? It will be so happy to have a little time to-gether away from the *obligeance* of so many—no-matter-how good—regulations. We might even try Saluda, if you will give Dr. Suitt the authority for allowing me time away from the hospital.

We think of you; and entertain ourselves and enjoy the summer days. I like Ashville better every year. Since Scottie has started a novel, and a months rest of tennis and loafing (after the excitement of the past few years, during which time her life has been as closely packed as possible) dont you think a country hotel in Saluda or Bryson City would be a very pleasant prospect for a month? We can bicycle, and swim and tennis + golf, and strike up a very profitable acquaintance; and I would be most grateful for the arrangement

Devotedly Zelda

232. TO SCOTT
[June 1939]

ALS, 4 pp.
[Highland Hospital, Asheville, North Carolina]

My Dearest Scott:

The hospital phoned this evening that Scottie rests well; is not very ill from the ether and is established as a successful case. I saw her this morning before she went into the operating room. She was very brave and cheerful—and prettier than I've ever seen her. So I'm glad everything was all right.

We've had some happy times: swimming and dawdling and vaguely planning. Scottie is writing a novel. I still think that if you would arrange with this hospital for us to spend the two weeks of her recuperation in Saluda or somewhere we would be very happy at swimming and tennis and getting beat into the scrubby-pine clad hill-sides by the sun "en vacances."

However, Mamma writes that she now suffers considerably with her leg, still cant leave the house and has had to get somebody in to look after her cooking which is quite an admission of defeat from Mamma. Needless to say, short of serious inconvenience, I want to see her sometime this summer. People her age do not survive the rigors of pain and Alabama heat in summer; and I grow restive that I am unable to offer what resources I have to the many enterprizes where they would be of service.

Saluda, with a nurse, would still be less expensive than hospitalization. I'm sure we could be very happy in Alabama. Those lazy summers are so fragrant of endless Time and Eternities of people and seasons waiting and the young people were very hospitable to Scottie.

If you feel that the heat would be ill-advised after her illness, maybe you're right. Since there arent any plans for her summer, and since there's nothing more gratifying or of a deeper urgency than the parental obligation, I wish that you would ask the doctors to let me have a month or as long as possible with her.

We both like swimming, at which she is become far above average. We both enjoy tennis at which she is now awfully good and much improved and we had a good time dubbing around a golf course here one day. I will phone Mrs. Flinn[16] and find out if there arent some available acquaintances; and maybe Noonie[17] knows some youth about the hillside.

Dr. Suitt has been more than kind. We've had many pleasant excursions and happy hours together; but it isnt the same as knowing that one is free to come and go without particular authorizations.

Dr. Suitt made the arrangements about the operation, and I am most deeply obliged to him for his courtesies if you want to mention it in your letters.

Don't worry about Scottie. She's fine, has never been prettier, and is as interesting and as agreeable a companion as one could want outside her virtues as progeny.

Take care of yourself. Scottie and I think of you, lament our expense account and trust that you will not exhaust yourself on our account—because we are far more in favor of having a good family and the happiness and warmth of human relationships than we are of any luxury that would have to be provided at the cost of such.

> Devotedly
> Zelda

---

16. Possibly Nora Flynn; she and her husband, Lefty, were friends of Scott's.
17. Newman Smith, Zelda's brother-in-law.

233. TO SCOTT   ALS, 2 pp.
[June 1939]   [Highland Hospital, Asheville,
                                       North Carolina]

Dearest Scott:

The flowers you sent Scottie are a white radiance: gladioli and some little feathery other things. Her room was a gala effect to-day; which makes it far nicer to be an invalid: when one is appropriate.

The nurse says that she is a most exemplary patient. It gives me the greatest pleasure to go in to see her every day. I take her things and look on and am very happy to have her here. She is always so redolent of many happy times and the good things of life.

People at this Hospital have been most considerate and have done so many nice things: telephoning, and rememberring. I expect that Scottie will be able to leave the hospital by next Monday. We will recuperate in as gentle a fashion as is prescribed. I wish that we could spend ten days in Saluda[,] watch Time loaf up and down the dusty streets and listening to the trains whistle.

Meanwhile, the pictures appearred and I am very proud and grateful about this, especially since it appears on the editorial page. I'm sure we could sell some pictures if we could have a show.

Scottie is writing a book: won't you send her Stevensons Art of Writing, or something to give her an idea of how much more there is to such than appears to the layman? Also, if you located The Art + Craft of Drawing: would it be asking too much that you send me a copy? Books of such particular implications would probably have to be orderred in Ashville —

    Devotedly
    Zelda

234. TO SCOTT   ALS, 4 pp.
[July 1939]   [Highland Hospital, Asheville,
                                       North Carolina]

Dearest Scott:

We are distressed at the seriousness of your illness. I have known since we were to-gether in New York that your lung was in as precarious an estate as is supportable; and was glad of the little money that you had saved ahead. It is very distressing that lungs do not get better:

Although Southern California is probably beneficial to tuberculosis, this part of the world is far more conducive to healing such illness. Why dont you come East as soon as you are able and see what can be done by the more attenuate sun of Tryon Valley. Almost anything could be cured amongst such timeless vineyards and amidst these sun-drenched rocks.

It is regrettable not to be able to [offer] you more than words of sympathy at such a time when some manifestation of our devotion would be so welcome.

— Scottie is very pleasantly established. No matter where she was, she would be unable to lead a very active life until the month is out. I have supper with her and spend the late afternoons planning and felicitating myself on having her near. Yesterday she went to an awfully nice bridge party; and to-day we're taking two girls to lunch. We'll be away over the week-end, and next week will no doubt pass as pleasantly as this. So please dont picture us perishing remote from civilization or bereft of any human contact. When Scottie is able to swim and play tennis, or golf, this will be a very pleasant life again.

Here is the board-bill. We still never have any money although we are very conservative on the subject. In any case, I have no alternative to spending the least possible and leaving the circumstance to your own discretion. Needless to say, I wouldn't even consider stretching matters to the extent of Alabama this summer, or until the pressure of so many unadvantageous circumstance has lessenned. I am more than happy to have Scottie here, and she seems to have made the adjustment to a life less entertaining than is her "habitude" with a very good will. It is so happy an estate to be on terms of intimacy again. We discuss things. She feels very badly about your illness, and is seriously disposed to be of whatever help that she is able.

My own resources are not as propitious as they might have been. Rosalind telegraphs rather desultorily that she wont be able to get up here till later, and Mamma isnt coming at all. Marjorie and Noonie are in Saluda. I wish there were more to contribute.

I am so sorry that you are sick.

> Devotedly
> Zelda

235. TO SCOTT   ALS, 4 pp.
[July 1939]   [Highland Hospital, Asheville,
                                 North Carolina]

Dearest D. O:

It is so happy to have Scottie near me. We've been cake baking and reconstituting all sorts of domestic adventures from the past. The boarding house is a very friendly affaire covered with vines and steeped, somehow, in the aura of uncatalogued memories, and Scottie is very comfortable—needless to say it is with the greatest pleasure that we have supper to-gether and loaf through the summer afternoons. Recuperatively speaking, there couldnt be many better places.

Scottie spends the day working on her novel: fooling a little at bridge: browning herself in the sunshine and, I hope, making steps toward the so-inevitable adjustment of more mature circumstance: the realization that everybody elses circumstance is not readily wieldable as ones own.

She is so nice: very communicative and not restive, and I am more than happy to remark that she is *most* considerate, and makes a nice effort to find life agreeable under what, to her, can but be a restrictive circumstance.

If it is inconvenient for you that she should visit California this summer:

1) Rosalind would be more than glad to have her, I know. She and Newman are going somewhere in this state, and Scottie is surely capable of finding entertainment.

2) It would make me *very* happy to go to Alabama with her for a month. I love those deep and moonlight midnights, and surely she could profitably employ some time where life is so steeped in reminiscences for me.

3) She could board with whichever of the Taylors you chose. Cousin Cecis house is empty, renovated and you know that she would be glad to have her.

4) Any arrangement you care to make with the Hospital about my going anywhere, or being with her, will make me very happy. *This last is, of cource, my first choice.* Outside of the ties of parental relationship, Scottie is such a satisfactory companion. Her interest[s] cover a big range, and she brings a very gratifying enthusiasm to life.

—Dear: I am so sorry about your health. Maybe you yourself

would be better off in this climate where the mountains might help you find more resistance again. Why dont you move to Arizona, or come back to Tryon—*Dont* just stay there and drift away; Besides, it must be not so happy to be sick alone. If you came East Scottie and I could see you more often and maybe a sense of old associations would contribute some minor solace. Meanwhile, I wish I had something to send you: Ashville book stores are one of the towns weekest points and I know you dont want any home-spun ties—

But I think of you, and would be so glad if I could help: or even offer some stray fragment of consolatory philosophy—

Devotedly
Zelda

236. TO ZELDA   TL (CC), 1 p.
                                 [Encino, California]
                                 July 13, 1939

Dearest:-

This came from Marjorie which ought to be reassuring about your mother. In this case wouldn't you rather wait till she came North and spend some time with her at Saluda than go down into that terrible heat? Conversely if Marjorie and Noonie come up first, you might go down, pick up your mother and bring her up to Saluda which might be better for her arthritis.

Let me know what you think.

Dearest Love,

237. TO SCOTT   ALS, 4 pp.
[July 1939]   [Saluda, North Carolina]

Dearest Scott:

Whenever I come to Saluda, the impersonal nostalgias that haunt the hot baked clay banks, the hot fragrance of the pines at noon, the crickets shrilling the summer days into Eternity remind me of vacations so many years ago at Mountain Creek. I wake up these fine mornings and think of Daddy and remember the happy times that our family spent here last year.

Scottie is engrossed in novel writing and I still collect data for essays. The square dance last night would, no doubt, in more than a figurative sense have swept us off our feet save the fact that this contingent is still invalided. It will be the end of July before Scottie is allowed any very exigent exertion. Dr. Suitt has been *very* kind and liberal about letting me be with her. We share the pleasantest of rambling suppers at her domicile on the corner and entertain ourselves as seems expedient with movies, or one-of-those-things. Scottie is doing a meritorious amount of good reading, is distressed (this confidentially) that you expect so much more than average of her marks, wants rather pressingly to achieve a job of some sorts. She's full of constructive energy, which is most gratifying.

We think of you, and wish there was some means at our disposal of ameliorating the pressure of life for you. Though we are not extravagant, we usually need money. The hospital advanced me $25 for this week end—which I will reimbourse from your next allowance. We owe ten dollars on the board bill. There isnt any way of doing any economizing short of eliminating pleasure and, after all, this is not the most entertaining of existences for the very young: though it is one of the most profitable of environments for the more mature.

I wont write you any more about Montgomery[.] I hadnt realized that we were in such a precarious financial estate. Personally, this has been a very happy summer for me: to have Scottie near and see her every day. She is amazingly resourceful about finding good ways to pass the days; and Time progress[es] somewhere in a not-too-regrettable fashion—

Devotedly
Zelda

over

It cost $25 a week at the boarding house: with my suppers, movies, busses, magazines and "junk." Scotties laundry is on my bill.

We gave an awfully pleasant lunch for 4 at Grove Park costing $10 (with movies)

This board is $12: train $2: 10 taxis $3 : porters $2—junk about $2 (stamps[,] paper[,] tooth-paste): $2.60 for some raspberry stain spilled on the merchandise at Ivey's—

It's very awkward to borrow from the hospital, so wont you send us the indispensibles rather than that these things should go over?

238. TO SCOTT
[July 1939]

ALS, 4 pp.
[Highland Hospital, Asheville,
North Carolina]

Dearest Scott:

I borrowed twenty-five dollars from the hospital to pay for the Saluda week-end; also Scottie owes ten dollars on the board bill. I dislike reiterating these so material necessities as much as you hate being nagged, but I believe I had rather face the bills than the unpaid creditors. Won't you please do something about the situation:

Meantime, I had a very pleasant time in Saluda: Scottie was bored to capacity, just as you had presaged, but managed to present an equitable front. The woods down there transport me into so many happy memories: the sun shine[s] in a more Biblical beam, the mornings are earlier and more dewy—the apples are sweeter in the mint beds[?] and the roads are long and dusty. Also I like sleeping in boarded houses and like to get up to the smell of smoke in the kitchen chimney.

Please believe me when I say that I had a letter from Mamma: Dr. Suitt also had one: saying that she was physically unable to make a trip this summer. Since our finances are so strained, of cource I want to wait until we are better able to make the trip. I want you to suit your own convenience; and not tax our resources, and send me whenever you can. As far as my personal requisites are concerned, this is being a very happy summer for me, being able to see so much of Scottie and finding her such good company. Newman told me that Mamma had lost money: she told me that she was financially able to come but physically unfit. I'll send her your note; maybe it will be of some inspiration in getting her to leave the heat.

Scottie feels very bad about being on probation: is beginning to realize the significance of 1/10 of a point and prays that you will not be too disappointed in her. Her life at present is such a welter of disappointments that I too trust that you will not judge her harshly. Wont you make-up? She has been so examplary about reading; is really working on her novel; is trying to write an article for Harpers; and really makes the most she can of her times here.

Also: she sent the nurses away as soon as possible, did not take the most expensive room, has been very punctilious in her relationship with me—and so, I believe deserves whatever leniency—with which I know you will treat the circumstance—

Please take care of the money either through me or Scottie as soon as you can. We simply haven't got any because she owes Ober the $50 *because* she wrote the article to pay bills encurred at Vassar last year. We need $100 sent care of Scottie

Love
Zelda

239. TO ZELDA TL (CC), 1 p.
[Encino, California]
July 24 1939

Dearest:-

I am enclosing a check for $15.00—didn't know Scottie had bartered away her fifty in advance. Sorry she's depressed about the marks. Have been depressed about her marks for two years so maybe she can stand a little of it.

Especially sorry to keep her on short rations but there has been difficulty in finding the sort of picture job that I could do at home in this state of indifferent health. However, that is evidently going to be solved this week and I will send you something by Friday.

It seems best on the whole to bring Scottie out here (the cheapest way) for three weeks or so and I see no reason why, a little later, you can't go to see your mother if she has definitely decided not to come out here. All other plans—Virginia Beach, etc., seem expensive and fundamentally unsatisfactory. This house is bearable five days out of seven and there is room for Scottie and she seems to have it on her mind to talk over her artistic and general plans with me—our recent meetings having been very short, usually confused (and sometimes not even amicable). I am so glad you've enjoyed her and I know she's enjoyed you. I hope I will be able to bring her East later in the summer for a reunion.

240. TO SCOTT
[c. July 24, 1939]

ALS, 2 pp.
[Highland Hospital, Asheville,
North Carolina]

Dearest D-O:

For my birthday, I love the purple asters and great white immaculate daisies and yellow gladioli that you sent me. Also, I am very happy to get the book on Art once more. I have always found it a most inspiring volumn, conducive to thought and of a very constructive guidance. I deeply appreciate your thinking of me so appropriately at a time when I know that you are harassed and pursued by all sorts of troubles.

We are going to somebody's dance and will perhaps give a picnic ourselves later on.

Maybe next year we will be able to celebrate something "en famille" again, and maybe next year we will be doing some very happy thing in remembrance of the times that we were born.

Meanwhile, I'm so glad to have Scottie with me. She's such fun, and seeing her about make me happy —

    With Love
    Zelda

241. TO SCOTT
[Late July 1939]

ALS, 6 pp.
[Highland Hospital, Asheville,
North Carolina]

Dearest Scott:

Summer billows over the sky and the lakes; every green square swoons to the sway of white swirling dress and Time itself is become a transient in Ashville. We patronize the swimming place and loaf through the busses and go to the movies every now and then, and life is very agreeable to me. Scottie still pursues her novel, a vast expansive correspondence, a coat of tan and the lovliness of her natural estate. I've never seen her so pretty before: also she is well disposed toward the social graces and the summer passes ingratiatingly. We'll begin tennis again to-day; such is so appropriate to these fine skies and bright green and blue concisions that one feels far more a part of the picture, when ones four sets are accomplished.

My paintings progress. I'm making some little pictures for Rosalind and for a friend who made me some frames and one for the little boy who lives in the lane—just in case he ever emerges. I still havent got any money at the hospital, which is going to leave me in lamentable estate at the next necessity for canvas-buying. If you know Carys address, I believe that I would like to start dickering about just who is likely to be interested in my painting, and argue with him concerning all my reasons why they ought to be of the deepest irresistibility to the public.

It is so gratifying that your lungs are healing. I still think maybe Tryon would be more conducive to happiness than anywhere. After all, its a very good thing to feel good when the mornings are bright and dewy and smoke is punguent on the morning air and the world is still raw material.

Thanks for the new check. There are so few days more: we will be very conservative, as we have been up to the present. There's really nothing around here to spend money on save movies, and swimming—yet it somehow manages to dribble away and so we are grateful for the new security.

It will be sad to see Scottie leaving. Thank you very much for such a pleasant summer. She is the best of company, and we managed to find enough people that she shouldn't perish of lonliness—and I loved having her near, and we enjoyed the consideration of all sorts of possibilities—

May I once more suggest, in case the California proves too much for you now:

Ceci, Rosalind or Montgomery for the remaining month.

Dearest: I trust that you will not resent this: in a letter to Scottie you wrote that she must consider Vassar as her home. She bears the best morale a child could possibly have considering the fact of the absence of the moral support that a conventionally established family conveys, and I think it's rather a needlessly painful punishment to remind her of the absence of material attributes which to a person of twenty-one every child has a right to: the sense of safety: no matter what our circumstance, any member of my family would more than gladly extend her whatever they had to offer in case of need. Wherever I am I am always happier, just circumstantially, as well as spiritually that she should be about—I know your family would want to do anything on earth for her. So, to me, it is regrettable that she should (she does not confess to such) ever have a sense of no place to go when she in actuality has as much devotion amidst her portion as most children do.

She is such a particularly brave and self-reliant child that it would be lamentable to allow a sense of the absence of stability to twist her mind with neuroses concerning the necessity to make a living: laudable as the ambition may be *per se*.

I do not criticize your letter: but I believe that the only right of a parent to share his tragedies with children under age is of a most factual nature — how much money there is and the technical name of his illness is about the only fallibilities that debutantes are equipped to encompass. The relationship of all these things to the child itself is a matter of his or her own personal orientation, and it doesn't do any good to let them know that one is harassed.

Nobody is better aware than I am, and, I believe, so is Scottie, of your generosity, and the seriousness of your constant struggle to provide the best for us. I am most deeply grateful to you for the sustained and tragic effort that you have made to keep us going;

As I told you, I wasnt critical, only trying to remind you of the devastating ravages that a sense of insecurity usually manages to establish when theres nothing to do about it

Love and gratitude Zelda

242. TO ZELDA   TL (CC), 1 p.
                                        August 2 1939

Darling:

As I write this I suppose Scottie is getting on the train. Again this morning some of her Eastern friends called up impatiently, so she will have some company her own age beside the little Brackett girls[18] whom I don't think she likes much.

This is nothing but a note to let you know I am thinking of you.

With dearest love,

P.S. Pierre Matisse is still the man to see about those pictures. I feel that Carrie Ross did his stuff. I'm trying to think of some way of

---

18. Probably the children of screenwriter Charles Brackett.

getting them attention. How many have you got that you would want to show? There seems to be a better market now than at any time since the depression. Wasn't it preposterous that the Germans sold off all their modern art for a song in Switzerland?

5521 Amestoy Avenue
Encino, California

243. TO ZELDA   AL (draft), 4 pp.[19]
[Early August 1939]   [Encino, California]

Dearest

I know you're going to miss Scottie and I hope August passes quickly for you. It seems strange that it's here—this last month has been too much of a hell for me to help much, but now I can see light at the end of the passage. It was like 1935–1936 when no one but Mrs Owens and I knew how bad things were and all my products were dirges + elegies. Sickness + no money are a wretched combination. But, as I told you, there has *not* at least been, an accumulation of debt + there are other blessings. I see that only the rich now can do the things you + I once did in Europe—it is a tourist class world—my salary out here during those frantic 20 months turned out to be an illusion once Ober + the governments of the U.S. and Canada was paid and the doctors began.

Keep well. I'm going to try to. I'm glad your mother's illness was a false alarm.

Have arranged for Scottie to have a piano near bye, tho not in this cottage. She seems to have had a happy time with you. I have written two long + two short stories and wait daily for Swanson[20] to find me a studio job that wont be too much of a strain—no more 14 hour days at *any* price. By the time you get this I hope I'll be paying the small (not formidable) array of bills that have accumulated. Here is another check to be used most sparingly—not on presents but nessessities of Scottie's departure ect. Her tickets + travelling money

---

19. This letter may not have been sent.
20. H. N. Swanson, an agent who was helping Scott obtain screenwriting assignments.

will reach there Tuesday morning if all goes well. Her rail fare Round Trip is only 78.50 round trip, with 5.00 extra fare both ways.

Dearest Love,

Of course you can count on going South in September. We could even meet you there.

And the editorial comment about your paintings was a real thrill to me. We must do something about that soon

---

244. TO ZELDA   TL (CC), 1 p.
                                      August 4, 1939

Dearest:-

Scottie arrives tomorrow and I hope she'll enjoy the weeks out here. She doesn't like heat much and of course this is subtropical, but there is a pool nearby belonging to the landlord and as I wrote you there are boys from the East, at least for the present.

Perhaps I was unwise in telling her so succinctly that she had no home except Vassar. On the other hand, she doesn't see the matter in relation to the past. When I tried to make a home for her she didn't want it, and I have a sick-man's feeling that she will arrive in a manner to break up such tranquility as I have managed to establish after this illness. Perhaps she has changed—but this is the first time in many years that you yourself have expressed pleasure in her filial behavior. I, too, have had that, though in short doses, ever since the spring of 1934. Perhaps the very shortness of the doses has been the fault and I hope this visit will be a remedy.

In theory I tend to disagree with you about doing her harm to know where she stands. Scottie at her best is as she is now with a sense of responsibility and determination. She is at her absolute worst when she lies on her back and waves her feet in the air—so incapable of gratitude of things arranged for (the golf at Virginia Beach, for instance, or the moving picture stuff here) has been accepted as her natural right as a princess. I was sorry for the women of fifty who applied for that secretarial job in Baltimore in 1932— who had never before in their lives found that a home can be precarious. But I am not particularly sorry for a youngster who is thrown on his own at 14 or so and has to make his way through school and college, the old sink or swim spirit — I suppose, *au fond*, the difference of attitude between the North and the old South.

Anyhow, we shall think of you and talk of you a lot and look forward to seeing you and wish you were with us. I will have done something by the time you get this about your expense money there.

Dearest love,

5521 Amestoy Avenue
Encino, California

245. TO SCOTT　　　　　　　　ALS, 2 pp.
[August 1939]　　　　　　　　　　[Highland Hospital, Asheville,
　　　　　　　　　　　　　　　　　　North Carolina]

Dearest D. O.

Scottie writes tales of glamorous swimming pools and strangers from the East; of driving lessons and divers interesting pursuits that make me as envious as possible. Bonne Chance!

A tennis tournament is in progress here; at which I am glorifying myself the best I have to offer. It's very exciting: and gives a more dynamic purpose to the afternoons; besides being very edifying as an exhibition of all the progress one has made at treading so many seasons into the hills.

My painting is not as dynamic as it was some time ago; but I am expecting further inspiration at any moment. There are only 6 of the more portentious project *accomplished*: one on the canvas. By the end of next winter I expect to have at [least] twelve more finished. However, there isnt any money: I owe the Hospital $25 for the trip to Saluda, and indeed my financial estate is only possible to discuss in the most negative of terms.

Dr. Carroll asked me to discuss with you plans for an autumn excursion. Dependent upon how much money there is, I want most urgently to go to Montgomery the first of September for a few weeks. Dr. Carroll is organizing a trip to the World's Fair: but I know that it could ill be afforded at present, and I feel that Mamma has a right to whatever going I am able to contribute. The doctor says he will plan entirely according to whatever advice you write him: so please be specific. I do not want to take a nurse. It simply doubles the expenses, and is no longer necessary.

Meantime take care of your health. I'm sorry about Ober. Was the break-up of a personal nature?[21]

Devotedly

Zelda

246. TO ZELDA TL (CC), 1 p.

August 16 1939

Dearest:-

I am glad Scottie made things sound smooth out here—actually the smoothness has been pretty superficial—a long struggle to make both ends meet. However, I AM ON SALARY FROM TODAY and if I can make a go of it (picture for Universal) the worst is over. I have been paying the grocer with short pieces for Esquire, meanwhile trying to get that detachment from physical and mental worries which is necessary for a good short story. There is one with the *Post* now which I hope will take us out of the red.

Scottie had an exciting first two days because of the Princeton boys who waited to see her. Our neighbors filled up their little pool and all in all she hasn't had a bad time but of course nothing like I have been able to give her in the past. I like her—she's come up a long way from last year. She has been conscientiously learning to drive on a heavily mortgaged Ford and has been writing a short story which seems to me pretty darned good as well as doing lyrics for a musical show.

Taking up the matters in your letter: I am writing Dr. Suitt in the same mail asking him to please do something about the swimming and that on Monday when the pay checks begin to arrive I will begin to get myself out of the red in the hospital. I repeat what I said before—that this catastrophe has not left us in that awful shape of 1936 and it even seems quite feasible that you will be able to go home to see your mother some time in September. I can't promise about the 1st of September, but I am doing my absolute best to make life comfortable for us all.

---

21. After his longtime literary agent, Harold Ober, refused Scott any further advances (which he took as a sign that Ober no longer believed in him), Scott broke with him. Scottie continued to live with the Obers, with whom she had a warm and loving home.

The World's Fair trip would seem to be out in the immediate future. It would come at the end of a list of absolute necessities such as taxes, insurance, living expenses, Vassar tuition, and your trip to see your mother. If things break beautifully anything is possible but I do not see it as a possibility for the early Autumn. My own plan is to get East, if possible, in November for a while at least.

Dearest love,

5521 Amestoy Avenue
Encino, California

247. TO SCOTT   ALS, 3 pp.
[c. August 15, 1939]   [Saluda, North Carolina]

Dear Scott:

I avail myself of this first opportunity to write you more frankly; while I am absent from the hospital.

First: the hospital is very expensive and, from my most unbiased point of view, hospitalization is of no urgency in my case. Dr. Carroll to be literal, Dr. Suit in Carrolls name, himself advises less introspection, more company, less brooding and dreaming: as you know it is extremely difficult to obtain any sort of social priviledge from those authorities. Although they have been generous, considerate and kind for a long time, nevertheless it deprives one of the sense of independence and of the right of spontaneous decision to have signed warrants planned ahead, for the most inconsequential of actions —

Mamma would be glad of company, and it would be a very constructive plan to let me visit her for 3 months beginning the first of Sept.

Whats the use of wasting so much money — when you are not situated so that any such extravagance is possible to be conveniently borne

Second: Scottie has a right to any sense of social warmth that her parents are able to convey; and even though she avails herself very little of the priviledge, I would like to be able to offer the kindness of a parental lodging.

I hope things are not of a very revolutionary nature; or even a very drastic policy — because you promised me long ago, last spring, that you'd help me to get out of this confinement by the next fall —

I'm spending two days in Saluda—It's good to hear the woods buzzing at high-noon, and good to smell the good things on the morning air—

I'm glad your summer is of a successful nature; and hope that you will find Scottie as engaging a companion as I did—

Please let me go home—

Devotedly

Zelda

Please answer discreetly.

248. TO ZELDA TL (CC), 1 p.

August 18 1939

Dearest Zelda:-

Got your letter from Saluda. Will absolutely try to arrange the Montgomery trip early in September. You letter made me sad, and I wish I could say "Yes, go where you want right away"—but it doesn't take into consideration the situation here. I will be much better able to grapple with the problem and with Dr. Carrol two weeks from now. A severe illness like mine is liable to be followed by a period of shaky morale and at the moment I am concerned primarily with keeping us all alive and comfortable. I'm working on a picture at Universal and the exact position is that if I can establish their confidence in the next week that I am of value on this job it will relieve financial pressure through the fall and winter.

Scottie is very pleasant and within the limits of her age, very cooperative to date—on the other hand, she's one more responsibility, as she learns to drive and brings me her work and this summer there is no Helen Hayes to take her on a glamor tour of Hollywood. All of which boils down to the fact that my physical energy is at an absolute minimum without being definitely sick and I've got to conserve this for my work. I am as annoyed at the unreliability of the human body as you are at the vagaries of the nervous system. Please believe always that I am trying to do my best for us all. I have many times wished that my work was of a mechanical sort that could be done or delegated irrespective of morale, for I don't want or expect happiness for myself—only peace enough to keep us all going. But your happiness I want exceedingly, just as I want Scottie's safety.

I am writing Dr. Carrol a long letter in a week's time of which I will send you a carbon. I have already written Dr. Suitt about the swimming.

    With dearest love,

5521 Amestoy Avenue
Encino, California

That fall, Zelda's family pressured Scott to let her leave the hospital, and Zelda began to press him, as well. Scott, who was sick and totally broke, began to resent the constant intrusions—requests that he see to Zelda's every need, in addition to urgings that new living arrangements be made for her. The tone of Zelda's letters changed from the happy optimism that characterized the summer to loneliness as winter approached.

249. TO SCOTT   ALS, 4 pp.
[Fall 1939]   [Highland Hospital, Asheville,
                        North Carolina]

Dear Scott:

I'm sorry about our present estate. So many years ago when we were first married and making Holiday about the Biltmore corridors, money was one of the things one simply stated the necessity for, went through the requisite ritual and waited. Now that 50¢ this way or that may, any day, begin to count it is become of vastly more relevance. In view of the fact that the war will probably make jobs a lot harder to get in California, wont you consider curtailing our expences as seems exigent? There is so little necessity for keeping me here: I would be of service in Montgomery besides being happy to be there, and keeping up two ménages is that much easier than keeping up three. Meantime, you promised me two years ago that you would pursue the matter of my going home. Time goes on, as you have perhaps remarked, and still I have no social status beyond that of a liability.

I play tennis, and paint pictures and go to the movies. There is occasionally a party. Last week the Hospital gave a most entertaining folk-dancing festival; and, as you know, we climb mountains and brood. It's an awfully nice place; do not think that I am ungrateful that I ask you most urgently to remember how long I have been devoting myself to the observance of the strictest of regimes: medical observation: and to remember that life is not an inexhaustible store of Efforts to no deeper purpose than that of ameliorating the immediate circumstance

I too am most grateful to the Finneys for their courtesies to Scottie. Has her party been cancelled? She seemed very controlled and reconciled to whatever curtailment had to be made when she was here. She is really of a very judicious temperament and makes adverse adjustment with a most commendable philosophy.

I suggested to you before that short of an actual job in Hollywood, this part of the world is far more conducive to good health: also it is cheaper — Why dont you consider it again?

Outside of offering suggestions, I am not in a position to be of any assistance —

Colleeen Moore's[22] dolls-house is now on exhibit in Ashville. I remember a most depressing evening of sitting around her house while people withheld their approbrium until they had placed what was wrong with each other — It would no doubt have made interesting reminiscence had I not forgot all save the aura of House-detective that pervaded the gathering

    Devotedly
    Zelda

250. TO SCOTT ALS, 2 pp.
[Fall 1939] [Highland Hospital, Asheville,
                                North Carolina]

Dear D. O:

It rains; and sleets; and is indeed as malevolent a time as ever attacked. The hills are steeped in cosmic regrets and the valleys are flooded with morose and aimless puddles.

However, the stores bloom and blossom and ingratiate themselves with the brightest of spring-times and the newest of aspirations. The drugstores are still fragrant of chocolate and aromatic of all sorts of soaps and bottled miracles. This town is so redolent of hushed

---

22. Hollywood actress, whom the Fitzgeralds met in Hollywood in 1927.

rendézvous: I always think of you when I wait in Faters for the bus or hang around Eckerts before a movie — or even after a movies, thus making orgy.

"The Hunchback of Notre Dame"[23] is the most magnificent fusion of music and action and the significance of lines that I have seen. The acting is far more than usually compelling: and the orchestration does not confine itself to the music but includes the whole performance.

There does not seem to be any news: which some people think of in terms of an advantage, but which, to me, presents itself vaguely in terms of disaster. Well anyway we're better off than the Finns + the Russians.[24]

I cant understand about your stories. The school that you started and the vogue which you began are still dictating the spiritual emulation of too many people for your work to be irrelevant: and certainly the tempo of the times ought to bring you some success.

Would it be a good idea if you tried Harold Ober again? That seems to me a most sensible way of handling the situation: Ober knows so much better than anybody else how to handle your work.

> Devotedly
> Zelda

Peter Liddle might be a lucky nom-de-plume.[25]

251. TO ZELDA   AL (draft), 9 pp.[26]
[Fall 1939]   [Encino, California]

Dearest Zelda:

It is two in the morning. I have been sleeping since ten. All day I've been working on a novel for which the magazine publishers have

---

23. 1939 film, starring Charles Laughton, Cedric Hardwicke, and Maureen O'Hara.
24. The Soviet Union invaded Finland in 1939.
25. Scott was considering writing under a pseudonym: "I'm awfully tired of being Scott Fitzgerald," he later wrote to Arnold Gingrich of *Esquire*; "I'd like to find out if people read me just because I am Scott Fitzgerald or, what is more likely, don't read me for the same reason" (*Life in Letters* 433).
26. Scott probably never sent this letter. The draft and a typescript are in the Bruccoli Collection at the Thomas Cooper Library of the University of South Carolina. This text is from *Correspondence* 557–559.

agreed to back me if they like the first twelve thousand words. It looks like a way out and Im putting everything I have into it. At twelve the mail came but certain letters I put aside unopened as I've done for a week—letters of quiet abuse from your family.

I am not very well—one lung is all gone now and I broke two fingers in the hand writing this when I tried to lift off my bed-desk by myself last Saturday. But of course that is all a secret because if the magazine knew I was not quite well it wouldn't help me write the novel. I care about the novel but not especially about anything else anymore. That a fifty dollar ticket to Montgomery would in some way purchase your eternal mental health is a proposition I will not debate. I wont even debate it with Dr Carrol—if he says it will, then Godspeed you. I should think that before Christmas—if I can get some peace—you could go south (to Montgomery) for a long trip *with* supervision. But the other story is too dreary—what would you do—because if you did go on your own I would fold up completely—for paints or amusements or clothes? Scottie would have to work + not be able to send you much for some time. Id lie very quietly in my grave out here but I think the spectre of you walking the streets of Montgomery in rags as the last of the Sayres, followed by curious urchins, would haunt me.

There'd be no one to help—even Newman hid behind his wife's skirts in an emergency. Just a horrible death in life.

For, Zelda, if you were capable of organizing anything you would do it there. What would I not give for the right to leisure—have you ever known me to have it? To be well, to be kept well, to have my pencil + paper bought for me, to not think of taxes and insurance and other peoples health and bringing up a child. I'd love to wake up some morning once and say: No cares today, no debts, no moneylenders, no mental prostitution, nothing between me and my canvas except my hand—and that well, not broken—the little finger trails across this page. I am not sorry for you this time—I envy you. And I am infinitely more sorry for my expiring talent which you tell me will be helped "by releasing you." That is equivalent to the great peace I should find if Scottie begged to contribute to the family fortunes by entering a steel mill or a whore-house.

You are a darling sometimes—I cant claim this distinction—but unfortunately you have given no signs that you can be anything more. And being a darling isn't enough. You've got to have the energy to sell your pictures—I can't forever find you Cary Rosses—and to live a literary life outside of mine. And where is that energy to proceed from? Are you to find it in Montgomery conversing with the shades of Mrs Mckinney? It is all right to conceive of life in terms of a vast nostalgia if it has an artistic purpose, or if it is a personal idiosyncracy like collecting old coins—but the world wont permit it unless it is self supporting. It's a luxury that even the rich, now, can scarcely afford. *We*—we consumptives, mistaken people, workers, die-ers, we must live—not at your expence, God knows, but in spite of you. We have our tombstones to chisel—and can't blunt our tools stabbing you back, you ghosts, who can't either clearly remember or cleanly forget.

I would rather do what I did in August—club the whole archaic Brenda Fraser[27] idea out of Scottie's mind, but separating her from her roommate—and have her indignation forever, than present the picture of a brood of unmatured pigs sucking at my nipples forever. If this be treason make the most of it. As a fighter, if she were contemporary, I admire your mother. In her present rôle of sinister old witch, I think she adds no dignity to anyone's stature. Why doesn't she get Tilde home? Or Rosalind?

Do you think she cares or ever has cared about you or your impersonal interest? Do you think she would ever quarrel with you for your impersonal good? She constructed herself on a heroic romantic model as a girl and you were to be the stuffed dummy—true or false, screwed or chaste, honest or bogus,—on which she was to satisfy her egotism. She chose me—and she did—and you submitted at the moment of our marriage when your passion for me was at as low ebb as mine for you—because she thought romanticly that her projection of herself in you could best be shown thru me. I never wanted the Zelda I married. I didn't love you again till after you became pregnant. You—thinking I slept with that Bankhead—making all your drunks innocent + mine calculated till even *Town Topics*[28] protested. I'd been drunk, sure—but find any record of me as a drunk at Princeton—or in the army, except one night when I retired to the locker room. You were the drunk—at *seventeen*, before I knew you—already notorious.

This is the very questionable element I bought and your mother asks to be given back—for some vague reason known fully in the depths of your family psychology. The assumption is that you were a great prize package—by your own admission many years after (and for which I have [never] reproached you) you had been

---

27. A leading debutante of the day.
28. Popular magazine of the 1920s, which specialized in gossip.

seduced and provincially outcast. I sensed this the night we slept to-
gether first for you're a poor bluffer and I loved you—romantically—
like your mother, for your beauty + defiant intelligence; but unlike
her I wanted to make it useful. I failed, as she did, but my intentions were a hell of lot purer and since you could have left me at
any time I'd like to discover the faintest basis for your family's
accusation that I drove you crazy. In so far as it was the conscious
work of man, that old witch drove you crazy. You were "crazy" in
the ordinary sense before I met you. I rationalized your eccentricities and made a sort of creation of you. But dont fret—if it hadn't
been you perhaps I would have worked with more stable material.
My talent and my decline is the norm. Your degeneracy is the
deviation

    (end of thought)

252. TO ZELDA

TL (CC), 1 p.[29]
October 6 1939

Dearest Zelda:-

Living in the flotsam of the international situation[30] as we all are,
work has been difficult. I am almost penniless—I've done stories for
Esquire because I've had no time for anything else with $100. bank
balances. You will remember it took me an average of six weeks to
get the mood of a Saturday Evening Post story.

But everything may be all right tomorrow. As I wrote you—or did
I—friends sent Scottie back to college.[31] That seemed more important than any pleasure for you or me. There is still two hundred dollars owing on her tuition—and I think I will probably manage to find
it somewhere.

After her, you are my next consideration; I was properly moved by
your mother's attempt to send for you—but not enough to go over-
board. For you to go on your first excursion *without* a nurse, *without*

---

29. Scott may have sent this letter in place of the more bitter one (no. 251).

30. On September 1, 1939, German soldiers invaded Poland, annexing Danzig and causing
Britain and France to declare war on Germany two days later.

31. The Murphys loaned Scott the money for part of Scottie's tuition.

money, without even enough to pay your fare back, when Dr. Carrol is backing you, and when Scottie and I are almost equally as helpless in the press of circumstances as you—well, it is the ruse of a clever old lady whom I respect and admire and who loves you dearly but not wisely.

None of you are taking this very well. Rosalind and Newman who wouldn't lend Scottie a few hundred for Vassar entrance, when, in 1925, I lent him five hundred—and you and I were living on a bank margin of *less than I lent*! It would, according to Rosalind, behind whom he hid, inconvenience them. I *borrowed* to lend him the money when his life-insurance policy lapsed! Live and learn. Gerald and Sar[a] *did* lend me the money!—and as gracefully as always.

I ask only this of you—leave me in peace with my hemorrhages and my hopes, and what eventually will fight through as the *right* to save you, the *permission* to give you a chance.

Your life has been a disappointment, as mine has been too. But we haven't gone through this sweat for nothing. Scottie has got to survive and this is the most important year of her life.

With Dearest Love Always,

5521 Amestoy Avenue
Encino, California

253. TO SCOTT
[October 1939]

ALS, 5 pp.
[Highland Hospital, Asheville,
North Carolina]

Dear Scott:
Needless to say; your letter somewhat hurt me. Very possibly you do not give thought to the fact that this hospital regimentation, while most excellent for whipping into shape, is very gruelling over long periods of time. Pleasure, twice a week—from my most unbiased attitude—is indispensable. The authorites have been *most* kind about sending me to the movies and advancing money for necessities; and I am deeply indebted to Dr. Carroll for his courtesy and consideration, and even generosity

However: Christmas is coming[.] I want to remember Scottie and Rosalind and Mamma—most imperatively, and there is a friend here that the social usage as well as my good-will would like to give something to.

I can charge in Gene Wests if you will drop her a note to that effect: but I would prefer that—if such is within possibility—you send me *direct* cash not through the Bank but care [of] Grove Park Inn. If you will write me that you want me to look up some friends of yours there; and will let me know when I will understand that there is a communication there for me. It's awful to be stripped of any sane resources of a vaguely charitable nature.

Especially since there is no minimizing the fact that I have a right to feel that I would be better off at home released from this five hours physical effort in the freezing cold—It is good for one year and agony for three. I am now well able to make a social in the bigger sense effort: Mamma would be happy to have me: if any trouble arose I could and would return here—and short of your possibly paranoiacal self-defensive reflex I cant see any legitimization of keeping me under hospitalization much longer.

I am indeed grateful that Scottie is having such a happy time. She is a very fortunate person in lots of ways and its good that the war hasnt hit her good fortune as yet. Is there any chance of seeing her during the holidays?

About yourself: I am appreciative of the difficulties of your circumstance. It's more than hard to work when you're sick—and I trust that life will not continue forever in the heaping of ashes. If you would let me do what is of a socially constructive; and personally desirable nature you would at least be released from the financial obligations of this very expensive place.

You wrote me an accusatory letter of distrust concerning *ambivalences*[?]. There is every reason to believe that I am more able to observe the social dictat[e]s than yourself—on the evidence of our *"vacations"* from the hospital—which have been to date a dread affair of doctors and drink and confirmation of the impossibility of any equitable reunion. Although you know this—and that the probabilities are much against our ever having any life together again—you are persistent in not letting me have a chance to exist alone—at least in comfort—in Alabama and make my own orientation. Or even in Ashville. *I might* be able to get a job: in any case living outside costs far less than living in, paying for medical supervision that is no longer requisite. I could board and do half time here for far less than I now cost; and I would be relatively happier. Wont you, in fairness, please consider this letter from some other basis than that I am your possible enemy and that your first obligation is self-defensive and answer me care of the Inn— because although there is no rule against "ad lib" patients communicating outside the hospital it might be questioned. I dont want to have my letters boiled down to a very optimistic evasion of all issues of a very relevant nature.

I trust that you will accord me the courtesy to acknowledge the justice of this presentation.

—After all: twenty dollars is the price of friends to dinner to you— and would keep me entertained a month.

    Sincerely
    Zelda

Oil paints cost $5 [a] canvas; and about $4 paint and oil—is a very expensive field and is therefore in an abeyance that I trust to be temporary—

I paint water colors

254. TO ZELDA   TL (CC), 1 p.
                              November 20 1939

Dearest Zelda:-

Things go along rather precariously here. I've gotten $100. ahead this week, enough to make it possible to submit the first two chapters of the novel to Collier's, I think. And this morning a barage of telegrams from Scottie asking for some quite necessary money (getting a coat out of storage, etc., plus transportation to Baltimore for the long awaited Peaches Finney party) which puts quite a dent in the sum.

Isn't it strange that a year ago there was so much and now suddenly it's as hard to come by as it was in 1936. I wish you had some merchandising instinct and could think of a way of selling some of your pictures. Couldn't you photograph enough of them to make up a sort of looseleaf booklet so that we could get someone interested?

Now please try not to worry me with any problems for a week as I need peace of mind desperately.

    With dearest love,

5521 Amestoy Avenue
Encino, California

255. TO SCOTT
[November 1939]

ALS, 4 pp.
[Highland Hospital, Asheville,
North Carolina]

Dearest Scott:

The world makes theatre for the most scintillant and rarified of weathers. The mornings are decorous and perfected and outlined in frost and the dusks are lonely and haunted and nostalgic, and lovely. These regions of such dramatic silhouette are the best of sets for whatever cosmic ———— constitutes the fall.

Thanks very much for the money. I will start painting again to-morrow with the greatest enthusiasm. I still dream of one-day launching these dynamics of the soul upon the public, and will keep my aspiration as life permits.

Won't you *please* do something about my trip home? I've got the money; as you know Mamma very much wants to see me. It is not improbable that having been confined to her house since last February she feels—as I do myself that there will not always be a home to go to. May I go at Thanksgiving; or do you prefer Christmas? I'm sure that Doctor Carroll will subscribe to whatever you suggest, if you will be kind enough to give him the authorization.

Meantime, its wonderful news about the novel. It must give you a most constructive and aspirational presentation of life to feel that you are progressing again. This ought to be a most auspicious time for books about the movies. In times of such stress, any field of glamour has an added desirability.

One last word of business flavor. My friends here have a weekly allowance for pleasure money. Would it be possible to arrange with the hospital for me to have three dollars a week (*not* to include paint-ing expense which is far more, and can go in my bills, or as you arrange). The money is for dinner in town, a movie, or to treat a friend to a soda occasionally. It is impossible to obtain access to any funds without the family's consent so wont you take care of this for me? It wont be possible to start on the fifty dollars just sent as allowance because I need it for Christmas presents, and to buy new canvas. But as you are able will you write Dr. Carroll about the pin-money.

Dont work too hard: you wont ever be able to replace your lungs, but you might some other time be able to write a book.

Rosalind write[s] of a glamorous winter for Scottie. She says there was a lovely picture of her in the paper. I'll try to corral one for us. I suppose the youth will turn more apostrophicly tragic and dramatic than even of our own time due to the strategic moment in which the[y] seek their destiny. I envy them.

Devotedly
Zelda

256. TO SCOTT   ALS, 2 pp.
[December 1939]   [Highland Hospital, Asheville,
                                        North Carolina]

Dear Scott:

Thanks for the money. Wont you wire me where to reach Scottie at Christmas? Is there any probability of her coming to Ashville? And still—what shall I do about giving her a present? Wont you wire me credit to Jean West? I'm sure she wouldnt press you for the bill.

Meantime: I paint on a small scale, and do the best I can to present life to myself in the glibbest possible terms. I most drearily [dearly?] want to live outside: I could still commute; if you want me to stay under medical jurisdiction, and such arrangement would be so much less expensive than persisting in this *join* that is not of any particular relevance any more. It seems to me that Carroll would be glad to be rid of the financial liabilities, at least.

Meantime: I haven't any superficial revelations to make and all the things I want to tell you are of so much import that I dont like to begin until circumstance is become less harassing.

Scottie must have been wreathed in dreams at the ball. It is, au moins, an inspiration to begin life under such auspices

The Ashville sky is treating us not unkindly; as yet there have been no casualities from blizzard or from cosmic threatenings: however I often envy you the blooming clouds of California—and am glad that at least you are warm—

Devotedly
Zelda

257. TO ZELDA   TL (CC), 1 p.
                                     December 6 1939

Dearest Zelda:-

I will somehow manage to pay that bill at Jean West's though she may have to wait a couple of months, but I am confused by this. Won't the hospital wonder where you got a new dress? The only thing would be to pretend that Rosalind sent it to you from Atlanta care of Jean West or that Rosalind authorized Jean West to make it for you. But for God's sake be careful because you know that Dr. Carroll would consider this wiring and writing me from outside as a complete breach of good faith on both our parts. I cannot write him directly because I know that the hospital would immediately deprive you of any leave. So it's much better for you not to telegraph me or communicate with me in any form at present except through legitimate hospital channels. It should be very apparent to you that since I am in the red with them I have no possible right to buy you clothes or outfits that you couldn't in any way accept through the hospital with their consent and cooperation. I am only too aware how much lack of money cripples a person.

This autumn is awfully important in Scottie's life and I want her to have a decent amount of clothes. Someone sent her a $25.00 bag and she changed it for an evening dress, but I assure you that however she may have appeared to you last spring this dose of poverty is making her very cautious about every penny she spends. She seems to be doing excellently at Vassar this year, at least I hope I can believe the good words that she writes me in her letters, but it is just simply impossible for me to outfit you this fall. Tuberculosis is much worse and I have been again confined to bed.

As I told you before, I do plan if it can possibly be managed, for you to go to Montgomery Christmas and equally to give you and Scottie a glimpse of each other. On the other hand if you play hooky you haven't a chance of getting away with it. The hospital will catch you up sooner or later. There is nothing that I have to communicate with you that isn't perfectly obvious. It boils down to the fact that I am very sick and very poor. If you are put "on bounds" again their whole attitude toward you will change in a minute.

Dearest love,

5521 Amestoy Ave.
Encino, California

258. TO ZELDA   TL (CC), 1 p.
                                      December 15 1939

Dearest Zelda:-

Writing you at length tomorrow. Think, hope, believe, but have no confidence ever that I am going to work in Metro within the next two days. I have left the Swanson agency. There's nothing like your old friends to hold you back.

      With dearest love always,

5521 Amestoy Avenue
Encino, California

259. TO SCOTT   ALS, 4 pp.
[December 31, 1939]   [Highland Hospital, Asheville,
                                   North Carolina]

Dear Scott:

Bright immutable skies discipline this last day of the year into whatever annals it has inspired: one is granted a momentary respite from the passage of time.

May the New Year bring you every happiness, good health, and lots of money. Aspiration and inspiration are also two attributes that one should be happy of their bestowal

I will be making resolutions: each year I promise to perfect myself according to the best of my circumstance: thinking of ways to be and how to be it. It is good to meet the most aspirational facet of the immediate possibilities, and good to feel that ones resources are being exploited to capacity.

I will be very happy to see Scottie: it must be wonderful to have the world making its debut; and maybe even more wonderful—if also more cruel to be growing up in a world of such changing horizons. That generation will certainly need all the resources that they have been able to amass: which should be quite a lot because our time was too appalled at its own mistakes to take any chances; and thus gave the children a little after the manner of the bitter but conquering baron: the most of the "standard" of the era that they could afford.

Dear: won't you please communicate with the hospital about letting me go? I am honestly well able to be out trying to "*debrouir*" [look after] myself; and want so dearly to make the effort.[32] There isnt forever left to either of us; and now, for the immediate instance I have a home to turn to while I organize an existence—which will not always be the case. There's no use evading these issues. It is extremely awkward to be without money but even more awkward not to be able to face the issue.

I now have *no* resources left; can't go to the movies because there isn't any money[.] Under such circumstance, wouldn't it be wiser and more economical that I should be at home where my time might be more profitably employed? Since I can't go to the movies? I ask you to acknowledge not only on the basis of your obligation to me—as your wife—but also on the terms of your social obligation: when there isn't any money one has to live some other way, under a more fitting circumstance. I know that Mamma will be very happy to have me at home.

Meantime: its good to be able to receive uncensored mail—I do believe I'm growing up.

There isnt any news: I havent seen our mutual friend any more but intend to look her up, sometime when I'm able to ask her to do something.

Devotedly
Zelda

260. TO SCOTT ALS, 2 pp.
[January 1940] [Highland Hospital, Asheville,
  North Carolina]

Dear Scott:
The wind seeps under the window ledge and all periods of rest visit these mountain[s] on the qui-vivre. For the last few days: the Cosmos has been exhausting its repetoire of bad times until this Sunday evening, the world is almost balmy and at peace again. Or so it would seem.

I have been vastly enjoying the rather[?] alive air of having ten

---

32. Zelda had gone home for Christmas without a nurse for the first time since her hospitalization.

dollars. I am going to pay a luncheon obligation and maybe buy something with whats left. I have always felt mean about spending your money when there isn't any; the conviction of the tragedy of human destinies has long haunted us both.

It is nothing short of miraculous that Scottie manages to fulfill her obligations with the days and months being told off on a rosary of day-coaches. It is a most impressive feat; and I'm so glad that scholasticly she is bringing more interest to bear on the situation; because she is so very alert and of such a comprehensive mind as goodness knows she ought to be considering the price of her education.

I had a very pleasant Christmas card from the Obers: and I believe that Scottie is still on amicable terms. I never quite knew what the row was about, but I suppose in these extremely difficult times agents also are having their bad moments.

Dont you know *somebody* in Ashville to whom you could give me an introduction and who might give me a job? It would be such salvation to be at work in any possible capacity.

Devotedly   Zelda

261. TO SCOTT   ALS, 3 pp.
[January 1940]   [Highland Hospital, Asheville,
                            North Carolina]

Dear Do-Do:

The least terminable of winters spins itself out into shop-worn editions of what winters ought to be: snow drifts and freezes in embryonic designs around the edges of things and time stalls laconicly along the scraped road-bed. It must be wonderful to earn ones living; and to be a person of positive policies again. Dr. Carroll has apportioned me a job which is of the deepest interest, if of somewhat gargantuan proportions. The windows of the assembly room in the new building are to have flower screens 8 × 4 ft — The job will probably take years: but painting for a public building such as this will be when Duke takes over is an ambitious and very compelling project.

The doctor says that he will pay me something for the work. Of course, he furnishes the materials.

When I first came here, I engaged myself in controver[s]y on the same subject. Dr. Carroll wanted screens for Homewood and I sent word that I ultimately would not subscribe to the commande[e]ring of professional talent. The fact that an artist is temporarily incapacitated ought not to make him fair game to anybody who is able. My talent has cost a lot in heart-ache and paint-bills; and I dont want to compromise myself on such a major project that will make it difficult to get away, should such opportunity arise—

The money gives me the possibility of roaming and romancing around town at will—the speculative possibilities of the urban scene are so vastly enhanced by money. The right to window-shop is, I suppose, the possibility of buying, and so its more fun to promener with the social guarantee than without.

The little bar (Dont be alarmed; it would be as good as my liberty should I ever be tempted thus) is now an antique shop. Ashville desperately needs some-sort of rendez-vous. I wish we could get backing for a coffee-shop. The college kids go to the drug-store; and the other people go home to forage. However, the new auditorium flourishes. It's a very impressive, very modern structure which bears a most official. All public structure is more appropriate if approaching the convertible barra[c]ks, assembly house nature, to me[?].

Scottie sent me a program of the Ballet Russe[.] This will never cease pulling at my heart-strings: not that I wish it would.

————————————

The news about your lungs is very gratifying. I'm so glad you're well enough again that life will, at least intuitively, be less of a burden. If your novel is good, there are probably so many happy still somewhere to be had. Why dont you revise everything; be [illegible]; and see what happens?

> Devotedly
> Zelda

I'll send on this article sometime this week.

262. TO ZELDA   TL (CC), 1 p.
                                       January 31 1940

Dearest Zelda:-

The article arrived and from a first brief glance I shall say that it is going to be rather difficult to sell. However, I will read it thoroughly tonight and report. Even a very intellectual magazine like the Forum or the Atlantic Monthly prefers their essays to contain some certain number of anecdotes or some dialogue or some cohesive and objective events. Of course, you might claim that your whole article was conversation and in a sense it is, but it is one person's conversation and thus does not contain much conflict. However I think it is damn good considering that your pen has been rusty for so long. Shall I suggest you some ideas which you might handle with more chance of realizing on them? Tell me.

Dear, I know no one in Asheville except a couple of secretaries and nurses and the clerks at the hotel. I was ill all the time I was there and confined to my room most of the time so I have no idea how you would make business contacts. This seems to be a great year for art and I wish you would drop a line to Carry Ross or someone about your new paintings and see if there is some interest. That would be a more practical way of getting things in motion than taking up something you're unfamiliar with.

All is the same here. I think I have a job for next week. I know I've finished a pretty good story—the first one adequate to the Post in several years. It was a hard thing to get back to. My God, what a fund of hope and belief I must have had in the old days! As I say I will write you more about the story tomorrow.

Dearest love,

5521 Amestoy Avenue
Encino, California

263. TO ZELDA   TL (CC), 1 p.
                                     February 6 1940

Dearest Zelda:-

I understand your attitude completely and sympathize with it to a great extent. But the mood which considers any work beneath their talents doesn't especially appeal to me in other people, though I acknowledge being sometimes guilty of it myself. At the moment I am hoping for a job at Republic Studios, the lowest of the low, which would among other things help to pay your hospital bill. So the fact that anything you do can be applied on your bill instead of on our jaunt to the Isles of Greece doesn't seem so tough.

However, I am disappointed, with you, that the future Ruskins and Elie Faurés and other anatomists of art will have to look at your windows instead of the mail hall. But something tells me that by the time this letter comes you will have changed your point of view. It is those people that have kept your talent alive when you willed it to sink into the dark abyss. Granted it's a delicate thing—mine is so scarred and buffeted that I am amazed that at times it still runs clear. (God what a mess of similes)[.] But the awful thing would have been some material catastrophe that would have made it unable to run at all.

Dearest love,

5521 Amestoy Avenue
Encino, California

264. TO SCOTT   ALS, 2 pp.
[February 1940]   [Highland Hospital, Asheville,
                                     North Carolina]

Dear Scott:

Thanks, again, for the money. I employ it very profitably buying "time" in Ashville. I sent Rosalind some flowers for Valentine: she remembered me so generously at Christmas; it gave me great pleasure to be able to let her know that I was thinking of her. I also sent Scottie two dollars; and I sent Mamma a present. So the money covered rather more ground than usual.

About the screens: we have reached a compromise. I am now going to make them out of *tempora*; it [is] a manner sheerly decoratif—which is a less distressing entertainment than having to think of my best and most exacting talents being buried in within the confines of psychotic morass. No matter how I felt about the uselessness and inappropriateness of the task; the reason I wrote you so pressingly was this: I do not believe, and Dr. Carol has lead me to believe that he is not averse to the idea, that it is necessary for me to stay in the hospital[.] I do not willingly subscribe to helping, or trying to help to pay bills which are entirely unnecessarily encurred. *We* could more profitably employ that money other wise; and with such effort as the screens will demand I might even make a living.

I am resentful; and within my right to resent this being buried alive when there isn't any adverse social judgment to substantiate the proceeding any longer. However, I grant you that theres nothing I can do about it—

Meantime the weathers fairly decent; and I await the spring with whatever equanimity I can find—

Devotedly
Zelda

265. TO ZELDA   TL (CC), 1 p.
March 8 1940

Dearest Zelda:-

It is wonderful to be able to write you this. Dr. Carroll has for the first time and at long last agreed that perhaps you shall try to make a place for yourself in the world. In other words, that you can go to Montgomery the first of April and remain there indefinitely or as long as you seem able to carry on under your own esteem.

So after four years of Dr. Carroll's regime interrupted by less than twenty scattered weeks away from the hospital, you will have the sense of being your own boss. Already I can share your joy and I know how Scottie will feel.

I am sorry your entrance will not be into a brighter world. I have no real finances yet and won't until I get a job. We have to live on those little pieces in Esquire and you know how little they pay. Scottie speaks of getting a job in Lord and Taylor's this summer but I do not want her to do that for all sorts of reasons. Maybe by the time you get home things will be brighter. So there we are.

    With dearest love,

5521 Amestoy Avenue
Encino, California

266. TO SCOTT   ALS, 4 pp.
[March 1940]   [Highland Hospital, Asheville,
                           North Carolina]

Dearest D. O

    The afternoons are long, and bleak; the winds blows itself off on the traditions of the Brontes, and Edgar Allen Poe: and time is become interminable.

    Mamma writes me, generously, again of defraying a trip home. *I did not ask* her; and since she is so spontaneously thoughtful and generous, I dont see why you wont let me accept a trip on a minimum scale.

    I'm trying to write a short story. It is entertaining; but maybe not as professionally coordinated as it should be. I'll send it to you as soon as its finished. I want to sell it to the American Magazine. The winter time is so much longer and more arduous than people of this tired uncatalogued era are equipped to bear with grace[.] The weather doesn't need to prove itself to me any more. I live in dread and deploration of sticking my nose out; and breathe a prayer on mercy whenever its time to go any place.

    Dear; since writing the above; your telegram has come. Needless to say, I rejoice at the prospect of thinking of myself in terms of capacity to aspirations again; instead of self-abnegation and obedience.

    I will be very, very happy to escape the spiritual confines of medical jurisdiction. Also, I will be very meticulous in my social conduct and promise not to cause any trouble: I will be able to have *vacation* with Scottie, maybe and do all sorts of half-forgotten pleasant things from such a long time ago.

    D. O: I am so deeply grateful to you for your constant thoughtfullness. This has been an awful time for you; and maybe, at last, we begin to emerge.

If what you do on Babylon is as significant as what you did for "Three Comrades" you probably wont have any more trouble.[33] Life is still interesting; and could be replete; and I think that we both have earned some.

The woods about here are haunted with uncatalogued memories in this pregnant abeyance before spring. It seems as if there ought to be some overwhelming compelling significance to drive one blindly seeking. To write a poem, or a book would be substitute.

I hear very seldom from Scottie: She sent me a program of the Russian Ballet and every now and then she writes accounts of glamorous activities. I'm so glad that she is fulfilling her academic obligations, and not wasting the effort that it cost to keep her there.

She was tentatively planning to get a job this summer which I think is quite a major idea. Lots of enviable careers have started before hers, and as it become[s] increasingly difficult to orient one-self in the world, there is the more need to begin.

> Again,
> Gratefully
> Zelda
> Needless to say; I'll be so happy to start as soon as I may—
> Devotedly
> Zelda

267. TO ZELDA   TL (CC), 1 p.
                                          March 19 1940

Dearest:-

It seems to me best not to hurry things

(a) I'd like you to leave with the blessings of Dr. Carrol—(you've consumed more of his working hours than one human deserves of another—you'd agree if you'd see his correspondence with me.) Next

---

33. Scott was preparing a film adaptation of his story "Babylon Revisited," but the movie was never made from his script, which he called "Cosmopolitan." A 1954 film, *The Last Time I Saw Paris*, was based on "Babylon Revisited," but the screenplay was not Scott's.

to Forrel he has been your eventual best friend—better even than Myer. (Though this is unfair to Myer who never claimed to be a clinician but only a diagnostician.)

But to hell with all that, and with illness

(b) Also you'd best wait because I will *certainly* have more money three weeks from now than at present, and

(c) *If* things develop fast Scottie can skip down and see you for a day during her vacation—otherwise you won't see her before summer. This is an *if*!

I don't think you fully realize the extent of what Scotty has done at Vassar. You wrote rather casually of two years being enough but it isn't. Her promise is unusual. Not only did she rise to the occasion and got in young but she has raised herself from a poor scholar to a very passable one; sold a professional story at eighteen[34] and moreover in very highbrow at present very politically-minded Vassar she has introduced with some struggle a new note. She has written and produced a musical comedy and founded a club called Omgim to perpetuate the idea—almost the same thing that Tarkington did in 1893 when he founded the Triangle at Princeton. She did this against tough opposition—girls who wouldn't let her on the board of the daily paper because, though she could write, she wasn't "politically conscious".

We have every reason at this point to cheer for our baby. I would do anything rather than deny her the last two years of college which she has now earned. There is more than talent there—a real genius for organization.

Nothing has developed here. I write these "Pat Hobby" stories—and wait.[35] I have a new idea now—a comedy series which will get me back into the big magazines—but my God I am a forgotten man. *Gatsby* had to be taken out of the Modern Library because it didn't sell, which was a blow.

With Dearest Love Always

5521 Amestoy Avenue
Encino, Calif.

---

34. Scott may be referring to "A Short Retort," an article defending modern youth, which Scottie published in the July 1939 issue of *Mademoiselle*.

35. Scott published a story about unsuccessful Hollywood screenwriter Pat Hobby in each monthly issue of *Esquire* from November 1939 until July 1941.

268. TO SCOTT
[March 1940]

ALS, 4 pp.
[Highland Hospital, Asheville,
North Carolina]

Dear D. O.

Life grows increasing[ly] involved. Dr. Carroll has written me from Florida that owing to my recent misdemeanor he doesnt know whether he will allow me to leave.[36] I dont accept that medical jurisdiction has the right of social judgment, and punishment—but I suppose theres no way of defeating a psychiatric authority short of running away

I'm so sorry about the episode: it is impossible to exist under this severest of regimentation for as long as I have and not take a few liberties. These were my first indiscretions since I've been on the road to mending. If you knew how dreary and miserable it is to be held accountable for the least of ones ice-cream sodas I know that you would forgive the social indiscretion. Meantime: Rosalind sent me some pretty Easter finery; the box made me very happy: gloves and a flower, handkerchiefs, two shirts and some stocking[s]. So one is purring; and contentedly enumerating the possessions.

Suns shine in Carolina: the weather is bursting with all sorts of cosmic effects and everybodys is very happy about the coming of Easter. In a little while Tryon Valley will be lovely and hushed and lost in a Heavenly haze of blossom and of truncate[?] isolated birdsong. Those were such happy times roaming about the virginal interstices of that lost and waiting little village.

 Devotedly
 Zelda

Would you be upset if I asked you for $15 and just left? These proceedings are so controversial that even the slightest move takes an eternity no matter what efforts one contributes[,] the individual, and mutual estates get worse: alas—the resources that were once at our disposition are dissipated by Time and other exigences. By now, you had a right to have contributed a classic of the most enduring proportions: and probably will yet.

---

36. Dr. Carroll's treatment included a strict diet, which Zelda appears to have violated while away from the hospital on one of her brief trips into Asheville.

By now: I had a right, just materially, to whatever rewards are still claimed by *new prototypes*.

They ought not to treat us like this —

I have never argued with you about Scottie: the fact remains that she has no expectations of a financial nature, and as little social security as is a tenable circumstance above absolute poverty: hence I think that she ought to at least be acquainted with the actuality; and look on work as a desirable and a progressive rather than as a social punishment.

———————————

Wont you send me $5 as soon as you can —

———————————

Devotedly
Zelda

269. TO ZELDA   TL (CC), 1 p.
                                     [Encino, California]
                                     April 11 1940

Dearest Zelda:-

I got your wire today asking for $5. and simultaneously one came from Dr. Carroll saying you were coming out. I don't know what the rail fare to Montgomery is, but I am sending you herewith $60., which I hope will take care of your ticket, baggage, etc. You are leaving bills behind you, I know, which I will try to take care of as soon as I can. I have sent Jean West $25. on account. Moreover I have sent a check to your mother for your expenses when you get to Montgomery.

Now as to the general arrangement: I am starting to work on this "speculation" job.[37] That is they are giving me very little money but if the picture is resold when finished the deal will be somewhat better. I hesitated about accepting it but there have been absolutely no offers in many months and I did it on the advice of my new agent. It is a job that should be fun and suitable to my uneven state of health. (Since yesterday I seem to be running a fever again) In any case we can't go

———————————

37. The screenplay of "Babylon Revisited," for which Scott was paid five hundred dollars a week, plus nine hundred for the film rights to his story.

on living indefinitely on those Esquire articles. So you will be a poor girl for awhile and there is nothing much to do about it. I can manage to send you $30., a week of which you should pay your mother about $15. for board, laundry, light, etc. The rest will be in checks of alternately $10. and $20.—that is one week the whole sum will amount to $35., one week $25., etc. This is a sort of way of saving for you so that in alternate weeks you will have a larger lump sum in case you need clothes or something.

You will be cramped by this at first—moreso than in the hospital, but it is everything that I can send without putting Scottie to work which I absolutely refuse to do. I don't think you can promise a person an education and then snatch it away from them. If she quit Vassar I should feel like quitting all work and going to the free Veteran's Hospital where I probably belong.

The main thing is not to run up bills or wire me for extra funds. There simply aren't any and as you can imagine I am deeply in debt to the government and everyone else. As soon as anything turns up I will naturally increase your allowance so that you will have more mobility, clothes, etc.

I am moving in town to be near my work.[38] For the present will you address me care of my new agent Phil Berg, 9484 Wilshire Boulevard, Beverly Hills, California. If you forget, "General Delivery, Encino" will be forwarded to me also. As soon as I have a new permanent address I will write you. I do hope this goes well. I wish you were going to brighter surroundings but this is certainly not the time to come to me and I can think of nowhere else for you to go in this dark and bloody world. I suppose a place is what you make it but I have grown to hate California and would give my life for three years in France.

So Bon Voyage and stay well.

Dearest love,

---

38. Scott did not move to 1403 North Laurel Avenue in Hollywood until the middle of June.

270. TO SCOTT ALS, 2 pp.
[April 1940] [Highland Hospital, Asheville,
North Carolina]

Dearest Scott:

Best wishes for the job. If not as remunerative perhaps such work should be far more interesting than having to lose yourself in another mans soul. It would indeed be wonderful to be a member in the best of standing again.

Of cource, I was sorry not to see Scottie[;] however this life is shop-worn and dreary and has about made it's last contribution; so maybe its better not to see her under unfortunate circumstance. It will be grand to see her in Montgomery; we'll be able to swim and play tennis and we might even enjoy—

I am so deeply grateful to you for arranging about home. No matter what problems one has to face it is so much more agreeable to face them without the pressure of ultimate authority figuring in the balast.

The sun is shining conscientiously; I still dabble on the same old story, and the world still doesnt bloom—nor even dream. However theres a suggestions of green on the horizons and the consolation of summer ahead.

Thanks again and again for the check; and all your courtesies. *Dont* send any more money care Mrs. Harlan unless I ask you; it might be inconvenient to her and my mail is still *ad. lib.* which means freedom from inspection—as I am myself 4 times a week—[39]

Devotedly
Zelda

---

39. In order to avoid her doctor knowing, Zelda had arranged for Scott to send money to her through an old friend who had moved to Asheville.

271. TO SCOTT   ALS, 2 pp.
[April 1940]   [Montgomery, Alabama]

Dearest D. O:

The very early morning is a mysterious and dangerous time fraught with the controlled purposes the day will hold: on review. The bus left Ashville at five o[']clock and is now soaring along th[r]ough houses and barn-yard[s] lethal and comforted by sleeping faiths and aspirations in abeyance.

Dr. Carroll gave me fourty dollars of the money. He is getting very old; is extremely irascible and difficult to treat with and I was afraid (from the indication of his manner) that if I pressed the issue I might not be allowed to leave. He very courteously said that if I wanted all the money that he would give it to me; but that I owed him two or three hundred dollars to his own personal account. Having felt the constant restraint of his (materially) omnipotent authority for the past four years, I was glad to get out in easy circumstance and considered it very ill-advised to protest. I deeply regret the twenty-dollars; will use to the best advantage whats left, and take care of myself in wise and mete manner.

I am most deeply grateful to you for sending me home. It is so happy and adventurous to be on the road again. I think of you and the many mornings that we have left believing in new places together. This country is so nostalgic with its imperative possibilities of escape from the doom of the mountains and its long engaging roads that it was made for travel. I am always glad to be going

Meantime: thanks again. Last night when I thought the situation over I tried to persuade the office to give me the other twenty dollars, but apparently they couldnt.

I wanted to pay Jean West; and a months board.

    Devotedly
    Zelda

Dear: on second thoughts: the hospital paid the bus ticket home so maybe we owed him the confiscated $20. I have $40—and will send Jean West $11 on account

272. TO SCOTT   ALS, 2 pp.
[April 1940]   [Montgomery, Alabama]

Dear Scott

Montgomery is as green and fragrant and as ingratiating as it was so many years ago. The back yard is graceful and fragrant and the house is cool and in tune with a very even inviolate cosmic tempo. It is a blessing to be out of the hospital where the properties of things are no longer absolute but assume also the desirabilities of relativity, and of free-will.

Mamma is lovlier than ever. Joe still cajoles the morning with the most gracious significances and Melinda[40] wheedles the hour to the happiness of fruitions. I've seen Livy, the Auerbachs and Katherine Ellsberry. It seems to me that the terms of my stay are not of a strictly social nature: and I want to acclimate myself to this free and somnolent paradise before I try to strike a working basis.

Again, I am most deeply grateful[?] to you for sending me home; and will try to merit my regained estate by the sincerest and most meritorious of cond[uct]

    Devotedly
    Zelda

Please dont fret over my extravag[ance]. There isnt anything to substanti[ate] any such assumption: My wants are modest: as the case requires and always[s][41]

273. TO ZELDA   TL (CC), 1 p.
                                    [Encino, California]
                                    April 19 1940

Dearest Zelda:-

I have no word yet that you've arrived in Montgomery.[42] I hope you are there by now and well ensconced and that things are as you'd like them. I enclose this week's $15. for expenses and $10. for extras.

---

40. Mrs. Sayre's household help.
41. The last line, written on the edge of the paper, is illegible.
42. For some reason, Scott apparently was not receiving Zelda's letters at this time.

The day before yesterday it looked as if things were going to be better. A better paid job intervened and I thought I could postpone the *Babylon* but it didn't work out that way. However, it might be a great deal worse. A few months ago I could not have paid for you to come out at all.

Do write me. I have a nice letter from Scottie about her play.

Dearest love,

274. TO ZELDA   TL (CC), 1 p.
[Encino, California]
April 27 1940

Dearest Zelda:-

Enclosed are checks for $15., for household and $20. for other expenses. Thanks for your cheerful letter. Try to write me when you get the checks so I will know they arrive on time. I try to mail them Fridays but if they don't get in the post till Saturday and there is any windstorm there may be a casual delay.

I am working on this "Babylon" moving picture. I can't make up my mind where to live this summer. After the valley which was so good for my lungs, Los Angeles seems very cityfied. But perhaps I can locate a high spot somewhere.

Scottie's play seems to be a great success. Things are working out for her much as I had hoped. The boys she goes with seem to be about the best available in that economic strata and I no longer get the horrors less [lest] she elope with some playboy. I think that whatever choice she makes she will be able to do it at leisure and she belongs to a cannier generation than ours.

I am sending you your watch. You've said many times that you wanted to give it to Scottie. While you were sick I didn't feel like giving away any of your possessions. If it gives you any pleasure keep it. If you want to give it to her all right. I've said nothing to her. Though it cost $500., I had it valued by a pawnbroker some years ago and he estimated its hock value at about $20.! And yet they say jewelry is a good investment.

With best to all the family.

Dearest love,

275. TO SCOTT ALS, 2 pp.
[May 1940] [Montgomery, Alabama]

Dear Scott:

Tilde sent me this from the N.Y Times. I am very proud of Scotties such aspirational activities; and happy that she is achieving distinction in so many fields. Wont you send the article back to me as soon as you've read it? Mrs McKinney will use it in the Montgomery paper — [43]

The town still blossoms and bowers. This is the most friendly of cosmoses; even the lay out of the town welcomes the advent of vagrant hearts, and June and I always feel somehow, more inclusive, corporeally in Montgomery.

I wish I had something to do. After I have been here a month I intend to try to find some sort of job. I may try short stories and might try magazine covers—because I seriously doubt that a person in this circumstance would get a job with so many people not knowing of what they are likely to be fed.

It's wonderful to be free from those so compelling obligations of hospital routine: it would seem impossible that a person could have been so exhausted as I was and still survive—

Thanks again for saving me. Someday I'll save you to[o]—
Devotedly
Zelda

276. TO ZELDA TL (CC), 1 p.
[Encino, California]
May 4 1940

Dearest Zelda:-

I sympathize with your desire to do something. Why can't you hire a cool room somewhere for a studio? All you'd need is an easel, a chair and a couch and I think you have an easel somewhere. I think

---

43. Piece in the *New York Times* about Scottie may have been in connection with the Vassar spring musical *Guess Who's Here*, for which she wrote the script.

with Marjorie's help you could get it for almost nothing and perhaps after next week I can help more (I go according to the fever—if it stays around 99 I feel rash, if it runs up over a degree at a daily average I get alarmed and think we mustn't get stony broke like last Fall. My ambition is to pay the Government who've laid off me so far. I don't know what they'd annex except my scrapbook.

Will return the clipping Monday—she's a smooth enough kid (for which I take most of the credit except for the mouth, legs and personal charm, and barring the wit which comes from us both)—anyhow she's the best kind a good deal of figuring out could do. She's not as honest as either you or me but maybe she didn't have as much to conceal.

I hope you're happy. I wish you read books (you know those things that look like blocks but come apart on one side)—I mean loads of books and not just early Hebrew metaphysics. If you did I'd advise you to try some more short stories. You never could plot for shocks but you might try something along the line of Gogol's "The Cloak" or Chekov's "The Darling". They are both in the modern library's "Best Russian Short Stories" which the local Carnegie may have in stock.

Don't waste your poor little income on wires to me—unless the money *doesn't* come.

Yours at about 99.7

P.S. Love to all. Excuse the bitter tone. I've overworked on the God damn movie and am in bed for the day.

277. TO ZELDA TL (CC), 1 p.
[Encino, California]
May 11 1940

Dearest Zelda:-
Sorry I wrote you such a cross letter last week and I miss getting an answer from you. Things are better. The awful cough I had died down, the temperature fell and I've worked hard this week with apparently no ill effect except that I'm looking forward tomorrow to a peaceful Sunday spent in bed with Churchill's "Life of Malborough". Funny that he should be prime minister at last. Do you

remember luncheon at his mother's house in 1920 and Jack Churchill was so hard to talk to at first and turned out to be so pleasant? And Lady Churchill's call on the Countess of Byng whose butler was just like the butler in Alice in Wonderland? I thank God they've gotten rid of that old rag scallion Chamberlain. It's all terribly sad and as you can imagine I think of it night and day.

Also I think I've written a really brilliant continuity. It had better be for it seems to be a last life line that Hollywood has thrown me. It is a strong life line — to write as I please upon a piece of my own and if I can make a reputation out here (one of those brilliant Hollywood reputations which endure all of two months sometimes) now will be the crucial time.

Have a cynical letter from Scottie about the Princeton Prom. Thank God I didn't let her start to go at sixteen or she would be an old jade by now. Tell me something of your life there — how you like your old friends, your mother's health, etc., and what you think you might do this summer during the hottest part. I should have said in my letter that if you want to read those stories upon which I think you might make a new approach to writing some of your own, order "Best Russian Stories", Modern Library Edition from Scribners and they will charge it to me.

Next week I'll be able to send you what I think is a permanent address for me for the summer — a small apartment in the h[e]art of the City. Next Fall if the cough is still active I may have to move again to some dry inland atmosphere.

Love to all of you and especially yourself.

Dearest love,

278. TO SCOTT   ALS, 2 pp.
[May 1940]   [Montgomery, Alabama]

Dear Scott:

Thanks for the money. I am so glad life uses you a little less ill: and pray that someday things will be fairer. I still maintain that you[r] reward is not anywhere near commensurate to your contribution

Mamma sends her love. The little house is peaceful, and fragrant of the prospect of June, and free of evil import in the clear morning sun. Life is so ingratiating sustaining oneself on the fragrance of strawberries and the beneficence of these deep lush May days. The roads bloom with butter-cups; the meadows flower with starry aspirations and the gardens aspire with poppies and gay staccato discipliners of the flow[e]ring summer.

I write you at least once a week *every* week; and last week I wrote you twice: so maybe Mr. Berg is a letter-eater amongst his other attainments.

Why dont you send stories to the Post again: they might be in a mood to consider favorably the premium that they created not so long ago. Surely the era that you discovered is not yet past—completed

Gratefully; devotedly
Zelda

279. TO ZELDA

TL (CC), 1 p.
[Encino, California]
May 18 1940

Dearest Zelda:-

It's hard to explain about the Saturday Evening Post matter. It isn't that I haven't tried but the trouble with them goes back to the time of Lorimer's retirement in 1935. I wrote them three stories that year and sent them about three others which they didn't like. The last story they bought they published last in the issue and my friend, Adelaide Neil on the staff, implied to me that they didn't want to pay that big price for stories unless they could use them in the beginning of the issue. Well that was the time of my two year sickness, T. B., the shoulders, etc., and you were at a most crucial point and I was foolishly trying to take care of Scottie and for one reason or another I lost the knack of writing the particular kind of stories they wanted.

As you should know from your own attempts, high priced commercial writing for the magazines is a very definite trick. The rather special things that I brought to it, the intelligence and the good writing and even the radicalism all appealed to old Lorimer who had been a writer himself and liked style. The man who runs the magazine now is an up and coming young Republican who gives not a damn about literature and who publishes almost nothing except escape stories about the brave frontiersmen, etc., or fishing, or football captains, nothing that would even faintly shock or disturb the reactionary bourgeois. Well, I simply can't do it and as I say, I've tried not once but twenty times.

As soon as I feel I am writing to a cheap specification my pen freezes and my talent vanishes over the hill and I honestly don't blame them for not taking the things that I've offered to them from time to time in the past three or four years. An explanation of their new attitude is that you no longer have a chance of selling a story with an unhappy ending (in the old days many of mine *did* have unhappy endings—if you remember). In fact the standard of writing from the best movies, like Rebecca,[44] is believe it or not, much higher at present than that in the commercial magazines such as Collier's and the Post.

Thank you for your letter. California is a monotonous climate and already I am tired of the flat, scentless tone of the summer. It is fun to be working on something I like and maybe in another month I will get the promised bonus on it and be able to pay last year's income tax and raise our standard of living a little.

Love to all and dearest love to you.

P.S. I am sending you the copy of the article you sent me about Scottie. You said something about giving it to Mrs. McKinney.

280. TO ZELDA   TL (CC), 1 p.
                                     [Encino, California]
                                     May 26 1940

Dearest Zelda:-

Do please write me when my checks come. This is the last day of the script and I'm pretty much all in, beautiful 99.6 fever and all. If this thing makes a hit it may make a difference in everything out here.

Will write fully in a few days.

Dearest love,

---

44. Director Alfred Hitchcock's highly successful 1940 film adaptation of Daphne du Maurier's novel *Rebecca*.

281. TO SCOTT ALS, 4 pp.
[May 1940] [Montgomery, Alabama]

Dear Scott:

I dont know what infamous trait causes Mr. Berg to dispose of the letters I send you. I write every Monday or Tuesday anyway acquainting you of how rejoiced I am at my renewed prosperity.

Mamma and I are having a very pleasant summer. It rains a lot and the garden breathes weeds and a sense of lost worlds, but its fun digging and watering and somehow a deep sense of romance and adventure lies behind the gate. No word from Scottie for some time but I believe that she intends to turn up here towards the end of June.

Her friends are planning a couple of weeks on the Florida coast: maybe she'd like to join the enterprize. Montgomery is cooler then I ever [k]new it at this time of year; even the pools aren't yet open so it may be a very tenable locale even as late as June. The young girls and honking automobiles inspire uncatalogued nostalgias and the deep green of the alleys sometimes make[s] me think of Cannes.

I'm so glad the picture is made; and will pray for reward; and wish you every success—

Devotedly
Zelda

The Little Theatre here has manifested an interest in "Scandalabra"[45]—would a copy of the play be possibly available?

Also Marjorie suggests that your Basil stories[46] ought to be good material for Mickey Rooney or maybe even Diana Durbin—They seem to be the sort of thing most deeply in demand. People (in general) just cant stand any more hysteria and fight shy of even the best if it promises to be depressing. Anything wholesome is a go: and any reassurance, spiritual or material that a person can offer in these times meets with a grateful respons[e]—

Devotedly
Zelda

(over)

Do let me know about my play and about the sea-shore—whether

45. Zelda wrote a play, *Scandalabra*, at La Paix in 1932, which was produced in Baltimore in 1933 and was unsuccessful. The Montgomery Little Theatre never took up the project. The play can be found in *Collected Writings* (199–267).
46. A series of stories Scott wrote in 1928 and 1929 about the ambitions and struggles of a young boy named Basil Duke Lee, who resembled Scott as an adolescent.

you think it advisable for either or both of us, or even the whole family to undertake such a project.

    Gratefully

    Zelda

282. TO SCOTT   ALS, 2 pp.

[May 1940]   [Montgomery, Alabama]

Dear Scott:

    Thanks for the money: one of the best things it buys is peace of mind; and I am alway[s] happy for a little surcease.

    The garden grows: poppies blow and scatter their seed under the big trees and Time sleeps under the lavender. I tend it faithfully and cherish my floral aspirations despite the somewhat recalcitrance of the beds that I planted.

    A few friends have been to see me. Most of the people we knew seem desperately engaged in keeping alive whatever keeps them alive. I havent been invited to any parties so I dont know what tempo the balls swing in. To this sort of town a beau is almost indespensible; but there dont seem to be any left. Pretty soon the pools will open; and I'm going to buy a bicycle.

    Mamma suggests that we spend a week at a Florida sea-side when Scottie arrives. Her *confreres* are gay and young and lovely and I know that she will have a good time.

    It is indeed edifying that things go better. I pray for the just reward of you[r] talent; and for a more proportionate acknowledgment of your contribution to American letters.

    Devotedly Zelda

Julia Andersons father died.[47]

---

47. This is written along the left-hand side of the first page of the letter.

283. TO ZELDA   TL (CC), 1 p.
                                 [Encino, California] ·
                                 May 31 1940

Dearest Zelda:-

Have finished my story and am going to rest for a week, perhaps somewhere further North. The Phil Berg Agency will always have my address. Have finally found a small apartment where I'll probably spend the summer but I don't expect to occupy it till the middle of June. From Scottie's letters I think she expects to join you about then, for the Florida expedition.

As you say in your letter, the problem does seem chiefly "how to keep alive" through these times but if this job of mine turns out well there will most certainly be others.

  With dearest love,

284. TO ZELDA   TL (CC), 1 p.
                                 [Encino, California]
                                 June 7 1940

Dearest Zelda:-

The Harvard Summer School idea seemed better for Scottie than her going to Virginia. You remember your old idea that people ought to be born on the shores of the North Sea and only in later life drift south toward the Mediterannean in softness? Now all the Montague Normans, Lady Willards, Ginnisses, Vallambrosas, etc., who loafed with us in the South of France through many summers seem to have dug themselves into an awful pit. I want Scottie to be hardy and keen and able to fight her own battles and Virginia didn't seem to be the right note—however charming.

I'll be sending you a semi-permanent address any day now.

  Dearest love,

285. TO ZELDA   TL (CC), 1 p.
                                      June 14 1940

Dearest Zelda:-

At the moment everything is rather tentative. Scottie is coming South about the 20th and after that wants to go to summer school at Harvard. If I can possibly afford it I want her to go. She wants an education and has recently shown that she has a right to it. You will find her very mature and well informed. My feeling is that we are in for a ten year war and that perhaps one more year at Vassar is all that she will have—which is one reason why the summer school appeals to me. If I can manage for a month than [then] perhaps I can manage the seashore for you in August—by which time you will have had a good deal of Montgomery weather. A lot depends on whether my producer is going to continue immediately with "Babylon Revisited"—or whether any other picture job turns up. Things are naturally shot to hell here with everybody running around in circles yet continuing to turn out two million dollar tripe like "All This and Heaven Too".

Twenty years ago "This Side of Paradise" was a best seller and we were settled in Westport. Ten years ago Paris was having almost its last great American season but we had quit the gay parade and you were gone to Switzerland. Five years ago I had my first bad stroke of illness and went to Asheville. Cards began falling badly for us much too early. The world has certainly caught up in the last four weeks. I hope the atmosphere in Montgomery is tranquil and not too full of war talk.

Love to all of you.

1403 N. Laurel Avenue
Hollywood, California

286. TO SCOTT   Wire[48]

> CA703 27 NT=MONTGOMERY ALA 18   1940 JUN 18 AM 11 50
> SCOTT FITZGERALD=
>   1403 NORTH LAUREL AVE HOLLYWOOD CALIF=
> I WONT BE ABLE TO STICK THIS OUT. WILL YOU WIRE
> MONEY IMMEDIATELY THAT I MAY RETURN FRIDAY TO
> ASHVILLE. WILL SEE SCOTTIE THERE. DEVOTEDLY
> REGRETFULLY GRATEFULLY=
>   ZELDA.

287. TO SCOTT   Wire

> V109   10=MONTGOMERY ALA 18   409P   1940 JUN 18 PM 2 48
> SCOTT FITZGERALD=
>   1403 NORTH LAUREL AVE HOLLYWOOD CALIF=
> DISREGARD TELEGRAM AM FINE AGAIN. HAPPY TO SEE
> SCOTTIE=
> DEVOTEDLY=
>   ZELDA.

288. TO SCOTT   Wire

> SV85 6=MONTGOMERY ALA 20   349P   1940 JUN 20 PM 2 57
> SCOTT FITZGERALD=
>   1403 NORTH LAUREL AVE HOLLYWOOD CALIF=
> SCOTTIE ARRIVED SAFE. EVERYTHING FINE. DEVOT-
> EDLY=
>   ZELDA.

---

48. Zelda apparently experienced a temporary concern (perhaps panic) about her ability to cope with Scottie's visit and so sent this telegram to Scott.

289. TO SCOTT ALS, 2 pp.
[June 1940] [Montgomery, Alabama]

Dear Scott:

Thanks once again for the money. Mammas old Jo[e] has been on the invalid list, so I'm grateful for the possibility of giving him a little. He's been here 24 years, and the family feels sorely stricken that anything should happen to him. Melinda still functions; and with Scottie here sometimes the house has quite an air of Pleasant Ave.

The garden is swathed in weeds, and in the poetic tradition of romantic regret. It gives me great pleasure to encourage the ageratum and to pamper the gladioli; but in these luxuriant summers things grow again before they can be cleared.

Scottie is having accolade: and a very picturesque time of midnight bonfires[,] barbecues and lots of expensive glamour that was non-extant when we grew up. She is so pretty and charming; I hope that she will stay a while—since Mamma says the *séjour* isn't too much for her—

Although eighty, she seems like a woman of sixty; running her own life as she always did and affords so much pleasure to all of us

    With gratitude and devotion
    Zelda

290. TO ZELDA TL (CC), 1 p.
June 29 1940

Dearest Zelda:-

Scottie seems to have had a fine time with you. I'm sorry she couldn't find a job there but maybe on the whole it's better for her to get the maximum of education that she still can under these war conditions. I didn't want her to go to Columbia because New York in summer is just a little too exciting for any serious work, and the same held true of Virginia. She seemed to feel that Harvard was a hardship because she knew so few people there, but for anybody with her ability to make friends I don't think it will be too difficult. I suppose you feel lonely without her. I'd like to take a look at her too and perhaps if things look better at the end of the summer we could all get together and see how the year has treated us.

Mrs. Owens is going to try to dig up that Scandalabra script for you. An item in the paper says that Shirley Temple may do the picture.[49] No other news. I'm being very quiet.

With dearest love,

1403 N. Laurel Avenue
Hollywood, California

291. TO SCOTT   ALS, 2 pp.
[June/July 1940]   [Montgomery, Alabama]

Dear Scott:

This may interest you: it seems that a strange apparition made its way about the Montgomery social structure and, apparently had a very pleasant time.

We loved having Scottie. She is prettier than ever and quite an adjunct and I want so much to have her back for a while before Vassar opens—Though I didn't have a chance to open any deep channels of "maternal advice" I somehow seemed to have made a *little* head way as to ingratiating myself—as she seemed quite sorry to leave. There is so much distress and suffering abroad that it is good and indeed spiritually indispensible to feel that one belongs somewhere and that there is still, at least, the warmth of parental relationship—

I am quite proud of Scottie. She is charming and lovely—

Meantime: Life pursues a billowy and dreamy course; and people here seem happy despite the fact that everyday a new country declares a new war—

Devotedly, gratefully
Zelda

---

49. "Cosmopolitan," Scott's screen adaptation of "Babylon Revisited"; in the end, producer Lester Cowan and Shirley Temple's mother were unable to agree on a financial arrangement.

292. TO ZELDA   TL (CC), 1 p.
                           July 6 1940

Dearest Zelda:-

I enjoyed reading the interview given out by our learned Scottie.[50] I'm glad to know she spends her time thinking about strikes, relief and starvation while feeling no slightest jealousy of the girls with silver foxes who choose to recline on country club porches. It shows that we have hatched a worthy egg and I do not doubt that someday, like George Washington, she will "raise that standard to which all good men can repair".

Seriously, I never heard such a bunch of hokum in my life as she sold that newspaper reporter but I'm glad she has one quality which I have found almost as valuable as positive originality, viz: she can make the most of what she has read and heard—make a few paragraphs from Marx, John Stuart Mill, and the New Republic go further than most people can do with years of economic study. That is one way to grow learned, first pretend to be—then have to live up to it.

She has just shown her keeness in another way by taking me for $100. more advance money for the summer school than I had expected to pay leaving me with a cash balance of $11. at date. Don't bawl her out for this. Leave it to me because it most certainly will come out of her allowance and it was honestly nothing but carelessness in getting the exact data from the summer school. However, it affects you to this extent that I'm going to ask you that if these checks reach you Monday not to cash them until Tuesday. It will be perfectly safe to cash them Tuesday because I'm getting a payment on the story at which I am back at work. The majority of the payment ($900.) goes to Uncle Sam, $300. goes against a loan already made against it and the rest will be distributed for our needs during the next three weeks—so please if you have any extra funds save them for any emergency. We have done our share of lending and giving over many years and we must all watch our money.

Tell me what you do. Cousin Ceci writes that my Aunt Elise died

50. Scottie was interviewed by the *Montgomery Advertiser*, while she was visiting her mother.

last April at the age of ninety. I was fond of that old woman and I hadn't yet assimilated her passing.

With dearest love always,

1403 N. Laurel Avenue
Hollywood, California

293. TO ZELDA   TL (CC), 1 p.
                                 July 12 1940

Dearest Zelda:-

You never tell me if you are painting or not, or what you are writing if anything. I spent a silly day yesterday with Shirley Temple and her family. They want to do the picture and they don't want to do the picture, but that's really the producer's worry and not mine. She's a lovely little girl, beautifully brought up and she hasn't quite reached the difficult age yet—figuring the difficult age at twelve. She reminds me so much of Scottie in the last days at La Paix, just before she entered Bryn Mawr. You weren't there the day of the Maryland Hunt Cup Race in the Spring of '34 when Scottie got the skirt and coat from my mother which suddenly jumped her into adolescence. You may remember that she wore the little suit till she was about sixteen.

It's hot as hell here today and I haven't been able to work. I too have had only one letter from Scottie but she seems to like Boston.

With dearest love,

1403 N. Laurel Avenue
Hollywood, California

294. TO SCOTT   ALS, 6 pp.
[July 1940]   [Montgomery, Alabama]

Dear Scott:

The money arrived; thanks for the bounty. The weekly stipend is always a great boon to the morale and puts one again in the humor, at least, for having things all right. I have been trying to (symbolicly as to clothes etc) observe the conventions with it; also to remember the poor in an appropriate scale. It's wonderful to be a femme d'affaires having wonderful missions of my own instigation again.

Mamma supports the heat as best she is able with the aid of fans and crushed ice and as much ease as can be attained. You have forgotten—as I had myself—what a drenching blistering affair this world is in summer: the streets as eclectic [electric?] with the intensity of these July mornings and by noon the heat is, of almost actuality, blinding. Mamma, I am thankful to say would be able to go to Carolina save that she is now 80 and feels any such departure from her daily routine would be too great a strain. She has $50 a month— is always trying to give most of it away but *could* support herself in a Carolina boarding house. This is a sweet little house; the garden is deep and romantic and aromatic tinged with Swinburnian suggestions and a lingering faded ritual-of-gardens. I am trying to grow tomatoes, since the flowers I planted have so ungraciously died— but my efforts so far are of a most unprofitable nature.

About sketching: of course I will take up my painting again sometime. Whatever I did now would be of a more desultory than remunerative nature. I work the garden: and spend two days a week at the Red Cross—and I am still under pressure of obligation to Dr. Carrol having signed a paper obligating me to 5 miles a day[51] and fantastic diets and generally lugubrious commiserations *au lieu de* joie-de-vivre. Do you suppose that he will live forever?

I am surviving very well: If Scottie comes back before Vassar (which of course I would love) it would be nice to give her a luncheon for the girls at the club. Unless, of course, such would be ill advised. Red Ruth is still extant—though grievously invalided for his sore foot—and he might under suasion arrange such an accomplishment.

Short of that—there isnt any way of returning her obligations. A picnic, however, might be within our means if we hired a truck; but such things are no good unless on an elaborate scale—Anyways it is very satisfactory to see her quietly and someday I hope and trust to convey to her a sense of *family* roots and tradition that makes life a so much *"fairer"* and more honorable arrangement.

Do tell me more about the Shirley Temple picture. To me, she is a most adequate interesting and even compelling personality.

Devotedly
Zelda

---

51. A stipulation regarding Zelda's release from the hospital was that she continue to walk five miles a day.

295. TO ZELDA   TL (CC), 2 pp.
                          July 20 1940

Dearest Zelda:-

Thanks for your letter about what you are doing. I do wish you were sketching a little if only to keep your hand in. You've never done any drawing at all in Alabama and it's so very different in flora and general atmosphere than North Carolina that I think it would be worthwhile to record your moods while down there. When times are a little calmer I think you ought to have a really inclusive exhibition of your pictures. Perhaps if the war is over next year it would be a good summer's job for Scottie to arrange it—I mean fill the place that Cary Ross did six years ago. She would meet all sort of interesting people doing it and I had an idea of suggesting it as her work for this August, but the war pushes art into the background. At least people don't buy anything.

I am sending you Gertrude Stein's new book[52] which Max Perkins sent me. I am mentioned in it on some page—anyhow I've underlined it. On the back of the wrapping paper I've addressed it and stamped it to Scottie. She might like to look it over too. It's a melancholy book now that France has fallen, but fascinating for all that.

Ten days more to go on the Temple picture.

With dearest love,

1403 N. Laurel Avenue
Hollywood, California

PRIVATE AND PERSONAL

Please write me a few lines about your mother's health. Is she well in general? Is she active, I mean does she still go down town, etc. or does she only go around in automobiles and tell me why you didn't go to Carolina this year. Was it lack of funds or is the trip a little too much for her.

---

52. *Paris France* (1940).

296. TO SCOTT   ALS, 2 pp.
[c. July 24, 1940]   [Montgomery, Alabama]

Dearest Scott:

The birthday flowers were beautiful: a colossal treasure box filled with dahlias and gladioli and all the grandiose beauties of midsummer gardens. You were sweet to think of me: being in Montgomery reminds me so often of the early days we knew each other. The vogue of the casual café seems to have vanished and the young people entertain themselves on a more formal, and even commendable scale. The South, apparantly from my somewhat remote observations is at last seeing the light of the popular romance on the score. I am so glad that Scottie had such a good time while here: it is gratifying that one is not completely forgotten even after so long a time.

These skies are so intense and tintillant that they are adamant overhead and underfoot the pavement tries its best to crack one's feet.

    Devotedly
    Zelda

297. TO ZELDA   TL (CC), 1 p.
        July 29 1940

Dearest Zelda:-

The Temple thing is this: she's too old to have a child's appeal and though they've put everything in her last pictures—song, dance, sleight of hand, etc.,—they fail to hold the crowd. In fact the very last is rather nauseous in its sentimentality.

So this "independent" producer Cowan, now of Columbia, shortly to be at Paramount, had the idea of a romantic drama for her and bought my *Babylon Revisited* last year for $900. for that purpose. I should have held out for more but the story had been nearly ten years published without a nibble. So then, in a beautifully avaricious way, knowing I'd been sick and was probably hard up, Mr. Cowan hired me to do the script on a percentage basis. He gives me—or *gave* me—what worked out to a few hundred a week to do a quick script. Which

I did and then took to bed to recuperate. Now he says he wants me to do another, and I'm supposed to be grateful because since I haven't done a movie for so long the conclusion is easy for this scum that I can't write. If you could see and talk for five minutes with the People I deal with you'd understand without words how difficult it is to master a bare politeness.

Anyhow I *think* it's been a good thing except for the health angle and if and when he sells Mrs. Temple and Paramount the script there'll be a little more money—if he doesn't think of a way to beat me out of it.

So that's the story. Tell me—did the watch come? You never mentioned it.

    With Dearest Love,

1403 N. Laurel Avenue
Hollywood, California

298. TO ZELDA   TL (CC), 1 p.
                                 August 3 1940

Dearest Zelda:
   This has been a hot, unsatisfactory day with lost [lots] of snags in the manuscript and nothing bright on the horizon except an awfully intelligent letter from Scottie about her courses and about Harvard which seems to have been a great success.

If things go even moderately well I think that I'll be able to send her to you for a week in September. She wants to pay a couple of visits first which will cost no more than the railroad fare and I imagine you will come South in early September. Have had no letter from you this week. I do hope all goes well.

    With dearest love,

1403 N. Laurel Avenue
Hollywood, California

299. TO SCOTT   ALS, 2 pp.
[August 1940]   [Montgomery, Alabama]

Dear Scott:

Thanks again for the money. It affords me pleasure, and the freedom of the city and lots of felicitous arrangements. I always write to thank you, and how you dont get my letters, I cant understand.

The red-cross is a cool and wind-blown barn where I sew labels in things and watch time passing from the face of the capitol clock. I spend two days a week there. Though swimming is become a "precieuse" entertainment for me—enjoying as I do the significance of line in the lean long bodies and the play of high hot noons over the water's edge—I sometimes go in. Red Ruth is still hobbling cheerily dramaticly and recklessly about, but there are so few of my old friends available that I mostly enjoy the garden and the *bien faisance* of being free from such restrictive routine as the hospital

Mamma is the best and most gracious of company. We linger over things: peaches + figs and the poignant fragrances of a summer already on the wane. I will start painting again as soon as I attain the vitality to both live, *and* aspire.

> Devotedly, and gratefully
> Zelda

300. TO ZELDA   TL (CC), 1 p.
      August 10 1940

Dearest Zelda:

Up to this last week I heard from Scottie regularly—but I think it was specifically because we were discussing courses at Vassar and also she was acknowledging her allowance. I've had no letter this week but I think the answer is quite simply that she's taking her examinations. I consider her as grown now, as having developed a great deal of common sense (knock wood) in these years and there is no use worrying about her except for some specific reason, as there is nothing I can possibly do at this distance.

I'm finishing the Temple script tomorrow. I would like to rest for a week but there's a nibble from Zannuck [Zanuck] which I may have to follow up. He is one producer I haven't quarrelled with, but give me time.

I had a very nice letter from your mother which I will answer this week.

  With dearest love,

1403 N. Laurel Avenue
Hollywood, California

301. TO SCOTT   ALS, 4 pp.
[c. August 14, 1940][53]   [Montgomery, Alabama]

Dear Scott:

The money arrived; for which I am duly grateful. I am afraid that I havent thanked you for unearthing the play: and I am most appreciative of the effort that I know this cost. Though I haven't seen anybody on the subject yet, I think that when the insistence of the weather here abates a little the *ms.* will hold the possibilities (at any rate) of much pleasure.

Meantime, Maxwell Field grows; the heat augments; and life moves along at a pleasantly uneventful tempo. I am become a regular customer at the swimming pool and though I have not attained a hue to set the fashion I am not entirely *blanc mange* any more.

The Gertrude Stein book both Mamma and I find extremely amusing and heart-breakingly remeniscent, for me. Isnt it devastating thinking that there isnt any France any more?

Meantime: it is always very gratifying to see Scottie. I trust that she will enjoy her sequel as much as the original theme.

There don't seem to be many young people about but I suppose upon shaking the cabbage-bush there will some appear.

Do you know, by any chance where my star-necklace is? Always my love, I always envested that necklace with a deep romantic appeal: endowed as it was with the property of story. Anyway, I would be glad of it and glad of my silver that sort of thing if there is

---

53. The envelope for this letter survives; it is postmarked August 14.

any—not avidly enough to warrant the causing of any confusion but glad—

People lots of times ask about you: and I always tell them tales of glamour and of renown—

I havent saved any money: so I havent any money saved—about which I feel very apologetic—

Devotedly
Zelda

302. TO ZELDA   TL (CC), 1 p.
                           August 15 1940

Dearest Zelda:-

I have the star necklace here and will send it to you parcel post tomorrow. You never told me about the wrist watch. Did you get it? About the silver, you may remember that one of the pieces—I'm afraid it was the mirror was stolen from a hat box which was in our baggage when I brought you to Asheville in April, 1936. I did everything possible to recover it but never could. There may be a piece or two—in fact I think there are—among the silver in Baltimore but it's pretty expensive to have it opened up and I'd rather wait until there is some pressing need of things. Is there anything else especially you would like from there?

I hope Scottie has written you. She is coming South, paying a couple of visits first. This picture has dragged on interminately though I'm not getting a cent out of it now. I'm simply gambling on the possibility of sale.

I'm glad you liked "Paris, France". It certainly is sad to think that that's all over—at least for our lifetime.

With dearest love,

1403 N. Laurel Avenue
Hollywood, California

303. TO ZELDA   TL (CC), 1 p.
                                      August 24 1940

Dearest Zelda:

By the time you get this Scottie will have leisurely started South—with two or three stops. I've missed seeing her this summer but we've exchanged long letters of a quite intimate character in regard to life and literature. She is an awfully good girl in the broad fundamentals. Please see to one thing—that she doesn't get into any automobiles with drunken drivers.

I think I have a pretty good job coming up next week—a possibility of ten weeks work and a fairly nice price at 20th Century Fox. I have my fingers crossed but with the good Shirley Temple script behind me I think my stock out here is better than at any time during the last year.

With dearest love,

1403 N. Laurel Avenue
Hollywood, Calif.

304. TO ZELDA   TL (CC), 1 p.
                                      August 30 1940

Dearest Zelda:-

It seems odd to be back in the studio again. Monday morning they called up to tell me they wanted me for a four weeks' job. I only get about half of what I used to but all of it is owed to everybody imaginable, the government, insurance, hospital, Vassar, etc. But four weeks pay does insure a certain amount of security for the next three months if I spread it over the time wisely.

I'm going to get a suit in two or three weeks and will send you the money for a dress as you must be short on clothes. I'm still running the fever and there's a couch in my office and while they insist on your physical presence in the studio there are no peepholes they can look into and see whether I am lying down or not. It gives me a very strange feeling to be back.

I suppose Scottie will be with you this week. She tells me that she has grown two years this summer. Do write me at length about her. I'm sorry to miss a glimpse of her at this stage of her life, but of course it seems much more important to stay here and keep her going. It is strange too that she is repeating the phase of your life—all her friends about to go off to war and the world again on fire.

    With dearest love,

1403 N. Laurel Avenue
Hollywood, California

305. TO ZELDA   TL (CC), 1 p.
                                   September 5 1940

Dearest Zelda:-
    Here's ten dollars extra as I thought due to Scottie's visit it might come in handy. Also I'm sending you Craven's "Art Masterpieces", a book of extraordinary reproductions that is a little art gallery in itself.
    Don't be deceived by this sudden munificence—as yet I haven't received a cent from my new job but in a wild burst of elation of getting it, I hocked the car again for $150.
    With dearest love, always,

1403 N. Laurel Avenue
Hollywood, California

306. TO SCOTT   ALS, 4 pp.
[September 1940]   [Montgomery, Alabama]

Dear Scott:
    Scottie arrived on a picturesque twilight, steaming into the station on a cider-blown day-coach from Atlanta. She had had breakfast and lunch there with Rosalind. Her voyagings are always the more persuasive from their impromptu quality—always seeming to be a very transitory interruption to the exigence of highly organized vacations.

She has had a wonderful, and perfected summer according to the best of summer traditions and seems (gratefully) happy and well to begin the more academic facets of life.

In the course of a long discussion Scottie suggested that it might be preferable to get a job for a year: This was *not* at my suggestion so dont attribute it to me in case you find yourself antagonisticly disposed. She thought the *Baltimore Sun* might offer possibilities. I told her that, judging from all your correspondence on the subject you would *much* prefer her to continue at Vassar; and advised that she write you concerning the project. Feeling as I do that an independent means of subsistence is almost indispensable to any constructive happiness, I nevertheless observe that you prefer that she first acquire the standard back-ground.

Montgomery is still tintillant in a blazing heat — Most people sip and fan and await the autumn surcease. I love the fading glories of summer over the cotton fields. Time is become traditions, for being so long disciplined by circumstance down here; and the past is, indeed, the actuality.

I am distressed, and regret, that you still have fever. One seems to live as well with tuberculosis as without — and maybe someday the suffering will be gone. It must be good to have a job. Two people have sent me clippings of the Shirley Temple exploit. It ought to be a very successful project — since you have dramatized the youth of the generation and she is about to take over —

Devotedly; grateful[ly]
Zelda

307. TO ZELDA TL (CC), 1 p.
September 6 1940

Dearest Zelda:

This is written in a big Saturday rush just to get you this money.

You know that to a certain extent I agreed with you on a metier for Scottie. When she was ten you were strong for Ballet — and later when she was fourteen I almost put her into the theatre. But now the dye is cast for a cultural education and situated as she is now she has an infinitely wider range of men to meet than she would in Baltimore or anywhere else. And except in cases of exceptional talent any newspaper would rather have a college graduate than a two year student.

With dearest love,

P.S. Naturally my hope is that with this job the strain of the last year will lift a little and life be more liberal for all of us

1403 N. Laurel Ave.
Hollywood, Calif.

308. TO SCOTT   ALS, 2 pp.
[September 1940]   [Montgomery, Alabama]

Dear Scott:

Thanks, most gratefully, for the money. I spose you want to know what I did with it: indeed, it would make a rather elaborate account. I buy things and accrue benefits and pay what I owe and enjoy as many controversial issues as a woman of big-business.

The autumn streets lead to new, and newly organized horizons; the gutters overflow with burnt gold leaves. The air is high and classic under bright impervious autumn skies and the mornings are hushed, and matinal resources mobilized now that the children are in school. The paper advertizes an art class at the museum which may engage my attentions; the red cross begs for workers; there are plenty of things to do. I may buy a bicycle later. I planted a garden-full of 25¢ worth of 15¢ worth of mustard, but the heat seethed and seered at the time, and we didnt prosper as truck-farmers.

Scottie had a very pleasant visit. She cant see any possible reason why she should keep me informed as to her whereabouts, so I dont know where she is, or why, or what to do about it if any: which is rather a disadvantage in a parental way.

A little cat pretty and poised and wild with as many antennae as a swamp lilly has adopted us. He's very obedient and persuasive and makes himself a happy home.

Devotedly
Zelda

309. TO ZELDA   TL (CC), 2 pp.
                                     September 14 1940

Dearest Zelda:-

Am sending you a small check next week which you should really spend on something which you need—a winter coat—for instance—or if you are equipped, to put it away for a trip when it gets colder. I can't quite see you doing this, however. Do you have extra bills, dentists, doctors, etc., and if so, they should be sent to me as I don't expect you to pay them out of the thirty dollars. And I certainly don't want your mother to be in for any extras. Is she?

This is the third week of my job and I'm holding up very well but so many jobs have started well and come to nothing that I keep my fingers crossed until the thing is in production. Paramount doesn't want to star Shirley Temple alone on the other picture and the producer can't find any big star who will play with her so we are temporarily held up.

As I wrote you Scottie is now definitely committed to an education and I feel so strongly about it that if she wanted to go to work I would let her really *do it* by cutting off all allowance. What on earth is the use of having gone to so much time and trouble about a thing and then giving it up two years short of fulfillment. It is the last two years in college that count. I got nothing out of my first two years—in the last I got my passionate love for poetry and historical perspective and ideas in general (however superficially), that carried me full swing into my career. Her generation is liable to get only too big a share of raw life at first hand.

　　Write me what you do?
　　With dearest love,

P.S. Scottie may quite possibly marry within a year and then she is fairly permanently off my hands. I've spent so much time doing work that I didn't particularly want to do that what does one more year matter. They've let a certain writer here direct his own pictures and he has made such a go of it that there may be a different feeling about that soon. If I had that chance I would attain my real goal in coming here in the first place.

1403 N. Laurel Avenue
Hollywood, California

310. TO SCOTT
[September 1940]

ALS, 4 pp.
[Montgomery, Alabama]

Dear Scott:

The money arrived, again. I'm always happy of the expectation of renewed possibilities latent within the Monday envellope; and generally in pressing need

You ask about my pursuits: Time broods over Montgomery with such detachment, and with so philosophic an acceptance that one simply does nothing in terms of rather dynamic negation; and is grateful. I am materially happy in the beneficent peace of Mammas humble circumstance and bask in the pleasurableness of leisurely fragrant breakfasts and suppers foraged out of the peaceful Dusk. I dont write; and I dont paint: largely because it requires most of my resources to keep out of the hospital. I've had such a difficult struggle over the last ten years that making the social-adjustment is more difficult than I had supposed and I content myself to drift through the dreamy beatitudes of Mammas little garden without worrying too much about the morrow. There's nothing I can do about it anyway: women of my age, and invalid history would have more than a struggle getting work in these times where sustenance itself is become more precious than one is wont to consider. I live: and am grateful and have no suggestions to offer: though I grant you that I would give anything within reason for a means of livlihood.

I finally wired Scottie to reassure myself of her continued existence. It seems that there is such a person—of considerable social promise and superior acumen and that there is some vague and promisory reassurance of a letter in the near future. She is certainly to be envied the most felicitous of circumstances with which life is showering her of late.

Here: all goes well. Marjorie and Noonie leave for Carolina next week; so my presence may be a comfort to Mamma during vacance. I see nobody except Livy Hart, Amalia Rosenberg + Mrs McKinney occasionally, but have a sense, always, of friendliness and freedoms in the constant yet casual encountering of old friends and associations from other eras.

Affectionately Gratefully
Zelda

311. TO SCOTT
[September 1940]

ALS, 2 pp.
[Montgomery, Alabama]

Dear Scott:

The book arrived. It is the most magnificent volume, and I am most deeply grateful to you for having remembered me so munificently. I thought of the many beautiful books on ballet, and pictures, and music that you have bought me and am grateful for you[r] so-constructive interest. The book is an education and I will cherish it as a most invaluable possession.

To-night is the first fall night[.] The moon is bright and cool and dispassionate and the shadows are remote and impersonally admonitory and the children have started to school; so the streets once more assume their academic context.

I always miss Scottie when she leaves, but am reluctant to try to prolong her visits as our hospitality is not as dynamic as the fun in Baltimore. She is a most gratifying companion; and brings a renewed appeal to the life of the rotogravures, a new faith in the advertisements and new desirabilities to the New Yorker et-cetera — besides the academic aspirations that accompany her *sejours* —

Again thanks — the book is a most invaluable acquisition.

Devotedly
Zelda

312. TO ZELDA

TL (CC), 1 p.
September 21 1940

Dearest Zelda:-

So glad you like the Art Book. I would like to hear of your painting again and I meant it when I said next summer if the war is settled down you ought to have another exhibition.

Scottie went to Baltimore as she planned and I finally got a scrap of a note from her but I imagine most of her penmanship was devoted to young men. I think she's going back with the intention, at least, of working hard and costing little.

I don't know how this job is going. It may last two months — it may end in another week. Things depend on such hair-lines here — one must not only do a thing well but do it as a compromise, sometimes between the utterly opposed ideas of two differing executives. The diplomatic part in business is my weak spot.

However, the Shirley Temple script is looking up again and is my great hope for attaining some real status out here as a movie man and not a novelist.

    With dearest love,

1403 N. Laurel Avenue
Hollywood, California

313. TO ZELDA   TL (CC), 1 p.
                              September 28 1940

Dearest Zelda:

Autumn comes—I am forty-four—nothing changes. I have not heard from Scottie since she got to Vassar and from that I deduce she is extremely happy, needs nothing, is rich—obviously prosperous, busy and self-sufficient. So what more could I want? A letter might mean the opposite of any of these things.

I'm afraid Shirley Temple will be grown before Mrs. Temple decides to meet the producer's terms of this picture. It wouldn't even be interesting if she's thirteen.

Tomorrow I'm going out into society for the first time in some months—a tea at Dottie Parker's (Mrs. Allan Campbell), given for Don Stuart's X-wife, the Countess Tolstoy. Don't know whether Don will be there or not. Earnest's book is the "book of the month."[54] Do you remember how superior he used to be about mere sales? He and Pauline are getting divorced after ten years and he is marrying a girl named Martha Gelhorn. I know no news of anyone else except that Scottie seems to have made a hit in Norfolk.

    Dearest love,

1403 N. Laurel Ave.
Hollywood, Calif.

---

54. Ernest Hemingway's *For Whom the Bell Tolls* (1940).

314. **TO SCOTT**   ALS, 4 pp.
[After September 24, 1940]   [Montgomery, Alabama]

Dear Scott:

Nobody knows what day, or time, it is here, in this dreamy world where days lose themselves in nostalgic dusk and twilights prowl the alleys lost in melancholic quest: so it is that your birthday passed before I thought to wire you.

Many happy returns of the day; and my deepest unpersonal[?] gratitude for the many happy times we spent to-gether—though it was long ago.—

For a long time I have had little sense of the passage of time due to being segregate[d] from life and its problems; now that I am once more in contact with routines, and rituals, that change, I witness so much of my generation (those that didn't particularly distinguish themselves) on the verge of irrelevance. For a long time it was as if a great many more than is usual with generations were going to be leaders, and brilliant people and move in dynamic traditions: But life itself has become so dramatic, and so imperative, than [that] no individual destiny can stand against its deep insistencies—save Hitler, or Mussolini.

So here we all are doing whatever we can about whatever we are able and trying to stay out of jail—while the ego is orienting itself in these forceful worlds of less "free-will."

Scottie seems to be happy about Vassar: most parents are happy in knowing that their children are categoricly provided for under the best of "pure-children" acts and life martials its resources. I pray in the name of justice[,] mercy and the beauties of a better-comprehended era. We have lived a long time amassing statistics and providing the means; and maybe sometime we shall have evolved a mete and reasoning appreciation of all this—

Scottie told me that your novel progresses—I am so glad that you are able—and know how much more life has to offer with something you care about to nurture.

The best of good luck for the coming year—

Thanks for all the nice things you've given me—

   Devotedly Zelda

315. TO SCOTT
[October 1940]

ALS, 4 pp.
[Montgomery, Alabama]

Dear Scott

Thanks for the money. This is $20 weather and it's good to be able to meet the exigence of nature. The skies crackle overhead and the streets echo staccato with the "alert" of children on their way to school. There isnt much to do but it requires a great deal more of attention than under a circumstance more *exigent* of its own.

Mamma and I have taken up a sporadic card-attack. We "fiddle" with bridge in the evenings and enjoy the peaceful de[s]cent of dusk over this long dreamy street so peaceful and remote from dissonance and congestion.

A lady is making me a deep-horizon blue suit and I am "secondarily" rummaging the town for a hat. There are always so many more "indespensibles" when one can afford—

Mary Goodwin Tabor took me on Sunday to the most heavenly hunting lodge, lethally floating through the dreamy pentameters of an Alabama pine-woods. It reminded me of Sheridan so many years ago—and its pale high academic concisions of summers long since absorbed by the history book. This war hasnt any romantic aspects and dreams arent being laid away in pine-fragrance and bird-song this time. I suppose the emotionalists have been unable to fabricate any super-structure of compensatory legend to sell the ghastliness of this debacle.

Surly nothing this country has done could deserve a Japanese invasion. Lets all go down to the Ritz and get some nice onion[?]-soup—

They say they are a nice-clean people.

—It must have been entertaining attending a conclave again. Are the people still as cultured as they are in Thomas Elliot[55] and polite enough to meet the requirements of "Alice in Wonderland"? or doesnt anyone care what happened to the Rover-boys any more?

Thanks again—
Zelda

---

55. Probably American-born poet and critic T. S. Eliot.

316. TO ZELDA   TL (CC), 1 p.
                                October 5 1940

Dearest Zelda:

Enjoyed your letter—especially the consoling line about the Japanese being a nice clean people. A lot of the past came into that party. Fay Wray, whose husband John Monk Saunders committed suicide two months ago; Deems Taylor who I hadn't seen twice since the days at Swopes; Frank Tuttle of the old Film Guild. There was a younger generation there too and I felt very passé and decided to get a new suit.

 With dearest love,

1403 N. Laurel Avenue
Hollywood, California

317. TO ZELDA   TL (CC), 1 p.
                                October 11 1940

Dearest Zelda:-

Another heat wave is here and reminds me of last year at the same time. The heat is terribly dry and not at all like Montgomery and is so unexpected. The people feel deeply offended as if they were being bombed.

A letter from Gerald yesterday. He has no news except a general flavor of the past. To him, now, of course, the Riviera was the best time of all. Sara is interested in vegetables and gardens and all growing and living things.

I expect to be back on my novel any day and this time to finish a two months' job. The months go so fast that even *Tender Is the Night* is six years away. I think the nine years that intervened between the *Great Gatsby* and *Tender* hurt my reputation almost beyond repair because a whole generation grew up in the meanwhile to whom I was only a writer of Post stories. I don't suppose anyone will be much interested in what I have to say this time and it may be the last novel I'll ever write, but it must be done now because after fifty one is different. One can't remember emotionally, I think except about childhood but I have a few more things left to say.

My health is better. It was a long business and at any time some extra waste of energy has to be paid for at a double price. Weeks of fever and coughing — but the constitution is an amazing thing and nothing quite kills it until the heart has run its entire race. I'd like to get East around Christmas time this year. I don't know what the next three months will bring further, but if I get a credit on either of these last two efforts things will never again seem so black as they did a year ago when I felt that Hollywood had me down in its books as a ruined man — a label which I had done nothing to deserve.

With dearest love,

1403 N. Laurel Ave.
Hollywood, Calif.

318. TO ZELDA   TL (CC), 1 p.
October 19 1940

Dearest Zelda:

I'm trying desperately to finish my novel by the middle of December and it's a little like working on "Tender is the Night" at the end — I think of nothing else. Still haven't heard from the Shirley Temple story but it would be a great relaxation of pressure if she decides to do it, though an announcement in the paper says that she is going to be teamed with Judy Garland in "Little Eva" which reminds me that I saw the two Duncan Sisters both grown enormously fat in the Brown Derby. Do you remember them on the boat with Viscount Bryce and their dogs?

My room is covered with charts like it used to be for "Tender is the Night" telling the different movements of the characters and their histories. However, this one is to be short as I originally planned it two years ago and more on the order of "Gatsby".

Dearest love,

1403 N. Laurel Avenue
Hollywood, Calif.

319. TO SCOTT　　　　　　　ALS, 4 pp.
[October 1940]　　　　　　　　[Montgomery, Alabama]

Dear Scott

Thanks for the money. You are so thoughtful to remember the costliness of the unusual—and in sending me the means of mastery. I am so happy to be able to show Scottie that I think of her always even if life has prevented of late the provision of a maternal and envelloping sanctuary as background and refuge. Still: Mamma's little house is as bright and cheerful a refuge as any I know and all her off-spring are welcome and awaited.

Montgomery is lost on a quietly ecstatic autumn; gutters rattle with the punguency of dry leaves and pavements crackle under the crystalline mornings. Every day I expect the front page of the papers to burst into flames but the news still pursues its relentless policies—and people all over the world, I suppose, are trying to stay out of it all.

Meantime, I now have $283 dollars that Uncle Reid left me when he died. Twenty-nine dollars of it I want to give to charity; I would like to buy a nice suit ($60 or so); and I am going to buy Mamma a ton of coal. The two hundred, or $150 left I would like to pay on the account at Doctor Carrolls—unless he has already been paid. I dislike as deeply as you do being in debt to those scoundrels and scallywags and the sooner we clear ourselves of their traces the better—So shall I send him the money direct, or maybe it would better to send it to you. It will give me great pleasure to be able to make this slight contribution so dont protest. It is greatly to our mutual advantage to be free of such encumbrement—

Its grand about the novel. It will indeed seem fair and free to taste of fame again; certainly I will pray for the success of the project—and await with the utmost eagerness the proofes—

　　　Devotedly
　　　Zelda

320. TO ZELDA TL (CC), 1 p.
October 23 1940

Dearest Zelda:-

Advising you about money at long distance would be silly but you feel we're both concerned in the Carrol matter. Still and all I would much rather you'd leave it to me and *keep* your money. I sent them a small payment last week. The thing is I have budgeted what I saved in the weeks at 20th to last until December 15th so that I can go on with the novel with the hope of having a full draft by then. Naturally I will not realize anything at once (except on the very slim chance of a serial) and though I will try to make something immediately out of pictures or Esquire it may be a pretty slim Christmas. So my advice is to put the hundred and fifty away against that time.

I am deep in the novel, living in it, and it makes me happy. It is a *constructed* novel like *Gatsby*, with passages of poetic prose when it fits the action, but no ruminations or side-shows like *Tender*. Everything must contribute to the dramatic movement.

It's odd that my old talent for the short story vanished. It was partly that times changed, editors changed, but part of it was tied up somehow with you and me—the happy ending. Of course every third story had some other ending but essentially I got my public with stories of young love. I must have had a powerful imagination to project it so far and so often into the past.

Two thousand words today and all good.

With dearest love

1403 N. Laurel Ave.
Hollywood, Calif.

321. TO ZELDA   TL (CC), 1 p.
                      October 26 1940

Dearest Zelda:-

Ernest sent me his book and I'm in the middle of it. It is not as good as the "Farewell to Arms". It doesn't seem to have the tensity or the freshness nor has it the inspired poetic moments. But I imagine it would please the average type of reader, the mind who used to enjoy Sinclair Lewis, more than anything he has written. It is full of a lot of rounded adventures on the Huckleberry Finn order and of course it is highly intelligent and literate like everything he does. I suppose life takes a good deal out of you and you never can quite repeat. But the point is he is making a fortune out of it—has sold it to the movies for over a hundred thousand dollars and as it's The Book-of-the-Month selection he will make $50,000 from it in that form. Rather a long cry from his poor rooms over the saw mill in Paris.

No news except that I'm working hard, if that is news, and that Scottie's story appears in the New Yorker this week.[56]

With dearest love,

1403 N. Laurel Avenue
Hollywood, California

322. TO SCOTT   ALS, 4 pp.
[October 1940]   [Montgomery, Alabama]

Dear Scott:

Thanks for the money. Atmosphere is very expensive in these times when breathing is become of more significance, and I always find plenty to buy—and lots of expenditures of irrelevant natures.

These day are lush and beneficent and steeped in the leas of summer-time. Childrens voices still flood along the dusk and Sun-

---

56. Scottie's story "A Wonderful Time" was published in *The New Yorker* in October 1940.

days bask before the church; and life floats gentle over the abeyance of Time and distress. I personally, am grateful to be warm, and out of the war.

Though I am vaguel[y] resentful of Earnests success (his work being neither as meritorious or as compelling as your own), I am also glad. Earnest also offer[s] at least a casual passing acknowledgment of the Christian Faith. I tried to get his book down town: 50 copies were out being rented, so we'll wait till one turns up. Tarkingtons new story in the Post seems of very little significance against the back ground of these dynamic times. I wish I could write a story that would coordinate the dominant bitterness and courage and conviction of traged[y] with the return to religious truths and the necessity for religious guidance that animates this most precarious world.

People ask about you whenever I see any; though I seldom go anywhere save to church. Also Scottie seems to have quite a clientele. Everybody here improves things: their minds, and things as bookreviews and such—and I dont know what parties there are because I am not envited to any.

Miss Booth and I went to a show—and I had lunch today with Lee Charles[?] at the church—Mamma, the family + I go to town lots of times to gauge the prospective aspirations by the predominant silhouette.

It's grand about your book. Please write—
Devotedly
Zelda

323. TO ZELDA   TL (CC), 1 p.
                                     November 2 1940

Dearest Zelda:
Listening to the Harvard and Princeton game on the radio reminds me of the past that I lived a quarter of a century ago and Scottie is living now. I hear nothing from her though I imagine she is at Cambridge today.

The novel is hard as pulling teeth but that is because it is in its early character-planting phase. I feel people so less intently than I did once that this is harder. It means welding together hundreds of stray impressions and incidents to form the fabric of entire personalities. But later it should go faster. I hope all is well with you.

With dearest love,

1403 N. Laurel Avenue
Hollywood, California

324. TO ZELDA TL (CC), 1 p.
November 9 1940

Dearest Zelda:-
Got into rather a fret about Scottie last week, which however came out all right. She went to the infirmary with grippe and then in spite of my telegrams to everyone there including the dean, Scottie and the infirmary itself, darkness seemed to close about her. I could get no information. Her weekly letter was missing. As I say, it turned out all right. She had been discharged and was probably out of town but I wrote her a strong letter that she must keep me informed of her general movements not that I have any control over them or want any because she is after all of age and capable of looking after herself but one resents the breaking of a habit and I was used to hearing about her once a week.
I'm still absorbed in the novel which is growing under my hand— not as deft a hand as I'd like but growing.

With dearest love always

1403 N. Laurel Ave.
Hollywood, Calif.

325. TO SCOTT ALS, 4 pp.
[November 1940] [Montgomery, Alabama]

Dear D. O.
Thanks for the money: I am always glad to be able to buy postage stamps and pay for a look at these bright autumn skies. The back

yard is punguent of dead leaves and many summers long merged in time: if it rains, sometimes, I will plant poppies for next spring and scratch around a little through the beds for lilly-bulbs. It is such lovely weather.

Meantime, its grand to know that your book progresses. I have been trying to write a short story: it comes so easy that I am a [little] suspicious. May I send it to you for your approval before I send it off? Although you may not like it, and may find it moralistic, it conveys a message that I would be most grateful to put across: that the story of life is of far deeper implication in religious terms.

Meantime, I dont do anything. Every now and then I call on Red Ruth (who is still terribly sick and incapacitated); Livye and I went to a show at the auditorium; every now and then a stranger pops up—but its been a long time since I lived here and most of my friends as long since swall[ow]ed up by a system, hither or yon. I go to church on Sundays at the Holy Comforter where I was baptized; and attend whatever prayer meetings there are.

I am eternally grateful to still have Mamma: a lone and middle-aged woman is a far pleasanter spectacle when merged in her traditions. To a man, I suppose the pressure of life is always supposed to be paramount but to a woman the poignancy of personal desirability is almost inescapably paramount.

It makes me sad to lose forever, in recapturing, the scenes of my youth. Most of us had rather always be children or at least always have the security + affection of a big family—

Devotedly
Zelda

326. TO ZELDA   TL (CC), 1 p.
                                 November 16 1940

Dearest Zelda:

I'm sitting listening to Yale-Princeton, which will convince you I spend all my time on the radio. Have had to lay off coco-cola hence work with an attack of avitaminosis whatever that is—it's like a weight pressing on your shoulders and upper arms. Oh for the health of fifteen years ago.

I'd love to see anything you write so don't hesitate to send it. I got the doctor's bill which has been paid today. I liked Scottie's little sketch, didn't you?

With dearest love

1403 N. Laurel Ave.
Hollywood, Calif.

327. TO SCOTT   ALS, 2 pp.
[November 1940]   [Montgomery, Alabama]

Dear D. O.—

Thanks for the money again—now that winter is here coal + gas + all the persuasions that a new season has to offer also exact their toll. Mamma's little house is so sunshine-y and so full of grace; the moated mornings remind me of twenty-five years ago when life was as full of promise as it now is of memory. There were wars then, and now, and, I suppose, as much Time as ever awaited its utilization: but the race had more gallantry at that time and the more romantic terms in which we took life helped us through. People are beginning to realize that there's no alternative to the truth now, and facing issues with the stern countenance of an indeed, necessitated and imperative right-eousness—that is, those with the good sense to be seeking salvation. There are still lots, I know who still find that it would be too awful to have to "believe it"—

I missed Scotties article: because I [k]new of it only through your letter; then the week was gone and it was too late: Have you a copy that I might see? I thought the thing last summer was very bright and engaging and promising:[57] and want her to write her novel—It's good practise at living if unprofitable otherwise.

Rosalind + Newman will be over for Mammas birthday: the 23rd—and I am looking forward to a happy reunion

Devotedly
Zelda

57. Scottie's story, "The End of Everything," published in *College Bazaar* in August.

328. TO ZELDA   TLS (CC), 1 p.
                          November 23 1940

Dearest Zelda:

Enclosed is Scottie's little story—she had just read Gertrude Stein's *Melanctha* on my recommendation and the influence is what you might call perceptible.

The odd thing is that it appeared in eastern copies of the New Yorker and not in the western, and I had some bad moments looking through the magazine she had designated and wondering if my eyesight had departed.

The editor of "Collier's" wants me to write for them (he's here in town), but I tell him I'm finishing my novel for myself and all I can promise him is a look at it. It will, at any rate, be nothing like anything else as I'm digging it out of myself like uranium—one ounce to the cubic ton of rejected ideas. It is a novel *a la Flaubert* without "ideas" but only people moved singly and in mass through what I hope are authentic moods.

The resemblance is rather to "Gatsby" than to anything else I've written. I'm so glad you're well and reasonably happy.

     With dearest love,
     Scott

P.S. Please send Scottie's story back in your next letter—as it seems
     utterly impossible to get duplicates and I shall probably want to
     show it to authors and editors with paternal pride.

1403 N. Laurel Ave.
Hollywood, California

329. TO SCOTT   ALS, 2 pp.
[Late November 1940]   [Montgomery, Alabama]

Dear Scott:

We have been *en fête* and with gala all week. Mamma was *80* on Saturday and Rosalind and Newman came over from Atlanta to bring us a good many happy reasons for having as many birthdays as possible. All of us bought a new rug and chair covers; and lots of people sent flowers and little pretty things. Tilde sent Mamma a beautiful new radio: which it is beginning to seem, may be our sole means of communication with California. I meant: the Texas floods are raging and your letter hasn't penetrated, but I suppose that it will show up in time.

Everything pursues its own ends and skies stay warm + beneficent—though winter time always leaves many vagrant nostalgias and a sense of more supply than demand of *Time* and of the portentousness of the weather.

Hope the book is getting along auspiciously—and that yourself and your job are prospering.

Zelda

330. TO SCOTT   ALS, 2 pp.
[November/December 1940]   [Montgomery, Alabama]

Dear Scott:

The money arrived; and is now largely in circulation. Thank you—I cant see what becomes of it, which is perhaps an iconoclastic habit of mine.

Mamma sends thanks for the congratulations: the birthday still resolves itself through these long sunshiny days into a great many new and as yet vagrant possessions and a house-full of flowers. One must have quite a few very definitive opinions at eighty; and a definite sense of accomplishment at having breathed, and pursued the effort, so consistently. "My Own Ends" still lead me far and wide but I do what I am able of what I would like and give daily prayers of gratitude for such a pleasant roof and such very "relevant" bounties—

Scottie seems to be having a good time. She writes tales of glamour[ou]s pilgrimadges hither + yon; and we are looking forward to seeing her at Christmas. Wouldn't it be too superior if we had a little cottage somewhere where she could put her last years theses and her next years hats—

Devotedly
Zelda

331. TO ZELDA   TL (CC), 1 p.
                          December 6 1940

Dearest Zelda:

No news except that the novel progresses and I am angry that this little illness has slowed me up. I've had trouble with my heart before but never anything organic. This is not a major attack but seems to have come on gradually and luckily a cardiogram showed it up in time. I may have to move from the third to the first floor apartment but I'm quite able to work, etc., if I do not overtire myself.[58]

Scottie tells me she is arriving South Xmas day. I envy you being together and I'll be thinking of you. Everything is my novel now — it has become of absorbing interest. I hope I'll be able to finish it by February.

With dearest love,

1403 N. Laurel Ave.
Hollywood, Calif.

332. TO ZELDA   TL (CC), 1 p.
                          December 13 1940

Dearest Zelda:

Here's why it would be foolish to sell the watch. I think I wrote you that over a year ago when things were very bad indeed I did consider pawning it as I desperately needed $200., for a couple of months. The price offered, to my astonishment was $20., and of course I didn't even consider it. It cost, I believe $600. The reason for the shrinkage is a purely arbitrary change of taste in jewelry. It is actually artificial and created by the jewelers themselves. It is like the Buick we sold in 1927 — for $200. — to come back to America in '31 and buy a car of the

---

58. According to Sheilah Graham, Scott saw his doctor in November, after a dizzy spell while at the corner drugstore. The doctor told him he had had a "cardiac spasm." Later that month, when he and Sheilah were going to a movie, he had another spell, whereupon he went home to bed. Since June 1940, Scott and Sheilah had lived near each other. After his dizzy spells, he moved into her apartment which was on the first floor. Sheilah and his secretary, Frances Kroll, planned to look for a ground-floor apartment for Scott.

same year and much more used for $400. If you have no use for the watch I think it would be a beautiful present for Scottie. She has absolutely nothing of any value and I'm sure would prize it highly. Moreover she never loses anything. If you preferred you could loan it to her as I think she'd get real pleasure out of sporting it.

The novel is about three-quarters through and I think I can go on till January 12 without doing any stories or going back to the studio. I couldn't go back to the studio anyhow in my present condition as I have to spend most of the time in bed where I write on a wooden desk that I had made a year and a half ago. The cardiogram shows that my heart is repairing itself but it will be a gradual process that will take some months. It is odd that the heart is one of the organs that does repair itself.

I had a letter from Katherine Tye the other day, a voice out of the past. Also one from Harry Mitchell who was my buddy at the Barron G. Collier Advertising Agency. And one week from Max Perkins who is keen to see the novel and finally one from Bunny Wilson who is married now to a girl named Mary McCarthy who was an editor of the New Republic. They have a baby a year old and live in New Canaan.

I will write you again early next week in time for Christmas.

    Dearest love,

P.S. I enclose the letter from Max, in fact two letters only I can't find the one that just came. They will keep you au courant with the publishing world and some of our friends.

1403 N. Laurel Ave.
Hollywood, Calif.

333. TO ZELDA   TL (CC), 1 p.[59]
                                December 19 1940

Dearest Zelda:
This has to be a small present this year but I figure Scottie's present as a gift to you both and charge it off to you accordingly.

59. The text of this letter appears in Andrew Turnbull's edition of Scott's *Letters*; but we have been unable to locate it. This transcription is Turnbull's (p. 133).

I am very anxious for Scottie to finish this year at college at least, so please do not stress to her that it is done at any inconvenience. The thing for which I am most grateful to my mother and father are my four years at Princeton, and I would be ashamed not to hand it on to another generation so there is no question of Scottie quitting. Do tell her this.

I hope you all have a fine time at Christmas. Much love to your mother and Marjorie and Minor and Nonny and Livy Hart and who-ever you see

Dearest love,

1403 N. Laurel Avenue
Hollywood, California

EPILOGUE

Happily, happily foreverafterwards — the best we could.
— ZELDA TO SCOTT, AUGUST 1936

On Saturday, December 21, 1940, Scott, who had been following the Princeton football games on the radio, settled down into his chair to read about the team in the alumni magazine. Sheilah Graham, who had been his companion for the last two years, was also reading, curled up on the sofa nearby. By all accounts, Scott was happy. No longer drinking, he had settled into a warm and comfortable domestic routine with Sheilah. He was proud of Scottie, and pleased that he could provide her with the kind of education that had meant so much to him at Princeton. Over the last decade, he had learned to live with the grief that Zelda's illness created, and he took solace in knowing that she, too, had settled into familiar domestic rituals and had her mother and sisters to care for her. Her letters reassured him that she found pleasure in her mother's house, in its garden and flowers, and in the little southern town in which she had been raised. Most gratifying of all, Scott's new novel, *The Last Tycoon*, was going well; out of the thirty episodes he had charted, he had completed seventeen. But that afternoon, Scott stopped reading, stood up, seemed to reach for the mantel, then fell onto the floor. When Sheilah returned after running for help, Scott was dead.

Scott had wanted to be buried near his father and the Keys and the Scotts in the cemetery of St. Mary's Catholic Church in Rockville, Maryland, a suburb of Washington, D.C. After a brief viewing in Hollywood, his body was sent by train to Baltimore. But because he was no longer a practicing Catholic, church authorities denied permission to lay Scott to rest in St. Mary's cemetery. An Episcopal minister officiated and he was buried in Rockville Union Cemetery instead. His funeral was attended by only about thirty people, including Scottie, a few of her Baltimore friends, the Obers, Gerald and Sara Murphy, Maxwell Perkins and his family, Scott's favorite cousin, Cecilia Taylor, and his brother-in-law Newman Smith. Zelda was too ill to be there, and Sheilah tactfully mourned her loss in private.

After Scott's death, Zelda lived intermittently between her mother's home and Highland Hospital, to which she returned during periods of relapse. In November of 1947, Zelda returned to the hospital for the last time. At midnight on March 10, 1948, the building in which she lived caught fire, and Zelda and eight other patients perished in the flames. Her body was so badly burned that it could only be identified by her slipper, which was found beneath her. Zelda was buried beside her husband on St. Patrick's Day.

But the story does not end there. In 1975, the Catholic Archdiocese of Washington overruled the earlier decision and the Fitzgeralds' remains were moved and reinterred in St. Mary's Church cemetery. The inscription on their stone bears the final words of *The Great Gatsby*: "So we beat on, boats against the current, borne back ceaselessly into the past." Those who visit the Fitzgeralds' grave today might remember what Scott and Zelda themselves said about a final resting place when any thought of death was but an imaginative projection into the future. As a young woman of nineteen, very much in love with life *and* with Scott, Zelda wrote to him enthusiastically in 1919:

> Why should graves make people feel in vain? I've heard that so much . . . but somehow I can't find anything hopeless in having lived—All the broken columnes and clasped hands and doves and angels mean romances—and in an hundred years I think I shall like having young people speculate on whether my eyes were brown or blue. . . . I hope my grave has an air of many, many years ago about it—Isn't it funny how, out of a row of Confederate soldiers, two or three will make you think of dead lovers and dead loves. . . .

Scott liked this description so much he used it nearly verbatim in his first novel, *This Side of Paradise*. But later he created an affectionate vision of his own about his and Zelda's grave. After visiting Zelda in the hospital in Baltimore in late September 1935, Scott wrote to a friend:

> It was wonderful to sit with her head on my shoulder for hours and feel as I always have, even now, closer to her than to any other human being. . . . And I wouldn't mind a bit if in a few years Zelda + I could snuggle up together under a stone in some old graveyard here. That is really a happy thought + not melancholy at all. (*Life in Letters* 290–291)

The Fitzgeralds' lives were unduly short; and they were tragic, but tragic in the best sense—in the sense that the human heart possesses hopes, dreams, aspirations, and infinite longings that cannot be fulfilled, but the great souls among us continue to desire and strive and work for these things despite all obstacles and failures. Therefore, their tragedy, while it does indeed evoke pity and fear, also inspires admiration and courage. The tragic view is ultimately an affirming one, urging us to love life and to desire it both because of and in spite of its persistent losses.

F. Scott and Zelda Fitzgerald, in the love that they shared and the suffering they endured, in their commitment to each other, their daughter, and their talents, and in the wealth of novels, stories, essays, paintings, and letters they produced in their short lives, have bequeathed to us and to subsequent generations a rich storehouse of intelligence, humor, loyalty, courage, and grace.

INDEX